OLDER WOMEN IN 20TH-CENTURY AMERICA

WOMEN'S STUDIES
FACTS AND ISSUES
(VOL. 3)

GARLAND REFERENCE LIBRARY
OF SOCIAL SCIENCE
(VOL. 122)

Volume 3

Women's Studies
Facts and Issues

Advisory Editors:

OLDER WOMEN IN 20TH-CENTURY AMERICA
A Selected Annotated Bibliography

Audrey Borenstein, Ph.D.

GARLAND PUBLISHING, INC. • NEW YORK & LONDON
1982

Library of Congress Cataloging in Publication Data

Borenstein, Audrey, 1930–
    Older women in 20th-century America.

    (Garland reference library of social science ; v. 122)
(Women's studies ; v. 3)
    Includes index.
    1. Aged women—United States—Bibliography.   2. Mid-
dle aged women—United States—Bibliography.   3. Geront-
ology—Bibliography.   I. Title.   II. Title: Older women
in twentieth-century America.   III. Series: Women's
studies (Garland Publishing, Inc.) ; v. 3.   IV. Series:
Garland reference library of social science ; v. 122.
Z7164.04B67   300s   [016.3052'6]   82-6082
[HQ1064]   AACR2
ISBN 0-8240-9396-8

Printed on acid-free, 250-year-life paper
Manufactured in the United States of America

This work is dedicated with love
to the memory of my grandmothers,
to my mother,
to my sisters,
to my daughter,
and to the granddaughters I hope for.

Peut-être, la sève reviendra. Une autre graine tombera et germera.
Marcel Mauss

Books by Audrey Borenstein

Custom: An Essay on Social Codes, trans. of *Die Sitte* by Ferdinand Tönnies. New York: The Free Press, 1961.

Redeeming the Sin: Social Science and Literature. New York: Columbia University Press, 1978.

Chimes of Change and Hours: Views of Older Women in 20th Century America, Rutherford, New Jersey: Fairleigh Dickinson University Press, 1982/83. (In press)

Older Women In 20th Century America: A Selected Annotated Bibliography

CONTENTS

ACKNOWLEDGMENTS

I wish to express my gratitude for the generosity of their assistance to me in the preparation of this bibliography to the Rockefeller Foundation for the Rockefeller Foundation Humanities Fellowship awarded for the academic year 1978–1979 in support of my research study, "The Older Woman as Seen Through Literature and Social Science," the librarians of the Sojourner Truth Library of the State University College of New York at New Paltz, for helping me obtain numerous works through their Inter-Library Loan service, Harriett Straus, for her interest, encouragement, and aid during the development of this project, and Professor Walter Borenstein, who fostered this undertaking from the first day that reference materials were gathered to the day of its completion.

Audrey Borenstein
New Paltz, New York
September 1981

INTRODUCTION

Throughout the decade of the 1970s, research activities in Gerontology were enlivened by the growing interest in the issues and concerns of older women in 20th-century North America and by the recognition that the humanities have a vital contribution to make to the study of aging. In appreciation of the confluence of these two recent developments, this bibliography was prepared to serve as a bridge between the humanities and the social sciences and is intended to promote cross-disciplinary and interdisciplinary studies on the much-neglected subject of older women.

A consensus has emerged from the growing numbers of published works about older women in the United States and from conferences, workshops, networks, and task forces as well as from informal study groups and from course offerings focusing on older women that "older women" are women in midlife and later life—that is, "older women" are women aged forty and over. In claiming the subject of aging to be at least as much the domain of women's interests as of men's, undertakings in research and advocacy are predicated upon two fundamental assumptions. One is that mature adulthood is inextricably joined to the later phases of the life cycle. The restriction of the term "older women" to women aged sixty-five and over obscures the vital connection between the circumstances, experiences, and perspective of a woman in her forties and fifties with her life and thought in the decades that follow; indeed, it casts more than a quarter of a century of a woman's life into a kind of limbo. To designate women in midlife as "older women" restores this vital connection. It also contributes to the shaping of the life course perspective that enhances our awareness of the continuity of life and of the interdependence of the generations. The second assumption is that older women are concealed in much gerontological research. Although the titles of countless publications in Gerontology are not at all indicative of this, the majority of the subjects in many studies of aging are women. The generic terms "elderly" and "older persons" conceal this important fact—a fact that in itself reflects the sex differential in life expectancy remarked by so many social observers throughout the course of this century.

That women ought to receive at least as much attention as men in gerontological studies was fully recognized only during the past decade in the United States. Early in the decade, in 1973, the title chosen for the 26th Annual Conference on Aging sponsored by the Institute of Gerontology in Ann Arbor, Michigan, was "Women: Life Span Challenges." Throughout the 1970s, national organizations were founded and advocacy projects were advanced that focused on older women in 20th-century North America. Among these are the Displaced Homemakers Network, the Gray Panthers National Task Force on Older Women, the National Action Forum for Older Women, the NOW National Older Women's Rights Committee, and the Older Women's League Educational Fund (OWLEF). Through OWLEF, a number of Gray Papers and other resource materials of special interest to older women have been published to promote both social action and research. Towards the end of the decade in 1979, at the first West Virginia University Gerontology Conference, older women and the rural aged were chosen as topics of special interest. In the first year of the new decade, the concerns of older women were made public at the federally sponsored White House Mini-Conference on Older Women, "Growing Numbers: Growing Force," which was convened in October 1980, in Des Moines, Iowa. About 200 of the 400 participants stayed on an extra day to found the national grassroots activist organization, the Older Women's League. There is every indication that older women will continue to be a focus of considerable social activism and research during the 1980s and beyond. This bibliography was prepared in response to the need for knowledge about a variety of issues and concerns of older women in 20th-century North America so as to inform and enhance social action programs and research undertakings.

Many anthropologists, psychologists, and sociologists engaged in teaching and research on the subject of women's aging are in search of sources providing literary perspectives on this subject—in women's autobiographies, diaries, essays, journals, letters and memoirs, and in fiction by women in which older women appear as major characters or as protagonists and in which themes of growing older are explored. Many humanists engaged in teaching and research on this subject are in search of sources providing information about theory and methodology in Gerontology and about research projects on older women conducted by oral historians and by scholars in the various subdisciplines of the social sciences. Furthermore, scholars in *all* disciplines are in search of reference materials on the subjects of creativity and productivity in the second half of life, on issues that are the subject of current debate (ranging from prolongevity to revision of the Social Security system), on the subject of activism against age prejudice and age discrimination, on general social criticism encompassing the issue of social inequality based upon distinctions between age strata, and on discussions of the injustices attendant upon these manifestations of "ageism." This bibliography was compiled with the intention of serving these diverse yet interrelated interests. It represents a gathering of what could be the first building blocks for a clearinghouse of information on this subject, which is multidisciplinary by its very nature.

Subject headings listed in the table of contents reflect a number of major research interests in two broad divisions of scholarly endeavor, the humanities and the social sciences. Humanistic perspectives on older women encompass autobiographies by older women and studies in older women's autobiography, critical studies of works by women of letters, personal documents of older women (diaries, essays, journals, letters and memoirs, as well as women's reflections on aging and word-portraits of older women), and fiction—novels, novellas and short stories—by and about older women. In the United States throughout this century, thousands of novels and short stories have been published in which older women appear as characters or in which aspects of women's aging are revealed. For this listing, selections were made of reasonably accessible works of fiction by women writers in which older women appear as characters and/or in which themes of aging are explored. This selection was guided by the effort to achieve balance in listing works of fiction published throughout the past decades of this century by writers from each of the regions in this country, each with her distinctive voice and point of view.

Humanistic perspectives on older women also encompass works on creativity and productivity in later life, arts and the elderly, historical perspectives on aging, researches in images of aging and the future of aging, and general humanistic perspectives on gerontological concerns. There are areas where the convergence of research interests of humanists and social scientists is especially evident. Creativity and productivity in later life is a subject that has long engaged the attention of psychologists. Arts and the elderly is the focus of interest of activists and advocates for the elderly and of psychologists and sociologists as well as humanists. Moreover, anthropologists, historians, philosophers, social gerontologists, and sociologists have complementary interests in historical perspectives on aging, images of aging, and the future of aging. In bringing their special perspectives to the subject of aging and the elderly, scholars in the humanities illuminate and deepen the central concerns of Gerontology.

Social scientific perspectives on older women encompass cross-cultural (anthropological) perspectives on aging, drawn both from works on the elderly in the United States (aging and ethnicity, and minorities and aging) and on the elderly in other societies; general studies and theory and methodology in Gerontology; housing and living environments for the elderly; studies in life-span development; works on middle age and on the problems and prospects of displaced homemakers; oral histories and studies in memory, reminiscence and the life review; psychological perspectives on aging; social and economic issues (employment, income, legal issues, pensions, poverty, retirement, Social Security, and volunteerism); and sociological perspectives on aging and on the problems and prospects of widowed women. The areas of social scientific research interests are contiguous with issues related to activism against ageism and general social criticism. Coming around by another path, the humanists are also concerned with issues related to action and advocacy because of their concern with aesthetic, moral, and spiritual values and with the positive aspects of aging. Complementary research endeavors are also notable in aging as seen in cross-cultural and historical perspectives, in studies of the housing and living environments for the elderly, and in the gathering of oral histories and inquiries into memory, reminiscence, and the life review. In over-arching the fields of specialization demarcated within the humanities and the social sciences, this listing provides readers with access to one another's work—to methods and styles of inquiry as much as to content and to conclusions or judgments based upon thoughts and observations and analyses. Therefore, it may conduce to the participation by individual researchers in an interdisciplinary symposium on central gerontological concerns as these pertain to women.

Of necessity, this undertaking has been an exercise in selection. Just as a bibliography of general works in aging specifically designating the topic "older women" would be no more than a few pages in length (as the length of the subsection in Gerontology entitled "Older Women—General" attests), so a bibliography of works related to the subject of older women in 20th-century North America, encompassing all publications in Gerontology that contain materials that have bearing on the issues and concerns of older women, would include thousands upon thousands of entries. In this work, which is the outcome of extensive research and teaching from an interdisciplinary perspective over a period of several years, selection of references was made on the basis of a number of considerations elucidated in the following paragraphs. Initially, it was intended that every work listed in this bibliography would be examined. It is the fate of overly ambitious projects that the reach will exceed the grasp: most, but not all the works listed here were read very closely, and annotations were composed on the basis of this careful examination of their contents. Those entries that were not read are marked with an asterisk (*), and brief annotations about their content are provided for those publications about which information in the form of abstracts, advertisements, or reviews was obtained. They were selected to be included here because they are cited in publications that *were* examined, and in which their value as reference materials for the development of one or another research project was indicated. A few of these entries that were not examined are full-length books or articles. But most are dissertations, theses, and papers presented at professional meetings—all of which are likely to contain especially useful compilations of out-of-the-way references—and government publications. This bibliography also includes a subject heading for selected bibliographies on the inter-related subjects of women and aging, which are explored in the publications cited throughout this work.

Subject headings in this bibliography denote selected major interests of researchers in the humanities and social sciences. The references listed under Housing and Living Environments—a subject of vital importance to older people—were compiled as a service for those researchers focusing on this growing field of study that was hitherto relatively unexplored and is only now receiving the attention it so richly deserves. An extension of the listings in social science would include subject headings in crime victimization, the economics of aging, health and medicine, education, law, the media, politics, and religion. A few publications on each of these topics were chosen to be included here. The selection of these publications was guided by two considerations—that they are indicative of recent research activity in these areas, and that they provide lists of references for further reading. Autobiographies, various personal documents and works of fiction, most of which were examined for this compilation, were selected if they met one or both criteria—that a life course perspective is taken in the work, or that it contains reflections on women's aging or on the experiences and special interests of older women in the United States in the 20th century. An extension of the listings of literary perspectives on older women would include other genres—in particular, drama and poetry—as well as additional autobiographies, personal documents and works of fiction. These could be gleaned from listings provided by enterprises engaged in the recovery of "lost" literature and from compilations of the publications of "little" magazines and small presses, as well as from publishers' backlists (which include numerous works now out of print) spanning this century. ·

Autobiographies, personal documents (except for personal essays), and memoirs are too diffuse to allow for useful annotations. In some, the writer weaves reflections on growing older throughout the work; in others, aging is the topic of a fragment of the whole; in still others, memory, wisdom,, or some other aspect of aging is a theme. Nearly all the autobiographies and personal documents listed here were examined closely (those not examined are indicated by an asterisk). Selection of autobiographies was based upon extensive reading of works in this genre. Hundreds of autobiographies by older women in 20th-century North America have been published since the turn of the century. Of these, a master list was compiled, and fifty autobiographies were read in the search for works that contain reflections on growing older and/or that were written from a life course perspective, by older women in a variety of occupations and professions, from all regions of the country, and of a wide diversity of ethnic, racial, religious, and social class affiliations. Selection of the works listed here was made with the objective of achieving a compilation that would represent a cross section of older women in terms of regional differences, differences in ethnic, racial, religious and social class backgrounds, and differences in work experience throughout the century. Researchers are provided with a broad spectrum of autobiographies from which a host of comparative studies (for example, in American history, women's perspectives on growing older, the changing world of women's work, and oral history) may be developed. The birth and death dates of the autobiographers and a note about the role each woman performed in public life serve to locate the memoirist in time and place. In addition, selected critical studies of autobiographies by *older* women are included in this section, with full annotations of the content of these pioneering works in a heretofore neglected area of studies in North American literature. Because there is no common agreement about the distinctions between literary genres—between autobiographies and memoirs, for example, or between oral memoirs as historical documents and as literature, or between novellas and "long" short stories—works are listed under subject headings in accordance with the author's designation of the genre or, in the absence of any indication of the writer's intention, in accordance with the consensus of critical opinion of scholars specializing in the study of the work of particular writers.

Some of the articles listed in this bibliography are cited as appearing in anthologies or in edited collections of articles. Many of these works were originally published in journals, and this is noted in the annotation in those cases in which the date of the original publication would be germane to the researcher's interest. Annotations of the reports from workshops conducted during the 26th Annual Conference on Aging, "Women: Life Span Challenges," held in Ann Arbor in 1973, are listed under the name of the recorder, since this was the system followed in the publication of the Work Group Reports. The names of the authors of dissertations, theses, and papers presented at professional meetings which were not examined are cited here as these appeared in publications consulted for the preparation of this work. Wherever this information was obtainable, the titles of the works and the place and date were checked in other sources for accuracy. Government publications and publications by organizations and agencies are listed under the name of the person indicated as the author or editor of the publication wherever such names were designated either in the work from which the reference was obtained, or in the publication itself if a copy was obtained for examination of its contents. In those cases in which a copy of the work was not obtained, and in which no name(s) of author(s) was or were provided, the work is listed as a publication of the agency or organization. In the cases of all publications annotated in this bibliography that include either an extensive bibliography or a listing of reference materials of lesser-known works or of works not commonly cited, this is noted as "extensive bibliography" or "bibliography" at the end of the annotation. Inasmuch as the professional degrees of some of the authors of these publications are listed in some cases but not in others, it was decided to omit degrees or other titles, with one exception: the M.D. is retained wherever the medical training of the author of the work appears to be relevant to the issues addressed in the materials cited here. Finally, under each subject heading that includes a listing of anthologies or edited collections of papers, some were selected to be annotated in full. These annotations provide the names of all contributors to the volume and the full titles of their papers, in order to acquaint the reader with the identities and research interests of those working in that particular field of study.

In every case throughout this bibliography, the annotation for the work cited is intended to be informational, that is, nonevaluative. This is so because of my conviction that every reader is quite competent to think for herself or himself and to form her or his own judgments about the issues and concerns of older women, and out of my respect for the very individual orientations and interests of readers consulting these pages. Variation in the length of annotations reflects the fact that the subject matter and reach of some publications are wide-ranging, whereas others are concentrated on a single topic or issue. Each annotation was composed with the intention of stating the essential content of the work in the idiom and with the point of view presented by the author of the work. The purpose of this formulation is to guide readers to works conducted by those in fields of specialization other than their own, to acquaint readers with the way work is written and presented by those in various fields of study, and to point to current trends in research along a broad spectrum of interests— from cognition in later life to humanistic geography—in aspects of women's aging. All annotations, however, have been carefully formulated so as to avoid the transposition of jargon, which does appear in some of the publications cited here. I have served as my own editor, removing both jargon and formulations that might reflect my own personal biases concerning any issue of current controversy. Thus, the phrasing of each annotation is intended to reflect the phrasing in the work that is annotated, and, wherever this was feasible, capitalizations, spelling, and variations in the designations of racial and ethnic groups are retained in the annotation in the same form in which they appear in the publication that is cited. Furthermore, familiarity with Gerontology publications has alerted me to the fact that there are a number of works in which the special concerns of older women are addressed—as an aside, or in a footnote, or in a brief section of a book or article ostensibly about something else. That is why certain works appear in this listing, with annotations including this information although their titles do not indicate contents which have any particular relevance to the subject of older women in 20th-century North America.

It has been said that the longest journey commences with a single step. This bibliography is a first offering toward the compilation of a definitive listing of works on the subject of women and aging. While works by male as well as female researchers are listed under many subject headings, only autobiographies by women and critical studies in women's autobiography and only personal documents and works of fiction written by women are included here. This is not to slight gerontological concerns of men and women taken together nor those of men exclusively but to right the balance of studies that, until only very recently, have not given older women the attention that is so long overdue. Inasmuch as humanistic and social scientific concerns are complementary, this bibliography should serve as a bridge to understanding among scholars in a variety of fields of study, as well as among women and men and older and younger people. The "see also" list of numbers designating other entries that follows each section of this bibliography is intended to serve as a useful system of cross-reference. Yet this bibliography is an invitation to discover the extent of the convergence of interests in this subject as much as a reflection of it. Therefore, the "see also" listing represents but a preliminary guide to interdisciplinary explorations—a guide that every reader may contribute to developing and refining through individual research projects.

As is well known, references generate references. Therefore, it is hoped that this work will seed research projects for many years to come. If it is put to use in the same interdisciplinary spirit in which it was prepared, it cannot but enhance our appreciation of the past in human experience as well as in scholarship. In this way we may illumine the ground where we now stand, and even, perhaps, carry the light forward for those who will come after us.

OLDER WOMEN IN
20TH-CENTURY AMERICA

I. ACTIVISM AGAINST AGEISM;
SOCIAL CRITICISM

A. General

1. Fischer, David Hackett. "Books Considered." *The New
    Republic* (December 2, 1978) 179(23):31-6. A review of
    The New Old: Struggling for Decent Aging and *Aging and
    the Elderly: Humanistic Perspectives in Gerontology*.
    Fischer states that the diversity of contemporary
    interests in aging becomes a unity if seen as a *move-
    ment*, both in the sense of something changing through
    time and as the latest of the great American reform
    movements. Because the latter have a continuing capacity
    for self-reform, their open, pluralistic structures
    making them adaptable to changing circumstance, many
    have lasted a very long time. Thus, society is in the
    process of permanent reform, which is the American al-
    ternative to permanent revolution. In Gerontology there
    has been a shift from concern with the *aged* to concern
    with *aging*, seen as a life-*process*, not a life *stage*.
    The emphasis today is on pluralistic networks of associa-
    tion which might respond to variations of individual
    taste; the attitude it opposes is not gerontophobia,
    but *ageism*. The age movement, like so many other
    American reforms, is becoming less radical but more
    militant, less unitary and more pluralistic, less ab-
    stract and more pragmatic, less communal and more indi-
    vidualistic, less egalitarian and perhaps more liber-
    tarian. Rumors about the death of liberalism are pre-
    mature.

2. Gray Panther *Network*. 3635 Chestnut Street, Philadelphia,
    Pennsylvania 19104. (1972-) Regular features of
    this publication are: news in brief; brickbats and bou-
    quets; letters; moving right along; on the road with
    Maggie; panther profile; book review; grassroots; local
    network directory.

3. Gross, Ronald, Beatrice Gross and Sylvia Seidman, eds.
    The New Old: Struggling for Decent Aging. Garden City,
    New York: Anchor Press/Doubleday, 1978. Sections in
    this book of readings are: Waiting for the End: Our
    Shameful Treatment of the Aged; The Graying of America:
    Demographic Perspectives; Ageism: The Last Segregation;
    Death: The Final Confrontation; Joys and Rewards of Old
    Age; Rallying Cries: Agendas for Action; The Struggle
    over Retirement; and Promising Programs and Projects
    with a listing of resources, information and help--
    publications, organizations and networks. In the Intro-
    duction, the editors state that, as fellow citizens, we
    must address the critical issues of aging together, and
    that the voices of older *women* are raised in protest
    against "Ageism: The Last Segregation."

4. Hessel, Dieter, ed. *Maggie Kuhn on Aging, a Dialogue
    Edited by Dieter Hessel.* Philadelphia: The Westminster
    Press, 1977. Maggie Kuhn, national convener of the
    Gray Panthers, discusses ageism, retirement communities
    and homes for the aged ("playpens and warehouses"),
    health, mandatory retirement, nutrition programs, the
    church's role with the aging, and other topics with
    students in the Advanced Pastoral Studies Program of
    the San Francisco Theological Seminary.

5. Kuhn, Maggie. "Grass-Roots Gray Power." In *The Older
    Woman: Lavender Rose or Gray Panther*, pp. 223-7, Marie
    Marschall Fuller and Cora Ann Martin, eds. Springfield,
    Illinois: Charles C. Thomas, 1980. This is the right
    "existential moment" for the Life Cycle Project to come
    to the churches and to society. There is need for pub-
    lic awareness both of the contributions the elderly can
    make and the forces and policies that demean them.
    Consciousness-raising can restore appreciation of the
    value of experience, and thus of the continuity of life.
    Its larger goal is self-determination, whereby those
    affected by decisions participate in making, enforcing
    and monitoring them. It opens up new options and is a
    means of personal as well as social liberation. It also
    helps the old deal with infirmities and fears, provides
    a new approach for professionals working with the elderly,
    prepares the elderly to function effectively as members
    of boards, committees and agencies that provide the
    services, enhances appreciation of the fact that people
    are sexual beings to the very end of life, and helps
    the elderly return to society as contributing members.
    This will expand the horizons of later life for those
    who will be tomorrow's elderly.

6.   Lasch, Christopher. "Aging in a Culture without a Future."
     Institute of Society, Ethics and the Life Sciences
     Report (August 1977) 7(4):42-4. A review of *No More
     Dying* and *Prolongevity*. Lasch identifies common features
     of two approaches to aging--the medical, exemplified
     by these books under review, and the social, through
     which the problem of old age is seen to be rooted more
     in modern society's intolerance of the old than in
     physical decline--and states that they are similar in
     that both rest on hope more than on a critical examina-
     tion of the evidence. In his view, old age could be
     made more bearable only if our social institutions were
     completely transformed, and there is a close association
     between irrational terror of old age and death and the
     emergence of the narcissistic personality dominant in
     our society.

7.   Levin, Jack, and William C. Levin. *Ageism: Prejudice and
     Discrimination Against the Elderly*. Belmont, California:
     Wadsworth Publishing Co., 1980. Contents are: Geron-
     tology: The Focus on Decline; Blaming the Aged; The
     Aged as a Minority Group; Reactions to Ageism; Proposals
     and Prospects for Change. In her Foreword, Maggie Kuhn
     states that this book is a significant summary of twenty
     years of research in Gerontology and an important
     "critic" of current theories and policies dealing with
     the issues of age. She believes that the ageism perva-
     sive in our society is documented well in this book,
     and that the authors have shown the impotence of re-
     tirement education and service programs which aim at
     the socialization of the victims to their fate.

8.   Rose, Arnold M. "The Subculture of the Aging: A Topic
     for Sociological Research." In *Middle Age and Aging:
     A Reader in Social Psychology*, pp. 29-34, Bernice L.
     Neugarten, ed. Chicago: The University of Chicago
     Press, 1968. Rose's statement of the interrelated
     hypotheses pointing to the rise of a subculture of
     elderly people in the U.S., his consideration of the
     general factors creating and influencing an aging sub-
     culture, description of the distinctive characteristics
     of this subculture, his observation of the growth of
     group-consciousness among the elderly and his prediction
     that sociologists would study this transformation of a
     social category into a social group. In 1962, in this
     paper first published in *The Gerontologist*, he stated
     that the elderly, heretofore a "low prestige segment"
     of the U.S. population, and therefore studied only by

those interested in "social reform," would have a
higher status in the future.

9. Rosenfeld, Albert, and Christopher Lasch. "Author's
    Back-Lasch." Institute of Society, Ethics and the
    Life Sciences *Report* (December 1977) 7(6):4, 39. In
    Rosenfeld's letter about Lasch's review of his book
    Prolongevity, he objects to Lasch's position that the
    theory that medical intervention and health measures
    played a major role in increasing life expectancy in
    the past century is a naïve one. In his reply, Lasch
    affirms that most historians and demographers incline
    to the view that improvements in diet, sanitation and
    general living standards, not improvements in medical
    technology, account for the prolongation of life ex-
    pectancy since the 18th century. Lasch also names the
    outstanding characteristic of the society of the
    "future" as stagnation which is dramatically manifested
    in the terror of aging.

10. Sommers, Tish. "A Free-Lance Agitator Confronts the
     Establishment." In *The New Old: Struggling for Decent
     Aging*, pp. 231-40, Ronald Gross, Beatrice Gross and
     Sylvia Seidman, eds. Garden City, New York: Anchor
     Press/Doubleday, 1978. In her testimony at a hearing
     held by the Administration on Aging, Sommers strongly
     criticizes the "social service" approach to helping
     the elderly, and says that out of self-interest as ·
     well as concern the helping professions may be over-
     selling the "pitiful plight" of seniors. In opposition
     to reinforcing dependency, and to the built-in disin-
     centives to work that now exist, and in criticism of
     laws and programs as they now operate and of the ex-
     ploitation of the labor of older persons that now
     obtains, she makes a number of proposals based upon
     autonomy and the right to self-sufficiency, with regard
     to transportation, employment and training programs.

*11. U.S. Congress. Senate. *Developments in Aging: 1979: A
      Report of the Special Committee on Aging, U.S. Senate*.
      Washington, D.C.: U.S. Government Printing Office,
      1980.

*12. U.S. Congress. House Subcommittee on Human Services of
      the Select Committee on Aging. *Future Directions for
      Aging Policy: A Human Service Model*. Committee Pub-

lication No. 96-226. Washington, D.C.: U.S. Government
Printing Office, 1980.

See also: 138, 143, 189, 193, 209, 229, 231, 234, 515, 628, 860.

B. Older Women

13. Bell, Inge Powell. "The Double Standard: Age." In
     Women: A Feminist Perspective, pp. 145-55, Jo Freeman,
     ed. Palo Alto, California: Mayfield Publishing Co.,
     1975. Women are considered to be made sexually un-
     attractive by aging much earlier than men; the most
     dramatic institutionalization of different age defini-
     tions for the sexes is the cultural norm governing
     age at marriage. With aging, women also experience a
     decline in prestige: a woman's primary role, that of
     mother, disappears during middle age. Economic loss
     is also a consequence of aging; whether women are
     more discriminated against in employment because of
     age is a subject that merits further study. Dollard's
     Caste and Class in a Southern Town was the basis for
     dividing this article into *sexual*, *prestige* and *economic
     loss*. Middle-class status does not cushion all of
     life's shocks for women.

14. *Broomstick: By, For, and About Women Over Forty*. 3543 18th
     Street, San Francisco, California 94110. (1978-).
     A monthly periodical with occasional double issues and
     four longer quarterlies.

15. Brown, Camie Lou. "Agism and the Women's Movement."
     In *Women on the Move: A Feminist Perspective*, pp. 225-7,
     Jean Ramage Leppaluoto, Joan Acker, Claudeen Naffziger,
     Karla Brown, Catherine M. Porter, Barbara A. Mitchell
     and Roberta Hanna, eds. Pittsburgh, Pennsylvania:
     Know, Inc., 1973. In this paper from the workshop of
     the book's title held in June, 1972, at the University
     of Oregon, Brown shows the resemblances between ageism,
     racism and sexism, provides examples of how she has
     seen ageism at work in the women's movement, and writes
     that women's quest for power in a sexist society should
     not be undertaken at the expense of other people who
     are oppressed.

*16. Bruère, Martha, and Robert Bruère. "The Waste of Old
      Women." *Harper's Bazaar* (March 1913) 47:115.

17. Feldman, Harold. "Penelope, Molly, Narcissus, and Susan."
     In *Looking Ahead: A Woman's Guide to the Problems and
     Joys of Growing Older*, pp. 73-80, Lillian E. Troll,
     Joan Israel and Kenneth Israel, eds. Englewood Cliffs,
     New Jersey: Prentice-Hall, Inc., 1977. When it is not
     unusual for people to live for ninety years, during
     the last third of life we may be "free at last." These
     four typologies suggest four ways of living that are
     not mutually exclusive: (1) Penelope, named after
     Ulysses' wife, derives meaning for her life from
     companionate relationships; (2) Molly (and one can
     be a Jewish mamma without being Jewish) finds meaning
     in life through children; (3) Narcissus types, who
     often like to live alone, are in search of self-
     affirmation; (4) Susans, named after Susan B. Anthony,
     find joy in serving a cause that needs them. Feldman
     proposes the establishment of ageism studies centers
     and provides examples of possible consciousness-raising
     courses to be taught in their programs.

18. *Growing Numbers, Growing Force. A Report From the White
     House Mini-Conference on Older Women (The Long Report).*
     San Francisco, California: Western Gerontological
     Society, and Oakland, California: Older Women's League
     Educational Fund, 1981. The 400 participants repre-
     sented a cross section of older women in the U.S.,
     younger advocates of older women's issues, and also
     some interested men; they were white, Black, Latina
     and Asian, ranging in age from their 20s to their 70s;
     some were disabled, and most had personally experienced
     the compounding effects of ageism and sexism. Contents:
     Opening Speakout; Workshop Reports: Insuring Adequate
     Income (Social Security, pensions, employment and
     training, means-tested programs, midlife planning for
     aging); Health Concerns of Older Women (cost and de-
     livery of health care; medical research and training;
     image of growing older female; long term care; alcohol
     and drug abuse); Quality of Life and Impact on Aging
     (The Demographics of Aging; The Family; Older Women
     Alone; Housing; Older Women as Victims of Violence
     and Fear); A Panel Discussion on Minority Women;
     Summary; Postscript; National OWL Agenda; Suggestions
     for Further Reading.

19. *Growing Numbers, Growing Force. Report from the White House Mini-Conference on Older Women. (The Delegates' Report)*. San Francisco, California: Western Gerontological Society, and Oakland, California: Older Women's League Educational Fund, 1981. Questions and answers on older women; excerpts from Keynote: Speak Out of Older Women; excerpts from general session: minority concerns of older women; summary of topics discussed in the work sessions, with a key proposal for each topic (Work sessions addressed fifteen topics, divided into three clusters: insuring adequate income; health concerns of older women; and quality of life and impact on aging). Conclusion on the significance and central themes of the Conference, and the formation of the Older Women's League to implement its program.

20. Hochstein, Rollie. "I'm Over 40." *Ms.* (November 1972) I(5):90-2. The full title is "Listen. I'm Going To Tell You Something, But I Want It To Remain Strictly Between Us. The Truth Is ... I'm Over Forty." Hochstein lies about her age not only to protect her "near and dear" (her spouse, mother and children), but also to protect herself from being the target of the age prejudices in our society as reflected in negative cultural connotations for the phrase "Older Woman."

21. *Hot Flash: A Newsletter for Mid-Life and Older Women*. School of Allied Health Professions, Health Sciences Center, State University of New York, Stony Brook, New York 11794. (1981-) This newsletter was conceived and born following "Health Issues of Older Women: A Projection to the Year 2000," the first national conference on the health issues of women over 40, in April, 1981.

22. "How To Fight Age Bias." *Ms.* (June 1975) III(12):91-4. A report on the activities of the Gray Panthers, *Prime Time*, a national newsletter edited by Marjory Collins; an excerpt from "Call for Action" by Tish Sommers (published in *Prime Time*); "Sisterhood Ages Well" by Tish Sommers, NOW Task Force on Older Women; a report on the NOW Task Force on Older Women, and a report on *No Longer Young: The Older Woman in America*, the 1973 Annual Conference on aging held at the University of Michigan, written by Janet Oliver; and a report on the Business and Professional Women's Organization financial aid programs for women.

23. Hunter, Jean E.   "Images of Woman." *Journal of Social
     Issues* (Summer 1976) 32(3):7-17. This paper surveys
     attitudes towards women in the classical civilizations
     of Greece and Rome, the religious teachings of the
     Judeo-Christian tradition, and in Western society
     during the Middle Ages.   Three images are predominant:
     woman as inferior, woman as evil, and woman as the
     love object.   Each supports a pervasive assumption
     that women and men differ not only in social roles
     but in their very nature.   Although women have chal-
     lenged prevailing conceptions of their role and worth
     since the Renaissance, every challenge has been met
     by recurrent appeals to earlier conceptions, and
     traditional images of women still retain their value
     to those who wish to appeal to them in defending
     the status quo.   For the social revolution of feminism
     to succeed, awareness and close study of traditional
     sources of these persistent images is necessary.

24. Janeway, Elizabeth.   "Breaking the Age Barrier." *Ms.*
     (April 1973) I(10):50-1, 53, 109-11. Many women who
     are now middle-aged believe that the proper role for
     women is the traditional one.   It is difficult for
     them to break away from their commitment to this role
     because their personal image and self-esteem are bound
     up with it.   To some older women, the Movement seems
     to be saying, "Your past doesn't mean a thing."   But
     the past cannot be written off this way.   The Movement
     offers older women the chance to take themselves
     seriously.   It is important to take full responsibility
     for one's life.   The Movement can bring isolation,
     including age-grade isolation, to an end, and older
     women can offer younger women an overview of what
     their lives have meant to them.

25. Jones, Ann, Recorder.   "Political Importance of the Older
     Woman."   In *No Longer Young: The Older Woman in
     America, Work Group Reports*, pp. 27-30.   Ann Arbor,
     Michigan: The Institute of Gerontology, The University
     of Michigan-Wayne State University, 1974.   Many older
     women want to use their greater free time productively.
     Areas related to women which need legislative action,
     including discrimination in pension and retirement
     benefits, will require changes in the law.   Women
     should also become involved in the revenue-sharing
     issue, and work to have more representation on govern-
     mental boards and commissions.   Directions for political
     activity are suggested; the politics of confrontation

is recommended; methods of organizing offices, councils
and commissions on aging are discussed; group pressure
by the elderly is recommended, and a number of techniques for effective action are suggested.

26. Kethley, Alice J. "Women and Aging: The Unforgivable
     Sin." In *Women On the Move: A Feminist Perspective*,
     pp. 39-45, Jean Ramage Leppaluoto, Joan Acker, Claudeen
     Naffziger, Karla Brown, Catherine M. Porter, Barbara
     A. Mitchell and Roberta Hanna, eds. Pittsburgh,
     Pennsylvania: Know, Inc., 1973. In this paper from
     the workshop of this book's title held in June,
     1972, at the University of Oregon, Kethley discusses
     the view of aging in America, which is a youth-oriented
     society, the problems of the elderly as a minority
     group in the U.S., and the special problems of aged
     women, a majority within the minority. She considers
     aging to be a challenge, a natural phenomenon and a
     privilege, and not a morbid topic or a disaster. She
     argues that we need knowledge about the entire life
     course, and that we should accept the value and worth
     of people of all ages and reflect this acceptance in
     our attitudes and actions.

27. Lewis, Myrna I., and Robert N. Butler. "Why Is Women's
     Lib Ignoring Old Women?" *The International Journal
     of Aging and Human Development* (1972) 3(3):223-31.
     The women's liberation movement has focused on issues
     that concern young and middle-aged women, but elderly
     women have much to contribute to its strength and
     viability. Discrimination against old women is in-
     herent in the Social Security system. Because of
     ageism combined with sexism, they are discriminated
     against by employers and members of the medical
     profession. Because of the sex difference in life
     expectancy, many live alone and have limited sexual
     outlets. Many suffer from the self-hatred that is
     common among victims of discrimination. But old women,
     whose numbers are increasing, have great potential
     politically and in terms of personal expression.
     Educational programs should be designed for them to
     explore late-life careers. They can develop a heightened
     sense of moral commitment and flexibility beyond their
     own egos, and can serve as models of aging for younger
     women.

28. Martin, Cora A. "Lavender Rose or Gray Panther?" In
     The Older Woman: Lavender Rose or Gray Panther, pp.
     55-8, Marie Marschall Fuller and Cora Ann Martin,
     eds. Springfield, Illinois: Charles C. Thomas, 1980.
     Two extremes of lifestyles that characterize older
     women are depicted. The lavender roses, "nice old
     ladies" in their 70s, were created by an early
     socialization that taught little girls in the 1900s
     to be obedient and quiet. Older women, when widowed,
     find it difficult to cope with today's impersonal
     social system. They are vulnerable to fraud and
     unaware of the benefits due them. Excerpts from
     two books about the personality development of women
     are quoted, one showing the dependency and passivity
     expected of women and the other questioning whether
     or not these qualities are "healthy." Many in the
     coming generation of older women are learning in-
     dependence. Although middle-aged women today still
     value traditional "femininity" and are reluctant to
     seem aggressive and competitive, they will need to
     learn political activism more than to master the
     rudiments of financial management or protective
     agencies. Planners for programs for the aged in
     the year 2000 can expect more gray panthers among
     their ranks.

29. National Action Forum for Older Women *Forum*. Co-directed
     by Jane Porcino, School of Allied Health Professions,
     Health Sciences Center, SUNY at Stony Brook, Stony
     Brook, New York 11794, and Nancy King, Center for
     Women Policy Studies, 2000 P Street, NW, Washington,
     D.C. 20036. (1978-)

*30. *Network News*. Displaced Homemakers Network, Inc., 755
     Eighth Street, NW, Washington, D.C. 20001. (1978-)
     Detailed information for programs seeking CETA funding
     for displaced homemakers.

31. Nudel, Adele. *For the Woman over 50: A Practical Guide
     for a Full and Vital Life*. New York: Taplinger
     Publishing Co., 1978. Nudel's book is the outgrowth
     of her having been active in the civil rights, antiwar
     and women's movements, of serving older people in
     institutional settings, of her own development as a
     woman over age forty, of her participation in an older
     women's consciousness-raising group, and of listening
     to the questions raised by older people at pre-retirement

panels. Chapters in this guidebook are on biological
aspects of aging; obtaining physical and mental health
care; "Forty-five Ways to Look and Feel Fantastic";
sex, relationships, divorce and remarriage; "Your
Changing Marriage"; relationships with aging parents;
widowhood; working; "Strategies for the Career Woman";
returning to school; and retirement. Bibliography
and list of state agencies on aging and regional
offices appended.

*32.   Older Women's League Educational Fund *Coverletter*, 3800
Harrison Street, Oakland, California 94611. A
quarterly newsletter of OWLEF.

*33.   Older Women's League Educational Fund. *How to Tame the
CETA Beast: An Advocacy Manual for Older Women.*
Oakland, California: Older Women's League Educational
Fund, 1979. An advocacy manual for older women to
help implement the displaced homemaker provisions
of CETA.

34.   *Our Own.* Older Women's Network, Inc., 3502 Coyote Creek
Road, Wolf Creek, Oregon 97497. Network newsletter.
(1977-)

35.   Preston, Caroline E. "An Old Bag: The Stereotype of the
Older Woman." In *No Longer Young: The Older Woman
in America*, pp. 41-5. Ann Arbor, Michigan: The
Institute of Gerontology, The University of Michigan-
Wayne State University, 1975. Preston asks if there
is a phrase or concept in our language that is more
contemptuous than the pejorative, invidious "an old
bag." She notes that older women in our society are
victimized by both sexism and ageism, and that there
is evidence that old people voice the same negative
stereotypes about the elderly that many young and
middle-aged people do. She reports some of the findings
of the Duke Longitudinal Study, cites the work by
Masters and Johnson concerning sexuality and aging,
points to Beauvoir's remark that late life can be
a time of liberation for women even more than for
men, and also cites statistics concerning sex
differences in marital status, retirement income and
vulnerability to age discrimination in hiring practices,
and Kassel's recommendation for polygynous liaisons
after age sixty.

36. Smeal, Eleanor. "A Challenge to Congress--NOW's Bill
     of Rights for Homemakers." *Ms.* (October 1979)
     VIII(4):84-5. Major provisions of the bill as out-
     lined by NOW President Smeal before the House Subcommittee
     on Retirement Income and Employment. Sections on
     educational rights for homemakers, economic rights
     for women in the home, and economic rights for women
     in transition. On page 85, Anne Witte ("Your Social
     Security--Don't Leave Home Without It") argues that
     the earnings-splitting arrangement is the most practi-
     cal means of covering both spouses equally. Her
     focus is on means for making the tax treatment of
     men and women more equitable.

37. Sommers, Tish. "The Compounding Impact of Age on Sex."
     In *The New Old: Struggling for Decent Aging*, pp. 123-36,
     Ronald Gross, Beatrice Gross and Sylvia Seidman, eds.
     Garden City, New York: Anchor Press/Doubleday, 1978.
     The compounding effects of ageism and sexism have not
     been clearly perceived because the aged are desexed
     in our society. In the U.S. the cult of youth affects
     both sexes, but the timing differs: women are seen as
     "old" much sooner than men. The empty nest syndrome,
     often concurrent with menopause, is a crisis of
     identity comparable to men's crisis at retirement,
     yet few take it seriously. Widowhood is a form of
     forced retirement, and women's chances for remarriage
     are poorer than men's. Women are victimized by "no
     fault" divorce laws, which have added to the growing
     numbers of unmarried older women in the U.S. Sommers
     discusses problems of labor force re-entry and the
     inequities of the Social Security system. She shows
     how there is a virtual blackout of services or benefits
     during women's middle years, how age discrimination
     is differently applied to men than to women, and how
     special protection for women is a myth in our society.
     She advocates working toward self-sufficiency and
     perceives ways older women are linking a reviving
     senior activism to women's struggle for equality.

38. Sontag, Susan. "The Double Standard of Aging." In *No
     Longer Young: The Older Woman in America*, pp. 31-9.
     Ann Arbor, Michigan: The Institute of Gerontology,
     The University of Michigan-Wayne State University, 1975.
     Old age is a genuine ordeal for both men and women,
     but growing older afflicts women more than men. In
     our society, well-being is equated with youth, but

it is much more important for women to be physically
attractive than for men, and beauty is identified
with youthfulness. Also, femininity is identified
with incompetence, helplessness, passivity, noncom-
petitiveness and being nice, and none of these qualities
improves with aging. Women are denied most of the
satisfactions men derive from work, which often
increase with age. Because women become sexually
ineligible much earlier in life than men do, aging
is a humiliating process of gradual sexual disqualifi-
cation for women. After early youth, women's sexual
value declines steadily. The single state is thought
to confirm women's, but not men's unacceptability.
Anxiety about aging is more common and acute among
middle-class and wealthy women. Thus, aging is defined
socially, not biologically, and the very women who
maintain their youthful appearance the longest are
the ones who feel the defeat of aging most keenly.
Women are more vain than men because of the relentless
pressure placed upon them to maintain their appearance
at a certain high standard. Unlike men, women are
identified with their faces; they pay much heavier
penalties than men for the normal changes inscribed
by aging on every human face. The vulnerability of
women is nowhere more clearly apparent than in the
pain, confusion and bad faith accompanying their
aging. It is to be hoped women will become indignantly
aware of the double standard of aging afflicting them
so harshly.

39.   Tuchman, Gaye, Arlene Kaplan Daniels and James Benét, eds.
      Hearth and Home: Images of Women in the Mass Media.
      New York: Oxford University Press, 1978. Preface by
      Daniels; Introduction on "The Symbolic Annihilation
      of Women by the Mass Media" by Tuchman; fourteen
      papers on television; women's magazines; newspapers
      and their women's pages; and television's effect on
      children and youth; a conclusion, "Will Media Treat-
      ment of Women Improve?" by Benét. Includes an annotated
      bibliography by Helen Franzwa on the image of women
      in television.

See also: 219, 242, 248, 250, 251, 255, 256, 258, 259, 261,
369, 380, 389, 462, 484, 557, 655, 719, 720, 726, 727, 728,
735, 748, 750, 754, 756, 757, 758, 759, 863, 869.

II. AUTOBIOGRAPHIES

A. Autobiographies By Older Women

40. Anderson, Margaret C. *The Strange Necessity (The Autobiography--Resolutions and Reminiscence to 1969).* New York: Horizon Press, 1969. (1891?-1973) Third volume of her autobiography; Anderson conducted *The Little Review*, first in Chicago and later in New York City and Paris.

41. Anderson, Mary. *Woman at Work, The Autobiography of Mary Anderson as Told to Mary N. Winslow.* Westport, Connecticut: Greenwood Press, 1951. (1872-1964) Anderson, labor leader and federal official, was Head of the federal Women's Bureau from 1920 to 1944.

42. Atherton, Gertrude Franklin Horn. *Adventures of a Novelist.* New York: Liveright, Inc., 1932. (1857-1948) Novelist, biographer, historian.

43. Austin, Mary. *Earth Horizon.* Boston: Houghton Mifflin Co., 1932. (1868-1934) Poet, critic, novelist, playwright.

44. Bailey, Pearl. *The Raw Pearl.* New York: Harcourt, Brace and World, Inc., 1968. (1918-) Singer.

45. Bowen, Catherine Drinker. *Family Portrait.* Boston: Little, Brown and Co., 1970. (1897-) Writer, biographer, historian.

46. Brooks, Gwendolyn. *Report from Part One.* Detroit, Michigan: Broadside Press, 1972. (1917-) Poet, novelist.

*47. Buck, Pearl. *My Several Worlds: A Personal Record*.
      New York: Day Co., 1954. (1892-1973) Novelist, short
      story writer.

 48. Butcher, Fanny. *Many Lives--One Love*. New York: Harper
      and Row, Inc., 1972. (1888-1974?) Reviewer of books
      and music; literary editor, Chicago *Tribune* for
      fifty years.

 49. Calisher, Hortense. *Herself*. New York: Arbor House,
      1972. (1911-   ) Novelist, short story writer.

 50. Chase, Ilka. *Past Imperfect*. Garden City, New York:
      Blue Ribbon Books, 1945. (1905-1978) Film actress,
      radio personality, author.

 51. Day, Dorothy. *The Long Loneliness, The Autobiography
      of Dorothy Day*. New York: Harper and Brothers, 1952.
      (1897-1980) Social reformer, writer.

 52. De Mille, Agnes. *Dance to the Piper*. Boston: Little,
      Brown and Co., 1952. (1905-   ) Dancer, writer.

 53. Deutsch, Helene, M.D. *Confrontations with Myself--An
      Epilogue*. New York: W.W. Norton and Co., Inc., 1973.
      (1884-   ) Psychiatrist.

 54. Duncan, Isadora. *My Life*. New York: Boni and Liveright,
      Inc., 1927, 1955. (1878-1927) Dancer.

*55. Duveneck, Josephine Whitney. *Life on Two Levels: An
      Autobiography*. Los Altos, California: William
      Kaufmann, Inc., 1978. (1891-   ) Autobiography of
      a distinguished California woman; "unique cultural
      history of our century."

 56. Ferber, Edna. *A Peculiar Treasure*. New York: Literary
      Guild, 1939. (1887-1968) Novelist, playwright.

 57. Fisher, Welthy Honsinger. *To Light a Candle*. New
      York: McGraw-Hill Book Co., Inc., 1962. (1880-1980)
      Missionary, educator (in China).

 58. Garden, Mary, and Louis Biancalli. *Mary Garden's Story*.
      New York: Simon and Schuster, Inc., 1951. (1877-
      1967) Opera singer.

*59. Gilman, Charlotte Perkins. *The Living of Charlotte Perkins Gilman: An Autobiography.* New York: D. Appleton-Century Co., Inc., 1935. (1860-1935) Lecturer, author.

60. Glasgow, Ellen. *The Woman Within.* New York: Harcourt, Brace and Co., 1954. (1893/94?-1945) Novelist.

61. Hayes, Helen, with Lewis Funke. *A Gift of Joy.* New York: M. Evans and Co., Inc. in association with J.B. Lippincott Co., 1965. (1900-   ) Actress.

62. Hellman, Lillian. *An Unfinished Woman--A Memoir.* Boston: Little, Brown and Co., 1969. (1905-   ) Playwright.

63. Hurston, Zora Neale. *Dust Tracks on a Road.* New York: Arno Press and The New York Times, 1969, reprinted from a copy in the collection of Howard University Library, copyright Hurston, 1942. (1901?-1960) Novelist, dramatist, folklorist.

Jones, Mother. See No. 69.

64. Keller, Helen. *Midstream: My Later Life.* Garden City, New York: Doubleday, Doran and Co., Inc., 1929. (1880-1968) Author, lecturer.

65. Lurie, Nancy Oestreich, ed. *Mountain Wolf Woman: Sister of Crashing Thunder, The Autobiography of a Winnebago Indian.* Ann Arbor, Michigan: The University of Michigan Press, 1966.

66. McCarthy, Mary. *Memories of a Catholic Girlhood.* New York: Harcourt, Brace and Co., 1957. (1912-   ) Novelist, short story writer, critic.

67. Mead, Margaret. *Blackberry Winter: My Earlier Years.* New York: William Morrow, Pocket Books, 1975. (1901-1978) Anthropologist, author.

68. Monroe, Harriet. *A Poet's Life (Seventy Years in a Changing World).* New York: The Macmillan Co., 1938. (1860-1936) Editor of *Poetry: A Magazine of Verse;* poet, dramatist.

Mountain Wolf Woman. See No. 65.

69. Parton, Mary Field, ed. *The Autobiography of Mother
     Jones*. Chicago: Charles H. Kerr Publishing Co.,
     1976, 3rd ed., revised. (1830-1930) Labor organizer.

70. Pesotta, Rose. *Bread Upon the Waters* (edited by John
     Nicholas Beffel). New York: Dodd, Mead and Co.,
     1944. (1896-1965) Labor organizer.

71. Peterson, Virgilia. *A Matter of Life and Death*. New
     York: Atheneum, 1961. (1904-1966) Critic, author.

72. Roosevelt, (Anna) Eleanor. *The Autobiography of Eleanor
     Roosevelt*. New York: Harper and Brothers, 1961.
     (1884-1962) Columnist, author, social reformer.

73. Roosevelt, (Anna) Eleanor. *This Is My Story*. New York:
     Harper and Brothers, 1937. (1884-1962) Columnist,
     author, social reformer.

74. Sanger, Margaret. *Margaret Sanger: An Autobiography*.
     New York: W.W. Norton and Co., Inc., 1938. (1883-
     1966) Leader of birth control movement, author.

75. Scudder, Vida. *On Journey*. New York: E.P. Dutton and
     Co., Inc., 1937. (1861-1954) Teacher, critic,
     editor, writer.

76. Van Hoosen, Bertha. *Petticoat Surgeon*. Chicago:
     Pellegrini and Cudahy, 1947. (1863-1952) Physician,
     surgeon.

77. Vorse, Mary Heaton. *A Footnote to Folly: Reminiscences
     of Mary Heaton Vorse*. New York: Farrar and Rinehart,
     Inc., 1935. (1874-1966) Writer, journalist.

78. Wharton, Edith. *A Backward Glance*. New York: D.
     Appleton-Century Co., 1934. (1862-1937) Novelist,
     short story writer, memoirist.

                    B. Autobiographies: Collections;
                          Critical Studies;
                       Variations on the Genre

79. Billson, Marcus K., and Sidonie A. Smith. "Lillian
     Hellman and the Strategy of the 'Other.'" In

Women's Autobiography: Essays in Criticism, pp.
163-79, Estelle C. Jelinek, ed. Bloomington:
Indiana University Press, 1980. (See No. 577 of
this Bibliography.) The memorialist's vision of
the outer world is as much a projection and refraction
of the self as the autobiographer's: the latent content
of the memoir is self-revelation. The strategy of
the "other" pervading *An Unfinished Woman* and
Pentimento proposes a dialectic between the memorialist
and time--past and present. The dialectic proposed
by this strategy--which allows Hellman to explore
the self from the distance of the "other," permits
her to see the self as the sum of all past experiences,
enables her to confront the unfulfilled desires of
her life through the process of conscious recall, and
provides her with yet another means to create drama--
results in a synthesis. This synthesis, that is, the
repossession of the past in the articulation of the
"other," becomes an act of renewal in the midst of
a sense of loss.

80. Blackburn, Regina. "In Search of the Black Female Self:
African-American Women's Autobiographies and Ethnicity."
In *Women's Autobiography: Essays in Criticism*, pp. 133-48,
Estelle C. Jelinek, ed. Bloomington: Indiana University
Press, 1980. Blackburn's concern is with the source
of the self-image of African-American women. Although
they led very diverse lives in the U.S., their identities
and self-conceptions are significantly shaped by their
blackness and their womanhood. The autobiographies
of Ossie Guffy, Delle Brehan, Zora Neale Hurston,
Pearl Bailey, Nikki Giovanni, Gwendolyn Brooks,
Lorraine Hansberry, Helen Jackson Lee, Maya Angelou,
Anne Moody, Angela Davis and Shirley Chisholm are
the texts for this study of black self-statement,
black pride, self-hatred and double jeopardy. (See
Nos. 44, 46 and 63 of this Bibliography.) Writing
autobiography is a declaration of a complex, multi-
dimensional, changing selfhood. This declaration by
these writers is a positive step toward bonding the
black and female self in America.

81. Bloom, Lynn Z., and Orlee Holder. "Anaïs Nin's *Diary*
in Context." In *Women's Autobiography: Essays in
Criticism*, pp. 206-20, Estelle C. Jelinek, ed.

Bloomington: Indiana University Press, 1980. (See
Nos. 608, 609 and 610 of this Bibliography.) The
concern of this study is how Nin's *Diary* corresponds
to definitions of autobiography in general; whether
or not it follows the standard conventions of autobiographical form and technique; and whether or not
it exhibits the characteristics of structure and theme
which typify the autobiographies of other leading
women writers. Autobiographies and diaries are
compared and contrasted, unique characteristics of
women's autobiographies are discussed, and it is
shown how, with respect to form and in their concern
with their identities as women and writers, the autobiographies of other leading women writers appear to
be more akin to diaries than to autobiographies written
by men. Nin's work follows the general conventions
of autobiographical writing and illustrates the
structural discontinuity and pervasive thematic
concerns that seem to typify women's autobiography.
That she could continue to affirm her creativity
despite decades of neglect and hostility is incredible.
Her *Diary* is distinctive in that, without imposing
any artificial structure on the material, she still
compels the reader to see her life and career as
unified and cohesive.

82. Breslin, James E. "Gertrude Stein and the Problems of
Autobiography." In *Women's Autobiography: Essays
in Criticism*, pp. 149-62, Estelle C. Jelinek, ed.
Bloomington: Indiana University Press, 1980. An
essay on *The Autobiography of Alice B. Toklas* by
Stein, whose desire to live and write in a continuous
present turns her against the retrospective act of
autobiography, and whose commitment to a continuous
present forces her to reject the notion of identity
altogether. For Stein, identity destroys creation,
as does memory. To *be*, rather than to *repeat*, one
must constantly break down identity. But how can
there be autobiography without identity? Autobiographies
are customarily defined as acts of self-representation.
But Stein is challenged to refashion the form to show
that she eludes or transcends the category of self or
identity. This book admits the conventions of memory,
identity, chronological time, in order to fight against
and ultimately to transcend their deadening effects.
At once an autobiography and a fiction, it is multivalent.
By renouncing a simple center and a continuous design,
by exploring the formal dilemmas of the genre, Stein
at once accepted, denied, and created autobiography.

83. Bruss, Elizabeth W. *Autobiographical Acts: The Changing Situation of a Literary Genre*. Baltimore: The Johns Hopkins University Press, 1976. Although the autobiographies considered here are by men (John Bunyan, James Boswell, Thomas De Quincey and Vladimir Nabokov), the Introduction and first chapter, respectively, present a criticism of the form and technique and development of the genre, and of autobiography "From Act to Text."

84. Demetrakopoulos, Stephanie A. "The Metaphysics of Matrilinearism in Women's Autobiography: Studies of Mead's *Blackberry Winter*, Hellman's *Pentimento*, Angelou's *I Know Why the Caged Bird Sings*, and Kingston's *The Woman Warrior*." In *Women's Autobiography: Essays in Criticism*, pp. 180-205, Estelle C. Jelinek, ed. Bloomington: Indiana University Press, 1980. (See Nos. 67 and 577 of this Bibliography.) Demetrakopoulos' essay is meant to re-establish the sacrality of feminine experience and to re-mythologize all human experience through the treatment of the development, characterization and significance of the matriarchal realm in women's autobiography. She shows the importance of (Jungian) feminine archetypes in these four autobiographies, and suggests that emphasis on their mothers in women's autobiography is due to innate and archetypal aspects of the woman's psyche, which were celebrated and codified long ago as the Eleusinian Mysteries, and that many kinds of women's autobiographies present strong developments of the emphasis on the matriarchal realm as the bedrock out of which a woman forges her identity. Woman's mythos is shaped in the writing of autobiography. It is the privilege of women to embody the consciousness toward which the image of mother/daughter duality strives--of matrilineal ongoingness as the symbol of hope for immortality, the continuity of the individual life.

85. Jelinek, Estelle C. "Introduction: Women's Autobiography and the Male Tradition." In *Women's Autobiography: Essays in Criticism*, pp. 1-20, Estelle C. Jelinek, ed. Bloomington: Indiana University Press, 1980. The publication of a large number of autobiographies in the 1930s led to revival of interest in their critical analysis, but critics discussed only their subject matter and they made moral judgments about their authors. Only after World War II did this mode

begin to receive consideration as a genre worthy of
serious critical attention. Jelinek compares the
content of women's and men's life studies and contrasts
stylistic aspects. She finds that most objective
theories of critics are not applicable to women's
life studies, calls attention to the "autobiographical
fallacy of self-revelation," and shows that self-
portraits by women are characterized by irregularity
rather than orderliness. The criterion of orderliness
is often not applicable to women's life stories. In
various times and countries, many more women than men
write discontinuous forms--diaries, journals and
notebooks--rather than autobiographies. These forms
are analogous to the fragmented, interrupted and
formless nature of women's lives. In the late 20th
century, experimentation in the genre may prompt
critics to modify their definitions and theories;
modifications are long overdue for judging women's
autobiographies.

86. Jelinek, Estelle C. Preface. In *Women's Autobiography:*
     Essays in Criticism, pp. ix-xii, Estelle C. Jelinek,
     ed. Bloomington: Indiana University Press, 1980.
     This book is a collection of 14 essays representing
     a cross section of criticism being written today on
     women's autobiographies, chosen because they view
     autobiographies primarily as literary works. The
     authors treated represent those most often read in
     courses in women's autobiography and in genre courses,
     as well as outside the university. All treat auto-
     biographies by English-speaking women, with far more
     by American than British writers; ten cover the 20th
     century predominantly. Eight describe or interpret
     the contents of the text, focusing on the self-image
     of the writer; six concentrate on more formal aspects.
     The methodologies emphasizing the writers' self-
     images include the historical, the sociological, the
     psychological, and the ethnic.

87. Limmer, Ruth. *Journey Around My Room: The Autobiography*
     of Louise Bogan, A Mosaic by Ruth Limmer. New York:
     The Viking Press, 1980. Deeply reserved, Bogan did
     not write her autobiography, nor was she likely to
     make known even the basic facts that appear in
     biographical compendia. The frame of this work is
     Bogan's story, "Journey Around My Room," inspired by
     Xavier de Maistre's *Voyage autour de ma chambre*.

Bogan's own "journey" is set in italics, opens certain
chapters, and opens and closes the book. A composition
of journals, notebook entries, poems (some never
published beforè), portions from her criticism, her
letters, a lecture, answers to questions, short stories,
recorded conversations, and scraps of paper, as a
continuous exploration of the question, "How did I
get here, below this ceiling, above this floor?"
Includes a chronology, illustrations, and notes on
sources.

*88. Mason, Mary Grimley, and Carol Hurd Green, eds. *Journeys:
Autobiographical Writings by Women*. Boston: G.K. Hall
and Co., 1979.

89. Showalter, Elaine, ed. *These Modern Women: Autobiographical
Essays from the Twenties*. Old Westbury, New York:
The Feminist Press, 1978. A reprint of 17 essays by
women and three responses by psychologists on the
subject of being a "modern woman" (a feminist) in the
Twenties, published in *The Nation*, 1926-27. The
essayists were invited by *The Nation* to explore the
personal sources of their feminism and to show how
their feminist ideals had stood up to the realities
and pressures of woman's life cycle. The median age
of the women was 40, and the age range from 58 (Mary
Austin) to 30 (Lorine Pruette). Contributors are
Inez Haynes Irwin, Mary Alden Hopkins, Sue Shelton
White, Alice Mary Kimball, Ruth Pickering, Genevieve
Taggard, Lorine Livingston Pruette, Kate L. Gregg,
Mary Hunter Austin, Crystal Eastman, Elizabeth
Stuyvesant, Lou Rogers, Phyllis Blanchard, Victoria
McAlmon, Garland Smith, Cornelia Bryce Pinchot,
Wanda Gág; psychologists are Beatrice M. Hinkle,
John B. Watson and Joseph Collins.

90. Smith, Lillian. "On Women's Autobiography." *Southern
Exposure* (Winter 1977) 4(4):48-9. Women have only
recently begun to break the million-year silence
about themselves. While they are exceptionally good
at writing memoirs, diaries and journals, no woman
has yet written a great autobiography. Women are
capable of abstract thinking, but like all artists
they are closer to human flesh and feelings; they
have great talent for the specific and concrete. To
write the perfect autobiography is to accept and bring
all the selves together. It is an ordeal in creation

of the self--a demiurgic and courageous quest for
the meaning of one's life. To bring the split selves
into unity is important for every individual in our
time.

91. Spacks, Patricia Meyer. "Selves in Hiding." In *Women's*
     Autobiography: Essays in Criticism, pp. 112-32,
     Estelle C. Jelinek, ed. Bloomington: Indiana
     University Press, 1980. The autobiographies of
     Emmeline Pankhurst, Dorothy Day, Emma Goldman, Eleanor
     Roosevelt and Golda Meir, all by women born in the
     19th century--who won not only fame but notoriety,
     each bitterly attacked for her public achievements--
     are stories of the tensions between private and
     public demands that have in common a distinctive tone.
     (See Nos. 51, 72 and 73 of this Bibliography.) All
     five books represent a female variant of spiritual
     autobiography. All are accounts of lives in which
     the women describe themselves as gaining identity
     from their chosen work; all reveal that the identity
     of public performance may cause its female possessor
     pre-existent uncertainties of personal identity.
     The failure to emphasize their *own* importance in a
     genre that implies assertion and display of the self
     is striking. Instead of using the cause ultimately
     to enlarge the sense of self, these women seem to
     diminish self in reporting their causes. Their
     heroism is undeniable, yet their stories convey a
     singular absence of personal satisfaction in achieve-
     ment. They use autobiography, paradoxically, partly
     as a mode of self-denial, and their strategies reflect
     both a female dilemma and a female solution of this
     dilemma.

92. Vorse, Mary Heaton. *Autobiography of an Elderly Woman*.
     Boston: Houghton Mifflin Co., 1911, Reprint Edition
     1974 by Arno Press, Inc. Vorse's mother was the model
     for this book. The work is a portrait of old age
     as seen from within, with reflections on the conventions
     and compensations of age and on intergenerational
     relationships. In retrospect, the narrator writes of
     her life as divided into four parts--childhood and
     girlhood, which now seem a dream; the years since her
     marriage, which seem real in comparison to this; the
     time when she was widowed and her (grown) children
     were becoming her comrades; and the present. She
     writes of the burden of the over-solicitousness of

grown children, the vivid memories she has of her own
mother now, her awareness of the past as both variable
and mysterious, the tyranny of convention ruling the
old and their great need to be released from it, her
refusal to sacrifice her individuality and lead a
packed-in-cotton-wool existence, and the sense of
the growing distance between the generations as one
ages. She believes that how one *should* grow old is a
question as deep as Life itself.

93. Winston, Elizabeth. "The Autobiographer and Her Readers:
     From Apology to Affirmation." In *Women's Autobiography:
     Essays in Criticism*, pp. 93-111, Estelle C. Jelinek,
     ed. Bloomington: Indiana University Press, 1980.
     From the 17th century on, women writers have shown an
     acute self-consciousness of the criticism they often
     aroused simply because of their sex. The autobiographies
     of professional women writers, British and American,
     exhibit an interesting pattern of response to this
     criticism. Up to 1920, they tended to establish a
     conciliatory relationship to their readers, attempting
     to justify their untraditional ways of living and
     writing so as to gain their audience's sympathy and
     acceptance. After 1920 they no longer apologized for
     their careers and successes, although a few were
     uneasy about violating cultural expectations for
     women. More recently published writers openly asserted
     their intellectual and aesthetic gifts and their
     serious commitment to the literary life. Comtemporaries
     like Mary McCarthy, Lillian Hellman and Maya Angelou
     have shown even greater self-confidence. (See Nos. 66
     and 577 of this Bibliography.) Their self-assertive,
     gender-affirming narratives are encouraging models
     for women readers, and give promise of a future when
     a woman's right to write will be assured.

See also: 314, 383, 387, 424, 554, 565, 566, 590, 872,
876, 885.

III. CREATIVITY AND PRODUCTIVITY IN LATER LIFE;
ARTS AND THE ELDERLY

A. General

94. Dennis, Wayne. "Creative Productivity Between the Ages
of 20 and 80 Years." In *Middle Age and Aging: A
Reader in Social Psychology*, pp. 106-14, Bernice L.
Neugarten, ed. Chicago: The University of Chicago
Press, 1968. Although women are not included in this
study, its findings--concerning the life curve of
productivity of 738 persons classified as artists,
scholars or scientists--all of whom lived to age 79
or beyond--are in contrast to Lehman's. (See No. 99
of this Bibliography.) Dennis attributes this to
differences in methodology. Dennis found the decline
in art much more marked than that in other endeavors,
that for almost all groups the forties were either
the most productive or only slightly lower than the
peak decade, and that for scholars, the seventies
were as productive as the forties. Differences in
output curves of the three groups may be because
productivity in the arts depends primarily upon
individual creativity, because the other two require
a greater period of training and greater accumulation
of experience and data, and because, unlike artists,
they can use accumulated data and receive assistance
from others.

*95. Jones, Jean Ellen. *Teaching Art to Older Adults:
Guidelines and Lessons*. Atlanta, Georgia: Georgia
Department of Administrative Services, 1980.

96. Kaminsky, Marc. *What's Inside You It Shines Out of You*.
New York: Horizon Press, 1974. In 1972, Kaminsky
became a group-worker with the Jewish Association for
the Services for the Aged and began a poetry workshop.

In working on the dream-poem with this group, one of
the things he learned was that old women's mourning-
dreams are true acts of creation. In the first
chapter, he writes of how each of his four grandparents
was his teacher. In subsequent chapters he writes
of the Thursday Poetry Group, which lasted for four
months; the beginning of autonomous creativity by
workshop members; his work with other clubs; Writing
and Healing (the poetry *workshop* is centered on the
making of the poem, and poetry *therapy* on the person);
work with memory poems; The Process of the Poetry
Group; and Songs of Healing. Part Two, The Sessions,
includes chapters on the Tuesday Group and the Young
Israel Group. Part Three presents The Poems.
Kaminsky states that the assignments poets use in
poetry workshops can call forth the full creativity
of the persons the poet works with, but even when
they do not, they are a form of "practice," preparing
the whole mind for the creative act.

97.   Koch, Kenneth. *I Never Told Anybody: Teaching Poetry
      Writing in a Nursing Home*. New York: Vintage Books,
      A Division of Random House, 1978. An account of
      Koch's poetry writing workshop, assisted by Kate
      Farrell, at the American Nursing Home in New York
      City. All the students were ill; most were in their
      70s, 80s and 90s, from the working class, and with a
      limited education. The method of teaching, which
      began with class collaborations, worked itself out
      as the class developed. In most cases, students
      dictated individual poems after the poetry idea was
      presented. The dictation was helpful because of
      physical disabilities and of limited education, which
      may have inhibited them in writing. Koch was unpre-
      pared for the directness, sensuousness and imaginativeness
      of some of the students' poems. Poems from this and
      other workshops are included.

*98. Kogan, Nathan. "Creativity and Cognitive Style: A
      Life-Span Perspective." In *Life-Span Developmental
      Psychology*, pp. 145-78, Paul B. Baltes and K. Warner
      Schaie, eds. New York: Academic Press, Inc., 1973.

99.   Lehman, Harvey C. *Age and Achievement*. Princeton:
      Princeton University Press, 1953. An influential
      study conducted by consulting lists of foremost
      achievements compiled by experts in each field, and

concluding that the peak period of creative production
in a wide variety of endeavors is reached in the
thirties. A very small number of women's names
appear in the listings Lehman canvassed. But Lehman,
who presents age-curves to illustrate the range of
ages of outstanding achievement in diverse fields
and the years during which the greatest volume of
work was accomplished, distinguishes between qualitative and quantitative achievement, emphasizes that
the age-curves depict *group*, not individual performance,
relies on the judgment of many experts rather than
on one, and, for the most part, studied the achievements of deceased rather than living people.

100. Lehmann, Phyllis. "The Aging and the Arts." *The
Cultural Post* (July/August 1977) 12:1, 4-5. Because
of negative stereotypes about them, the aged have
probably been more isolated from cultural institutions
than even the poorest, most disadvantaged of younger
Americans. But this is changing. Since 1973, the
National Center on the Arts and Aging has acted as a
catalyst for bringing together leaders in the arts
and the field of aging. Examples are provided of
outreach programs in the U.S. involving older people
in the arts as audiences, volunteers or employees,
and as participants.

*101. Luce, Gay Gaer. *Your Second Life (Vitality and Growth
in Middle and Later Years)*. New York: Delacorte
Press/Seymour Lawrence, 1979. The author founded
SAGE, Senior Actualization and Growth Explorations,
in 1974.

102. McLeish, John A.B. *The Ulyssean Adult: Creativity in
the Middle and Later Years*. Toronto: McGraw-Hill
Ryerson Ltd., 1976. McLeish's view is that many
regenerative and creative powers that are unused
form part of the equipment of the person all
throughout life, that in the later years life can
be lived actively and creatively, and that many
older adults are inhibited from accomplishments that
would glorify the later years because they subscribe
to modern myths and negative conventions about the
decline and fall of creativity. Two major types of
late-life creators are Ulyssean One, who begins new
creative enterprises in later life, and Ulyssean
Two, the older adult who remains creatively productive

within her or his own familiar arena of life and
work from middle age onward. Both types maintain a
sense of quest and are remarkable for their courage
and resourcefulness. Creativity is a *universal*
resource. This book contains many examples of
women Ulysseans.

103.   Maslow, Abraham. *Motivation and Personality*. New
       York: Harper and Row, 1970. Maslow, founder of
       humanistic psychology, inspired the human potential
       movement. In this work, he explores the possibilities
       of "self-actualization," and takes the point of view
       that later life is the time for the fullest realiza-
       tion of human potential and that the autobiographies
       by and the biographies about people who played a
       prominent role in public life are excellent sources
       for the study of ways to achieve this.

*104.   Sunderland, Jacqueline T., Norma Jean Taylor and Peter
       Smith, eds. *Arts and the Aging: An Agenda for Action*.
       Washington: The National Council on the Aging, Inc.,
       1977. Reports from the first national conference
       in Minneapolis in 1976 on making the arts accessible
       to the aging and includes suggestions for initiating
       and developing arts programs for the aging at every
       level. NCOA publication #7707.

105.   Vickery, Florence E. *Old and Growing: Conversations,
       Letters, Observations, and Reflections on Growing
       Old*. Springfield, Illinois: Charles C. Thomas,
       1978. Founder and executive director of the San
       Francisco Senior Center, the first community-
       sponsored social and educational program for older
       adults in the U.S., Vickery explores the changes of
       later life in family and work relationships, socio-
       economic status and the maintenance of health and
       well-being, in terms of their potential for enhanced
       self-awareness and personal growth. This book
       examines the new tasks of later life, sexuality
       and aging, the need for love and relatedness in old
       age, ways of coping with loneliness, bereavement
       and death, and ways of developing a positive viewpoint
       on aging. Vickery believes today's elderly can and
       should work to change negative images of old age,
       and that growing numbers of people now recognize the
       possibilities for meaning and creativity in late life.

*106. Yglesias, Helen. *Starting: Early, Anew, Over, and
        Late*. New York: Rawson, Wade, 1979. Yglesias,
        who wrote her first novel when in her 50s, writes
        a fragment of her autobiography through which she
        discovers many common obstacles to self-fulfillment,
        and follows this with sketches of other people who
        started out early or late or changed course in
        midlife, among them Grandma Moses, Mother Jones
        and Alberta Hunter.

See also: 194, 199, 223, 230, 232, 235, 236, 237, 324, 352,
414, 542, 563, 633, 740, 870.

                        B. Older Women

107. *Art News* (January 1971) 69(9). The entire issue is
        devoted to women artists, and includes articles by
        Linda Nochlin, "Why Have There Been No Great Women
        Artists?", "Dialogue" by Elaine de Kooning with
        Rosalyn Drexler, "Moving Out, Moving Up" by Marjorie
        Strider, "Do Your Work" by Louise Nevelson, "Social
        Conditions Can Change" by Lynda Benglis, "The
        Double-Bind" by Suzi Gablik, "Women Without Pathos"
        by Eleanor Antin, "Artists Transgress All Boundaries"
        by Rosemarie Castoro, "Sexual Art-Politics" by
        Elizabeth C. Baker and "The Odd American" by Rodrigo
        Moynihan. Nochlin's lead article and commentaries
        by others could serve as sources for a study of
        older women artists.

108. *Arts in Society* (Spring-Summer 1974) 11(1). This
        issue grew out of the conference on Women and the
        Arts at Wingspread, the Johnson Foundation Conference
        Center near Racine, Wisconsin, September 13-15, 1973.
        Contents: A Shift in the Balance by Linda Heddle
        and Monika Jensen (Editorial); Images of Women by
        Elizabeth Janeway, with New Images of Women: A
        Responsibility for Artists? and Imagery in Public
        Education, discussion leaders May Stevens and
        Gertrude Hernan; Inner Reality of Women by Ravenna
        Helson, with Developing Creativity and Imagery in
        Communication Media, discussion leaders Agnes Denes
        and Perry Miller Adato; Making Cultural Institutions
        More Responsive to Social Needs by Grace Glueck,

with Volunteering: Is It Worthwhile?, Men and Women
as Partners in Change, Changing the Values and
Practices of Cultural Institutions, and The Ethics
of Power, discussion leaders Cynthia Pitts, Allyn
Roberts, Lois Jones Pierre-Noel and Sister Mary
Austin Doherty; How Feminism in the Arts Can Implement
Cultural Change by Linda Nochlin, with Developing
Careers in the Arts, and Higher Education and Women,
discussion leaders Doris Freedman and Margaret
Mahoney; and Keep Your Hands on the Plow: Hold On!
by Fannie Hecklin; The Male Artist as Stereotypical
Female by June Wayne, A Reexamination of Some Aspects
of the Design Arts from the Perspective of a Woman
Designer by Sheila de Bretteville, and Social Organi-
zation and Design: Interview with Clare Spark-Loeb,
Sheila de Bretteville, and Dolores Hayden; Poetry.

109. Callen, Anthea. *Women Artists of the Arts and Crafts
      Movement: 1870-1914*. New York: Pantheon Books, 1979.
      This history of women in the Arts and Crafts movement
      in England and America, includes an introduction on
      class structure and the arts and crafts elite, and
      chapters on design education for women; ceramics;
      embroidery and needlework; lacemaking; jewellery and
      metalwork; woodcarving, furniture and interior
      design; hand-printing, book-binding and illustration;
      and a conclusion on feminism, art and political
      conflict. Photographs; Appendix I, Biographical
      Notes on Selected Craftswomen; Appendix II, A
      Comparative Note on Women's Wages; select bibliography.

110. Cunningham, Imogen. *After Ninety*. Seattle: University
      of Washington Press, 1977. Most of the photographs
      collected for Cunningham's last book (born in 1883,
      she died in 1976) were taken specifically for this
      book--a direct confrontation with the issues of life
      for those who were literally or spiritually "after
      ninety."

111. Frym, Gloria. *Second Stories: Conversations With Women
      Whose Artistic Careers Began After Thirty-Five*, with
      Photographic Portraits by Debra Heimerdinger. San
      Francisco: Chronicle Books, 1979. Interviews with
      ten women--a painter, printmaker, novelist, sculptor,
      writer, playwright, poet, photographer, singer and
      songwriter, and a dancer--whose artistic careers
      began after age 35.

112. Hedges, Elaine, and Ingrid Wendt. *In Her Own Image:*
     Women Working in the Arts. Old Westbury, New York:
     The Feminist Press, 1980. In this anthology of women's
     testimony about their artistic aspirations and achieve-
     ments, older as well as younger women artists are
     represented in each of the four thematic sections--
     Household Work and Women's Art, Obstacles and
     Challenges, Definitions and Discoveries, and
     Women's Art and Social Change. A variety of forms
     of artistic work by women artists living in different
     periods of history and with a diversity of national,
     ethnic, racial and economic backgrounds, are presented
     in each of the four sections.

113. Hudson, Jean Barlow. "The Double Enemy." *Broomstick*
     (March 1980) II(4):5. Hudson, who moved 35 times in
     as many years of marriage, lived in 11 foreign
     countries and many states in the U.S., and had four
     children, the last one at age 50, began to write
     novels at age 60. She battles the "double enemy" of
     old ways of living she thinks should change and the
     difficulties of learning a new career she ought to
     have been practicing and learning over the past 25
     to 30 years. She sees 15 good years remaining to
     her as a novelist.

114. Janeway, Elizabeth. "Images of Women." *Arts in Society*
     (Spring-Summer 1974) 11(1):9-18. Janeway discusses
     the problematical relationship of image to self, and
     states that women's first task in re-creating woman's
     image is calling on the energy and reality of the
     self within the image. Self and image are inter-
     dependent and co-exist in a creative tension. Women
     must change the false images by speaking out. For
     the first time in history, social change is altering
     our experience faster than that of men. Janeway
     finds a powerful positive value in social change.
     A new and valid image of woman can only be created
     out of our lived experience, our confrontation with
     history. In *art* we can find the very process of
     creativity itself, which we shall use to re-shape
     our image. Quoting Suzanne Langer on creativity,
     Janeway writes that we should proceed as if we were
     artists, putting aside the old image of the "good
     woman" and seeing ourselves as good *artists*.

115. Kallir, Otto. *Grandma Moses*. New York: Harry N.
     Abrams, Inc., 1973. Biography of the author; 135
     color and 70 black and white photographs.

116. Kaminsky, Marc. "What's Inside You It Shines Out of
      You." In *The New Old: Struggling for Decent Aging*,
      pp. 209-28, Ronald Gross, Beatrice Gross and Sylvia
      Seidman, eds. Garden City, New York: Anchor Press/
      Doubleday, 1978. A selection from Chapter Two of
      the book of this title. After five months of sessions
      with the elderly women in the Thursday Poetry Group,
      the poet discovered he was doing not poetry therapy
      nor poetry workshops, but poetry *groups*, where the
      person was found in the poem and the poem in the
      person. Most poems were made by presentation of a
      catalyst-poem followed by concentrated conversation
      by the women for whom Kaminsky acted as scribe.
      Their poems--"spontaneous utterance poems" and
      "conversation poems"--developed by the making of
      the group, and the group by the making of the poems.
      Each woman had her own perspective of the value of
      the group; this excerpt tells the story of how it
      helped a member change her life.

117. Kotz, Mary Lynn. "Georgia O'Keeffe at 90: A Day with
      Georgia O'Keeffe." *Art News* (December 1977) 76(10):
      37-45. Kotz introduces her portrait with the
      observation that the artist today is anything but
      old, that her conversation is like that of a 40-year-
      old woman except for her remarkable memory, which she
      uses with wit, clarity and breadth of description.
      Kotz finds O'Keeffe to be as joyful as she has ever
      been in her desert environment, and to be both
      vibrant and sturdy.

118. Lyons, Harriet. "May Wilson: Reborn at 61." *Ms.*
      (April 1973) I(10):110-11. Wilson, an habitué of
      Times Square photo booths, superimposes her 25¢
      self-portraits on portraits of other people. (Some
      examples are printed here.) Six years ago, at age
      61, she decided to begin a new life. She had a 9th
      grade education, was married at age 19, and raised
      two children. In 1966, her husband told her he had
      plans that did not include her. She left their
      estate in Maryland and went to New York City. She
      had been making art since 1948, working on paintings
      and assemblages in a studio above the family garage.
      Her artistic efforts were not taken seriously by her
      family or friends. She now lives in a two-room
      apartment filled with art, and is visited often by
      younger friends. Her new life is one of exuberance
      and spontaneity.

119. McDowell, Barbara, and Hana Umlauf, eds. "Older
     Women." *The Good Housekeeping Woman's Almanac*,
     pp. 95-108. New York: Newspaper Enterprise
     Association, Inc., 1977. Topics are: The Best Is
     Yet to Be; Aging Isn't a Disease; How Long Will You
     Live?; What Is Menopause?; Age Is No Bar to Beauty;
     Love Life After Menopause; Facing Financial Problems;
     How to Spend and Where to Save; Avoiding Loneliness;
     and Success Past Sixty. In this last section are
     portraits of Antonia Brico (1903-), conductor;
     Sonia Delaunay (1885-), artist; Millicent Fenwick
     (1910-), Congresswoman; Dorothy Fuldheim (1893-),
     TV anchorwoman and author; Ruth Gordon (1896-),
     actress and writer; Maggie Kuhn (1906-), retired
     social worker and founder of Gray Panthers; Anne
     Morrow Lindbergh (1906-), writer; Anna Mary Moses
     (1860-1961), artist (see No. 115 of this Bibliography);
     Annie Peck Smith (1850-1935), classics scholar,
     lecturer and mountain climber; Malvina Reynolds
     (1900-), composer, and, after 60, singer of her
     own songs; Mercy Otis Warren (1728-1814), who began
     her three-volume history of the American Revolution
     after she was 50; and examples of "More Young
     Oldsters"--Bertha and Harold Soderquist, who joined
     the Peace Corps when she was 76 and he 80; 76-year-
     old Hattie Carthan, "Brooklyn's Tireless Tree Lady,"
     and Rita Reutter, elected Homecoming Queen of Florida
     Technological University in Orlando at age 58.

120. Miller, Jennifer. "Quilting Women." *Southern Exposure*
     (Winter 1977) 4(4):24-8. Historical sketch of the
     making of bedcovers, "the first true art form in
     America," with interviews with quilters. Focuses
     on the creativity of quilting.

121. Miller, Luree. *Late Bloom: New Lives for Women*. New
     York: Paddington Press, Ltd., 1979. Countless women
     have shown that maturity is a time when doors open.
     Miller presents profiles of late-bloomers drawn from
     their own stories. She writes that they were candid
     about that crucial time in their lives when they
     confronted the certainty that they alone were responsible
     for their own lives, for they saw that the chances
     were excellent that their lives would be very long.
     Many wanted to record their experiences for their
     daughters. Sections include: Survivors with Style;
     Doing What One Loves; When a Woman Holds a Family
     Together; Brave Women Alone; Women Defining Themselves;
     Women Supporting Women.

122.   Mitchell, Margaretta. "Introduction." In *After Ninety*,
        pp. 9-23, Imogen Cunningham. Seattle: University of
        Washington Press, 1977. Photographer, teacher and
        writer Margaretta Mitchell presents a vivid portrait
        of Cunningham as a self-disciplined, hard-working,
        independent and straightforward artist with boundless
        energy and an unforgettable character. Mitchell finds
        this project to be one of the most unusual ever
        undertaken by a photographer, not only because so few
        artists live and work to such a fine old age but
        also because it is rare for an artist of any age
        in our culture to confront this stage of life without
        fear or condescension but with self-identification
        and with compassion. Cunningham, who achieved the
        creation of her own character at the last of life,
        and who was not discovered until she was in her 80s,
        was "a living symbol of youth in old age." (See
        No. 110 of this Bibliography.)

123.   "Mother and Daughter Back in School." In *The Older
        Woman: Lavender Rose or Gray Panther*, pp. 209-10,
        Marie Marschall Fuller and Cora Ann Martin, eds.
        Springfield, Illinois: Charles C. Thomas, 1980.
        Story about a 70-year-old woman and her 93-year-old
        mother, who are enrolled in the University of Wis-
        consin-Whitewater's "Live In and Learn Program,"
        first published in *Aging* in 1976-77. Mother and
        daughter drive to the campus on Mondays from their
        home 40 miles away, and return there on Thursdays.
        They live in adjoining dorm rooms on campus. One
        fall they were the only two participants in the
        program, although about 100 senior citizens audited
        classes and lived at home.

124.   Munro, Eleanor. *Originals: American Women Artists*.
        New York: Simon and Schuster, 1979. This book is
        an outgrowth of the television series "The Originals/
        Women in Art," produced by WNET/Thirteen. Munro's
        studies of visual artists are compositions of biography,
        autobiography, interview, profile and her own inter-
        pretations. She describes herself as "an art critic
        emboldened to say something about psychology" or
        "a mutual searcher" whose experience is in the
        aesthetic rather than the scientific field. She
        sought out women of three generations or four "waves"
        working in various media, and arrives at general
        statements about women's art at this time in history

in her notes on "A Century of History" and in the
Afterword. The artists she sees as pioneers are:
"Methods and Matriarchs"--Mary Cassatt and Georgia
O'Keeffe; Women of the First Wave: Elders of the
Century, including Hedda Sterne and Sari Dienes--Lee
Krasner, Alice Neel, Louise Nevelson, Isabel Bishop,
Louise Bourgeois, Helen Lundeberg, Jeanne Reynal
and Alma W. Thomas; Women of the Second Wave:
Mavericks at Midway, including Grace Hartigan, Jane
Freilicher and Fay Lansner--Helen Frankenthaler, Lila
Katzen, Joan Mitchell, Elaine de Kooning, Nell Blaine,
Miriam Schapiro, June Wayne and Mary Frank; Women
of the Third Wave: Sisters of the Crossroads, including
Elise Asher and Sheila de Bretteville--Anne Truitt,
Lenore Tawney, Sylvia Stone, Beverly Pepper, Betye
Saar, Sheila Hicks, Barbara Chase-Riboud and Lee
Bontecou; and Women of the Fourth Wave: Humboldt's
Daughters--Jennifer Bartlett, Faith Ringgold, Eleanor
Antin, Jackie Winsor, Michelle Stuart, Connie Zehr,
Betty Klavun and Patricia Johanson. Selected general
and selected artists' bibliographies; photographs
of artists; color pages of art works ("Portfolios
of Color").

125.   Nevelson, Louise. *Dawn + Dusks--taped conversations*
       with Diana MacKown. New York: Charles Scribner's
       Sons, 1976. At age 77, the noted sculptor talks
       about creativity and about her own development as
       an artist and her commitment to her work.

126.   Peterson, Karen, and J.J. Wilson. *Women Artists:*
       Recognition and Reappraisal from the Early Middle
       Ages to the Twentieth Century. New York: Harper and
       Row/Harper Colophon Books, 1976. The authors, whose
       academic training has been in comparative literature,
       use an interdisciplinary approach in this "book *of*
       art *by* women." They present a general historical
       overview of women artists working in the Western
       tradition--the Middle Ages; the 15th through 17th
       centuries; the 18th century; the 19th century; "New
       Forms and Stranger": 1890-1920; The Present Moment.
       Appendix: Ladies of the Jade Studio: Women Artists
       of China. Reproductions, bibliography.

127.   Riley, Matilda White. "Old Women." *Radcliffe Quarterly*
       (June 1979):7-10. The 13 million women aged 65 and
       over in the U.S. have more to offer society than

society is ready to receive, yet many are deprecated
and patronized, and sometimes even feared; too many
have great problems and difficulties. But the lot
of older women is not fixed, and it is likely that
they will fare much better socially and economically
in the future. Forerunners are needed for these
transformations, just as Riley's mother and her
generation at Radcliffe pioneered early in higher
education for women. Riley foresees a time when
many older women will play major roles in the creative
and performing arts, in politics and in city life,
and will make a significant difference in the productivity of the economy. Coping creatively, they will
avert what might have become a disastrous consequence
of the demographic revolution.

128.   Snyder-Ott, Joelynn. *Women and Creativity*. Millbrae,
        California: Les Femmes Publishing, 1978. Artist and
        teacher Snyder-Ott compares her reconstruction of
        women's vital contributions to art with the work of
        an archeologist excavating buried treasure. Her
        explorations take her from a meditation on female
        iconography at Stonehenge to reflections on her own
        experiences as an artist and art educator. She sees
        the feminist art movement of the 1970s as a con-
        tinuation of the struggle of women artists in earlier
        centuries. Photographs; selected bibliography.

129.   Stein, Ellen. "That Civilizing Spirit." *Southern
        Exposure* (Winter 1977) 4(4):65-9. Young brides of
        the Bicentennial year are not claiming the civilized
        essence of their heritage. The women of the Asheboro
        garden clubs are generally in their 50s or older;
        the fourth generation has declined to carry on.
        Generations of women built the fine library system
        of Randolph County. As they grow older, the work
        they did as private volunteers may be performed by
        hired public servants. The most talented young
        women trained through the personalized, women-
        centered 4-H/home extension system are going into
        industry rather than serving as community resources.
        There may be no one to replace the older women who
        do the volunteer work of the community.

130.   Thompson, Fred. Introduction and Bibliography. In
        The Autobiography of Mother Jones, pp. iii-xlii,
        Mary Field Parton, ed. Chicago: Charles H. Kerr

Publishing Co., 1977. (See No. 69 of this Bibliography.)
Thompson states that Mary Harris Jones (d. 1930)
wrote this account of her labor union activities
when she was a very old woman, and that her memories
summarize the long story of labor organization not
only by her decades of involvement but also by the
variety of her experiences. He states that the
main body of this book is a facsimile of the original
1925 Kerr edition, which is a wholly undocumented
record of an old woman's uncertain memories, and that
he has expanded his introduction to the 1972 edition
here to add detail to her story and to provide a
skeleton sketch of the growth of the labor movement
in which she was involved. He suggests Mother Jones
may have been born in 1839 and not in 1830. He
states that it is not known how the main body of
this book was prepared, but nonetheless it is a great
piece of working class literature. That Mother Jones
also became a legend, he writes, is an important fact
of history in itself.

131.   Walker, Alice. "In Search of Our Mothers' Gardens."
       Southern Exposure (Winter 1977) 4(4):60-4. Walker
       writes that the deeply spiritual women that poet
       Jean Toomer saw in the South in the early 1920s were
       not, as he called them, "Saints." They were Artists,
       driven to madness because there was no release for
       their creativity. The answer to the question about
       what it meant for a black woman to be an artist
       three or four generations ago has an answer "cruel
       enough to stop the blood." Black women must identify
       with the living creativity of these women of earlier
       generations. For Walker's own mother, overworked
       as she was, being an Artist has always been a daily
       part of life: her creativity with her flowers is
       "work her soul must have."

132.   Zabel, Morton Dauwen. Epilogue. In *A Poet's Life:
       Seventy Years in a Changing World*, pp. 459-76,
       Harriet Monroe. New York: The Macmillan Co., 1938.
       In this epilogue to Monroe's autobiography, Zabel
       notes that Monroe (b. 1860) launched *Poetry* in 1912,
       braving public skepticism and risking her personal
       reputation, when she was of an age when most people
       think that the moment for action has passed. (See
       No. 68 of this Bibliography.)

See also: 333, 336, 337, 339, 345, 348, 382, 397, 403, 404, 410, 411, 425, 426, 485, 487, 501, 569, 575, 582, 593, 614, 642, 660, 674, 744, 859, 872.

IV. CROSS-CULTURAL PERSPECTIVES
ON AGING

A. U.S.--Anthropological Perspectives;
Aging and Ethnicity;
Minorities and Aging

133. Armitage, Sue, Theresa Banfield and Sarah Jacobus.
"Black Women and Their Communities in Colorado."
Frontiers (Summer 1977) II(2):45-51. Excerpts from
oral histories about black communities in Colorado
from interviews with six black women give insight
into the support networks of various black communities
and show why the "Exodusters'" vision of autonomous,
self-sufficient black communities remained alive.

134. Ashley, Yvonne. "'That's the Way We Were Raised': An
Oral Interview with Ada Damon." *Frontiers* (Summer
1977) II(2):59-62. Ada Damon, Ashley's father's
aunt, whose oral history is transcribed here, is
Navajo and was born in 1900 south of Shiprock, New
Mexico, on the Reservation--at a time when Navajo
weaving was at a peak and the government began a
policy of forcing children into boarding schools.

*135. Center on Pre-Retirement and Aging of Catholic University
of America and the National Center for Urban Ethnic
Affairs. *Symposium on Older Americans of Euro-
Ethnic Origin*. Washington, D.C., 1979.

*136. Chapman, Sabrina Coffey. "A Social-psychological
Analysis of Morale in a Select Population: Low-
income Elderly Black Females." Diss., Pennsylvania
State University, 1978.

137. Clark, Margaret. "The Anthropology of Aging: A New
Area for Studies of Culture and Personality." In
Middle Age and Aging: A Reader in Social Psychology,

pp. 433-43, Bernice L. Neugarten, ed. Chicago: The
University of Chicago Press, 1968. Although anthropologists have long relied on the aged as a source of
much of their data and claimed the study of cultural
patterning of the human life cycle as a special
concern, they are relative newcomers to aging studies.
Clark identifies the major contributions to cross-
cultural perspectives on aging and the intellectual
orientations and value judgments that may account
for a dearth of culture and personality studies of
later life and for the failure to appreciate that
the transition from adult to elderly status is a
critical period of socialization. Two case histories
from the Studies in Aging of the Langley Porter
Neuropsychiatric Institute are presented (one of an
older woman), and a comparative study of mentally-
healthy and mentally-ill samples is cited, in her
discussion of difficulties in acculturation and of
conflict *within* American culture caused by the need
for major reorientations in values as people in the
U.S. grow old. Clark suggests that old age in the
U.S. may represent a dramatic cultural discontinuity,
and that to learn if traumatic aging is specific to
our culture, anthropologists should study aging in
societies where the values our elderly are pressed
to adopt in later life are already the *core* values
of the culture.

138.   Clark, Margaret. "Cultural Values and Dependency in
       Later Life." In *Aging and Modernization*, pp. 263-74,
       Donald O. Cowgill and Lowell D. Holmes, eds. New
       York: Appleton-Century-Crofts, 1972. Many observers
       of American life have remarked the isolating and
       anxiety-provoking effects on the person of our
       singular definition of freedom as independence. In
       the end, many elderly in the U.S. must make an un-
       happy choice between denial on the one hand and self-
       recrimination on the other. In our culture, morality
       is intimately bound up with self-reliance, and self-
       reliance tied to work and productivity and to social
       and economic independence. Types of dependency are
       described to show how certain cultural patterns
       serve to define the aged in the U.S. as dependent.
       Research in San Francisco indicates there can rarely
       be any happy prolonged dependence between the gener-
       ations. But some people escape being bound by their
       culture, and many elderly in San Francisco resolved
       the conflict between freedom and involvement and
       thus were freed for further growth.

139. Clark, Margaret, and Barbara Gallatin Anderson.
     *Culture and Aging: An Anthropological Study of Older
     Americans*. Springfield, Illinois: Charles C. Thomas,
     1967. A study of the perceptual world of the aged
     based on interviews with 435 members of two larger
     samples of San Franciscans selected in 1959 for
     extensive longitudinal study by the Langley Porter
     Institute Studies of Aging. Vignettes of subjects
     show the varieties of aging. Research shows major
     areas the aged see as potential sources of stress.
     Certain trends in our culture history--the weakness
     of kinship ties, the rapidity of industrial and tech-
     nological change, the marked increase in the numbers
     of elderly, and the dominant emphasis on productivity
     --contribute to the normless position of American
     elderly. Major topics are the subjects in their
     cultural setting; personal and social systems and
     functioning; values and social perceptions of the
     aged; Self and Society in Old Age: Beyond Disengagement,
     and aging adaptation in our culture. Concludes that
     those who survive best in later life are those able
     to substitute alternatives for the primary values
     of our culture--conservation rather than acquisition
     and exploitation; self-acceptance rather than con-
     tinuous struggle for self-advancement; being instead
     of doing; congeniality, cooperation, love and
     concern for others rather than control of others.
     Concludes that the traditional female role provides
     some lasting benefits for even the elderly poor
     women in the U.S. Sample gave no evidence of an
     emerging activism among elderly Americans. Includes
     epilogue by Florida Scott-Maxwell, and appendices
     on the study sample and measurement of morale.

140. Coles, Robert. *The Old Ones of New Mexico*, with
     photographs by Alex Harris. Albuquerque: University
     of New Mexico Press, 1973. Words and photographs
     of Spanish-speaking elders of the American Southwest.
     Introduction; photographs; chapters on: Two Languages,
     One Soul; Una Anciana; La Necesidad; The Age of a
     Reputation; and The Old Church, The Spanish Church,
     The American Church.

141. Fogel, Helen. "Mainstream Women." In *Looking Ahead:
     A Woman's Guide to the Problems and Joys of Growing
     Older*, pp. 167-9, Lillian E. Troll, Joan Israel and
     Kenneth Israel, eds. Englewood Cliffs, New Jersey:

Prentice-Hall, Inc., 1977. The cases of 56-year-old
"Bernice" and 45-year-old "Alice" illustrate the
preoccupations and perspectives of middle-aged
"mainstream women."

142. Golden, Herbert M. "Black Ageism." In *Dimensions of
      Aging: Readings*, pp. 259-64, Jon Hendricks and C.
      Davis Hendricks, eds. Cambridge, Massachusetts:
      Winthrop Publishers, Inc., 1979. Golden states that
      attempts to apply research findings based on undif-
      ferentiated comparisons of black with white elderly
      will be ineffective. Race should be regarded as an
      independent variable in research intended to serve
      policy and/or planning objectives.

143. Henry, Jules. *Culture Against Man*. New York: Vintage
      Books, Random House, Inc., 1963. Part Three of the
      late anthropologist Henry's book is entitled Human
      Obsolescence, and is about three hospitals for the
      aged--one public, Municipal Sanitarium ("Muni San"),
      and two private, Rosemont ("Hell's Vestibule") and
      Tower Nursing Home. These represent the kinds of
      fates awaiting most who become sick and obsolete in
      our culture. The section on Tower, where women out-
      number men four to one, is sub-titled The Aged Upper-
      Middle-Class Woman. Henry states that *culture
      outlasts body and mind*. Thus, even after she is
      immobilized, the American upper-middle-class woman
      is concerned with appearance and status, and the
      culture determines the channels she follows in
      expressing her capacity to hurt and to hate. Henry
      finds that the orientation toward aging and death
      in the U.S. is unique.

*144. Jackson, Jacquelyne Johnson. "The Blacklands of
       Gerontology." *The International Journal of Aging
       and Human Development* (August 1971) 2(3):156-71.

 145. Jackson, Jacquelyne Johnson. "Comparative Life Styles
       and Family and Friend Relationships Among Older Black
       Women." *The Family Coordinator* (October 1972)
       21(4):477-85. This report on a comparison of selected
       instrumental and affective relationships of older
       married (74) and spouseless (159) black women in
       Durham, North Carolina, with their oldest children
       and closest friends, found many similarities despite
       the differences in marital status. Among these were

similarities in contact frequency and satisfaction
with children and friends, mutual assistance between
the mothers and their oldest children, and relationships of closeness, identification, and agreement
with their oldest children. Presence or absence of
spouse may be significantly related to such variables
as number of close friends; sharing commercial
recreation with friends; dependence on or participation with children in emergencies and shopping;
mutual assistance patterns between mothers and
youngest children; choices between spending more time
with friends or kin; and specific preferences for
greater affinal or consanguineal contact.

146. Jackson, Jacquelyne Johnson. "Marital Life Among Aging
      Blacks." *The Family Coordinator* (January 1972) 21(1):
      21-7. The research finding that matriarchy is *not*
      the dominant spouse pattern among black families is
      confirmed in this interview study of 135 older (over
      age 50) married, predominantly low-income Southern
      urban blacks. Although data were reported by the
      subjects only, the study does include both husbands
      and wives. A younger sample showed greater variation
      by sex in their responses. Marriage is not the
      dominant pattern among elderly black females; more
      attention should be given to those supportive familial
      patterns available for aged black men and women
      without spouses.

147. Jackson, Jacquelyne Johnson. *Minorities and Aging*.
      Belmont, California: Wadsworth Publishing Co., 1980.
      Lifetime Series in Aging editor Alan D. Entine notes
      that Johnson identifies nine prime minority groups as
      a focus for this book--Black American women and men,
      American Indian women and men, Asian American women
      and men, Hispanic American women and men, and Anglo-
      American women, and presents much information and
      many issues concerning them for the first time.
      Johnson writes that the impact of ethnicity upon
      aging is an important issue in the field; that
      minority aging has been isolated in recent years, and
      hence many courses offered under this rubric are
      really about race and ethnic relations; and that
      students of aging need to move toward an inter-
      disciplinary approach. Contents: Demographic Aspects
      of Minority Aging, Physiological Aspects of Aging,
      Mortality and Life Expectancy, Patterns of Aging

Minorities, Psychological Aspects of Minority Aging,
Social Aspects of Minority Aging, Aged Minorities:
Dominant Social Problems and Federal Policies, and
The Future of Minority Aging. Each chapter ends
with notes, and suggested exercises and annotated
readings. Tables, glossary, selected bibliography
with two sections--aging and minorities, and general
works on aging.

148.   Jackson, Jacquelyne Johnson. "Negro Aged: Toward Needed
       Research in Social Gerontology." *The Gerontologist*
       (Spring 1971, Part II) 11(2):52-7. Building upon
       her earlier critiques of literature about aging and
       aged Negroes (to 1967), Jackson surveys social
       gerontology literature on Negroes and presents a
       selected bibliography of the most useful researches
       available, critically evaluates researches on the
       Negro aged, and states a number of the most important
       research problems or areas on this subject in need
       of further study. Sections on Social Gerontology
       and the Negro, 1950-1967; 1967-1969; extensive listing
       of references.

149.   Jackson, Jacquelyne Johnson. "Older Black Women." In
       *Looking Ahead: A Woman's Guide to the Problems and
       Joys of Growing Older*, pp. 149-56, Lillian E. Troll,
       Joan Israel and Kenneth Israel, eds. Englewood
       Cliffs, New Jersey: Prentice-Hall, Inc., 1977.
       Jackson surveys demographic and social characteristics
       of older black women in the U.S. Headings: The
       Physical Environment, Income and Work (for both,
       some trends are progressive and others regressive),
       The Family, and Health. She states there is a
       paucity of gerontological knowledge about older
       black women, and that methods for studying inter-
       relationships between race and aging are inadequate.
       Both may be corrected in the coming years because of
       growing numbers of older black women in the U.S.

150.   Kalish, Richard A., and Sharon Moriwaki. "The World
       of the Elderly Asian American." In *Dimensions of
       Aging: Readings*, pp. 264-77, Jon Hendricks and C.
       Davis Hendricks, eds. Cambridge, Massachusetts:
       Winthrop Publishers, Inc., 1979. Asian Americans
       are stereotyped as people without pressing problems,
       whose needs are met within the ethnic group and
       whose values have made accommodation to their North

American homeland simple. This paper focuses on the psycho-social aspects of the past and present living situation for today's elderly Chinese and Japanese Americans on the Pacific Coast. The first generations are growing old in a foreign culture. Few studies report on significant *generational* differences among Asian Americans. We should not make villains of today's middle-aged child because the world for him or her is different from that of predecessors and successors. The immigration experience of Asian Americans is unique for many reasons. They were perceived to be unassimilable; discrimination against them was codified in law; and there is a movement today, primarily by the young, to establish a Pan-Asian American movement--an effort to overcome ancient angers and historical antagonisms unparalleled by that made by other ethnic activist groups. The demand for services exceeds the supply. The authors state they are not as pessimistic about the future as they are distressed about the past.

151. Kalish, Richard A., and Sam Yuen. "Americans of East Asian Ancestry: Aging and the Aged." *The Gerontologist* (Spring 1971, Part II) 11(2):36-47. Research and services involving elderly Asian-Americans must be understood in the context of their common origins in high civilizations very different from those of the Occident, and their common experiences as immigrants to the U.S. But the three largest nationality groupings from East Asia discussed in this paper--Chinese-, Japanese- and Filipino-Americans --are each very distinctive in traditions, language, religion and history in the U.S. Also, each ethnic group is heterogeneous, and the correlation between age and generation no longer obtains. This paper discusses the interrelationships between the need for services and the need for research, reviews the relevant literature, presents data and describes current research on each group, and develops a guide for future research in theory building on topics that would improve understanding (the role of dependency is one) and evaluation research.

152. Kent, Donald P. "The Negro Aged." *The Gerontologist* (Spring 1971, Part II) 11(2):48-51. The questions Du Bois raised in the 1890s about the conditions of the Negroes are still largely unanswered so far as

the aged are concerned. Kent discusses demographic,
social and economic characteristics of the Negro
("our largest visible minority") and Negro aged. He
states that the youth-centeredness of American
society may be even more exaggerated within Negro
society, and that aged black females are more disadvantaged than their white or male counterparts;
and lists questions calling for further research.

*153.   Lacklen, Cary. "Aged, Black, and Poor: Three Case
         Studies." *The International Journal of Aging and
         Human Development* (August 1971) 2(3):202-7.

154.   Levy, Jerrold E. "The Older American Indian." In
        Older Rural Americans: A Sociological Perspective,
        pp. 221-38, E. Grant Youmans, ed. Lexington:
        University of Kentucky Press, 1967. Contemporary
        conditions of the aging Indian, both male and female,
        are represented by the case of the Navajo of Arizona,
        New Mexico, Utah and Colorado (the largest single
        Indian tribe in possession of the largest reservation)
        with some contrasting material from other tribes.
        Major topics are: The Aged in Aboriginal America,
        and Current Developments: The Navajo Example.

155.   Lindsay, Inabel B. "Coping Capacities of the Black
        Aged." In *No Longer Young: The Older Woman in America*,
        pp. 89-94. Ann Arbor, Michigan: The Institute of
        Gerontology, The University of Michigan-Wayne State
        University, 1975. Most elderly blacks grew up in a
        society affording them limited educational and em-
        ployment opportunities, restricted housing in urban
        ghettoes or rural slums and reliance on folk medicine
        because of the unavailability of medical and financial
        resources; and because of sex differences in longevity,
        a great percentage of older black women are left
        alone to shoulder family responsibilities. They
        have been remarkably successful at this. Recent
        research discloses special strengths of black families
        as adaptability of roles, strong kinship ties, and
        strong orientations to religion, work and achievement.
        Older blacks share their resources generously,
        however meager, with kin and friends. For many
        elderly blacks today, the black church is a means
        of spiritual sustenance and a center for social
        relationships. The case of an elderly widowed black
        woman is cited as a vivid example of coping capacity.

156. Maldonado, David, Jr. "The Mexican American Grows
     Old." In *The Later Years: Social Applications of
     Gerontology*, pp. 37-43, Richard A. Kalish, ed.
     Monterey, California: Brooks/Cole Publishing Co.,
     1977. Myths of the extended family have blinded
     both social scientists, and practitioners who provide
     services, to the present crisis of the Chicano aged.
     Since World War II, the Mexican American community
     has been changing from a rural to an urban society.
     Chicanos left the farm for the city, and farm work
     for more skilled jobs, higher wages, and education.
     These changes have created pressure to break up the
     extended family and to strengthen the nuclear unit.
     Some elderly Chicanos have not experienced the
     dramatic social change since World War II, but most
     were socialized to an agrarian way of life and did
     not expect to live in old age in the city or in a
     small town far from their children. Myths--that
     the Chicano family is a patriarchal structure, or
     that aging Chicanos do not experience stress--
     maintain images that no longer reflect true conditions.
     The general society, having a dated knowledge of
     Chicano culture, believes the Chicano family can and
     will provide for its older members. Younger Chicanos
     are having an increasingly difficult time doing so.
     But both old and young recognize the tension and
     transition, and are making adjustments.

157. Moore, Joan W. "Mexican-Americans." *The Gerontologist*
     (Spring 1971, Part II) 11(2):30-5. The distinctive
     age structure of Mexican-Americans, among whom there
     are comparatively few elderly people, is a result
     of at least four factors--mortality patterns, fer-
     tility patterns, and patterns of immigration to the
     U.S. and repatriation to Mexico. A profile of the
     Mexican-American aged in 1960 shows their markedly
     low level of educational attainment. Mexican-
     American women generally go on bearing children much
     later in life than do Anglo women. Data suggest
     that the Mexican-American aged of the next genera-
     tion will continue to be poor, and that it will be
     another thirty years before they are as well-
     educated as the Anglo elderly of today. Existing
     research is limited, and does not represent the
     minority viewpoint or the significance of the local
     situation with enough clarity to justify general
     statements. A comparative frame of reference is of
     prime importance because of variations in history
     and status.

*158. National Center on the Black Aged. "A Fact Sheet:
       Comparison of Black and White Older Women--Age
       65+." Washington, D.C., 1980.

159. "The Older Native American." In *The Later Years:
      Social Applications of Gerontology*, pp. 43-5,
      Richard A. Kalish, ed. Monterey, California:
      Brooks/Cole Publishing Co., 1977. Statistics about
      Native Americans are often inadequate, inaccurate,
      or unavailable. A survey of the Library of Congress
      catalogue files revealed that there are about 417
      cards on Indian legends and pottery, but none at all
      for "income" or "population." There is confusion
      surrounding the definition of "Indian." By all
      standards, American Indians, and especially the aged
      in that group, are one of the most deprived segments
      in our population. Per capita income for Indians
      is only about 1/3 the national average. Existing
      programs for elderly Indians continue to be uncoordi-
      nated and fragmented. A low level of visibility for
      the unique problems of aged Indians is a major by-
      product of this dilemma. Thus, many Indians of all
      ages never receive the full benefits of these programs.
      A high-level advocate for elderly Indians and the
      coordination and publicizing of all programs aimed
      at helping them are recommended. Only about 6% of
      the total population of Indians are elderly, reflecting
      the low life expectancy (46 years) of this population.
      Inadequate nutrition, dilapidated housing, insufficient
      medical services, poor transportation systems and
      other problems must be met to raise their life ex-
      pectancy. The appalling lack of acceptable housing
      for Indians, the alarmingly high unemployment for
      older Indians and Indians in general, and the hunger
      or malnourishment that are a way of life for most
      older Indians are documented. Poor health for
      Indians is intensified by bad roads, poor communica-
      tion, inaccessible health care facilities and a
      high turnover of medical personnel.

160. Palmore, Erdman. "United States of America." In
      *International Handbook on Aging: Contemporary
      Developments and Research*, pp. 434-54, Erdman Palmore,
      ed. Westport, Connecticut: Greenwood Press, 1980.
      In the U.S., rich resources and gerontological
      knowledge do not appear to be matched by attitudes
      toward and treatment of the elderly. In part, this
      may be due to the heterogeneity of the aged population,

and in part to the youth cult developed in an earlier
frontier society. But recognition and concern for
the aged is growing at an unprecedented rate.
Since the late 1940s, the growth in Gerontology
and programs for the aged has been dramatic--and
this has been mutually reinforcing. Both are related
to the increasing numbers of the elderly and to the
expansion of governmental support for welfare and
social services and for research. Topics include
demography, a review of the nine basic human rights
for older Americans in the Bicentennial Charter for
Older Americans (1976, Federal Council on the Aging),
and biological, psychological and social science
research. Lists the three major sources of information on aging--Aging Research Information Service,
Keyword Indexed Collection of Training Resources
in Aging, and National Clearinghouse on Aging. The
U.S. has led most of the world in gerontological
research but has tended to lag in the practical
application of Gerontology to the solution of problems
of aging. But the outlook for the future appears
promising.

161. Richek, Herbert G., Owen Chuculate and Dorothy Klinert.
"Aging and Ethnicity in Healthy Elderly Women."
Geriatrics (May 1971) 26(5):146-52. Fifty women,
35 Indians and 15 Caucasians, in their 70s were
interviewed in this preliminary study of ethnicity
and disengagement. Each woman initially completed
a self-report inventory providing measures of
positiveness of perceptions of eight aspects of
the phenomenal world, and then again with the
thoughts and feelings that prevailed during the
"happiest" age in her life. Concludes that the
disengagement process differs for these two groups
in those areas of the life space pertaining to
children, authority, work, parents, and hope.

*162. Rubenstein, Daniel. "An Examination of Social
Participation Found among a National Sample of
Black and White Elderly." *The International Journal
of Aging and Human Development* (August 1971)
2(3):172-88.

163. Schlegel, Alice. "Situational Stress: A Hopi Example."
In *Life-Span Developmental Psychology: Normative
Life Crises*, pp. 209-15, Nancy Datan and Leon H.
Ginsberg, eds. New York: Academic Press, Inc., 1975.

Research among older Hopi women reflecting their
early socialization from 1910-1930 indicates that
the stress period built into the life cycle of the
Hopi woman is the adolescent stage, roughly between
puberty at age 12 and marriage at age eighteen.
Hopi women experience stress in adolescence because
of the radical restrictions on freedom, the inten-
sification of the mother's disciplinary role, and
the pressure put upon the girl to find a husband.
Normal reactions to stress are moodiness and
irritability; a pathological reaction is depression,
an apathy that can rob the victim of her appetite
and will to live. Every society appears to place
stress on its members at certain stages of the life
cycle. In urban areas of the U.S., these stages
seem to be early adolescence, young adulthood, and
old age. For the Hopi, it is adolescence for women
and young adulthood for men. The Hopi passes into
old age without much social recognition of the fact,
and with little or no change in status.

164. Seltzer, Mildred. "Jewish-American Grandmothers." In
      *Looking Ahead: A Woman's Guide to the Problems and
      Joys of Growing Older*, pp. 157-61, Lillian E. Troll,
      Joan Israel and Kenneth Israel, eds. Englewood
      Cliffs, New Jersey: Prentice-Hall, Inc., 1977. Social
      and personality characteristics of Jewish-American
      grandmothers. Seltzer observes that old women of
      all ethnic groups may have more in common with one
      another than with younger members of their own
      families, and that the strength that enabled them
      to survive until old age in a hostile environment
      may be the very characteristic upon which negative
      stereotypes are based.

165. Sowell, Thomas. "Ethnicity in a Changing America."
      Daedalus (Winter 1978) 107(1):213-37. Note pages
      220-5, in which Sowell states that age is often
      overlooked in explaining inter-ethnic differences,
      and that median age differences among American ethnic
      groups are substantial in themselves and also in
      their impact on a wide range of socioeconomic
      variables. Theories which attempt to explain dif-
      ferences between any two ethnic groups or between a
      given ethnic group and the "national average," run
      the risk of explaining too much if they do not first
      eliminate those differences due to differences in
      age distribution. Age may be an important "hidden"

factor in gross ethnic data on personal incomes,
fertility, the economic rate of return on education,
death rates, crime rates and unemployment statistics.
Present conditions and policies cannot be evaluated
without making age distinctions in ethnic data.

*166. Swanson, William C., and Carl L. Harter. "How Do
       Elderly Blacks Cope in New Orleans?" *The Interna-
       tional Journal of Aging and Human Development*
       (August 1971) 2(3):210-16.

*167. Wolf, Beverly Hungry. *The Ways of My Grandmothers*.
       New York: William Morrow and Co., Inc., 1980. Wolf,
       a member of the Blood tribe of the Blackfoot nation,
       returned to the reserve in western Canada after
       years away at school learning the English language,
       and asked the older women about their lives and
       memories of tribal legends and customs. Photographs;
       "a rare record of the American Indian heritage."

*168. Wylie, F.M. "Attitudes toward Aging among Black
       Americans: Some Historical Perspectives." *The
       International Journal of Aging and Human Development*
       (February 1971) 2(1):66-70.

 169. Yung, Judy. "'A Bowlful of Tears': Chinese Women
       Immigrants on Angel Island." *Frontiers* (Summer 1977)
       II(2):52-5. Visiting the Immigration Station in
       1975, Yung was deeply touched by the poetry and other
       records scratched on the walls by the detainees.
       The experiences related in this article are based
       upon oral history interviews with women detained
       there between 1910 and 1941.

See also: 3, 4, 5, 6, 7, 8, 9, 11, 12, 80, 131, 201, 278,
279, 282, 290, 294, 298, 302, 303, 313, 321, 334, 359, 384,
499, 500, 502, 504, 506, 508, 509, 510, 511, 513, 514, 516,
517, 520, 525, 527, 528, 530, 531, 532, 533, 534, 535, 546,
645, 655, 664, 701, 707, 747, 766, 767, 776, 815, 841, 857,
872, 883, 885.

            B. World--Anthropological Perspectives;
                 Aging in Other Societies

 170. Amoss, Pamela T., and Stevan Harrell, eds. *Other Ways
       of Growing Old: Anthropological Perspectives*.

Stanford, California: Stanford University Press,
1981. Foreword by Carl Eisdorfer; Introduction: An
Anthropological Perspective on Aging by Amoss and
Harrell on human universals, cultural variation,
demographic factors, subsistence economy, property,
politics, knowledge, the experience of aging, and
implications for the position of the aged in human
societies; and chapters on Evolutionary Perspectives
on Human Aging by Kenneth M. Weiss; "Nepotists"
and "Altruists": The Behavior of Old Females Among
Macaques and Langur Monkeys by Sarah Blaffer Hrdy;
"The Old People Give You Life": Aging Among !Kung
Hunter-Gatherers by Megan Biesele and Nancy Howell;
Old Age Among the Chipewyan by Henry S. Sharp; The
Elderly Asmat of New Guinea by Peter W. Van Arsdale;
Old Age in Gwembe District, Zambia by Elizabeth
Colson and Thayer Scudder; Respected Elder or Old
Person: Aging in a Micronesian Community by James
D. Nason; Growing in Respect: Aging Among the Kirghiz
of Afghanistan by M. Nazif Shahrani; Growing Old in
Rural Taiwan by Stevan Harrell; Old Age in a South
Indian Village by Paul G. Hiebert; and Coast Salish
Elders by Pamela T. Amoss.

171.   Arnhoff, Franklyn N., Henry V. Leon and Irving Lorge.
"Cross-Cultural Acceptance of Stereotypes Towards
Aging." *The Journal of Social Psychology* (June 1964)
63(First Half):41-58. A detailed report of the
results of a study whereby students from six countries
--the U.S. (423), Japan (184), Puerto Rico (246),
Sweden (305), Greece (336), and England (245),
completed The Attitudes Towards Old People Questionnaire, checking a 100-item list of statements
about old people. The major contribution of the
data is that they enable social scientists to place
attitudes towards aging in the U.S. in their proper
perspective. The aging and the aged have been,
remain, and will be a problem, and attitudes
towards agedness in the U.S. are not unique. In
many instances, they are more favorable than attitudes
held by people living in other countries.

172.   Benet, Sula. *How to Live to Be 100: The Life-Style of
the People of the Caucasus*. New York: The Dial
Press, 1976. Work based on an investigation involving
frequent trips to cities, towns and villages in the

Caucasus ranging from 6 weeks' to 4 months' duration
between 1970 and 1975; includes "A Visit with the
Oldest Woman in the World"--139-year-old Khjaf
Lazuria (died 2/14/75) whom Benet found to be a
striking contrast to old people in the U.S. who often
give up on life while in their 60s. She would have
found incomprehensible or laughable the notion that
she should cease having interests, desires or
feelings because she had reached a certain age.
Topics: field work experience; the land and people
of the Caucasus; the demography of longevity;
hospitality and etiquette; folk medicine; nutrition
and longevity; Sex; Joy in Privacy, Shame in Public;
the changing family; Life's Rhythm: Conclusions About
Longevity; and Some Recipes from the Long-Living
People of the Caucasus. Photographs.

*173. Bergman, Simon. *A Cross-National Perspective on
Gerontology: Lectures by Simon Bergman.* Denton,
Texas: Center for Studies in Aging, North Texas
State University, 1979.

174. Burgess, Ernest W., ed. *Aging in Western Societies.*
Chicago: The University of Chicago Press, 1960.
This survey of the problems of the elderly and the
solutions for their welfare adopted in Western
societies includes an overview by Burgess in Section
One on aging in Western culture, and papers on
population (Philip M. Hauser and Raul Vargas),
employment and retirement (Seymour L. Wolfbein and
Ernest W. Burgess), income maintenance and medical
insurance (Wilbur J. Cohen), housing and community
services (Wilma Donahue), physical health (Vera J.
and Jerome S. Peterson), mental health (Robert W.
Kleemeier), the family (Burgess), Life Beyond Family
and Work (Robert J. Havighurst), research on aging
(John E. Anderson) and a chapter on Résumé and
implications (Burgess). Part Two, Selected Case
Studies, includes papers on old age and invalidity
insurance and pensioners and medical-care insurance
in 11 European countries (no authors cited), Swedish
housing design (Wilma Donahue), Old People's House-
work Scheme (Helen L. Slater), An Important Swedish
Epidemiological Study and A District Mental Health
Service (Robert W. Kleemeier), A Case Study of Family
Relations (Jean-René Tréanton), The Three-Generation
Rural Family in Italy (Angela Zuccino), Relations with
Their Children of Parents in an Old People's Home,

translated from "Pro senectute," Duty of Children to
Support Parents (Max Rheinstein), Clubs for Older
People in an English Community (Bertha James),
Clubs for Older People in the Netherlands (Robert
J. Van Zonneveld), a paper on the Nuffield Foundation
by John C. Beavan and a paper on The Condition of
the West German Pensioner Before the Social Reform
by Ludwig von Friedeburg. Part Three consists of
selected statistical tables.

175. Cowgill, Donald O., and Lowell D. Holmes, eds. *Aging
and Modernization*. New York: Appleton-Century-Crofts,
1972. Includes chapters on A Theory of Aging in
Cross-Cultural Perspective (by Cowgill), on aging
among the Sidamo of Southwest Ethiopia, the Igbo,
the Southern African Bantu, the Samoans, aging in
Thailand, Santo Tomás Mazaltepec, among the Salt
River Pima, in Japan, the USSR, Ireland, Austria,
Israel and on Israeli kibbutzim, in Norway and in
the U.S.; and papers on "Cultural Values and Dependency
in Later Life" by Margaret Clark and on a world perspective on role changes in widowhood by Helena
Znaniecki Lopata. (See Nos. 138 and 849 of this
Bibliography.)

176. Diamond, Stanley. "Nigerian Discovery: The Politics
of Field Work." In *Reflections on Community Studies*,
pp. 119-54, Arthur J. Vidich, Joseph Bensman and
Maurice R. Stein, eds. New York: John Wiley and
Sons, Inc., 1964. Of the Anaguta, Diamond writes
that he quickly came to appreciate the older people's
deeply experienced and incised faces, each one of
which was "a tapestry, a work of art, a map to be
read." He states that they were the most expressive
and fully human faces he had ever seen, and he compares them most favorably with the faces of the
elderly that are familiar even in the cities of
the West.

*177. Fry, Christine L., ed. *Dimensions of an Anthropology
of Aging*. New York: Praeger, 1981.

*178. Ganschow, Thomas W. "The Aged in a Revolutionary
Milieu: China." In *Aging and the Elderly: Humanistic
Perspectives in Gerontology*, pp. 303-20, Stuart F.
Spicker, Kathleen M. Woodward and David D. Van
Tassel, eds. Atlantic Highlands, New Jersey:
Humanities Press, Inc., 1978.

179. Harlan, William H. "Social Status of the Aged in Three
      Indian Villages." In *Middle Age and Aging: A Reader
      in Social Psychology*, pp. 469-75, Bernice L. Neugarten,
      ed. Chicago: The University of Chicago Press, 1968.
      The commonly held assumptions that the status of the
      aged was or is higher in pre-industrial than in
      urban-industrial societies and that current problems
      of the aged are due to urban-industrialism are examined
      in the light of studies of the aged in villages in
      North India, Burail and Rattan Garh, and of data
      from Dube's monograph on Shamirpet in South Central
      India. In Burail, interviews of 50 men over age 60
      indicate that status as head of the joint family is
      not automatically retained by reason of age alone,
      but depends upon several factors, among them marital
      status and inter-generational and interpersonal
      relationships. Also, neither formal nor informal
      village leadership is vested in the old men of the
      village; those who occupy positions of leadership in
      extra-family affairs do so by virtue of attributes
      other than age. In Rattan Garh, 60 women over age
      50 were interviewed, and it was found that patterns
      of family organization are quite at variance with
      ideal norms. As in Burail, the loss of status by
      old women began not with widowhood but often with
      the arrival of a daughter-in-law in the household.
      Many old women were bitter about their status. Older
      women, especially those of a low socioeconomic position,
      occupy a very tenuous status in old age, and their
      difficulties are neither new nor the consequences
      of outside forces. In Shamirpet, Dube found dis-
      crepancies between the ideal norms governing family
      life and the actual practices. Respect is shown the
      elderly on ritual occasions, not in everyday life.
      Abuse may be heaped upon parents, who dominate the
      family only until middle age. Harlan concludes that
      the status of the elderly is not high in any of these
      three villages, and proposes three heuristic princi-
      ples to be followed in re-examining current assumptions
      about the origins of the problematic status of the
      elderly.

*180. Holmes, Lowell D. "Trends in Anthropological Gerontology:
       From Simmons to the Seventies." *The International
       Journal of Aging and Human Development* (1976)
       7(3):211-20.

181.   Iglitzin, Lynne B., and Ruth Ross, eds. *Women in the
       World: A Comparative Study.* (Studies in Comparative
       Politics #6) Santa Barbara, California: Clio
       Press, 1976.   Part One: Conceptualizing the Cross-
       Cultural Study of Women; Part Two: Women in Europe
       and the U.S.; Part Three: Women in the Developing
       Countries; Part Four: Women in Nations Mobilized for
       Social Change.   In 1974, twenty-five participants
       from the U.S., Canada, Western Europe, China, and
       the Middle East joined with fellows of the Center
       for the Study of Democratic Institutions and the
       University of California, Santa Barbara in a dialogue
       entitled: "Social and Political Change: The Role of
       Women."   The papers presented by conferees constitute
       the core of this book.

182.   Mead, Margaret.   "Weaver of the Border."   In *In the
       Company of Man: Twenty Portraits of Anthropological
       Informants*, pp. 175-210, Joseph B. Casagrande, ed.
       New York: Harper Torchbooks, 1964.   The life story
       of Mrs. Phebe Clotilda Coe Parkinson (b. 1863,
       Samoa), the daughter of a woman who was a member of
       a chief's family in Western Samoa and a father who
       was the nephew of an American bishop.   Of this woman,
       still a reigning power at age 65 in her in-between
       world where Mead first met her in 1928, the widow
       of a bilingual, half-English, half-German surveyor
       and amateur ethnologist reared in the princely
       household of Schleswig-Holstein, and mother of 12
       children, Mead wrote that she demonstrated what a
       Polynesian could do with values that are European
       "when they are grafted on to a firm belief and pride
       in Polynesian blood."

183.   Myerhoff, Barbara G., and Andrei Simič, eds. *Life's
       Career--Aging: Cultural Variations on Growing Old.*
       Beverly Hills: Sage Publications, Inc., 1978.   Cross-
       cultural perspectives on aging. Contents: "Old
       Age in a Life-Term Social Arena: Some Chagga of
       Kilimanjaro in 1974" (Sally Falk Moore); "Winners
       and Losers: Aging Yugoslavs in a Changing World"
       (Andrei Simič); "Youth and Aging in Central Mexico:
       One Day in the Life of Four Families of Migrants"
       (Carlos G. Vélez); "A Symbol Perfected in Death:
       Continuity and Ritual in the Life and Death of an
       Elderly Jew" (Barbara G. Myerhoff); "El Senior
       Citizens Club: The Older Mexican-American in the
       Voluntary Association" (José Cuellar); Introduction

by Simić, and Conclusion by Simić and Myerhoff,
exploring the three major themes of continuity,
the sexual dichotomy, and aging as a career. On
pp. 236-40, "The Sexual Dichotomy in Aging," it
is noted that power reaches a peak at different times
for men and women in each culture, and one sex fills
the vacuum left because of declining power of the
other.

184. Palmore, Erdman, ed. *International Handbook on Aging:*
      Contemporary Developments and Research. Westport,
      Connecticut: Greenwood Press, 1980. A major reference
      for comparative studies. Articles on 28 countries,
      most of which have substantial organizations, pro-
      grams and research on aging—Austria, Canada, Chile,
      Denmark, West Germany, Finland, France, East Germany,
      Greece, Hungary, Ireland, Israel, Italy, Japan,
      Mexico, The Netherlands, New Zealand, Norway, Poland,
      Rumania, South Africa, Switzerland, Union of Soviet
      Socialist Republics, United Kingdom, U.S.A., Uruguay,
      Venezuela and Yugoslavia. Three Appendices: Inter-
      national Directory of Organizations Concerned with
      Aging; International and Regional Organizations on
      Aging; and The International Development of
      Academic Gerontology.

185. Piovesana, Gino K. "The Aged in Chinese and Japanese
      Cultures." In *Dimensions of Aging: Readings*, pp.
      13-20, Jon Hendricks and C. Davis Hendricks, eds.
      Cambridge, Massachusetts: Winthrop Publishers, Inc.,
      1979. There is no such thing as "Oriental culture":
      Indians, Chinese Tibetans and Japanese have distinctive
      ways of thinking and attitudes. This paper discusses
      traditional attitudes toward aging only in China
      and Japan, where Confucianism has enhanced the posi-
      tion of the old man in both societies. Age has
      received its most detailed explanation in the context
      of family relationships, and aged parents are deserving
      of the most consideration. Piovesana defines
      reverence and filial piety in Confucianism and
      explores the topics of ancestor worship and aging,
      the Confucian tradition in Japan, and aging and
      the family in Chinese and Japanese societies.

186. Simmons, Leo W. *The Role of the Aged in Primitive*
      Society. New Haven: Yale University Press, 1945.
      Conspectus of the status and treatment of the aged
      in 71 societies (16 in North America, 10 in Central
      and South America, 14 in Africa, 3 in Europe, 16 in
      Asia and 12 in Oceania and Australia). Topics: the

assurance of food; property rights; prestige; general
activities; political and civil activities; the use
of knowledge, magic and religion; the functions of
the family; reactions to death. Simmons cautions
that this has been a neglected subject in ethno-
graphies, that sources are scattered and often
very incomplete, and that 71 tribes are too few
to justify relying on any single statistical co-
efficient. But he states that much greater confidence
may be placed in the general trend of large numbers
of coefficients bearing on a major hypothesis, and
in this respect data and findings are often impressive.
Some findings are that sex differences are striking
in property rights (women have fared better among
collectors, hunters, and to a lesser extent fishers
than among farmers and herders in prestige), and
in political and civil activities, where old men have
been overwhelmingly favored over old women in important
offices in most societies. Simmons also reports that
midwifery has been much more often the work of aged
women than of aged men; that the domestic authority
of aged women has followed more irregular trends
than that of aged men; that in the matter of family
care and support, the aged of both sexes have fared
almost alike in both patrilineal and matrilineal
societies; and that witchcraft when seen as "shamanism
gone awry" may explain in part why old women have
been persecuted as witches more often than aged men.
Description of research procedure; appendices on
statistical correlations and an index to correlations; bibliography.

187.   Talmon, Yonina. "Aging in Israel, A Planned Society."
        In *Middle Age and Aging: A Reader in Social Psychol-
        ogy*, pp. 461-8, Bernice L. Neugarten, ed. Chicago:
        The University of Chicago Press, 1968. A report of
        a research project conducted in 12 collectives which
        found a major source of strain of aging to be the
        ambivalent position of old age in a future-oriented,
        youth-centered society. Life is work-centered and
        productivity highly valued. Retirement is gradual,
        thus requiring continuous readjustment. In aging,
        members grow more dependent on the community and
        need more services. Since up-to-date specialized
        training is at a premium, long experience is a
        liability. The pattern of familial continuity en-
        hances close parent-children ties, but engenders
        much strain in the occupational sphere. Gradual

withdrawal from work enhances the importance of the
family to the elderly. Grandchildren become a
major preoccupation, especially for aging women.
Ties between aging parents and children are firmly
based on reciprocal services. Due to the over-
emphasis on planning, members do not fully realize
the need for a deliberate cultivation of flexibility
in role. Women are more unfavorable toward and
critical of the position of the aged in the collective
than are men because women have less chance of a
balanced and well-ordered old age. Analysis also
showed that members' parents, who are not as imbued
with faith in youth, work and productivity as
elderly members who are founders, and who are more
marginal and who do not have as high expectations
as they, are more contented with life in the
collective.

See also: 189, 265, 266, 359, 384, 396, 402, 405, 409, 795,
845, 849, 853.

V. GERONTOLOGY

A. General Studies;
Demographic Perspectives on Aging

188.   Atchley, Robert C. *The Social Forces in Later Life:*
An Introduction to Social Gerontology, 3rd ed.
Belmont, California: Wadsworth Publishing Co.,
Inc., 1980. In this third edition of his text,
Atchley includes more material on middle age than
had appeared in the earlier editions, and adds
material on life styles, employment problems in
middle and later life, and fear of crime; adds major
sections on ageism and age prejudice; adds a new
chapter on how inequalities associated with social
class, race, ethnicity, and sex influence aging;
further refines his introductory chapter to provide
a better overview of theory in social gerontology;
and adds a new section on employment in the field of
aging to his epilogue. Contents: Part One: Introduction; The Scope of Social Gerontology. Part Two:
The Aging Individual: Biological Aging; The Psychology
of Aging; The Social Psychology of the Aging Individual.
Part Three: Age Changes in Situational Context: The
Changing Social Context of Later Life; Health;
Finances; Employment and Retirement; Activities;
Death, Dying, Bereavement, and Widowhood; Personal
Adaptation to Aging. Part Four: Societal Responses
to Older People: General Social Responses to Aging;
Social Inequality; The Economy; Politics and Govern-
ment; Community; Moorings in the Community: Religion
and Voluntary Associations; Primary Relationships:
Family, Friends, and Neighbors. Epilogue; appendices
on demography and methodology; extensive bibliography.

189.   Beauvoir, Simone de. *The Coming of Age*, trans. Patrick
O'Brian. New York: Warner Paperback Library, 1973.
Encyclopedic study of old age and an impassioned

social criticism of the treatment of the elderly in
contemporary societies. Divided into two major sections: Old Age Seen from Without (Old age and
biology; The ethnological data; Old age in historical
societies; Old age in present-day society) and The
Being-in-the-World (The discovery and assumption of
old age; The body's experience; Time, activity,
history; Old age and everyday life; Some examples
of old age). Four appendices: The hundred-year-olds;
Who cares for the aged?; The condition of aged workers
in the socialist countries; Some statistical data
upon sexuality of old people.

190.   Binstock, Robert H., and Ethel Shanas, eds. with the
        assistance of Associate Editors Vern L. Bengston,
        George L. Maddox and Dorothy Wedderburn. *Handbook
        of Aging and the Social Sciences*. New York: Van
        Nostrand Reinhold Co., 1976. One of three handbooks
        of aging published as part of the multidisciplinary
        project in compiling materials on the biological,
        psychological and social aspects of aging. Part
        One: The Social Aspects of Aging--Chapters on Scope,
        Concepts and Methods in the Study of Aging; Age and
        the Life Course; Part Two: Aging and Social Struc-
        ture--Chapters on Aging and World-Wide Population
        Change; Societal Development and Aging; Aging in
        Non-industrial Societies; Generations and Inter-
        generational Relations: Perspectives on Age Groups
        and Social Change; Social Stratification and Aging;
        Part Three: Aging and Social Systems--Chapters on
        Age Strata in Social Systems; The Family Life of
        Old People; Housing and Living Environments of Older
        People; The Economy and the Aged; Work and Retirement;
        Leisure and Lives: Personal Expressivity Across the
        Life Span; Aging and the Law; Political Systems and
        Aging; Part Four: Aging and Interpersonal Behavior--
        Chapters on Personal Characteristics and Social
        Behavior: Theory and Method; Social Networks and
        Isolation; Status and Role Change through the Life
        Span; Death and Dying in a Social Context; Part Five:
        Aging and Social Intervention--the Political Dilemmas
        of Intervention Policies; Strategies of Design and
        Research for Intervention; Income Distribution and
        the Aging; Aging, Health, and the Organization of
        Health Resources; Aging and the Social Services;
        The Future of Social Intervention.

191. Blau, Zena Smith. *Old Age in a Changing Society*. New
York: New Viewpoints, a Division of Franklin Watts,
Inc., 1973. (2nd ed. 1981 not examined.) Topics
are old age in a changing society; aging, widowhood
and retirement; parents and children; the significance of friendship; structural constraints on
friendship; changes in identity; the influence of
intimates on identity change; illness and work
alienation in old age; patterns of response to aging
and new roles for later life. Blau concludes with
a theoretical essay on role exit. Data are derived
from the Elmira study of older people, the Kips Bay
study of the health needs of older people in New
York City, and the study of associates of Kips Bay
respondents. (See No. 294 of this Bibliography.)
States that for most people, the anchoring points of
identity in adulthood are the family and work. An
unanticipated finding was that retirement has more
detrimental effects on the morale, associational
life and self-concept of older people, particularly
older men, than does widowhood. Also found that
friendship becomes more important in late life, when
kinship and work ties are severed, and that women
are less devastated than men by widowhood since they
fulfill their intimacy needs primarily in close
friendships with other women rather than in marriage,
as men do; but chances for forming new friendships
in late life are limited for the working-class woman
by meager financial resources and by the likelihood
that her life is limited to kin and neighbors. Blau
points out that "intimacy at a distance" can be "a
euphemism for pseudo-intimacy" and that "voluntary
retirement" for "health" or "personal" reasons may
be a face-saving device for older workers. She
states that women who seek further education in
middle age are innovators of an emergent social
pattern that will be adopted by the coming generation
of women.

192. Bouvier, Leon, Elinore Atlee and Frank McVeigh. "The
Elderly in America." *Population Bulletin* 30(3),
Washington, D.C.: Population Reference Bureau, Inc.,
1975. Demographic characteristics of the elderly;
economic and social statistics; present status of
the elderly; help for the elderly--federal efforts,
private and voluntary organizations, White House
Conferences on Aging, and the momentum for change
and recent legislation; national efforts and state

and local groups *of* the elderly *for* the elderly;
prospects of older people in the U.S.; and U.S.
elderly in world perspective.

193.   Butler, Robert N., M.D. *Why Survive? Being Old in
       America*. New York: Harper and Row, 1975. The title
       of the first chapter, The Tragedy of Old Age in
       America, names the subject of this Pulitzer prize-
       winning book by gerontologist and psychiatrist Butler.
       Poverty, age discrimination, exploitation and isola-
       tion are the subjects of chapters entitled How to
       Grow Old and Poor in an Affluent Society, What About
       My Pension?, The Right to Work, No Place to Live, No
       Time to Wait, The Unfulfilled Prescription, "They
       Are Only Senile," Houses of Death Are a Lively
       Business, Victimization of the Elderly, and
       Pacification and the Politics of Aging. In the
       last chapters, Butler writes of The Gift of Life, and
       of the need for enlarging the value of that gift by
       "loosening up life"--by making work, education and
       leisure run concurrently and continuously throughout
       the life course. In Growing Old Absurd, he proposes
       the development of a new sensibility toward old
       age through activism and the arts and argues that
       we still have the possibility of making life a work
       of art. Four appendices, on sources of gerontologi-
       cal and geriatric literature, and on organizations,
       government programs and government agencies for the
       elderly, and other national organizations and pro-
       grams in the field of aging. Extensive bibliography.

194.   Comfort, Alex. *A Good Age*. New York: Crown Publishers,
       Inc., 1976. An encyclopedia of gerontological con-
       cerns. Topics are presented in alphabetical order,
       from Ageism to Youth (with a concluding section on
       The Prudent Diet). Examples are: Alcohol, Arthritis,
       Bereavement, Bloody-mindedness, Brain, Cancer,
       Centenarians, Creativity and Disengagement, through
       Vitamins, War and Wrinkles. Illustrations and
       quotations focus on the possibilities for achieve-
       ment in later life. Bibliography.

195.   Cutler, Neal E., and Robert A. Harootyan. "Demography
       of the Aged." In *Aging: Scientific Perspectives
       and Social Issues*, pp. 31-69, Diana S. Woodruff and
       James E. Birren, eds. New York: D. Van Nostrand Co.,
       1975. A discussion, with tables and graphs, of
       historical trends in life expectancy; age composition

of the population; the basic demographic processes
of fertility, mortality and immigration; demographic
indicators--the dependency ratio, sex ratio and
birth cohort; some demographic characteristics of
the present elderly U.S. population--residential
distribution, economic characteristics, living
arrangements and educational attainment; concluding
remarks.

196. Datan, Nancy, and Nancy Lohmann, eds. *Transitions of
      Aging.* New York: Academic Press, Inc., 1980. Pro-
      ceedings of the 1st West Virginia University Gerontology
      Conference (1979). Papers: Gisela Labouvie-Vief,
      "Adaptive Dimensions of Adult Cognition"; Nancy
      Lohmann, "Life Satisfaction Research in Aging: Impli-
      cations for Policy Development"; Andrew C. Ostrow,
      "Physical Activity as it Relates to the Health of
      the Aged"; Carol B. Giesen and Nancy Datan, "The
      Competent Older Woman"; Lillian E. Troll, "Inter-
      generational Relations in Later Life: A Family System
      Approach"; Helena Z. Lopata, "The Widowed Family
      Member"; David Gutmann, Jerome Grunes and Brian
      Griffin, "The Clinical Psychology of Later Life:
      Developmental Paradigms"; Gayle B. Thompson, "Economic
      Status of Late Middle-Aged Widows"; Graham D. Rowles,
      "Growing Old 'Inside': Aging and Attachment to Place
      in an Appalachian Community"; M. Powell Lawton,
      "Environmental Change: The Older Person as Initiator
      and Responder"; Sheldon S. Tobin, "Institutionaliza-
      tion of the Aged." (See Nos. 302, 307, 337, 428,
      626, 830 and 850 of this Bibliography.)

197. Davis, Richard H. "The Role of Television." In *The
      Later Years: Social Applications of Gerontology*, pp.
      244-9, Richard A. Kalish, ed. Monterey, California:
      Brooks/Cole Publishing Co., 1977. Numerous surveys
      indicate that the use of print media for information
      service by those of little education, the culturally
      disadvantaged, and the elderly is far less than use
      by other subpopulations. Television is the most
      frequently chosen source for news, and older age
      segments choose information programs over enter-
      tainment programs. Older people view local news
      programming in still greater numbers than network
      national news. Topics: broadcasting and the older
      audience, and the values of television.

198.   Field, Minna. *The Aged, the Family, and the Community.*
       New York: Columbia University Press, 1972. In the
       Preface, Field notes that her book went to press at
       the same time as the conclusion of the deliberations
       of the 1971 White House Conference on Aging, and
       discusses the delegates' recommendations. Chapters,
       with illustrative cases--many from the life histories
       of elderly women--are: Introduction; Who Are the Aged?;
       The Impact of Social Changes on the Generations;
       Economics of Aging and Family Relationships; Patterns
       of Living Accommodations; Ill-Health and Family Rela-
       tionships; Impact of Extended Leisure Time; Social
       Work with the Elderly; Looking to the Future. In
       the last chapter, Field lists the National Objectives
       for Older Americans as set forth in the Older Amer-
       icans Act and discusses needed steps to economic
       betterment and needs for improved medical care and
       living arrangements and for satisfying leisure time;
       new roles; achievement of coexistence with younger
       family members; future role of social work; the need
       for research; and the impact of social attitudes.
       She states that the attitude of our youth-work-
       achievement-oriented society is the most serious
       impediment to adequate planning and purposeful
       activity.

199.   Hall, G. Stanley. *Senescence: The Last Half of Life.*
       New York: D. Appleton and Co., 1922. Hall's classic
       work on "the last half of life" is introduced with
       the view that human life has five chief stages--
       childhood, adolescence, middle life or the prime
       (from age 25 or 30 to age 40 or 45), senescence,
       "which begins in the early forties, or before in
       woman," and senectitude, "the post-climacteric or
       old age proper." The book, which contains many
       passages on aspects of women's aging, takes a highly
       favorable view of older women and of the possibili-
       ties for growth in later life for both women and
       men. It includes chapters on The Youth of Old Age,
       The History of Old Age, Literature By and On the
       Aged, Statistics of Old Age and Its Care, Medical
       Views and Treatment of Old Age, the Contributions of
       Biology and Physiology (with an extensive report of
       the work of Professor Steinach, whose rejuvenation
       treatment inspired Atherton's *Black Oxen* (see No.
       452 of this Bibliography), a Report on Questionnaire
       Returns (from older women as well as men), and Some
       Conclusions, and The Psychology of Death. Hall had

received nearly two-score letters from old people suggesting that he write this book--letters addressed to him through the editor of the *Atlantic Monthly* and written in response to an article he published there anonymously on "Old Age" (in the January, 1921, issue).

200. Harris, Charles S., Research Coordinator. *Fact Book on Aging: A Profile of America's Older Population.* Washington, D.C.: The National Council on the Aging, Inc., 1978. Profile of the elderly in America. Topics: Demography, Income, Employment, Physical Health, Mental Health, Housing, Transportation, and Criminal Victimization. Tables, charts and references.

201. Hendricks, Jon, and C. Davis Hendricks. *Aging in Mass Society: Myths and Realities*, 2nd ed. Cambridge, Massachusetts: Winthrop Publishers, Inc., 1981. Part One includes chapters on The Spectrum of Aging (with sections on age grading, ageism and the historical foundations of Gerontology), The Age-Old Question of Old Age (aging in historical context), and Aging in Advanced Industrialized Societies. Part Two, Theories of Aging, includes chapters on Physiological Changes over Time and Theories of Social Gerontology; Part Three, Dimensions of Aging, has chapters on Psychological Processes in Later Life; Health Status in the Later Years; Work, Finances and the Golden Years; Dilemmas of Retirement; Family Life and Living Arrangements; the everyday concerns of aging (social involvement; sexuality in later life; time, religion and death); The Aged in the Political Arena; and Minority Groups in the Later Years (elderly Blacks, Hispanic Americans, American Indians and Asian Americans); and Part Four, Looking Ahead, consists of a chapter on The Prospects of Aging, including sections on the elderly of tomorrow, Preparing the Way--Institutional Reforms (Social Security, legislative response, flexible retirement, and prognosis on health) and Gerontology as a Vocation. Each chapter has a listing of pertinent readings. Includes a Glossary and Index.

202. Huyck, Margaret Hellie. *Growing Older: What You Need to Know About Aging.* Englewood Cliffs, New Jersey: Prentice-Hall, Inc., 1974. Topics: ways of defining and measuring aging, social expectations, biological changes, human sexuality, parents and children, friends

and lovers, work and leisure, personal space,
personality and self-concept, successful aging, and
new perspectives on aging.

203. Kalish, Richard A., ed. *The Later Years: Social
      Applications of Gerontology.* Monterey, California:
      Brooks/Cole Publishing Co., 1977. Includes Kalish's
      "The Musicians of Bremen: An Adaptation," Herbert
      A. Shores's "A Plea from the Older Individual," and
      papers on demography and ethnicity and aging; psycho-
      social views of the older person; finances; retirement;
      health and illness; politics and the law; family,
      religion, adult education and television; housing and
      transportation; social and health services; institu-
      tional living. Appendices are: The Contributors, and
      Some Organizations Serving the Elderly in the U.S.

204. Neugarten, Bernice L. "Age Groups in American Society
      and the Rise of the Young-Old." *Annals of the
      American Academy of Political and Social Science*
      (September 1974) 415:187-98. The numbers of old
      persons in the U.S. will continue to rise sharply.
      In all industrial societies, young and old must adapt
      to changes resulting from added longevity. Middle
      age has become a newly delineated stage in the life
      cycle. Another division may be imminent--that of
      the young-old (aged 55 to 75) and the old-old
      (aged 75 and over). The young-old differ from the
      middle-aged mainly by the fact of retirement. More
      than 15% of the total population, the young-old are
      relatively healthy and affluent. The family is still
      an important part of their daily life, and many still
      have a living parent. They are much better educated
      than the old-old and are a highly active political
      group. They will probably develop a wider range of
      life patterns with regard to work, education and
      leisure. The young-old in 1990 will probably exert
      a potent influence upon government. The age group
      of the old-old is growing at an increasing rate.
      Most will probably live independently, but will
      need suportive services to enable them to live as
      fully as possible. The young-old could become major
      agents of social change in building a society in
      which age is irrelevant. They have great potential
      for creating an attractive image of aging and for
      improving age norms and attitudes.

205. Riley, Matilda White, and Anne Foner, in association
      with Mary E. Moore, Beth Hess and Barbara K. Roth.
      Aging and Society, Volume one: An inventory of
      research findings. New York: Russell Sage Foundation,
      1968. Introduction: A Synopsis; Part One--Socio-
      cultural Contexts: The Population; Work and Retirement;
      Finances; Education; The Residential Setting; The
      Family. Part Two--The Organism: The Nature of Aging;
      Mortality and Morbidity in the Population; Physical
      Changes; Behavioral Changes. Part Three--The
      Personality: Personality Dimensions and Needs; The
      Self; Life Attitudes; Life Satisfaction; Mental Dis-
      order and Deviance. Part Four--Social Roles: The
      Structure of Roles; Work and Retirement; Political
      Roles; Religious Roles; Voluntary Associations;
      Leisure Roles; Family; Friends and Neighbors;
      Roles in Institutions.

206. Riley, Matilda White, John W. Riley, Jr., and Marilyn
      E. Johnson, eds., in association with Anne Foner and
      Beth Hess. *Aging and Society*, Volume two: Aging
      and the professions. New York: Russell Sage
      Foundation, 1969. Introduction; Papers on aging
      and social work; aging and medicine; aging and nursing;
      aging and public health; aging and manpower develop-
      ment; aging and financial management; aging and
      architecture and planning; aging and the law; aging
      and the ministry; aging and education; aging and
      mass communications.

207. Riley, Matilda White, Marilyn Johnson and Anne Foner,
      eds. *Aging and Society*, Volume three: A sociology
      of age stratification. New York: Russell Sage
      Foundation, 1972. Part One: Introduction--Elements
      in a model of age stratification; Interpretation of
      Research on Age; Notes on the Concept of a Population.
      Part Two: Age Stratification in Selected Aspects of
      Society--The Polity; the Work Force; The Community;
      Higher Education and Changing Socialization; Age,
      Aging, and Age Structure in Science; Friendship.
      Part Three: The Nature of Age Stratification; Age
      Strata in the Society; The Life Course of Individuals;
      The Succession of Cohorts. Appendix: Some Problems
      of Research on Age.

208. Riley, Matilda White, and Joan Waring. "Age and Aging."
      In *Contemporary Social Problems*, 4th ed., pp. 355-
      410, Robert K. Merton and Robert Nisbet, eds. New

York: Harcourt Brace Jovanovich, Inc., 1976. This
chapter has four sections. The first presents a
conceptual model to help define the major sets of
social factors at work: a sociological perspective
includes a discussion of age dynamics, societal
dynamics, age stratification and intrinsic strains
and imbalances. Section two addresses some social
problems arising from age stratification, among them
social inequalities and age segregation and generational conflict. The third section is concerned
with the problems that arise from role changes
accompanying aging and explores the strains and hidden
sufferings that may accompany transitions at every
stage from entering nursery school to widowhood and
death. The fourth section addresses some of the
possibilities and difficulties of social interventions
directed toward the correction of these social problems, and includes discussions of dispelling myths
and misperceptions, redistribution of work, education
and leisure over the life course, social change and
cohort analysis, and constraints on intervention.

209.   Smith, Bert Kruger. *Aging in America*. Boston: Beacon
Press, 1973. This book includes an Introduction by
Bertram S. Brown, M.D., Director, National Institute
of Mental Health; a Prologue, "An Old Woman Speaks,"
(see No. 592 of this Bibliography), an Epilogue, "A
Young Person Responds," an Appendix on The 1971
White House Conference--and Beyond; Notes; Information
on Aging; and an Index. Chapters, drawing extensive-
ly from case study materials, are: The Aging--Who
Are They?; Needs We Share; Some Problems Among the
Old (race and poverty, health and care)--and Some
Possibilities for Meeting Them (programs in
Ypsilanti, Big Spring, Texas, South Carolina, Topeka,
Kansas and elsewhere, demonstrating that the
community concept is both workable and useful);
The Masking of Emotions (psychological problems in
intergenerational relationships, new dilemmas--as
the situation of the "children" of retirement
age who are still responsible for very old parents,
and some positive possibilities); How the Individual
Can Prepare; How the Challenge Might Be Met--Some
Examples (nutrition programs, ACTION, other programs
and how to locate help); Personal Responsibility.

210. Soldo, Beth J. "America's Elderly in the 1980s."
     Population Bulletin 35(4), Washington, D.C.: Popula-
     tion Reference·Bureau, Inc., November 1980. Demo-
     graphic facts and forecasts. Topics: The Clock
     Starts Ticking; Defining the "elderly" (they are an
     extremely diverse group, spanning a 30- to 35-year
     age range); Demography of Today's Elderly (survivors
     of the 1900-1910 cohort have smaller families on the
     average to rely on than those born one to two decades
     earlier or later): Numbers (there was an eightfold
     increase in the past 80 years, but the effect of
     the small Depression-era cohorts will slow the growth
     of the elderly to 7% in the 1990s and 10% in the
     first decade of the 21st century); Proportion of
     total population; Differences within the older
     population (age, sex and race; note that 6 of every
     10 elderly are women, a relatively recent phenomenon);
     Geographic distribution (including discussions of
     "gray ghettos" and differences between Snowbelt and
     Sunbelt states); Death and Illness (note that over
     time, male-female differences in life expectancy
     have widened); Use of health care resources. Quality
     of Life: Education, Employment, Income, Expenditures,
     Housing, Marital status, living arrangements and
     family help. Help for the Elderly: the public
     sector response; Evaluating the public sector
     response; Response from the private sector; 1981
     White House Conference on Aging; Recent legislative
     changes. Initiatives for Change: Challenges of an
     Aging Society: Whose responsibility?; Financing
     Social Security; Discriminating against older women;
     Health care and the elderly. Aging in International
     Perspective: Care of the elderly in developed
     countries; Care in developing countries.

211. Tibbetts, Clark, ed. *Handbook of Social Gerontology:*
     Societal Aspects of Aging. Chicago: The University
     of Chicago Press, 1960. The "first attempt to
     identify and structure a new field of research and
     learning--social gerontology." Part One, The Basis
     and Theory of Societal Aging, includes an introductory
     chapter by Tibbetts on Origin, Scope, and Fields
     of Social Gerontology, and papers on demography,
     aging in preindustrial societies, The Technological
     and Societal Basis of Aging, The Impact of Aging on
     the Social Structure, and The Aging Individual.
     Part Two, The Impact of Aging on Individual Activities
     and Social Roles, includes papers on health; income

security; changing status, roles and relationships;
patterns of work-life; patterns of retirement, and
the uses of leisure. Part Three, Aging and the
Reorganization of Society, includes papers on the
family; the economy; health programs; housing and
community settings; governmental functions and the
politics of age; voluntary associations; and religion
and the church.

*212.   U.S. Congress. Senate. Special Committee on Aging.
        Developments in Aging: 1979, Part I. Report No.
        96-613, 96th Congress, 2nd Session, 1980.

*213.   U.S. Department of Commerce. Bureau of the Census.
        *Demographic Aspects of Aging and the Older Population
        in the United States*. Washington, D.C.: U.S. Govern-
        ment Printing Office, 1978.

 214.   Younger, Evelle J. "The Older Person as Victim." In
        The Later Years: Social Applications of Gerontology,
        pp. 209-15, Richard A. Kalish, ed. Monterey,
        California: Brooks/Cole Publishing Co., a Division
        of Wadsworth Publishing Co., Inc., 1977. One of the
        first publications focusing attention on crime and
        the elderly, edited from "The California Experience:
        Prevention of Criminal Victimization of the Elderly"
        by Younger in *The Police Chief*, 1976. In 1971,
        when the White House Conference on Aging reported
        that crime is a major concern, those in the California
        Attorney General's office became convinced that
        criminal victimization of the elderly had been
        largely ignored. For physical, economic and psycho-
        logical reasons, the elderly are especially vulnerable.
        Their fear of crime has become almost epidemic. Fear
        must be combatted by demonstrating the concern of
        law enforcement officials and by convincing the
        elderly they are not powerless to prevent victimiza-
        tion. Crimes against the elderly discussed in this
        article include crimes of force, buncos and confidence
        games, medical quackery, and consumer fraud. Four
        years of leadership in this area have yielded
        promising results in local crime prevention programs.

See also: 160, 729, 731, 765, 866, 877, 878, 879, 880, 881.

B. Historical Perspectives;
Images of Aging; Future of Aging

215. Achenbaum, W. Andrew. "The Obsolescence of Old Age."
In *Dimensions of Aging: Readings*, pp. 21-38, Jon
Hendricks and C. Davis Hendricks, eds. Cambridge,
Massachusetts: Winthrop Publishers, Inc., 1979. In
this excerpt (Chapter 3) of his *Old Age in the New
Land* (see No. 216 of this Bibliography), Achenbaum
states his thesis that the period between 1865 and
1914 represents a watershed in which general ideas
about the worth of old people changed from positive
perceptions to disesteem. He shows that this was a
result of the impact of new scientific, bureaucratic,
and popular ideas that converged with innovations in
medical practice, the economic structure, and American society in general, in sections on changes in
theory and practice in health and medicine, and
sections entitled "Not all of the centenarians are
paragons of all the virtues," "the superannuated
man" (on the idea of the economic obsolescence of
old age), and "old age, like death, is merely
incidental," and finds irony in the unprecedented
devaluation of the worth of old people. Notes for
this chapter include many references to articles
and books by and about women on the subject of aging.

216. Achenbaum, W. Andrew. *Old Age in the New Land: The
American Experience Since 1790*. Baltimore: The
Johns Hopkins University Press, 1978. Part I of
this history is entitled "Changing Perceptions of
the Aged's Roles in 19th-Century America," Part II,
"The Demographic and Socioeconomic Dimensions of
Old Age," and Part III, "Contemporary Old Age in
Historical Perspective." In Part I, Achenbaum
concurs with the judgment that there never was a
"golden epoch" in the history of old age, and he
dissents from the view that "modernization" has
proceeded inevitably and unidirectionally. He
finds many resemblances between the images of old
age extant from 1790 to 1860, but a striking
difference in the *perception* (not actual social
status) of old people then and now. Perceptions of
the worth of the elderly did not remain static, and
their problems were not denied, but they were seen
in a positive light. A subtle change from a
"republican" mode of thought to a "romantic" view

ultimately although inadvertently affected perceptions
of the worth of the aged. A disesteem for the aged
may be traced to the convergence of new ideas with
innovations in medical practice, in the economy,
and in society in general. In Part II, Achenbaum
discusses the divergence between the rhetoric and
realities of growing old in 19th-century America (a
divergence that is a motif in this book, and that he
believes obtains in the U.S. to this day). Here he
focuses on the actual position of older people rather
than on perceptions of their value and functions.
He emphasizes the critical distinction between the
intellectual and social history of old age in the
U.S., and avers that ideas about the worth and
functions of the old have a life of their own. Part
III has chapters on the ways old age became a
national problem, on Social Security ("a crucial
watershed") and on old age in the U.S. since Social
Security. Old age remains a serious "problem" in
the U.S. today, but the ways old age and the needs
of the elderly are defined are historically novel.
In Conclusion: Toward the Year 2001, Achenbaum
discusses three crucial roles historians could play
in the future--as social scientists, policy analysts
and humanists. Foreword by Robert Butler; Appendix
on methodology; selected bibliography.

217.   Achenbaum, W. Andrew, and Peggy Ann Kusnerz. *Images
       of Old Age in America: 1790 to the Present*. Ann
       Arbor, Michigan: The Institute of Gerontology, The
       University of Michigan-Wayne State University, 1978.
       This publication of the prints and photographs and
       much of the text of the exhibit of this same title
       prepared by the Institute of Gerontology at The
       University of Michigan, includes a preface by
       Achenbaum on the historian's perspective, a preface
       by Kusnerz on the pictorial librarian's perspective,
       and Details of Visuals. The sections on images of
       old age in America are: Introduction; 1790-1864;
       1865-1934; and 1935 to the Present. Achenbaum
       discusses the contributions of scholars in the
       humanities to gerontological research and the
       complex relationship between perceptions and realities
       of growing old. He suggests that an examination of
       these images and of our own assumptions about aging
       can contribute to an enhancement of the meaning and
       dignity of the lives of older people. Kusnerz
       reviews the problems encountered in the search for
       information in graphic form. She notes that visuals
       from a variety of contexts--popular periodicals,
       books, sheet music, newspapers and fine art prints
       and photographs--are included here, in order to

represent many viewpoints from American culture
on old age.

218. Birren, James E., and Vivian Clayton. "History of
Gerontology." In *Aging: Scientific Perspectives
and Social Issues*, pp. 15-27, Diana S. Woodruff and
James E. Birren, eds. New York: D. Van Nostrand
Co., 1975. Encompasses early inquiries into aging
(the three themes--antediluvian, hyperborean and
rejuvenation--in myths about aging and death),
early and later empirical periods of the scientific
era, a section on the growing interest in Gerontology,
and a section on Aging in the Future.

219. Davies, Leland J. "Attitudes Toward Old Age and Aging
as Shown by Humor." *The Gerontologist* (June 1977)
17(3):220-6. Report on a representative sample of
363 jokes about aging and 187 jokes about death taken
from six anthologies. A reading of several thousand
jokes indicated many revealed negative views and sex
differences in attitude toward later life. Jokes
referring to aging were all more negative in attitude
for sexual, physical, social and, to a lesser degree,
mental changes of aging. The emphasis on older men-
younger women in sexual jokes, the negative jokes
about old maids, and the sexual bias in age conceal-
ment jokes demonstrated a strong difference in
attitude toward aging of the sexes. Male aging,
especially in regard to sexual functioning, is
considered much more positively than female aging.
There is a very strong negative stereotype of the
old unmarried woman. Concluding section on Need
for Intervention.

220. Fischer, David Hackett. *Growing Old in America*. New
York: Oxford University Press, 1977. Early America
(1607-1820) was an era of growing *gerontophilia*,
in which old age was exalted (except for slaves,
paupers and some old women--as, poor widows), sometimes hated and feared, but more often honored and
obeyed. The period of deep change (1780-1820),
during the era of the American and French revolutions,
was marked by a transformation in attitudes toward
old age and in the life experiences of the old.
This transition was followed by an era of growing *gerontophobia* (1780-1970), a period in which youth was
celebrated and the aged often became victims of prevailing attitudes and social arrangements. From 1910 to
1970, a second period of deep change took place,
when old age was seen as a social problem and an
elaborate system of social welfare was developed to
deal with it. Today, a fifth period of age relations

may be dawning, which might be built upon an ideal
of *gerontophratria*, a brotherhood of generations.
Nine categories of evidence are presented--the custom
of "seating the meeting" according to age, which
ended around 1830 and was replaced by a stratification based upon wealth; "age heaping"; shifts in
fashion in costume; changing linguistic patterns--
most pejorative terms for old men began to appear in
the late 18th century, and praise words for the aged
to disappear in the same time period (it is noted
that virtually every term of abuse used for old women
appears to be as old as the English language itself);
changes in group portraits of American families;
the disappearance of the modified system of primo-
geniture by the early 19th century; the sharp decline
in the proportion of children given the same names
as their grandparents between 1790 and 1830; literary
evidence; and the growth of retirement, a change
that led to the establishment of mandatory retirement
in most occupations by the late 19th century. In
the Introduction, Fischer reviews the history of
old age in prehistoric societies, in the ancient
world, and in medieval Europe; in Old Age Becomes
a Social Problem, he discusses the problem of
poverty, and the history of pension legislation
and of geriatrics and social gerontology; in A
Thought For the Future, he proposes a national
inheritance system and calls for a recognition of
old people as autonomous individuals and for an
ethic of creativity to coexist with the work ethic.

*221. Fowles, Donald G. *Some Prospects for the Future
       Elderly Population*. U.S. Department of Health,
       Education and Welfare, Statistical Reports on Older
       Americans, No. 3. Washington, D.C.: U.S. Department
       of Health, Education and Welfare, 1978.

222.   Hareven, Tamara K. "The Last Stage: Historical Adult-
       hood and Old Age." *Daedalus* (Fall 1976) 105(4):13-27.
       An historical overview of the changing meanings of
       aging and advanced old age from the late 19th century
       to the present. Problems of old age and aging in the
       U.S. are examined in terms of more fundamental
       historical discontinuities in the life course than
       demographic changes, industrialization or the "cult
       of youth." The absence of dramatic transitions to
       adult life allowed a more intensive interaction among
       different age groups within the family and the

community, thus promoting a greater sense of continuity
and interdependence among those of all ages. Retirement at a specific age, an invention of the 20th
century, represents the most drastic development in
the emergence of old age as a separate life stage.
In the late 19th and early 20th centuries, work
careers--which extended over the life course and
were often disorderly--and family organization were
clearly intertwined, and reciprocity among family
members all through life was essential for survival
in old age. The major changes that have led to the
isolation of older people in society today were
rooted not so much in changes in family structure
or living arrangements as in the transformation and
redefinition of family *functions*. Socioeconomic
changes of the past century gradually led to a
segregation of work from other aspects of life, and
to a shift from the predominance of familial values
to an emphasis on individualism and privacy. These
changes are due to the segmentation of the life course
into more formal stages, of more uniform and rigid
transitions from one stage to the next, and of
the separation of age groups from one another.

223. Harris, Louis, and Associates, Inc. *The Myth and
     Reality of Aging in America*. Washington: The
     National Council on the Aging, Inc., 1975. In
     the Foreword, NCOA President Albert J. Abrams calls
     attention to the findings that most older people in
     the U.S. have the desire and potential to be productive,
     contributing members of society; that most feel their
     economic and social conditions are better than the
     general public perceives them to be, although a
     sizeable minority, including millions of elderly
     people, still live at or below the poverty line;
     that 97% of Americans believe that Social Security
     payments to the elderly should automatically increase
     with increases in the cost of living; that 81% of
     the public believe the federal government has the
     responsibility to use general tax revenues to help
     support older people; and that 86% are opposed to
     mandatory retirement. Contents include sections on
     public attitudes toward and image of old age and the
     elderly, the social and economic contributions of
     people over age 65, preparation for and the experience
     of being older, the accessibility and use of community
     facilites by the public aged 65 and over, portrayal
     of the elderly by the media, and the politics of old

age; includes three appendices on methodology.
Data derive from 4,254 in-person household interviews in 1974 of a representative cross section of
the American public aged 18 and over, with additional
representative samples of the public aged 65 and over,
of people aged 55 to 64, and of elderly blacks.
Presents considerable evidence of a discrepancy
between the *experience* of life after 65 and expectations of it by those under that age. Other significant
findings: defining the elderly as a deprived group
can do both old and young a disservice; older people
themselves have accepted negative stereotypes of
the elderly, and most see themselves as exceptions
to a perceived average; like the young, three of
every four older people say they would prefer to
spend most of their time with people of all different
ages; there is a great potential manpower among older
Americans and a serious need in the U.S. for career
planning and job training programs for people of all
ages; for one in three elderly poor, serious health
problems, inadequate income and fear of crime make
life a difficult struggle.

224.   Hendricks, Jon, and C. Davis Hendricks. "The Age Old
       Question of Old Age: Was It Really So Much Better
       Back When?" *The International Journal of Aging and
       Human Development* (1977-78) 8(2):139-54. It is
       commonly assumed that the aged in modern industrial
       societies fare less well in many respects than did
       their pre-industrial counterparts. This paper
       examines archaeological, historical and literary
       evidence on demographic changes, the standard of
       living, and the status of the aged and attitudes
       toward the aged from prehistoric times through the
       pre-Christian and Christian eras and the Middle Ages
       and the Renaissance (which marks the beginning of
       profound changes in population structure) to the
       modern era, and concludes that, even though many
       supportive aspects of the pre-industrial world are
       absent in contemporary society, it is likely that
       ambivalence toward the elderly is a long-standing
       tradition.

225.   Neugarten, Bernice L. "The Aged in the Year 2025."
       In *The Older Woman: Lavender Rose or Gray Panther*,
       pp. 332-43, Marie Marschall Fuller and Cora Ann
       Martin, eds. Springfield, Illinois: Charles C.
       Thomas, 1980. One scenario for the future is an

"equilibrium" society in which the size and age
distribution of the U.S. population will stabilize,
the social system will become more equitable, and
older persons will receive their fair share of
whatever goods are produced. But whatever happens,
the numbers of the aged will increase dramatically.
If death rates remain about the same, the aged
population will be even more heavily weighted toward
women, and toward widowed women, by 2025. If they
decline, the "old-old" (age 75+) will be almost one
out of two of the aged. If birth rates remain low,
those aged 65+ will constitute about 16% of the
population by 2025. It is likely the age of retirement will continue to decline up to the year 2000,
but there may be a turnabout by 2025; however, the
economic burdens on the society are likely to increase because of growing numbers of the "old-old."
The four- and five-generational family (*not household*) will be the norm by the year 2000, and especially
so by 2025. The trend toward separate households
may or may not continue. Families will probably
want more options in the settings and type of care
available for an aged family member whose health is
failing. The future of the intergenerational family
network will depend also upon changing attitudes
toward marriage and divorce. There has been a
fragmentation of the family with regard to its
child-rearing role; it remains to be seen if this
will also become true of the *parent-caring* role.
By 2025, the trend toward the appearance of a
leisure class of young-old may be reversed, with
people remaining in the labor force perhaps up to
age 75.

226.   Palmore, Erdman. "The Future Status of the Aged." In
       The Older Woman: Lavender Rose or Gray Panther, pp.
       323-31, Marie Marschall Fuller and Cora Ann Martin,
       eds. Springfield, Illinois: Charles C. Thomas, 1980.
       The National Center for Health Statistics, available
       since 1961, and data from the Census Bureau indicate
       that the relative status of the aged in health,
       income, occupation and education is rising and
       probably will continue to rise for the rest of the
       20th century. Factors accounting for improvements
       are the slowing in rates of change for the younger
       cohorts and the increase in both government and
       private programs to improve the status of the aged.
       Since present programs are having beneficial effects,

these data justify their continuation or expansion.
The data also contradict the theories that the status
of the aged continues to decline in modern societies,
that age stratification is becoming more significant,
and that the aged are becoming more like a disadvantaged minority group.

*227.   Seltzer, Mildred, and Robert Atchley. "The Concept of
        Old: Changing Attitudes and Stereotypes." *The
        Gerontologist* (Autumn 1971) 11(3):226-30.

228.   Sherr, Virginia T. "Benjamin Franklin and Geropsychiatry:
        Vignettes for the Bicentennial Year." In *The Older
        Woman: Lavender Rose or Gray Panther*, pp. 79-87,
        Marie Marschall Fuller and Cora Ann Martin, eds.
        Springfield, Illinois: Charles C. Thomas, 1980. As
        a prolific writer, scientist and humanist, Benjamin
        Franklin was a true multidisciplinarian. He may
        have anticipated the dilemma for older women created
        by the statistical imbalance between the sexes in
        later life. He believed that older women and young
        men are ideally suited to one another, and listed
        eight reasons why old women make good lovers, in
        his "Old Mistresses Apologue." Sherr writes that
        sexuality as related to aging is becoming acknowl-
        edged as a real issue in 1976, and that this is in
        part a matter of personal autonomy, civil rights,
        and the politics of a climate that tends to impose
        on older people the idea that they are in a futureless,
        stereotyped position. She also finds that the
        Bicentennial is coming to accept the therapeutic
        value of cultural foods and alcohol as a social
        stimulant for the institutionalized elderly. She
        quotes a letter, "Consideration for the Old Folks,"
        that Ben Franklin once wrote his sister, noting his
        point that *appearances* as well as realities should
        be attended to in conduct toward old people. Sherr
        also discusses the benefits for the elderly of the
        EMI Scanner, the 1976 report by Jacobs on the
        diagnosis and treatment of normal-pressure hydro-
        cephalus, which augurs well for preventive psycho-
        neurologic intervention, mobile outreach units,
        home health visitors, and discoveries about the
        effect of prolonged immobilization that counteract
        mislabeling of patients as senile or psychotic. She
        concludes that the challenge in 1976 both to the
        elderly and those helping them is similar to that
        faced by Dr. Franklin's peers two centuries ago "when
        they rebelled against being programmed without
        representation."

229. Stannard, David E. "Growing Up and Growing Old:
      Dilemmas of Aging in Bureaucratic America." In
      *Aging and the Elderly: Humanistic Perspectives in
      Gerontology*, pp. 9-20, Stuart F. Spicker, Kathleen
      M. Woodward and David D. Van Tassel, eds. Atlantic
      Highlands, New Jersey: Humanities Press, Inc., 1978.
      Stannard notes that a person's worth is defined in
      terms of the criteria for valuation adopted in a
      particular society, and that social change in the
      U.S. for at least the past twelve decades has been
      in the direction of specialization in work, with-
      drawal of the family from active participation in
      community life, and bureaucratization; as a consequence,
      there is the vacuum of an open-ended liminal period
      awaiting all of us at the end of the life cycle. In
      a society that measures worth in terms of ability to
      produce and consume, those who have had these
      abilities taken away *with no future prospect for
      their return* are caught in a very complex dilemma
      that is all the worse because they were seemingly
      willing participants in creating this non-status
      situation. Stannard finds both the activity and
      disengagement theories to be deficient because they
      are not grounded in societal reality. He shows the
      plight of the aged by drawing from some material in
      the last part of his *The Puritan Way of Death*, and,
      citing unemployment and poverty rates by age, finds
      that in our society the threshold to old age is
      crossed at increasingly younger ages.

See also: 1, 171, 201, 353, 355, 363, 426, 515, 603, 644,
678, 680, 798.

               C. Humanistic Perspectives on Aging

230. Berg, Geri, and Sally Gadow. "Toward More Human
      Meanings of Aging: Ideals and Images from Philosophy
      and Art." In *Aging and the Elderly: Humanistic
      Perspectives in Gerontology*, pp. 83-92, Stuart F.
      Spicker, Kathleen M. Woodward and David D. Van
      Tassel, eds. Atlantic Highlands, New Jersey:
      Humanities Press, Inc., 1978. The negative evalua-
      tion of aging implicit in the "facts" given by the
      sciences is expressed and applied by medical science
      in its treating of aging as a disease. The humanities

disclose *positive* meanings of aging. The slowing
process may be a way of opening time; other changes
may express the intricacies that are possible for
one for whom reality has become more richly textured
and may mean that aging is a clarification of the
essential form one's life is to be given. Aging
may mean the chance to decide freely what meaning
the coming death will have for the life that remains.
For most artists, growing old is an enriching,
deepening experience. A dialectic between abstract
ideals and concrete immediacy of images is needed
to encompass the complex possibilities of the
experience of aging.

231.   Butler, Robert N. Afterword. In *Aging and the Elderly:
       Humanistic Perspectives in Gerontology*, pp. 389-91,
       Stuart F. Spicker, Kathleen M. Woodward and David
       D. Van Tassel, eds. Atlantic Highlands, New Jersey:
       Humanities Press, Inc., 1978. Butler finds it
       unsurprising that a range of feelings about the
       elderly from ignorance and ambivalence to hatred
       and distaste are found in the works of artists,
       writers and humanists, as in the general culture.
       He observes that Beauvoir's work--which has the
       deficiencies of incomplete scholarship, ideology,
       élitism and subjectivity about aging--reinforced many
       stereotypes, although her aim was to improve the
       treatment of old people in Western civilization,
       and he states that students, artists, scientists
       and humanists must all form their own attitudes
       through the depth of individual relationships with
       older people. He would like to see more attention
       given to humanizing old age, and suggests that the
       vision of humanists should reach beyond contemporary
       life to the future of aging.

232.   Erikson, Erik H., and Joan M. Erikson. Introduction:
       Reflections on Aging. In *Aging and the Elderly:
       Humanistic Perspectives in Gerontology*, pp. 1-8,
       Stuart F. Spicker, Kathleen M. Woodward and David
       D. Van Tassel, eds. Atlantic Highlands, New Jersey:
       Humanities Press, Inc., 1978. The Eriksons reflect
       on their participation in the "Human Values and
       Aging" project, note the rarity and hence the need
       for the study of the connotations of the life stages
       and of life as a whole within the dominant world
       view, and state that Integrity and Wisdom connote an
       active *adaptation* and not a passive *adjustment* to the

conditions of development, and that Despair in some
balance with the forces of Integrity is an essential
component for the last stage, since people develop
through conflict. Their central point here is that
what remains true for the last stage in life is in
the *epigenetic nature* of the life cycle from its
beginning. They suggest that people in their 40s
and 50s can begin to face the issue of neglected
potentialities and recommend endeavors to balance
the specializations of modern life, perhaps through
community centers serving people of all ages, and
the development of skills in work with clay, glass,
metal, textiles, leather and wood; in a world of
machine-made objects, this would give new dimensions
to things and words.

*233.   Freeman, Joseph T. *Aging: Its History and Literature*.
         New York: Human Sciences Press, 1979.

234.   Gruman, Gerald J.   "Cultural Origins of Present-day
         'Age-ism': The Modernization of the Life Cycle."
         In *Aging and the Elderly: Humanistic Perspectives
         in Gerontology*, pp. 359-87, Stuart F. Spicker, Kath-
         leen M. Woodward and David D. Van Tassel, eds.
         Atlantic Highlands, New Jersey: Humanities Press,
         Inc., 1978. Topics are (1) the contemporary aging
         crisis; (2) the discovery of age-ism; (3) the
         modernist transformation (in the 1890s, a hierarchy
         of ages, races, and stages of development was invoked
         to justify domestic and foreign policy); (4) the
         positivist ideology of age and the revolt that failed,
         with sub-sections on pre-positivist views on age and
         aging, a section in which Gruman discusses Sir
         James Crichton-Browne's rebuttal against age-ism
         (and Osler's lecture) which was based on assumptions
         inherited from Renaissance humanism and the En-
         lightenment, age stages in positivism (Gruman finds
         that the intellectual foundation for disengagement
         theory was presented more than a century ago),
         rebellion, and the development from neo-positivism
         to disengagement theory; and (5) modernization theory
         and the re-engagement of the elderly. Gruman states
         that the re-engagement theory offered here is intended
         to challenge the basic assumptions of neo-positivist
         ideology, and presents a redefinition of moderniza-
         tion (a process which has been underway since at
         least the Renaissance) in which the aged do have a
         future as they become re-engaged at the frontier of

modern cultural adaptation and realization through
historical time. Extensive bibliography.

235. *Human Values and Aging Newsletter.* Institute on the
      Humanities, Arts, and Aging, Brookdale Center on
      Aging of Hunter College, 440 East 26th Street,
      New York, New York 10010. (1979-) A bi-monthly
      Newsletter under the auspices of the Value Dilemmas
      in the Aging Society Project. Regular features,
      as *Case Studies*, *Book Reviews*, and *Essays*, focus
      on moral dilemmas faced by professional practioners,
      as well as on positive aspects of aging.

236. Moss, Walter, G. "Aging in Humanistic Perspective, An
      Essay." In *Humanistic Perspectives on Aging: An
      Annotated Bibliography and Essay*, pp. 1-6. Ann
      Arbor, Michigan: The Institute of Gerontology, The
      University of Michigan-Wayne State University, 1976.
      An essay on the contributions the humanistic
      disciplines can make to gerontology (with examples
      from history and many genres of literature), the
      foundations of a humanistic gerontology (drawing
      from the insights of humanistic psychology, aging
      might be seen as potential growth of the mind and
      the spirit) and on what the humanities in general
      give to older people (helping one achieve transcendence
      and ego integrity, and emphasizing the potential
      positive aspects of aging--growth of the spirit,
      of wisdom and of experience--rather than the negative
      aspects of physical decline). Annotated bibliography
      (see No. 876 of this Bibliography) of Aging Around
      the World (Non-fiction, past and present); Reflec-
      tions of the Aging (Autobiographies by Older Authors);
      Literature on Aging and the Aged: Drama, Essays,
      Novels, Poetry, Short Stories; Reflections on Death;
      Films and Videotapes; Toward a Humanistic Gerontology:
      Other Explorations (comments on additional sources).

237. Philibert, Michel. "Philosophical Approach to
      Gerontology." In *Dimensions of Aging: Readings*, pp.
      379-94, Jon Hendricks and C. Davis Hendricks, eds.
      Cambridge, Massachusetts: Winthrop Publishers, Inc.,
      1979. The study of human aging must be comparative,
      dialectical, hermeneutical and interventive. Phili-
      bert considers the deliberate rejection and ignorance
      of pre- and non-scientific literature on aging to
      be ruinous to the study of aging. In his view, the
      call for (more) research was answered by four main
      "scientific tribes"--physicians, biologists,

psychologists and sociologists, who accepted the
misconceptions of aging, science and history current
in the 1930s and who did not appreciate the
importance of *qualitative* changes that were affecting
the experience of aging, and its conditions and
meaning for society and the individual. Philibert
perceives the development of a "dangerous trend"
toward "gerontologocracy." He distinguishes between
Western and Eastern approaches within the context
of a philosophical approach to Gerontology, and
presents the Eastern view as one in which aging is
seen more as a cultural and spiritual process than
a biological one and as a process of continued
opportunity for further growth in wisdom and in
social prestige and authority. He calls for a new
concept of aging (actually a rejuvenation of an old
one) which would restore the positive aspects of
aging and old age, and through which the aging
would be treated as partners and teachers, not as
students or objects of study.

238. Spicker, Stuart F., Kathleen M. Woodward and David D.
      Van Tassel, eds. Editors' Foreword. In *Aging and
      the Elderly: Humanistic Perspectives in Gerontology*,
      pp. vii-viii, Stuart F. Spicker, Kathleen M. Woodward
      and David D. Van Tassel, eds. Atlantic Highlands,
      New Jersey: Humanities Press, Inc., 1978. The
      humanities have a vital contribution to make to the
      study of aging, which is a subject too vast to be
      left solely to the physical and social scientists.

239. Van Tassel, David D. Preface. In *Aging and the
      Elderly: Humanistic Perspectives in Gerontology*,
      pp. v-vi, Stuart F. Spicker, Kathleen M. Woodward
      and David D. Van Tassel, eds. Atlantic Highlands,
      New Jersey: Humanities Press, Inc., 1978. Van Tassel
      states that this collection of essays by humanists
      on aspects of human aging represents the first
      fruit of a project that was conceived in 1972 and
      supported in 1974 by the National Endowment for
      the Humanities under the title "Human Values and
      Aging: New Challenges to Research in the Humanities."
      He based the project upon the fundamental assumption
      that an important body of material does exist and
      that humanists ought to be studying this vast,
      untapped source of human experience as recorded in
      history, literature, folklore, artifact and art,
      created by past generations and cultures. If

scholars in the humanities locate, bring to light
and refine these materials, this would give new
perspectives to gerontology, broaden the horizons
of each humanistic discipline and enhance appreciation
and understanding of the later stages of life. The
volume has five sections: The Western Heritage:
Images and Ideals; Dementia, Competency and Senescent
Meditation; Aging, Death, and Destiny; The Polity
and the Elderly: Modernization, Revolution and
Equity; and Theoretical Considerations. Afterword
by Robert N. Butler. (See No. 231 of this Bibliography.)

240. Whitehead, Evelyn Eaton. "Religious Images of Aging:
      An Examination of Themes in Contemporary Christian
      Thought." In *Aging and the Elderly: Humanistic
      Perspectives in Gerontology*, pp. 37-48, Stuart F.
      Spicker, Kathleen M. Woodward and David D. Van
      Tassel, eds. Atlantic Highlands, New Jersey:
      Humanities Press, Inc., 1978. An examination of
      the use made of central images and religious themes
      in treating three challenges central to the personal
      experience of aging--establishing a basis for self-
      worth less dependent upon economic productivity or
      social role; interpreting the significance of one's
      own life; and coming to terms with the changes and
      losses of aging. Whitehead cautions that the six
      religious images discussed here--personal salvation,
      hope, religious sense of time and personal history,
      God's unconditional love for the individual, spiritual
      discipline of "emptiness" and "letting go" and image
      of the Christian as pilgrim-on-the-way--should not
      be allowed to deteriorate at the political level
      into catch-phrases used to sanction individual
      resignation or communal passivity in the face of
      society's less-than-adequate response to its
      elderly members.

See also: 215, 216, 217, 220, 245, 353, 361, 362, 381, 542,
551, 868, 876.

                         D. Older Women--General

*241. Anderson, Mrs. Eddie Neely. "Fifteen Hundred Women
       Look at Life After Forty." Diss., Columbia
       University, 1952.

242. Bart, Pauline B.   "Emotional and Social Status of the
      Older Woman." In *No Longer Young: The Older Woman
      in America*, pp. 3-21. Ann Arbor, Michigan: The
      Institute of Gerontology, The University of Michigan-
      Wayne State University, 1975. Bart observes that
      adult socialization and aging are areas of study in
      which there are many more female than male scholars,
      and that most recent books about aging have been
      written by women who are feminists. These scholars
      consider aging to be a problem because they are
      critical of society and believe that it should be
      changed. Bart presents demographic characteristics
      of women over 45, and discusses "pioneers" (women
      who had the opportunity to have contact with feminist
      ideas and the suffragist movement), "professionals"
      (who are too young to have experienced the first
      movement of feminists), school "returnees,"
      "Penelopes" (traditional husband-centered women who
      are no longer young) and "Portnoy's Mothers" (child-
      centered women whose children are grown).

243. Beeson, Diane.   "Women in Studies of Aging: A Critique
      and Suggestion." *Social Problems* (October 1975)
      23(1):52-9. Challenges the prevailing assumption
      in social gerontology that major life changes as
      retirement and widowhood are less problematic for
      women than for men. Attributes the basis for these
      evaluations to role theory and an "over-socialized
      conception of woman." Contrasts scholarly accounts
      of women's experience of aging with those expressed
      in non-academic publications in which a double sexual
      standard of physical attractiveness, the trauma of
      widowhood, economic and social psychological problems
      of older women, and the significance of female
      menopause are explored, and for which supporting
      statistical and demographic data are available.
      Recommends a phenomenological approach through which
      the symbolic world of the aging woman is studied
      without prior commitment to specific concepts or
      definitions of the situation.

244. Block, Marilyn R., Janice L. Davidson, Jean D. Grambs
      and Kathryn E. Serock. *Uncharted Territory:
      Issues and Concerns of Women Over 40*. College
      Park, Maryland: University of Maryland Center on
      Aging, 1978. (Revised publication entitled *Women
      Over Forty: Visions and Realities* by Marilyn R.
      Block, Janice L. Davidson and Jean D. Grambs,

Springer, 1981, not examined.) A curriculum guide
to a course on women over 40, comprised of 14 modular
units: Images of Older Women; A Demographic Profile
of the Older Woman; Menopause and Sexuality; Health
and Medical Issues; Mental Health and Related Issues;
Life Patterns; Family Relationships; Social Networks;
Widowhood and Death; Older Women and the Legal System;
Employment and Retirement; Social Security and Pensions; Continuing Education; Ethnic and Racial
Variations. Includes an annotated filmography of
more than 100 films, and a bibliography of approximately 1,000 books and articles on older women.

245.   Borenstein, Audrey. *Chimes of Change and Hours: Views
of Older Women in 20th Century America*. Rutherford,
New Jersey: Fairleigh Dickinson University Press,
1982/83. (In press.) Humanistic exploration of the
values of creativity, freedom and social responsibility
in the lives of 20th-century older American women as
seen through Social Gerontology, Sociology, Anthropology, Psychology, History, Oral History and
American literature. Three major sections with
three chapters in each. Part One presents social
scientific perspectives on older women in 20th-
century America from American History, Anthropology,
Oral History, Psychology (Analytical Psychology and
Social Psychology), Social Gerontology and Sociology.
Chapters are: Older Women in a Changing Society,
Women in the Second Half of Life, and Voices from
Oral Histories: Self-Portraits of Older Women.
Part Two presents literary perspectives on women's
aging, and consists of a chapter on women's reflec-
tions on aging recorded in their personal documents
and essays (autobiographies, diaries, journals,
letters, memoirs, notebooks and general nonfiction)
entitled Times Remembered and Time's Passage: Written
Memoirs and Reflections, a chapter entitled Aspects
of Aging: Selections from the Works of Five Women
Writers (Gertrude Atherton, Ellen Glasgow, Zora
Neale Hurston, May Sarton and Edith Wharton), and
a chapter entitled Older Women in Selected 20th
Century American Fictions. Part Three includes
a chapter on creativity in the second half of
women's lives, a chapter comprised of transcripts
of oral history interviews with nine older women
artists, and a summary chapter on interdisciplinary
study, "Older Women as Seen Through Social Science
and Literature: Views from a Bridge."

246. Fuller, Marie Marschall, and Cora Ann Martin, eds.
Introduction. In *The Older Woman: Lavender Rose
or Gray Panther*, pp. xi-xv. Springfield, Illinois:
Charles C. Thomas, 1980. The neglect of the topic of
older women is compared with the neglect of 59% of
a tribe by an anthropologist who also fails to note
sex and age differences among its peoples. The
reasons for this neglect are: the search for universals in social science, which may bias perception;
the focus of most theories on a narrow spectrum of
the life cycle; the age bias in most research samples;
the fact that the norm for statistical analysis has
been male; the sex bias in our language; and the
predominance of older men in positions of power in
scholarly circles and, possibly, among those who
are theorists, researchers and professors. Social
factors also promote neglect: the visibility of
older women is limited by transportation and living
patterns, and older women have not been present in
such large numbers until fairly recently in history.
The topics in the anthology include: Profile of the
Older Woman, Socialization, Biological Facts and
Fallacies, Social Bonds, Social Institutions,
Alternative Life Styles, and Looking Ahead.

247. Fuller, Marie Marschall, and Cora Ann Martin, eds.
Preface. In *The Older Woman: Lavender Rose or
Gray Panther*, pp. vii-x. Springfield, Illinois:
Charles C. Thomas, 1980. The purpose of this anthology
is to bring together a current description of the
lives of older women, their special problems and
special needs. Articles are limited to those
published in the 1970s and in most cases based upon
1970s data. With some exceptions, readings are
about women aged 65 and over, and identify the polar
extremes of the aggressive gray panther or retiring
lavender rose. In some vital areas--as, religion--
material was limited; in others--as, economics--it
was abundant. The editors assume this book will be
most useful for undergraduate classes in gerontology
and in women's studies. They teach courses in both
areas, but in first looking for articles to include
here, were surprised to find so few on older women.
They discovered that some titles obscure the fact
that older women are the subjects, concealed within
the generic "he" and older "person." For many reasons,
older women have been and remain unseen. The editors
find that courses on the older woman are being
developed on many campuses.

248. *Generations--Special Issue on Older Women.* "Women
      and Aging." (Tish Sommers, Guest Editor.) Western
      Gerontological Society (August 1980) IV(4):1-40.
      This special issue on older women includes "Older
      Women and Our Language," "If We Could Write the
      Script," "Women--the Elder Majority," "Looking
      Forward ... Looking Back," "Social Security and
      Women," "American Mid-Life Women," "The National
      Displaced Homemakers Network," "The Older Woman
      Living Alone," "Quadruple Jeopardy: Old, Poor, Female,
      Black," "Five Older Women," "Sexism and Ageism: Health
      Care Obstacles," "Breast Cancer Needs More Research,"
      "Caring for Brain-Damaged Husbands," "Support Groups,"
      and a mock report to a mythical world conference on
      women in the year 2010. Regular features are
      President's message, resource list, book reviews,
      WGS and older women, and 1980 meetings and conferences.

249. Goodchilds, Jacqueline D. "Young Women, Old Women,
      and Power." In *Looking Ahead: A Woman's Guide to
      the Problems and Joys of Growing Older*, pp. 207-9,
      Lillian E. Troll, Joan Israel and Kenneth Israel,
      eds. Englewood Cliffs, New Jersey: Prentice-Hall,
      Inc., 1977. The very techniques for concealing
      victory that placed some women of the 1950s genera-
      tion in line for power-holding status are, once
      that status is attained, the very practices that
      will insure a brief reign. Men enjoy greater esteem
      as they age; women do not. If this is to change in
      the future, the bond between age and power may have
      to be broken. But that would mean the ruling élite
      would be made up of old men and young women--an
      irony Goodchilds notes here.

250. Jacobs, Ruth Harriet. *Life After Youth: Female, Forty
      --What Next?* Boston: Beacon Press, 1979. Jacobs
      outlines the social experiences of the cohort of
      females born in 1924 in her Introduction, and
      organizes her book, with some revisions, according
      to the typology she presented in *Social Policy* in
      1976--nurturers; unutilized nurturers (including
      displaced homemakers); re-engaged nurturers; chum
      networkers and leisurists; careerists--employed and
      unemployed; seekers; faded beauties; doctorers;
      escapists and isolates; and advocates and assertive
      older women. These types, "constructs for analytical
      purposes," show the roles available to most older
      women today. Jacobs recommends a social climate,

social policy and social concern more favorable
to older women, and advises women to be change
agents rather than change victims.

251. Jacobs, Ruth Harriet. "A Typology of Older American
      Women." *Social Policy* (November/December 1976)
      7(3):34-9. Jacobs states that large numbers of
      older women in the U.S. are underemployed and under-
      paid, underfinanced and underhoused, undervalued,
      and underloved, *even*, at times, by *themselves*. She
      quotes Robert N. Butler as having said that older
      women are deserving of special study. Her purpose
      in this article is to present a more extensive
      typology of older women than currently exists. Her
      13 types include nurturers (excellent candidates for
      unemployment), unemployed nurturers (among them the
      displaced homemakers), re-engaged nurturers (re-
      engagement is effected through paid or volunteer
      employment, and for far fewer older women, remarriage;
      Jacobs stresses the need for retraining and counseling
      for those re-entering the labor force); chum
      networkers and/or leisurists (whose identity is
      based upon spending time with other women in like
      circumstances); careerists; retired careerists (who
      are apt to be living in poverty); seekers; advocates;
      faded beauties; doctorers; escapists (alcoholics and
      suicides); isolates; and assertive seniors. She
      proposes that all these types be drawn together in
      a creative way.

252. Kastenbaum, Robert, and Deborah Simonds. "Those
      Endearing Young Charms: Fifty Years Later. In
      *Looking Ahead: A Woman's Guide to the Problems
      and Joys of Growing Older*, pp. 196-206, Lillian E.
      Troll, Joan Israel and Kenneth Israel, eds. Englewood
      Cliffs, New Jersey: Prentice-Hall, Inc., 1977. It is
      more accurate to think of process, of the "working"
      of charms, than of "having" charms. We read charm
      from our own response, our sense of delight,
      indulgence and well-being. Human survival is most
      at risk at the extreme points of the life span; the
      vulnerable young and old need something "extra,"
      and charm is such an "extra." This paper suggests
      ways charm may diminish with aging, and how the
      future course of charm may be affected by sex role
      typing and by early choices of personal life style.
      It suggests that charm may be viewed as the least
      restricted form of power, identifies negative and

positive aspects of "being an old charmer," and
concludes that the charm older women can exercise
promises a valuable and distinctive mode of intergenerational affinity.

253. Matthews, Sarah H. *The Social World of Old Women:*
      Management of Self-Identity. Beverly Hills, California:
      Sage Publications, Inc., 1979. This social psycho-
      logical study conducted in the 1970s used participant
      observation, interviewing and archival research. The
      subjects are white widows aged 70 and over who live
      alone and are mothers. Matthews takes the reality-
      constructionist perspective on identity, and uses
      exchange theory and labeling theory to clarify the
      meaning of "oldness" to the social actors. She
      argues that old age is a socially constructed
      category. She finds that self-identity and self-
      presentation are problematic for old women, and
      discusses strategies (not always consciously planned)
      that may be adopted in encounters with others and
      with self. She finds settings to be a vital component
      in maintaining self-identity. There are newcomers
      and residents in settings, and each role has conse-
      quences for self-identity. Data support the finding
      that the old widow's offspring are of paramount
      importance to her. But from an exchange perspective,
      it is found that, while the extended family structure
      is intact, the *quality* of relationships is affected
      adversely by the low status of old women who have a
      weak power base from which to demand treatment as
      equals. Old women use strategies to cope with the
      uncertainty of death. To protect self-identities in
      a senior center where they are defined by the staff
      as postadults, they use confrontation and role
      distance. Matthews found a similarity between all
      strategies used to maintain acceptable self-identities
      --that they lead to increased isolation--but suggests
      that two forces in society, the Gray Panthers and
      the Women's Movement, may increase the visibility
      of options. Appendices on Interview Guides.

*254. Meltzer, Leslie Marilyn. "The Aging Female: A Study
      of Attitudes Toward Aging and Self-Concept Held by
      Pre-Menopausal, Menopausal and Post-Menopausal
      Women." Diss., Adelphi University, 1974.

255. *No Longer Young: The Older Woman in America.* Ann
      Arbor, Michigan: The Institute of Gerontology, The

University of Michigan-Wayne State University, 1975.
Proceedings of the 26th Annual Conference on Aging,
sponsored by the Institute of Gerontology in Ann
Arbor in 1973, on the topic *Women: Life Span
Challenges*. Individual papers on: Status of
Older Women Today; Mechanisms for Change; Resources
for Change; Status of Women: 1993-1998. Biographical
notes on participants.

256. *No Longer Young: The Older Woman in America--Work Group
Reports from the 26th Annual Conference on Aging*.
Ann Arbor, Michigan: The Institute of Gerontology,
The University of Michigan-Wayne State University,
1974. Work Group Reports from the conference on
Women: Life Span Challenges, on: The Woman Alone;
Sexuality and Alternative Life Styles; Psychotherapy
and Counseling; Biological Realities and Myths; Low
Pay/Low Status; Political Importance of the Older
Woman; Life Span Behavior Patterns--Class and Ethnic
Variations; Service Needs; Literature and Myths;
Self Image and Roles; Family Relationships; Volunteer-
ism; Economic and Legal Status; Continuing Education
and Second Careers; Retirement: Career and Non-Career;
Media: Use and Misuse; Gerontology Trends and Career
Perspectives. List of recorders and list of
moderators and resource persons.

257. *Older Women: The Economics of Aging*. The Women's
Studies Program and Policy Center at George
Washington University in conjunction with The
Women's Research and Education Institute of the
Congresswomen's Caucus, 1980. This working paper
"is designed primarily for use by policymakers and
other interested parties to define the economic
status of older women and to analyze the factors
affecting this status" and includes public policy
options that might be helpful in meeting the needs of
older women. Section I, The Aging Profile, addresses
the topics of sex, age, race and ethnicity, marital
status, living arrangements and income. Section II,
Factors Contributing to the Limited Incomes of Older
Women, develops the topics of socialization, economic
impact of marital dissolution, limited employment
opportunity, and limited income from public programs
and private pensions. The topics in Section III,
Policy Options for Older Women, are: To Develop
Comprehensive Data, To Promote Public Awareness,
To Insure Income Adequacy, To Encourage Employment,
and To Improve Service Program Design and Delivery.
Bibliography and Appendix.

258. Payne, Barbara, and Frank Whittington. "Older Women:
An Examination of Popular Stereotypes and Research
Evidence." *Social Problems* (April 1976) 23(4):488-504.
Older women are negatively stereotyped and socially
devalued. Many researchers have not distinguished
between the sexes in analysis of their data. But a
number of negative stereotypes of older women can
be examined through analysis of studies in which sex
is used as an independent variable. In the areas of
health and longevity, marital status and family roles
and leisure activities, most negative stereotypes of
older women are found to be false and misleading.
Proposals are that researchers be attentive to sex
differences and similarities, bias reflecting cultural
stereotypes, and the varieties of older women. A
number of promising areas for future research are
identified.

*259. Rubenstein, Hildette. "'Aging in Myself and Others':
Older Women's Perspectives." Diss., Northwestern
University, 1979.

260. Trager, Natalie P. Introduction. In *No Longer Young:
The Older Woman in America*, pp. vii-xii. Ann Arbor,
Michigan: The Institute of Gerontology, The University
of Michigan-Wayne State University, 1975. The public
focus has shifted from Women's Lib to Watergate and
inflation since the 26th Annual Conference on Aging
on *Women: Life Span Challenges* in 1973, but the view
that the 1973 conference material is no longer
relevant overlooks the fact that it was addressed
to women 45 years of age and older. Trager discusses
the objectives of the conference and the papers
presented, and observes that women's longer life span
requires them to plan for their own economic and
emotional security in old age, that there will be
more surviving females who are poor in the future,
and that women must depend upon their own efforts
more and more to provide for the essentials of life.
She states that she is impressed with how little the
lot of many of our older females has been improved
in the past century, but also that the variety of
collective solutions to problems common to the
elderly reflects the variety of older people in our
society, and avers that the present cohort of the
elderly is a tough one, comprised of survivors of
America's worst Depression.

261. Trager, Natalie P. Introduction. In *No Longer Young: The Older Woman in America, Work Group Reports*, pp. ix-xv. Ann Arbor, Michigan: The Institute of Gerontology, The University of Michigan-Wayne State University, 1975. Trager discusses considerations of preplanning for the conference, which focused on the sociological, psychological, economic and legal situations of women aged 45 and older, and reports on major contributions of each of the 17 workshops, among which the student gerontology seminar is said to have been in some ways the most positively oriented and optimistic.

262. Troll, Lillian E., Joan Israel and Kenneth Israel, eds. *Looking Ahead: A Woman's Guide to the Problems and Joys of Growing Older*. Englewood Cliffs, New Jersey: Prentice-Hall, Inc., 1977. Individual papers are grouped in sections entitled: Introduction; The Body; The Soul; New Worlds; Differences; Help; Power.

263. Williams, Blanch. "A Profile of the Elderly Woman." In *The Older Woman: Lavender Rose or Gray Panther*, pp. 5-8, Marie Marschall Fuller and Cora Ann Martin, eds. Springfield, Illinois: Charles C. Thomas, 1980. Demographic characteristics of elderly women, including numbers and percentages of the U.S. population, life expectancy, geographic distribution, race, education, employment, income, marital status and living arrangements, as of July 1, 1974, in this publication of an article appearing in *Aging*, 1975.

See also: 13, 14, 15, 17, 18, 19, 20, 22, 24, 25, 26, 27, 28, 29, 31, 32, 34, 35, 37, 38, 228, 335, 336, 337, 338, 339, 345, 346, 347, 366, 381, 390, 391, 392, 398, 399, 405, 407, 410, 411, 412, 413, 416, 418, 421, 423, 521, 543, 558, 559, 591, 595, 597, 612, 613, 620, 638, 639, 641, 644, 646, 651, 654, 656, 657, 658, 722, 724, 732, 738, 750, 754, 755, 758, 759, 780, 805, 819, 837, 862, 864, 865, 867, 868, 872, 884.

E. Theory and Methodology

264. Cowgill, Donald O. "Aging and Modernization: A Revision of the Theory." In *Dimensions of Aging: Readings*, pp. 54-68, Jon Hendricks and C. Davis Hendricks, eds. Cambridge, Massachusetts: Winthrop

Publishers, Inc., 1979. An extension and development
of the theory of aging stated in Cowgill and Holmes's
Aging and Modernization. Modern health technology,
modern economic technology, education and urbanization were found to initiate a chain reaction tending
toward the diminution of the status of the aged.
But new evidence suggests that this trend may
"bottom out" in advanced stages of modernization,
after which the relative status of the aged begins
to improve. This trend is evident in the most
modernized nations today.

265.   Cowgill, Donald O. "A Theory of Aging in Cross-Cultural
       Perspective." In *Aging and Modernization*, pp. 1-13,
       Donald O. Cowgill and Lowell D. Holmes, eds. New
       York: Appleton-Century-Crofts, 1972. Doubt about
       the general validity of disengagement, quasi-minority
       and subculture theories of aging has recently
       heightened interest in cross-national and cross-
       cultural research. This paper sets forth a number
       of propositions about aging that are treated as
       hypotheses in the chapters in the book. Some identify
       universal conditions (as, that older populations have
       more females than males), and others specify conditions
       that vary from society to society (as, a *systematic*
       variation is that modernized societies have higher
       proportions of older women and of widows). The
       variations are related to an independent variable,
       the degree of modernization. Interrelated factors
       in modernization are level of technology, degree
       of urbanization, rate of social change, and degree
       of westernization. The major hypothesis is that the
       role and status of the aged vary systematically with
       the degree of modernization of society, and that
       modernization tends to detract from the relative
       status of the aged and to undermine their security
       in the social system.

266.   Cowgill, Donald O., and Lowell D. Holmes. "Summary and
       Conclusions: The Theory in Review." In *Aging and
       Modernization*, pp. 305-23, Donald O. Cowgill and
       Lowell D. Holmes, eds. New York: Appleton-Century-
       Crofts, 1972. This paper includes a list of
       "universals" and "variations" and concludes that,
       for the most part, modernization theory has
       "survived the test" of review in light of a cross-
       national and a cross-cultural perspective. Certain
       propositions may need to be modified or deleted,

but these are more than counter-balanced by
serendipitous findings which extend and strengthen
modernization theory.

267. Cumming, Elaine. "Further Thoughts on the Theory of
Disengagement." In *Aging in America: Readings in
Social Gerontology*, pp. 19-41, Cary S. Kart and
Barbara B. Manard, eds. New York: Alfred Publishing
Co., Inc., 1976. Modifications of the disengagement
theory, presented as a system of hypotheses, are
intended to make the theory better able to describe
and predict both the range and limits of the aging
process. In its original form, the theory was too
simple, did not take departures from the modal case
into account, and did not and does not concern itself
with the effects of poverty and illness on old age.
Cumming suggests some characteristics of aging
people that might make an important difference in
their patterns of disengagement. She discusses the
effect of disengagement on two temperamental types
related to introversion and extroversion, the subjective experience of the onset of disengagement
during middle life, and disengagement as a social
imperative and a response to changing roles. Sex
differences are postulated, among them women's
propensity toward adopting either instrumental *or*
socio-emotional roles. Disengagement from central
life roles is different for women because women's
roles are essentially unchanged from girlhood to
death, and therefore transitions are easier for
women to make; also, the problems raised by widowhood
are more easily resolved than those raised by retirement. If these sex differences are significant,
there should be a visible contrast in men's and
women's ability to cope with the disengagement
process. Two examples from study samples are provided
to show that women are better able than men to find
roles in social systems. Comparative suicide rates
for men and women in later life are cited to show
that at the age when disengagement is postulated to
occur, women's suicide rate declines and men's
increases. Perhaps as women age, they move from a
little too much constraint to the right amount of
freedom, whereas men move from too much of the one
to too much of the other.

268. Cumming, Elaine, and William Henry. *Growing Old: The
Process of Disengagement*. New York: Basic Books

Publishing Co., Inc., 1961. A report of the disengagement theory of aging developed from the Kansas
City Study of Adult Life and of the data upon which
the theory is based. The sample consisted of healthy
men and women with reasonably adequate means who
resided in Kansas City; those in the panel were aged
50 to 70, and those in the quasi-panel were aged 70
to 90. The tentative theory is that aging is an
inevitable, mutual withdrawal, resulting in decreased
interaction between the aging person and others in
his or her social systems. A completed aging process
results in a new equilibrium between the individual
and society--one marked by a greater distance and
an altered type of relationship than that which
obtained in middle life. Includes a discussion of
an "implicit theory of aging" based upon the idea of
the desirability of an ever-expanding life, and
chapters on evidence for disengagement in the social
structure and in changes in attitude and orientation;
personality variations with age; the issue of successful
aging; retirement and widowhood; case studies; the
very old; a formal statement of the theory, and the
relationship of the theory to intergenerational ten-
sion, the structure of the life span, and time and
death. Findings suggest that, following a plateau
in the late 40s and through the 50s, there is a
crisis, marked by anxiety, between 60 and 65,
followed by contentment. Again, in the 70s, there
is a restlessness and irritability. If this is not
resolved by death, it may lead to a period of
tranquility and satisfaction in very old age for the
survivors. The study suggests that disengagement
is more difficult for men than for women *in American
society*, that it is modern science in part that
makes ours "a woman's world" in old age, and that,
although the disengaged older man is thoughtful and
reflective and the disengaged older woman is active
and carefree, this is only a stage: in their 80s and
90s, both sexes display "the same pattern of dependency,
self-satisfaction, self-centeredness, and placidity."
Foreword by Talcott Parsons; six appendices; bibliography

269. Hendricks, Jon, and C. Davis Hendricks. "Theories of
      Social Gerontology." In *Dimensions of Aging: Readings*,
      pp. 191-208, Jon Hendricks and C. Davis Hendricks,
      eds. Cambridge, Massachusetts: Winthrop Publishers,
      Inc., 1979. This paper is an explication of the
      principal theories of social gerontology that have

gained adherents since the first was formulated in
1960: disengagement theory (according to which women
have fewer stresses than men because they have
traditionally had ready access to socioemotional
roles that are not as subject to age-grading and
organizational imperatives as the instrumental roles
with which men have primarily identified) and re-
visions of the theory; the activity perspective;
the aged as a subculture; social-psychological
perspectives on personality and patterns of aging;
and the emergent theories emphasizing an ecological
perspective--the exchange model, the social breakdown
theory--and the sociology of age stratification.

270. Jacobs, Jerry. "Some Theories of Aging: A Test of
Goodness of Fit." In *Fun City: An Ethnographic
Study of a Retirement Community*, pp. 72-84. New
York: Holt, Rinehart and Winston, Inc., 1974.
Chapter 5, "Some theories of aging: A test of
goodness of fit," considers a number of the more
popular concerns and theoretical positions toward
aging in general and retirement in particular, and
the extent to which the expectations generated by
these theories, both explicit and implicit, fit the
life styles of residents of Fun City. (See No. 288.
of this Bibliography.)

271. Palmore, Erdman. "When Can Age, Period, and Cohort
Be Separated?" *Social Forces* (September 1978)
57(1):282-95.. All research on aging processes,
human development, differences between generations,
age stratification, cohort analysis, or trends over
time within any specific group must confront the
problem of distinguishing between age, period, and
cohort effects, or any interpretation of results
will be dubious if not erroneous. Most previous
efforts to deal with this problem have resulted in
errors due to a combination of conceptual confusion
and methodological inadequacy. To avoid this, three
levels of analysis must be kept distinct: measuring
differences, inferring effects, and imputing causes
(Summary Table, p. 294). The three differences that
must be measured are longitudinal, cross-sectional,
and time-lag. The inference of effects is based on
the fact that each difference is composed of only
two of the three possible effects: age, period, and
cohort. Only under specified conditions and with
certain assumptions is it possible to separate and

estimate the values of these three effects. The imputation of specific causes for these effects must be based on evidence from outside this model. This method is compared with others, and three previously published sets of data are re-analyzed to illustrate its utility.

272.   Riley, Matilda White. "Age Strata in the Society." In *Aging and Society*, volume 3: A Sociology of Age Stratification, pp. 397-452, Matilda White Riley, Marilyn Johnson and Anne Foner, eds. New York: Russell Sage Foundation, 1972. A cross-sectional view of the age strata of society. Riley states that age stratification "rests upon the inexorable processes of cohort flow through the society and of individual aging within these cohorts." Bibliography

273.   Riley, Matilda White. "Social Gerontology and the Age Stratification of Society." *The Gerontologist* (Spring 1971, Part 1) 11(2):79-87. Society is stratified by age as much as by social class or racial or ethnic identification, and it undergoes continuous change partly because of the inexorable process of cohort succession. Each birth cohort has a distinctive character because of its size and because of the social characteristics and the experiences of the people who belong to it. Those who are in the age category "65 and over" are members of a cohort that is remarkable for its longevity, that has the highest proportion of foreign-born in the U.S., and that has been "much-studied."

274.   Rose, Arnold M. "A Current Theoretical Issue in Social Gerontology." In *Middle Age and Aging: A Reader in Social Psychology*, pp. 184-9, Bernice L. Neugarten, ed. Chicago: The University of Chicago Press, 1968. A critique of disengagement theory, including a review of publications by its proponents, revisionists and critics, in which Rose identifies new trends in the U.S. counteracting the forces impelling toward disengagement of the elderly, and suggests these are ignored by disengagement theorists because their work is based on functionalist theory. He argues that, in the case of the elderly, the facts of social life are too complex and varied to be encompassed in the functionalist notion of equilibrium, and states that cultural history and human interactions are better guideposts.

275. Streib, Gordon F. "Are the Aged a Minority Group?" In
Middle Age and Aging: A Reader in Social Psychology,
pp. 35-46, Bernice L. Neugarten, ed. Chicago: The
University of Chicago Press, 1968. Streib reviews
the sociological literature on the concept of
minority group, specifies the criteria for defining
a minority group--members are identified as such
throughout the life cycle; members are thought less
deserving of respect and consideration than others;
there is a sense of group identity; there is a
readiness to organize as a political pressure group;
members have differential access to power, privileges
and rights; members are economically and socially
deprived--and examines the empirical data to determine whether or not the aged constitute a minority
group. His conclusion is that they do not, that age
is a less distinguishing group characteristic than
others such as sex, occupation and social class,
and that from the standpoint of conceptual clarity
and empirical fact, the idea of the aged as a
minority group obfuscates understanding.

See also: 8, 175, 179, 188, 201, 207, 208, 234, 304, 551, 721,
723, 798, 801, 810, 818, 821, 822, 829, 830, 851.

VI. HOUSING AND LIVING ENVIRONMENTS

276. Bahr, Howard M., and Gerald R. Garrett. *Women Alone: The Disaffiliation of Urban Females*. Lexington, Massachusetts: D.C. Heath and Co., 1976. A report of research results of the last two years of the Columbia Bowery Project, a study of homelessness and disaffiliation conducted in New York City from 1963 to 1970. This book is based upon an analysis of interviews with 383 middle-aged and elderly women, most of whom were residents of three census tracts in Manhattan, and 52 of whom were clients of a shelter for homeless women—female counterparts of studies of homeless men in a previous project at Camp LaGuardia. The major concern of this book is with disaffiliation —living alone, not employed, and not having membership in voluntary associations—not with aging. But the majority of disaffiliates are women, and the dearth of research on them is especially distressing because the personal consequences of disaffiliation appear to fall most heavily upon females. The general picture among women who live alone is a decline in involvement accompanied by a sense of futility and personal insecurity. Topics: measuring disaffiliation, the research sites, activities and problems of women living alone, correlates of affiliation and lifetime patterns of affiliation in work, the family, voluntary associations and religion; the women's shelter, social characteristics of its residents, and drinking patterns of homeless women; summary and speculations; appendices on methodology; an historical sketch of the Women's Emergency Center, and "Reactions to Disaffiliation among Aged Women: The Novelists' View" (Appendix D). Disaffiliated women in the tract samples have many problems for which the remedies are obvious; their outlook for reintegration is fairly positive. Action programs are suggested to reduce involuntary disaffiliation among the Shelter women.

277. Calkins, Kathy. "Time: Perspectives, Marking and
      Styles of Usage." *Social Problems* (Spring 1970)
      17(4):487-501. A report on views of time and styles
      of time usage by patients in a physical rehabilita-
      tion center, a setting in which time is abundant.
      Conventional time markers are problematic for many
      clientele, who are elderly, poor, chronically ill
      and/or mentally incapacitated. Styles of time usage
      are passing time, waiting, doing time, making time,
      filling time and killing time. Retirement community
      settings are suggested as the most significant area
      of comparative study of meanings and patterns of
      time usage.

278. Cantor, Marjorie H. "Effect of Ethnicity on Life
      Styles of the Inner-City Elderly." In *Demensions
      of Aging: Readings*, pp. 278-93, Jon Hendricks and
      C. Davis Hendricks, eds. Cambridge, Massachusetts:
      Winthrop Publishers, Inc., 1979. Cantor reports
      goals, population, methodology and findings of a
      cross-cultural study of the urban elderly poor living
      in the inner city that was undertaken by the New
      York City Office for the Aging in 1970. The final
      sample of 1,552 respondents was highly representative:
      49% were white, 37% black, and 13% Spanish-speaking.
      Data on age, sex, ethnicity, religious affiliation,
      socioeconomic status, marital status, living arrange-
      ments, health and nativity are provided. New York
      City has more older people living alone than other
      communities in the U.S., and their problems are
      especially acute in inner-city neighborhoods. The
      highest incidence of single-person households was
      found among the most frail segment of the white
      population, especially among widowed or single women
      aged 70 and over. Cantor discusses the extent and
      nature of family relationships and suggests that in
      the future Spanish elderly will experience the same
      dilemma of role crisis faced by their peers and
      that growing numbers of blacks will live alone in
      old age. She identifies the white elderly as "truly
      New York's hidden poor."

279. Cantor, Marjorie H. "Life Space and the Urban Elderly."
      In *The Later Years: Social Applications of Gerontology*,
      pp. 281-7, Richard A. Kalish, ed. Monterey,
      California: Brooks/Cole Publishing Co., 1977.
      Selected findings of a comprehensive cross-cultural
      survey of the elderly living in the inner or central

city of New York are reported. Inner City (the 26
poorest neighborhoods) elderly comprise about 35% of
all older New Yorkers. Of the 1,552 respondents,
49% are white, 37% black, and 13% Spanish-speaking,
principally Puerto Rican. Findings are that the
elderly of the Inner City are long-term residents,
that with the glaring exception of medical care, the
Inner City neighborhoods of New York provide within
easy proximity most essential services needed by the
elderly, that familial bonds are strong and there
is evidence of mutual affection and assistance between the generations, that friends and neighbors
are of vital importance in the life of urban elderly,
that 8% of the sample have no personal support
system of any kind, and that, despite negative
feelings about the city, most respondents think it
offers them rich choices and can satisfy their needs.

280. Carp, Frances Merchant. *A Future for the Aged: Victoria
Plaza and Its Residents.* Austin: The University of
Texas Press, 1966. A study of older people's
reactions to changed housing and recreation
facilities. Major purposes: (1) assessment of
the impact of changed housing on older people (those
who had lived in this nine-story building for a
period of one year or more were compared in 1961
with a similar group who had applied unsuccessfully
for apartments there), (2) identification of background and personality traits associated with
differences in adjustment to life in Victoria Plaza,
and (3) study of the processes of interpersonal
contact, group formation and leadership emergence.
The collection of baseline (pre-housing change),
demographic, attitudinal, and personality-test data
on all applicants precluded confusion of selection
and housing effects. Of the 352 applicants for
public housing originally studied, 204 were later
selected to live in Victoria Plaza. Applicants were
not representative of the aged population of San
Antonio in racial or ethnic origin, had an average
age of 72, and were 21% male and 79% female. Findings
were that there was an overwhelmingly favorable
reaction to the new facility. Chapters on why the
studies were made; how the people were selected;
what they were like; the housing they had and the
housing they wanted; selection of tenants by the
San Antonio Housing Authority; reactions to Victoria
Plaza and the senior center; changes in life style

and adjustment; social processes in Victoria Plaza;
measures of tenant morale or adjustment; methodology
of prediction of morale or adjustment; predicting
adjustment; some implications of the studies.
Four methodological appendices.

281.   Carp, Frances M. "Housing and Living Environments of
        Older People." In *Handbook of Aging and the Social
        Sciences*, pp. 244-71, Robert H. Binstock and Ethel
        Shanas, eds., with the assistance of Associate
        Editors Vern L. Bengston, George L. Maddox and
        Dorothy Wedderburn. New York: Van Nostrand Reinhold
        Co., 1976. A definitive review of research on this
        subject. Evidence of growing sophistication in
        research in this area is cited; conceptual models
        are moving toward the dynamics of field theory.
        Ambiguous and variable definitions of "older person"
        and "housing and living environments," and constant
        alterations in the living environment and population
        of older persons, contribute to the difficulty of
        arriving at valid generalizations. The U.S. was
        slow to undertake the task of housing its older
        citizens, compared to other industrialized nations.
        Justifiable conclusions from studies of the effects
        of living in these new settings are discussed. Only
        3% of older persons participate in HUD programs;
        the size and shape of the remaining need are unknown.
        Federally subsidized low-cost housing and retirement
        communities, taken together, affect the lives of a
        small fraction of the older population. Topics also
        include: location of residence; households of the
        elderly (independent living is more prevalent and
        increasing more rapidly among women--three times as
        many women as men live alone, and the trend of
        increase toward maintenance of independent house-
        holds is much sharper among women); types of housing;
        groups at special risk (the greater numbers of older
        women and their attraction to public housing combine
        to saturate these living situations with females,
        while old men drift to old hotels and rooming houses,
        and the result is a tendency toward sex as well as
        age stratification among the old); effects of
        living environments; the needs for creating a
        wider variety as well as a larger supply of beneficial
        living environments, and for a technology for commu-
        nication between researchers and potential users
        of research findings. Carp concludes that existing
        data do not warrant generalizations about the effects

of age segregation in living situations on life
style and well-being: "The longer experience in
other Western countries calls into question the
wisdom of constructing disproportionate amounts
of age-specific housing."

282. Carp, Frances M. "The Mobility of Retired People."
In *The Later Years: Social Applications of
Gerontology*, pp. 269-80, Richard A. Kalish, ed.
Monterey, California: Brooks/Cole Publishing Co.,
1977. Major topics in this paper, based upon data
collected from a sample of 709 elderly persons, 17%
Afro-American, 57% Anglo-American and 26% Mexican-
American in San Antonio in 1968-69, are: growing
old in the city, the study of transportation needs,
habits and preferences of older people, mobility
behaviors and attitudes, older people's use of
various means of transportation, and expressed and
latent transportation need. A striking finding is
the brevity of trips taken by the elderly. The
car provided more transportation than any other
mode, and car owners had relatively few transportation problems, but access to cars was limited among
this group. In general, the data indicate that
retired people go out infrequently, that they make
little use of community resources except for basic
maintenance (medical and food), and that they are
minimally mobile in regard to informal social
contacts. Suggests that the low rate of direct
expression of dissatisfaction with transportation
may be defensive, perhaps an adaptive response to
strongly inhibiting and unchangeable circumstances
and a means of keeping self-respect.

*283. Elder-Jucker, Patricia Louisa. "Effects of Group
Therapy on Self Esteem, Social Interaction and
Depression of Female Residents in a Home for the
Aged." Diss., Temple University, 1979.

*284. Faucher, Ted Allen. "Life Satisfaction Among Elderly
Women in Three Living Arrangements." Diss.,
University of Kansas, 1979.

285. Fontana, Andrea. *The Last Frontier: The Social
Meaning of Growing Old*. Beverly Hills: Sage
Publications, 1977. Includes chapters on physiological and social determinants of growing old,
perspectives on the meaning of leisure, and three

chapters based on ethnographic data gathered through
in-depth interviewing and participant observation
study. Research was conducted in three settings:
middle- and upper-class elders in and around a
senior citizen center; lower-class elders in a
metropolitan setting; a convalescent center where
Fontana took a job as a janitor ("housekeeper")
to study the effects of institutionalization on
growing old. Three of the four types derived from
data at the senior center--the relaxers, the joiners
and the do-gooders--include cases of elderly women;
the "waiters" were all men. The elderly poor,
studied through spending research hours sitting on
park benches, in hotel lounges and in recreation
halls, as well as in making rounds to old people's
homes with a volunteer meal service worker, included
older women among the Sitters, but not the Drifters,
as examples of types of "waiters"--those who wait
for Godot (there is no meaning to their waiting)
and those who wait for God (whose waiting has
implicit meaning). At the convalescent center,
where various patterns of interaction are presented,
examples of the Prisoners and the Others include
Mrs. Leister, who, as one of the Others, was seen
"before she had set in place the last brick that
would forever entomb her alive inside the wall."
Concludes that various theories of growing old each
seem to fit some persons and not others.

*286. Hochschild, Alene Russell. "A Community of Grandmothers."
       Diss., Department of Sociology, University of
       California at Berkeley, 1969.

 287. Hochschild, Arlie Russell. *The Unexpected Community:
       Portrait of an Old Age Subculture*. Berkeley:
       University of California Press, 1973. A participant
       observation study of the community life of and
       sororal bond forged between 43 old people living at
       Merrill Court, a small apartment building near the
       shore of San Francisco Bay. The 35 widows who
       created the moral atmosphere at Merrill Court, met
       after they applied for this public housing, and
       formed a community described by Hochschild "as a
       mutual aid society, as a source of jobs, as an
       audience, as a pool of models for growing old, as a
       sanctuary and as a subculture with its own customs,
       gossip, and humor." Hochschild, in portraying the
       widows' activities, norms, and relationships with

one another, with kin (an entire chapter focuses on
Family Ties and Motherly Love), and with those in
the world beyond Merrill Court, suggests that their
subculture may be seen as a "rear-guard counter-
culture" and that the times are ripe both for the
sibling bond and for old age communities of the type
she discovered at Merrill Court.

288. Jacobs, Jerry. *Fun City: An Ethnographic Study of a
Retirement Community.* New York: Holt, Rinehart and
Winston, Inc., 1974. Fun City, developed in the
1960s for retirement-age persons, is an unincorporated
town about 90 miles from a large metropolitan area,
with about 6,000 residents. Streets appear deserted
day and night; the homes have "gray on gray"
architecture, and the norm of inoffensiveness
results in "gray on gray" social interaction. Only
a "visible minority" lead Fun City's "active way
of life," participating formally in the many clubs
and activities, and interacting informally in the
shopping center area. The "invisible majority"
lead a passive way of life. The residents are white
and middle class; single women outnumber single men
about three to one. Jacobs discusses why residents
came to Fun City, and why they remain there. In
the last chapter he reviews theories of aging,
stresses the need for and rarity of participant-
observer studies of life styles of the aged,
concludes that for most residents, Fun City is a
"false Paradise," which he thinks is true of
segregated retirement communities in general, and
recommends integrating retirement settings with
existing natural settings. (See No. 270 of this
Bibliography.)

289. Johnson, Sheila K. *Idle Haven: Community Building
Among the Working-Class Retired.* Berkeley:
University of California Press, 1971. A case study,
using interviewing, participant observation and
sociometric techniques, of community building among
elderly, working-class, white urban Americans,
conducted in the 1960s at Idle Haven, on the eastern
side of San Francisco Bay. About half the residents
of the adult park are over age 60; about 40% are
in their 40s and 50s--typical for Californian but
not all U.S. mobile-home residents. Of the 102
married couples, 45 were in either a second or
third marriage for one or both partners, and many

of these childless marriages had a romantic, private
quality. In discussing the park and its people, the
search for community, family and friendship ties,
patterns of mutual aid, and leisure and life style,
Johnson reports, among other findings, that most of
the neighboring was done by women, although men were
also involved in neighborly exchanges, that 58% of
the women were retirees, that women who entered the
park as widows had a much harder time making friends
and were less active in park activities than married
women or those widowed after moving there, and that
mutual aid was governed by reciprocity and friendship rather than by the impersonal criteria of the
job market. She found women decidedly easier to
interview than the men, and notes that women parti-
cipated much more extensively than men in park
activities, were more often in leadership roles,
and were more fully occupied in private hobbies
than men. She states that even if mobile-home
parks like Idle Haven disappear in the next few
years, the needs of those to whom they appeal are
not likely to disappear. Two appendices, on the
Wally Byam Caravan Club and on her interview schedule.

290.   Kahana, Eva, and Asuman Kiyak. "The Nitty-Gritty of
        Survival." In *Looking Ahead: A Woman's Guide to the
        Problems and Joys of Growing Older*, pp. 172-7,
        Lillian E. Troll, Joan Israel and Kenneth Israel,
        eds. Englewood Cliffs, New Jersey: Prentice-Hall,
        Inc., 1977. Community services for the elderly
        have been increasing, but most provide referral and
        advice rather than direct help. This paper reports
        findings of a survey of available services, and of
        interviews with elderly persons, family members and
        friends they mentioned, and representatives of
        agencies, in two Detroit communities, one Jewish
        and one Polish. Few service programs were found.
        Specific needs reported by older women were for
        household maintenance and repair services and for
        legal, job and family counseling. Agency represen-
        tatives stressed needs for better transportation,
        for legal, retirement and personal counseling, and
        for health care. Family and friends mentioned
        services and emotional support. As women live into
        old age and have physical problems, friends and
        families may no longer be able to provide sufficient
        supports for continued independent living. Imaginative
        services and programs will be needed to help them
        survive in the community.

291. Kart, Cary S., and Barbara B. Manard. "Quality of Care
      in Old Age Institutions." In *Dimensions of Aging:
      Readings*, pp. 224-32, Jon Hendricks and C. Davis
      Hendricks, eds. Cambridge, Massachusetts: Winthrop
      Publishers, Inc., 1979. Reviewing research on the
      quality of care, Kart and Manard conclude that a
      fundamental problem is that many concerned with the
      issue fail to distinguish between different types
      of facilities offering different levels of care.
      No universal schema for categorizing OAIs has been
      developed. While researchers have identified the
      characteristics of a good OAI, "researchers,
      practitioners, and regulators are operating in an
      unfocused vacuum when it comes to making an OAI
      good." Extensive bibliography.

292. Kastenbaum, Robert, and Sandra E. Candy. "The 4%
      Fallacy: A Methodological and Empirical Critique
      of Extended Care Facility Population Statistics."
      In *Aging in America: Readings in Social Gerontology*,
      pp. 166-74, Cary S. Kart and Barbara B. Manard,
      eds. Port Washington, New York: Alfred Publishing
      Co., Inc., 1976. References to the 4% figure as
      the percent of elderly in the U.S. in nursing homes
      and other extended care facilities are made
      repeatedly in journals, books, classes, conferences
      and governmental deliberations. Often this statistic
      is used to redirect attention to the 96% of the
      elderly who are not institutionalized. This perpetu-
      ates an elementary and serious error, that is, the
      failure to recognize that the data are cross-
      sectional, and do not provide any information about
      how many people will have resided in extended care
      facilities at some point in their lives. Nor do
      cross-sectional data provide information about the
      probabilities of institutionalization for an
      individual. Two small studies are reported which
      reveal the 4% statistic to be fallacious. It was
      found that, from the point of view of the individual,
      there is one chance in four, not one in 25, of
      being in an extended care facility at some point
      in life, and one chance in five, not one in 40, of
      entering a nursing home. If misleading use of the
      4% statistic is abandoned, this may contribute to
      the abandonment of destructive attitudes and
      practices. The true extent of the problem of
      institutional care is of greater magnitude than
      is generally assumed.

*293. Ketchin, Statia Ainsley. "Housing the Elderly: A
       Survey of Housing Support Services for the Elderly
       in the 50 States." M.A. thesis, George Washington
       University, 1980.

294.   Kutner, Bernard, and David Fanshel, Alice M. Togo and
       Thomas S. Langner. *Five Hundred over Sixty: A
       Community Survey on Aging.* New York: Russell Sage
       Foundation, 1956. A report of an interdisciplinary
       interview study of 500 non-institutionalized persons
       (312 women, 188 men) aged 60 to 90 (average age 70),
       residents of the Kips Bay-Yorkville section of New
       York City, that was initiated to locate problems
       and needs of the elderly in a major urban center.
       The aim of the study, dealing with problems of
       personal adjustment, factors affecting or affected
       by health, the use of community health services and
       attitudes toward health and social centers, was to
       suggest ways of approaching the problems of aging in
       other social and cultural contexts. Part One deals
       with a survey of aging; Part Two, with patterns of ad-
       justment in old age (measuring adjustment; marriage and
       adjustment; employment and adjustment; morale and the
       social self; and activity, isolation and adjustment
       --note that ethnic group variations in social
       isolation were found to reflect cultural differences
       with respect to in-family ties); Part Three, Health
       in Old Age, consists of chapters on health status
       and orientations, the use of community health
       resources, and attitudes toward the use of community
       facilities. Part Four, Trends and Programs, has
       chapters on trends in services for the aged in New
       York City, and programmatic interpretations.
       Methodological appendices.

295.   Lally, Maureen, Eileen Black, Martha Thornock, and
       J. David Hawkins. "Older Women in Single Room
       Occupant (SRO) Hotels: A Seattle Profile." In
       The Older Woman: Lavender Rose or Gray Panther,
       pp. 304-16, Marie Marschall Fuller and Cora Ann
       Martin, eds. Springfield, Illinois: Charles C.
       Thomas, 1980. These 16 older women living in ten
       hotels in downtown Seattle come from a variety of
       backgrounds, and do not display the extent of social
       deviance reported in other studies. Most have been
       in paid employment most of their adult lives, and
       half worked in male-dominated occupations. Five
       lived in downtown hotels all their adult lives; only
       three mentioned fear of crime or violence. Independence

and self-sufficiency were extremely important to all these women. They are seen as a population of contrasts. They express concern about their economic situations, but are optimistic about the future. They are better educated than average for their age cohort, but live in near poverty in low-income neighborhoods. Almost all have serious health problems, but they assert their independence and desire to be on their own. They boast of solitary independent lives, yet a few admit they are lonely. They claim to have chosen SRO residence, but prefer not to associate with those who live in the area. Their belief system allows them to continue to perceive themselves as purposeful and in control of their own destinies. A prominent feature of the life-style accompanying this belief system is the restrictive nature of their social networks. A number of promising approaches are recommended in the delivery of social and health services to these women.

296. Lawton, M. Powell, and Thomas O. Byerts. "Planning Physical Space." In *The Later Years: Social Applications of Gerontology*, pp. 261-8, Richard A. Kalish, ed. Monterey, California: Brooks/Cole Publishing Co., 1977. Planning for housing for the elderly involves a number of considerations with regard to facilities and resources and circulation routes. Existing housing stock is a neglected topic, although 70% of the elderly are homeowners, and most wish to remain where they are. Other topics discussed which are related to facilities and resources are mobile home parks, boarding houses (criteria for site selection and factors involved in conversion of existing structures), the consequences of size for social participation, the provision for services, and provision for changes to be expected over time. Walking (criteria for pedestrian design and housing location, the concept of "ideal distance to facilities," the fear of crime, parks as resources for the elderly) and public transportation are the major concerns of the discussion of circulation routes, since these are the most frequent forms of transportation for the elderly.

297. Montgomery, James E. "The Housing Patterns of Older People." In *The Later Years: Social Applications of Gerontology*, pp. 253-60, Richard A. Kalish, ed.

Monterey, California: Brooks/Cole Publishing Co.,
1977. It has been estimated that persons over 65
spend 80 to 90% of their lives in the domestic
(home) environment. Others have shown that the
life space of the elderly tends to diminish with
age. Thus, the quality of the housing environment
becomes increasingly significant in the lives of
older persons and families. Those over age 65
constitute a group with a wide variety of personalities, life styles and needs. This paper presents an
overview of income and housing of older persons, a
statement about their housing needs, and a study
of housing alternatives. The elderly living on low
fixed incomes cannot afford to buy modestly priced
homes or to rent modestly priced apartments. Their
alternatives are mobile homes, continuing to live in
but to neglect maintenance of their homes, renting
rundown quarters, or living in federally subsidized
housing. The dwelling units occupied by the elderly
are often old, in a state of disrepair, and lacking
in plumbing and/or heating amenities. Many older
persons are "over-housed" in terms of number of
rooms and square footage. Many more older families
live in central city and rural areas than in the
suburbs, and in rural areas many live under highly
adverse conditions. Older persons do not move as
often as those of other age groups. Some basic
needs are: independence, safety and comfort,
wholesome self-concept, a sense of place, related-
ness, environmental mastery, psychological stimulation
and privacy. Housing alternatives examined here
include remaining in one's own home, age-mixing or
age segregation, retirement communities, and
congregate homes.

298.   Myerhoff, Barbara. *Number Our Days*. New York: E.P.
       Dutton, 1978. Inside view of elderly Jewish members
       of a senior citizens center in California, most of
       whom are aging well. Aging is seen as a career
       rather than as a series of losses. Myerhoff depicts
       the complexity, vitality and flexibility of the
       counterworld of the center, and its members' wisdom,
       their penchant for ceremony and symbol, and the
       grandmothers' tales, speeches and exchanges of the
       Living History Class (a forum for reminiscence).
       She finds that survivors' guilt makes it impossible
       to live the unexamined life, and that the old women
       are more active, capable, energetic and authoritative
       than the old men.

*299.   Pincus, Allen Melvin. "Toward a Conceptual Framework
        for Studying Institutional Environments in Homes
        for the Aged." Diss., University of Wisconsin, 1968.

300.   Roeper, Peter J., Recorder. "Sexuality and Alternative
        Life Styles." In *No Longer Young: The Older Woman
        in America, Work Group Reports*, pp. 5-8. Ann Arbor,
        Michigan: The Institute of Gerontology, The University
        of Michigan-Wayne State University, 1975. The
        discussion indicated that major problems in the
        living situation for older people today are alienation,
        loneliness and lack of communication, and that a move
        toward communal living might begin to resolve these
        problems. Ignorance of and prejudice toward sexual-
        ity in later life were documented, and typical
        problem situations were presented: the problem of
        an unmarried couple living together in hiding and
        shame, the problem of elderly women inhibited by
        their religious convictions from gratifying sexual
        needs, and problems due to the population imbalance
        between the sexes.

301.   Rosow, Irving. *Social Integration of the Aged*. New
        York: The Free Press, 1967. This book reports the
        methodology and findings of the landmark study of
        local friendships of 1200 elderly people in the
        Cleveland area, who lived in apartments in buildings
        classified into three groups according to the pro-
        portion of households with an older member--Normal,
        1-15%, Concentrated, 33-49%, and Dense, 50% and
        more. In Chapter One, Rosow argues that the aged
        do not need special housing so much as decent
        ordinary housing at an affordable price, and predicts
        that the number of local friends and the amount of
        interaction with neighbors will be directly related
        to the residential concentration of the aged. Analysis
        of the data supported two basic propositions--that
        middle-class people have significantly more friends
        than those in the working class, and that there is
        a greater local dependency for friendships on the
        part of the working class. Age (over 75), sex
        (women), and marital status (unattached) are strong
        sensitizing variables, especially in combination,
        favorably predisposing people to take advantage of
        social opportunities of age-dense localities. Five
        groups, comprising 88% of the sample, were abstracted,
        on the basis of amount of contact with neighbors and
        desire for more friends--the Cosmopolitan, the

Phlegmatic, the Isolated, the Sociable, and the
Insatiable. Study also includes an analysis of
reference groups (neighbors do provide long-term
help to solitary people who are ill, but only in
Dense areas) and identification with the aged
(residential density stimulates identification in
the working class and willingness to affiliate with
the aged, but has no effect in the middle class), and
considerations for future research. Appendix on
Housing Dissatisfaction.

302.   Rowles, Graham D. "Growing Old 'Inside': Aging and
       Attachment to Place in an Appalachian Community."
       In *Transitions of Aging*, pp. 153-70, Nancy Datan
       and Nancy Lohmann, eds. New York: Academic Press,
       Inc., 1980. Two areas have been neglected by
       researchers studying relationships between the
       aging and the environment--the subjective dimensions
       of the *lifeworld* of the old person, and the old
       person's attachment to a *rural* place. Recent work
       by humanistic geographers reveals the importance
       of a sense of place for well-being in old age.
       Rowles's paper is informed by Relph's insideness-
       outsideness dualism. Reporting on his work with a
       panel of 12 old residents of Colton, an Appalachian
       mountain community, who range in age from 62 to 91
       years, Rowles develops the hypothesis that physical,
       social and autobiographical insideness provide crucial
       supports in old age. The sense of "insideness" is
       reflected by the old people's reluctance to leave
       Colton, even though it is one of Appalachia's dying
       towns. For long-time elderly residents, Colton has
       become literally an extension of the self. The
       young-old do not feel autobiographical insideness
       in Colton, although they may feel an affinity for
       another place. This generational difference is
       significant for understanding the evolving relation-
       ship between the old and the rural setting. An old
       person who migrates surrenders the support to
       autobiographical insideness given by living in the
       place where important life-events occurred. As an
       accommodative strategy, insideness "is threatened
       by the increased mobility and alienation from place
       that marks contemporary cultural change and that is
       transforming rural society." Extensive bibliography.

303.   Shapiro, Joan Hatch. *Communities of the Alone: Working
       with Single Room Occupants in the City*. New York:

Association Press, 1971. The "problem" SRO is one
with a deteriorating building, inadequate management
and tenants who are socially or physically sick. In
the nine SROs studied in detail beginning in 1964,
most tenants are over 40, and the population is
racially mixed. It was found that the lives of all
but a few SRO tenants are actively intertwined,
which sharply contradicts the stereotype of the
single, unattached person as reclusive. The most
common constellation was the matriarchal quasi-
family in which the dominant woman tends to feed,
protect, punish and set norms for the alcoholic
"family" members. Other older women tenants include
lesbian pairs and triangles, women who watch and
report daily activities, and elderly, family-less
whites (Irish, Italian and Jewish) who had become
stranded by poverty and age in the same neighborhoods
where they had grown up. The SRO is a survival
culture, consisting of interlocking near-groups.
The black alcoholics tended to be the core group
most heavily committed to the programs in the nine
buildings. All active leaders and organizers in
every building were Negro, and all but one were
women. The difference between Negroes and whites
in attitudes toward dependence was profound. The
Negroes had a well-developed capacity to help and
be helped and to exchange things and feelings with
generosity and joy. The whites did not. The
programs in the form used here seemed tailored
to the needs and strength of the Negro population.
Contents: SRO as a Village Community, The Entry
Phase, Programs, The Process of Resolving Differences,
Referral and Relocation and Separation. Conclusions;
Recommendations; Appendix on the history of SROs
in New York City.

304. Stephens, Joyce. *Loners, Losers, and Lovers: Elderly
Tenants in a Slum Hotel*. Seattle: University of
Washington Press, 1976. In her field work at the
Guinevere, an SRO slum hotel, Stephens found that
most of the aged poor tenants (average age 67) live
in the cheapest rooms, which lack cooking or refrig-
eration facilities. Tenants were unanimous in their
suspicion of and hostility toward nursing homes, and
were willing to pay the price of isolation and
loneliness to maintain independence, privacy and
freedom. The hotel management played a significant
part in their survival measures; the manager had his

spies, and a clear distinction was made between
permanent guests and transients. Gossip was
pervasive, and sometimes gave rise to long-standing
vendettas; there were no loyalties. Chapter Seven
is on Men and Women (the sex ratio was 97 males to
11 females, which is not unusual). Women have more
vulnerability, suffer more extreme isolation and
loneliness, and have less capacity to cope than their
male counterparts. Romances between elderly tenants
are rare: men are wary and suspicious of the women,
and women are bitter and resentful toward the men;
each sex assumes the other is exploitative. In
the SRO world, aged women suffer more acutely than
aged men from role loss, and women's adjustment to
the SRO is more fragile and tenuous. Women do not
relate well to one another, but are mutually hostile
and jealous. Stephens concludes that alienation and
loneliness among the aged are not due to "disengagement," but are strategies for survival, and that
specific populations of elderly should be studied
in their natural settings.

305.   "Swope Ridge Nursing Home: Prevention and Rehabilitation."
       In *The Later Years: Social Applications of Gerontology*,
       pp. 359-66. Richard A. Kalish, ed. Monterey,
       California: Brooks/Cole Publishing Co., 1977.
       Swope Ridge, a non-profit nursing home in Kansas
       City, Missouri, has been challenging the concept of
       custodial care since it opened its doors in 1957.
       No resident is admitted with the idea he or she is
       a terminal patient. The physical environment is
       designed to promote social activity. Physical
       therapy is the primary phase of the rehabilitation
       program. Residents are given the opportunity to
       learn new skills and to relearn old ones. A list
       of activities offered during one month illustrates
       the range of services available to residents, who
       have a role in the decision-making process. A
       Volunteer Program was developed in 1964; the entire
       staff is exposed to a continuous in-service education
       program; and outpatient services to the community
       have been available since 1970. A Health Care
       Complex was in the planning stage at the time this
       article was published in the Congressional Record
       in 1971.

*306. Teski, Marea Cecile Panares. "Reality Structure and
       Social Interaction in a Retirement Hotel." Diss.,
       Cultural Anthropology, Indiana University, 1976.

307.   Tobin, Sheldon S. "Institutionalization of the Aged."
        In *Transitions of Aging*, pp. 195-211, Nancy Datan
        and Nancy Lohmann, eds. New York: Academic Press,
        Inc., 1980. A discussion of the salient findings
        from Tobin and Leiberman's intensive longitudinal
        study reported in *Last Home for the Aged: Critical
        Implications of Institutionalization* (1976). The
        oldest of the old are likely to become institution-
        alized. Most reside in proprietary nursing homes,
        and this situation is unlikely to change. The
        best of contemporary long-term facilities was
        chosen so as to focus on the irreducible effects
        of life in an institution. Topics: attitudes
        preceding admission, institutionalization as a
        family process (children of aging parents are
        themselves likely to be elderly or nearly so, and
        families can do little to avoid feeling guilty and
        the elderly feeling abandoned), the effects of
        institutional life, residents and the families
        (mythicizing living children and significant figures
        from the past functions to make the past more real
        and more poignant), the latent meaning of changes
        after institutionalization, an assessment after
        one year, the prediction of vulnerability to the
        stress of institutionalization, the association
        between passivity of the patient and negative out-
        comes, and relocation stress. Extensive bibliography.

308.   Tulloch, G. Janet. *A Home Is Not a Home (life within
        a nursing home)*. New York: The Seabury Press, 1975.
        Documentary fiction about life in a nursing home,
        with a Foreword by Senator Charles H. Percy. In
        her Preface, Tulloch writes that it is only partially
        true that Joady is herself and that this is her life.
        Tulloch, born with cerebral palsy, writes that Joady
        was 43 years old when she entered the Home, among
        whose patients (all women) are 34-year-old Cathy,
        pretty and intelligent and afflicted with MS, and
        Essie, in her 80s, who has a malignancy, and who
        grieves over her alcoholic daughter. Tulloch writes
        of the Blanche DuBois in the Home--there were many
        Blanches "doomed to vegetation because they had not
        learned to fight during their vital years"--of Church
        in the home ("an abomination"), administration
        parties, plastic flowers, a birthday greeting
        card, assembly line medicine, death ("Noisy Exit"),
        the torment of a nurse who had worked there for
        43 years, and a visit with friends 600 miles away
        at Christmastime.

*309. U.S. Department of Commerce, Bureau of the Census.
       *1976 Survey of Institutionalized Persons: A Study
       of Persons Receiving Long-Term Care.* Washington,
       D.C.: U.S. Government Printing Office, 1978.

 310. U.S. Department of Housing and Urban Development. *How
       Well Are We Housed? 4. The Elderly.* Washington,
       D.C.: Government Printing Office, 1978.

*311. U.S. Department of Housing and Urban Development. *How
       Well Are We Housed? 2. Female-Headed Households.*
       Washington, D.C.: Government Printing Office, 1978.

*312. White, E.A. "Environment as Human Experience: An
       Essay." M.A. Thesis, Clark University, 1973.

 313. Youmans, E. Grant, ed. *Older Rural Americans: A
       Sociological Perspective.* Lexington: University of
       Kentucky Press, 1967. In the Introduction, Youmans
       observes that few researchers have studied older rural
       populations systematically, and that the papers in this
       volume provide a sociological perspective on elderly
       rural Americans, intended primarily for social
       gerontologists, social scientists and others
       interested in rural gerontology, and for organiza-
       tions and individuals who are developing programs for
       the rural elderly. The first five chapters focus
       on perspectives and social roles (work, family and
       community, and disengagement among older rural and
       urban men), the four succeeding chapters are concerned
       with the social, economic, housing and health condi-
       tions of the rural elderly, and the subjects of the
       remaining four chapters are, respectively, elderly
       American Indians, elderly rural Spanish-speaking
       people of the Southwest, elderly rural blacks, and
       programs for the rural elderly.

See also: 571, 576, 582, 625, 634, 678, 680, 684, 685, 703, 705,
708, 711, 715, 717, 784, 790, 851.

VII. LIFE-SPAN DEVELOPMENT

A. General

314. Back, Kurt W., ed. *Life Course: Integrative Theories
      and Exemplary Populations.* Boulder, Colorado:
      Westview Press, Inc., 1980. AAAS Symposia Series,
      Selected Symposium No. 41. Provides interdisciplinary
      perspectives on the human life course as a unit.
      Part One presents an overview from disciplines con-
      cerned with understanding the human life course, and
      includes Tamara K. Hareven, "The Life Course and
      Aging in Historical Perspective"; James Olney,
      "Biography, Autobiography and the Life Course";
      Toni Antonucci, Lois M. Tamir and Steven Dubnoff,
      "Mental Health Across the Family Life Cycle";
      Halliman H. Winsborough, "A Demographic Approach
      to the Life Cycle." Part Two, which includes studies
      of special populations in which integration of a
      variety of experiences over time can be achieved,
      includes Robert J. Havighurst, "The Life Course of
      College Professors and Administrators"; Pamela J.
      Perun and Denise Del Vento Bielby, "Structure and
      Dynamics of the Individual Life Course"; Eleanor
      Walker Willemsen, "Terman's Gifted Women: Work and
      the Way They See Their Lives" (see No. 348 of this
      Bibliography); and Barbara Myerhoff, "Life History
      Among the Elderly: Performance, Visibility and Re-
      Membering." Part Three, Conclusion, proposes new
      methods appropriate to a science of human life in a
      form suitable for students, faculty and professionals
      in human development, demography, and gerontology,
      based on these approaches, in Kurt W. Back, "Mathe-
      matics and the Poetry of Human Life and Points
      In-Between."

315. Britton, Joseph H., and Jean O. Britton. *Personality
      Changes in Aging: A Longitudinal Study of Community*

Residents. New York: Springer Publishing Co., Inc.,
1972. A report of a longitudinal (1956-65) three-
wave interviewing study of survivorship, change and
continuity of elderly residents of a Pennsylvania
village of 1,000 persons and the surrounding township
of another 1,000 persons--"normal" adults living in
their natural surroundings. Twelve appendices with
information on methodology.

316.   Erikson, Erik H.   "Generativity and Ego Integrity."   In
       Middle Age and Aging: A Reader in Social Psychology,
       pp. 85-7, Bernice L. Neugarten, ed.   Chicago: The
       University of Chicago Press, 1968. Erikson's formula-
       tion of eight stages of ego development from infancy
       to old age, each one of which represents a choice or
       a crisis for the expanding ego, includes stage 7,
       middle adulthood, in which the issue is the development
       of *generativity* (expansion of ego interests and a
       sense of having contributed to the future) versus a
       sense of ego stagnation, and stage 8, late adulthood,
       in which the issue is a sense of *ego integrity* (a
       basic acceptance of one's life as having been inevitable,
       appropriate, and meaningful) versus a sense of
       despair (fear of death). Reproduced from Erikson's
       Childhood and Society (1963).

317.   Erikson, Erik H.   "Human Strength and the Cycle of
       Generations."   In *Insight and Responsibility*, pp.
       111-57, Erik H. Erikson.   New York: W.W. Norton and
       Co., Inc., 1964. In this, the fourth in a series
       of lectures on the theme of the illumination of
       clinical insight on the responsibilities of each
       generation for all succeeding ones, Erikson speaks
       of *Hope, Will, Purpose* and *Competence* as the
       rudiments of virtue developed in childhood; of
       Fidelity as the adolescent virtue; and of *Love,
       Care* and *Wisdom* as the central virtues of adulthood,
       as interdependent qualities. He also speaks of the
       three different systems in which these virtues are
       anchored--*epigenesis* in individual development; the
       sequence of generations; and the *growth of the ego*.

318.   Frenkel-Brunswik, Else.   "Adjustments and Reorientation
       in the Course of the Life Span."   In *Middle Age and
       Aging: A Reader in Social Psychology*, pp. 77-84,
       Bernice L. Neugarten, ed.   Chicago: The University
       of Chicago Press, 1968. A report of research con-
       ducted under the leadership of Charlotte Buhler to

determine the principles of life-span development.
Research materials consist of 400 biographies of
persons from various nations, social classes and
vocations; letters, diaries and other personal
documents; and interviews with working-class people.
Data were grouped into (1) the external events of
life--97 dimensions were identified, (2) internal
reactions to these events, and (3) the accomplishments
and productions of people. Psychological phases of
the life course were identified, each demarcated by
a turning point. Transition to the fourth period,
which begins on the average at age 48.5, is marked
by psychological crises (there is a tendency to
change, discontent and complete negation; a high
point in the destruction of one's own creative work
is found at the beginning of this period, but
independent creative work often culminates, and
social activities are shifted into a new field since
the philanthropic activities begin first at this
time). A fifth period, which begins on the average
at age 63.8, is often introduced by complete retirement.
Sickness is the turning point in 44.5%, and death
among close associates in 33% of the cases studied.
There is a sharp decline in factual and social
dimensions, but an increase in hobbies. Retrospection
and the death cult are characteristic of this period.
A preoccupation with politics reappears. A factor
in psychological development appears to be independent
of the biological function. Some vital functions,
like knowledge, experience and training, counteract
the biological decline. In the first half of life,
our subjective experience is determined primarily by
our needs, in the sense of expansion of the individual.
In the second half of life, the individual regards
as more important certain tasks he has set for himself
or tasks set for him by society or those which come
from some code of values. At around age 45, "needs"
become less important, and the duties directed by
our ideals and our conscience or laid down by
authority and practical demands play a more dominant
role. Transference from the field of needs to the
field of duties, which is dictated by society and by
inner developmental factors, is a *transference in
dominance*. The ability to take on another attitude
toward life is a character trait that is almost a
necessity for success.

319.   Gutmann, David.   "Parenthood: A Key to the Comparative
       Study of the Life Cycle."   In *Life-Span Developmental
       Psychology: Normative Life Crises*, pp. 167-84,
       Nancy Datan and Leon H. Ginsberg, eds.   New York:
       Academic Press, Inc., 1975.   Adulthood is related
       to species survival as well as to self-actualization.
       For both sexes, parenthood is the point at which
       individual satisfaction intersects with the needs
       of the species, and for most adults, it is the
       ultimate source of the sense of meaning.   The parent-
       centered perspective provides insight into the meaning
       of empirical findings of sex-role changes in later
       life in a variety of cultures, that is, that men
       become more dependent and affiliative in later life
       and tend toward diffuse sensuality, whereas women
       age psychologically in the opposite direction,
       becoming more aggressive and domineering and less
       sentimental and less interested in communion.   Through
       these changes in sex roles, the normal unisex of
       later life is established.   Aging brings new beginnings,
       especially for women.   As parents become middle-aged
       and their children assume responsibility for their
       own security, the chronic sense of parental emergency
       phases out, the psychological structures established
       by both sexes in response to this emergency are dis-
       mantled, and the sex-role reversals that shape the
       transcultural data take place.   Both sexes can then
       live out the potentials and pleasures they had to
       relinquish early on in serving their particular
       parental task, and each sex becomes to some degree
       what the other sex used to be.   "Masculine" and
       "feminine" traits pertain to *parenthood* and are
       distributed by *life period*.   Parenthood may serve
       as a basis for a comparative psychology of the
       life cycle.

*320.   Haan, N., and D. Day.   "A Longitudinal Study of Change
       and Sameness in Personality Development, Adolescence
       to Later Adulthood."   *The International Journal of
       Aging and Human Development* (1974) 5(1):11-39.

321.   Kimmel, Douglas C.   *Adulthood and Aging: An Inter-
       disciplinary, Developmental View*.   New York: John
       Wiley and Sons, Inc., 1974.   Kimmel adopts a developmenta
       approach to adulthood, bringing an interdisciplinary
       perspective to adult development by emphasizing the
       interaction of psychological, social and physiological
       aspects of growing older, and includes six case

examples ("interludes" between the chapters) to
bridge theoretical concepts and living reality.
Two of these case studies are of older women--a
67-year-old black grandmother who lives in Harlem,
and an 89-year-old woman who came to the U.S. 43
years ago and who now lives in a nursing home.
Eleven photographs, including Degas's *Old Italian
Woman* as a Frontispiece.

322. Lowenthal, Marjorie Fiske, Majda Thurnher, David
      Chiriboga, et al. *Four Stages of Life: A Comparative
      Study of Women and Men Facing Transition.* San
      Francisco: Jossey-Bass, Inc., 1975. Self-actualization
      theories are put to the test through a study of
      people thought to be representative of "mainstream
      Americans." The sample consists of 216 people,
      most of whom are Caucasian and from the middle and
      lower-middle classes. The four stages are: high
      school seniors, men and women married less than one
      year who had not yet started a family, middle-aged
      parents whose youngest child was a high school
      senior, and older persons planning to retire within
      two to three years. All were in the process of
      self-assessment, but most--especially at the third
      stage--did not seem able to see very far ahead. One
      conclusion was that complexity of personality is
      maladaptive for older people, which may be due to
      the closing off of avenues for self-expression in
      our society. Women at the third stage were in a
      more critical period of their lives than were those
      of any other group. When they spoke of stress,
      they focused on their children; they seemed to be in
      despair about their marriages. Women at the fourth
      stage were not so distraught; they were more
      accepting of themselves. But the more enterprising
      among them seemed likely to dissipate their energies
      and gifts on their families. They tended to express
      renewed energies at the expense of personal develop-
      ment, by a growing dominance over family members.
      This study finds evidence for a psychological
      transformation in the second half of life, whereby
      men give greater recognition to feelings and women
      to instrumentality. It states that the most com-
      pelling need is for a life-course orientation in our
      social and educational institutions.

*323. Maas, Henry S., and Joseph A. Kuypers. *From Thirty to Seventy: A Forty-Year Longitudinal Study of Adult Life Styles and Personality*. San Francisco: Jossey-Bass, Inc., 1974. A follow-up study of older women and men studied initially in the 1930s as parents of Berkeley infants chosen for the longitudinal analysis.

324. Neugarten, Bernice L. "Adult Personality: Toward a Psychology of the Life Cycle." In *Middle Age and Aging: A Reader in Social Psychology*, pp. 137-47, Bernice L. Neugarten, ed. Chicago: The University of Chicago Press, 1968. Neugarten states the need for a personality theory that encompasses the entire life cycle. In commenting on the salient issues of adulthood with examples from middle age, she states the need for a theory emphasizing the executive functions of the personality, and one that can help account for the growth and maintenance of cognitive competence and creativity as well as help to explain the conscious use of past experience. The middle years--the decade of the 50s for most--are an important turning point. Men become more receptive to affiliative and nurturant promptings, and women more receptive to aggressive and egocentric impulses; men cope with the environment in increasingly abstract and cognitive terms, and women in increasingly affective and expressive terms. Older persons of both sexes move toward more egocentric, self-preoccupied positions and attend increasingly to personal needs. Ego functions are turned inward with aging; awareness of approaching death can serve as an impetus for a new and final restructuring. This paper also shows the limitations of any theory of personality that is based primarily upon a biological model of the life span, and suggests that age norms and the age-status system form a cultural context for studying adult behavior and personality changes and differences.

325. Neugarten, Bernice L., and Nancy Datan. "Sociological Perspectives on the Life Cycle." In *Life-Span Developmental Psychology*, pp. 53-69, Paul B. Baltes and K. Warner Schaie, eds. New York: Academic Press, Inc., 1973. The socio-historical context of human development is the focus of this paper, in which sociological concepts contributing to the under-standing of human personality--the social system,

social role, socialization and re-socialization--
are reviewed, the life cycle is discussed from each
of three dimensions of time--life time (chronological
age), historical time and social time (which under-
girds the age-grade system of a society), researches
on age norms as a system of social control and of age
stratification are reviewed, and the changing rhythm
of the life cycle in the U.S. is presented as an
illustration of the interrelationship between
historical time, social time and life time. Over
the past 80 years, a striking difference has been
developing between men and women with respect to
the timing of family and work cycles. The age of
economic maturity has been deferred for men, but
not for women. They are younger than men when
entering the labor force, work much longer than
before, and are older than men when they retire.
New rhythms of social maturity also affect parent-
child and grandparent-grandchild relationships,
and intergenerational patterns of mutual aid.

326. Newman, B.M., and P.R. Newman. "Later Adulthood: A
Developmental Stage." In *Dimensions of Aging:
Readings*, pp. 126-43, Jon Hendricks and C. Davis
Hendricks, eds. Cambridge, Massachusetts: Winthrop
Publishers, Inc., 1979. In this excerpt from
Development Through Life, the authors emphasize
the continued potential for growth in the years from
age 50 until death, and state that the search for
personal meaning is the primary integrating theme
of this life stage. The developmental tasks are
the redirection of energy to new roles and activities
in the family and work spheres, the acceptance of
one's life, and the development of a point of view
about death. The psychosocial crisis is integrity
vs. despair, and the central process for resolution
of the crisis is introspection. Retirement and
grandparenthood are examples of events in later life
which bring about a redirection of energy to new
roles. Reminiscence appears to lend continuity to
the older adult's self-concept. The authors discuss
an integration of research findings concerning
changes in cognitive functions with aging, and the
patterns of changes in self-esteem observed among
older adults and the sources of self-esteem most
relevant to the aged. They present a model for a
multi-age day care program as an application of the
principle of providing new roles for older people.

327. Peck, Robert C. "Psychological Developments in the
      Second Half of Life." In *Middle Age and Aging: A
      Reader in Social Psychology*, pp. 88-92, Bernice L.
      Neugarten, ed. Chicago: The University of Chicago
      Press, 1968. Peck suggests dividing the second half
      of life and the Eighth Stage (Erikson: see No. 316
      of this Bibliography) of Ego-Integrity vs. Despair
      into Middle Age and Old Age periods, which may occur
      in different time sequences for different persons.
      In Middle Age, the stages and tasks are: Valuing
      Wisdom vs. Valuing Physical Powers (based on
      personality analysis of thousands of business
      people, mostly men); Socializing vs. Sexualizing
      in Human Relationships; Cathectic Flexibility vs.
      Cathectic Impoverishment; and Mental Flexibility
      vs. Mental Rigidity. In Old Age, the stages and
      tasks are: Ego Differentiation vs. Work-Role Pre-
      occupation (for many women, this stage may be reached
      in middle age, when grown children depart); Body
      Transcendence vs. Body Preoccupation; and Ego
      Transcendence vs. Ego Preoccupation. People working
      on the same stage may vary widely in chronological
      age; hence, future researches in aging should be
      based on samples of people at the same "stage in
      life."

328. Pressey, Sidney L., and Raymond G. Kuhlen. *Psychological
      Developments Through the Life Span*. New York: Harper
      and Brothers, 1957. The topics in Part One,
      Abilities, Tasks, and Achievements, are growth,
      change, and decline in physique; growth and change
      in abilities as shown by tests; development of
      abilities as indicated by achievement and by mental
      disease; education through the life span; and the
      work life. Part Two, Dynamic and Social Development,
      includes chapters on changing motivation during the
      life span; emotional development; satisfactions in
      life activities; moral, sociopolitical, and religious
      values and behavior; social interaction; and hetero-
      sexual development, marriage and family relationships.
      Part Three, with a chapter on retrospect and prospect,
      is entitled Preface to a "Life-Span" Psychology of
      the Future. Preface and each chapter followed by
      a bibliography.

*329. Riley, Matilda White, ed. *Aging from Birth to Death:
      Interdisciplinary Perspectives*. Boulder, Colorado:
      Westview Press for American Association for the
      Advancement of Science, 1979.

330. Self, Patricia A. "The Further Evolution of the Parental Imperative." In *Life-Span Developmental Psychology: Normative Life Crises*, pp. 185-9, Nancy Datan and Leon H. Ginsberg, eds. New York: Academic Press, Inc., 1975. Our society now demands that persons be flexible with regard to parental duties. In spite of their early sex-role training, many persons seem to adapt successfully to the current transition in sex roles. This implies that sex roles are learned and not innate. In order for further successful evolution of the human species to occur, recognition of the intellectual, social and emotional needs of all persons of all ages and both sexes seems imperative. Parenting is only one of many important events occurring between ages 20 and 50. Gutmann's parental imperative (see No. 319 of this Bibliography) may have been more important to the human species in its earlier evolutionary history than it is in modern civilization. People in urban societies are now moving away from a recognition of persons based on expectations of sex-appropriate behavior and toward an appreciation of individual differences among persons.

331. Sheehy, Gail. *Passages: Predictable Crises of Adult Life*. New York: E.P. Dutton and Co., Inc., 1976. Sheehy collected 115 life stories of men and women aged 18 to 55 for this book in which her objectives were to locate changes in inner life, to compare the developmental rhythms of men and women, and to examine the predictable crises for couples. Sections: Part One: Mysteries of the Life Cycle; Part Two: Pulling Up Roots; Part Three: The Trying Twenties; Part Four: Passage to the Thirties; Part Five: But I'm Unique (with chapters on men's life patterns and women's life patterns); Part Six: Deadline Decade; Part Seven: Renewal.

332. Troll, Lillian. "Issues in the Study of Generations." *The International Journal of Aging and Human Development* (1970) 7:199-218. Delineates five separate concepts of "generation"--as ranked descent, age-homogeneous group, developmental stage, time span and Zeitgeist. Examines dimensions of the analysis of generations in the family. Explores major dimensions of the problem of the "generation gap" as well as the issue of change and the implications of study of generations for the gerontological

concern of life-span development. Suggests focusing
on the issue of social change in the context of
development over the entire life-span.

See also: 101, 102, 105, 139, 268, 593, 603, 604, 606, 607,
623, 662.

B. Older Women

333.   Carsman, Evaline P. "Education as Recreation." In
       *Looking Ahead: A Woman's Guide to the Problems and
       Joys of Growing Older*, pp. 140-6, Lillian E. Troll,
       Joan Israel and Kenneth Israel, eds. Englewood
       Cliffs, New Jersey: Prentice-Hall, Inc., 1977.
       Although educational programs must service students
       who want to upgrade their skills in order to become
       employed, the opportunities for self-enrichment
       provided by liberal arts curricula are an added
       bonus. Older women's participation in education can
       serve to re-create them, to make them new persons
       with new social roles and world-views. The need to
       grow, which is nourished and enhanced by the search
       for knowledge, does not cease at any age. The
       extent to which the needs of older people for
       continuing education will be met depends ultimately
       upon public policy.

334.   Darrow, Susan T., Recorder. "Life Span Behavior
       Patterns--Class and Ethnic Variations." In *No
       Longer Young: The Older Woman in America, Work
       Group Reports*, pp. 31-5. Ann Arbor, Michigan: The
       Institute of Gerontology, The University of Michigan-
       Wayne State University, 1974. Women of all social
       classes and races are ill-prepared for old age, which
       most must face alone. Poverty and race are a double
       burden for the black woman: the majority have few
       social, economic and medical resources in old age.
       Widows are in social limbo, since their social class
       is assigned on the basis of their husbands' or
       fathers' occupations. There is evidence that middle-
       class women fare better than lower-class women in
       the later years. Research indicates that the presence
       of age peers is more important for the morale and
       life adjustment of older people than the presence
       of kin. Both social service programs for elderly

black women and programs to eliminate poverty and
racism are needed. Research into the social,
cultural and ethnic patterns related to old age,
and the development of social supports for widows,
are recommended, as well as the provision of peer
contact and work involvement for the elderly. Social
and economic changes may facilitate the development
of greater independence for women over the life course.

*335. Datan, Nancy, and Rodeheaver, D. "Dirty Old Women:
The Emergence of the Sensuous Grandmother." Invited
Contribution to Symposium "Socialization to become
and old woman." Mildred Seltzer, Chairman, American
Psychological Association, San Francisco, 1977.

336. Elliott, Grace Loucks. *Women After Forty*. New York:
Henry Holt and Co., 1936. Author of "Understanding
the Adolescent Girl," Elliott states that *Women
After Forty* originated in work with adolescent girls,
since it was found that the problems of the mother
in adjusting to middle life were often a major factor
in the difficulties of the daughter. In her view,
the transition period of middle life is comparable
in importance and difficulty with that of adolescence.
The book's material, gathered chiefly to formulate
educational proposals of benefit to those now younger,
is based upon study of the psychological literature
on personality development and problems, and study
of current interpretations of Christianity pertinent
to this subject; upon interviews with psychologists,
psychiatrists, analysts and leaders in adult education
in England and on the Continent as well as in the
U.S.; upon a questionnaire study of women between
the ages of 45 and 60; upon discussions with married
and unmarried women over 40 on the subject of later
life; and upon Elliott's consultations with middle-
aged and elderly women. She emphasizes the continuity
of life, and states that many people do their best
work and are most creative in their later years.
Chapters: The Significance of the Last Half of Life
(she takes the Jungian viewpoint that the question
of the meaning of life is of prime importance in
the years of maturity and later life); Crises in
Middle Age; Achievement in Later Life (the function
of age in modern society is the most important question
for society as well as for the individual; to be
satisfying, work in later life must provide for a
broadening of interests and sympathies; society has

closed doors to the opportunities of later life for
women who have been family-centered); The Transition
in Middle Age; Maturity and Immaturity in the Last
Half of Life; Deprivation of Basic Needs; Psychological
Assumptions and the Last Half of Life; The Rhythm
of Life: Religious Interpretations and the Last Half
of Life; The Completion of Life. Elliott takes the
position that middle age and later life can be rich
and gratifying, and that one's attitude in facing
whatever life brings is far more important than the
conditions of one's life. She believes that the
foundation for the human and cultural achievements of
life, almost half of which is lived when the procreative functions have ceased, is the capacity to trans-
form energy from procreative channels to the creative
union with other lives in all the aspects of personality.

337.   Giesen, Carol Boellhoff and Nancy Datan. "The Competent
       Older Woman." In *Transitions of Aging*, pp. 57-72,
       Nancy Datan and Nancy Lohmann, eds. New York:
       Academic Press, Inc., 1980. The stereotype of the
       old as dependent, passive, incompetent and incapable
       of coping with the problems and crises of life is not
       confined to non-professionals. Positive consequences
       of this image are care and concern for the aged, but
       these are countered by negative traits associated
       with aging and by patronizing attitudes. Because
       of the double standard, aging is seen to have more
       negative consequences for women than for men. But
       negative qualities associated with aging are inaccurate,
       and the negative stereotype is based upon two mis-
       conceptions--the idea that today's older woman has
       not had to acquire a level of competence similar to
       that required of older men, and the notion that
       women's competence diminishes with aging. Interviews
       gathered over 1½ years as part of two studies in
       stress and coping strategies re-affirm that "life
       brings change, change brings growth--and with growth,
       competence." Most of these West Virginia women
       believed they had become *more* competent over the
       years, and now could deal more effectively with
       their lives. As children, they performed competently
       in tasks that were their share of responsibility
       for their family's welfare. They entered young
       adulthood confident they could learn and perform
       the tasks of marriage, parenthood, and wage earning.
       Most felt that becoming a parent was a major source
       of change in their lives and that they had "grown
       up" because of it. Most learned to be competent as

wage earners and also learned home skills traditionally associated with masculine roles. Competence
and capability of women who spent 40 or more years
coping with a harsh environment and economy is not
relinquished in late adulthood. There is no retirement
for these women; as the demands of parenthood diminish,
these tasks are replaced by instrumental activity
in other areas of their lives.

338. Kline, Chrysee. "The Socialization Process of Women."
In *The Older Woman: Lavender Rose or Gray Panther*,
pp. 59-70, Marie Marschall Fuller and Cora Ann
Martin, eds. Springfield, Illinois: Charles C.
Thomas, 1980. A review and analysis of research
findings in studies of women's work roles, housewife
roles and retirement roles suggests that the
socialization process of American women, which
creates *impermanence* in the form of role loss and
repeated adjustment to change in the life situation,
facilitates women's adjustment to later life.
Adequate re-engagement procedures in the work world
have not been developed because of the myth that
modern workers--men as well as women--experience
continuity in the work role and have steady careers
from education to retirement. It is recommended
that women's activist groups reconsider the objective
of attaining a rigid, lifelong goal. If impermanence
and discontinuity over the life cycle have a positive
effect on adjustment to old age, then a new system
of career flexibility ought to be adopted by women
and men.

339. Livson, Florine B. "Patterns of Personality Development
in Middle-Aged Women: A Longitudinal Study." *The
International Journal of Aging and Human Development*
(1976) 7(2):107-15. Two groups of women are identified
in a sample of 24 women studied throughout adolescence
and at ages 40 and 50, who scored above the mean on
the index of psychological health--the *traditionals*,
gregarious and nurturant, who have minimal conflict
between their personalities and social role, and
the *independents*, more autonomous and more in touch
with their inner life, who are conflicted at 40,
when intellectual skills decline, but who resolve
the crisis by age 50, when they move into the stage
of intimacy achieved by age 40 by the *traditionals*.
Independents interrupt their development in the middle
adult years, but leap forward by age 50; *traditionals*

show steady personality growth from adolescence to
middle age. The key factor is the fit between a
woman's life style and personality. *Traditional*
personalities fit conventional feminine roles.
Disengagement from mothering stimulates the
independents to revive their more assertive goal-
oriented skills. These are two examples of successful
paths a woman can take from adolescence to middle
age if traditional roles for women are part of her
social world and become part of her expectations of
herself. Young women today have more options in
their choice of life styles. But middle age can
call forth suppressed parts of the self.

340. Rose, Arnold M. "The Adequacy of Women's Expectations
      for Adult Roles." *Social Forces* (October 1951)
      30(1):69-77. This paper focuses on the hypothesis
      that the adequacy of the advance expectations for
      future adult roles is a function of the definiteness
      and specificity of these roles, and uses consistency,
      degree of specificity and realism as the criteria
      of adequacy of expectations. The particular
      hypothesis is that because of the social changes
      accompanying the Industrial Revolution, the roles
      of middle-class urban women are less specific and
      less definite, and thus her pre-adult expectations
      less adequate, than those of men. Major differences
      between the sexes are that women's change of function
      was slower and less complete than men's, there was
      more opposition to women acquiring new functions,
      and new roles for women have never become clear and
      definite. Data from a study of 256 college students
      about expectations for the adult role are presented
      to support the conclusion that there is a certain
      inconsistency, lack of definiteness, and lack of
      realism about expectations for adult roles among a
      significant proportion of women college students.
      This suggests that future research would reveal that
      these inadequacies in expectation would create
      problems for adult women.

341. Schlossberg, Nancy K. "Lifelong Learning." In *Looking
      Ahead: A Woman's Guide to the Problems and Joys of
      Growing Older*, pp. 133-9, Lillian E. Troll, Joan
      Israel and Kenneth Israel, eds. Englewood Cliffs,
      New Jersey: Prentice-Hall, Inc., 1977. Comments made
      by adult women students at the University of Maryland
      reflect some reasons why women of all ages are re-

turning to college campuses. This paper discusses two of the barriers confronting the mature returning woman student--age bias and limited support services.

*342. Sears, P.S., and A. Barbee. "Career and Life Satisfaction Among Terman's Gifted Women." In *The Gifted and the Creative: A Fifty Year Perspective*, J. Stanley, W.C. George and C.H. Solano, eds. Baltimore: The Johns Hopkins University Press, 1977.

343. Sinnott, Jan Dynda. "Sex-Role Inconstancy, Biology, and Successful Aging." In *Dimensions of Aging: Readings*, pp. 144-9, Jon Hendricks and C. Davis Hendricks, eds. Cambridge, Massachusetts: Winthrop Publishers, Inc., 1979. Sinnott proposes to extend Kline's hypothesis (see No. 338 of this Bibliography) that the inconstancy of roles in women's lives accounts for their relative resilience in adapting to changes in later life. This paper, based on a review of a number of studies, suggests that the ability to show *life-span variations in sex roles* indicates a general flexibility that is associated with more successful aging and a longer life span. The relationship between androgyny and successful aging seems to be a part of a larger pattern of increasing and decreasing sex-role differentiation at different points along the life course.

344. Troll, Lillian E. "Poor, Dumb, and Ugly." In *Looking Ahead: A Woman's Guide to the Problems and Joys of Growing Older*, pp. 4-13, Lillian E. Troll, Joan Israel and Kenneth Israel, eds. Englewood Cliffs, New Jersey: Prentice-Hall, Inc., 1977. There are redundant older women because of the revolution in health and life style of the past century which has enabled so many women to live past their time of traditional usefulness. Most women over 35 who are alive today have been trained from earliest infancy to be servants of men, but they are discovering that this is not a lifetime role and thus are in danger of becoming obsolete. Older women today are in transition. Because their mothers and grandmothers do not present useful models of womanhood, they must be pathfinders. Their daughters and granddaughters will benefit from the trails they mark. Data Troll gathered on generational differences in three-generation families show that the conditions of today's aging women may be temporary and transitional.

345. Troll, Lillian E., Helen Lycaki and Jean Smith.
      "Development of the Cognitively Complex Woman over
      the Generations." In *No Longer Young: The Older
      Woman in America*, pp. 81-7. Ann Arbor, Michigan:
      The Institute of Gerontology, The University of
      Michigan-Wayne State University, 1975. In the past,
      cognitively complex women were thought to be exceptions;
      today, a new image is emerging. This paper inquires
      into the means of assessing this putative historical
      change. Generational shift data based on interview
      responses of three-generation lineages of 88 women,
      largely lower-middle to working class in origin but
      upwardly mobile, are presented. Three cognitive
      style components were selected for study--the dimensions
      of Objectivity, Differentiation and Categorization.
      One reported shift was that the middle generation of
      women is more objective and less egocentric than
      either of the others. Interpretations are given
      from both an ontogenetic and phylogenetic viewpoint.
      For Differentiation and Categorization, it was found
      that the scores are progressively larger for each
      younger generation. These overall average genera-
      tional shifts are embedded in substantial family
      resemblances. Path analysis revealed a direct-line
      path from Objectivity of the grandmother to Objectivity
      of her daughter, but also a diagonal path of trans-
      mission from Objectivity of the grandmother to
      Differentiation in her daughter in the second
      generation. The paths for Differentiation of the
      first generation to cognitive style ratings in the
      second generation are more complex. The curious
      finding is reported that the chronological age of
      the grandmother has most pathways coming from it to
      the characteristics of her daughter, but that it is
      the education of these daughters that is the source
      of most paths to the characteristics of the youngest
      generation. Widening the world for women of one
      generation leads to progressively more cognitively
      complex women in a later generation. A long period
      of time is required to produce cognitively complex
      women. The process of development during the adult
      years should not be neglected: opening the horizons
      for adult women could lead to expectations of
      increased development in cognitive complexity in
      their own lifetime.

346. Uits, Carolee, Recorder. "Self Image and Roles." In
      No Longer Young: The Older Woman in America, Work

Group Reports, pp. 43-6. Ann Arbor, Michigan: The
Institute of Gerontology, The University of Michigan-
Wayne State University, 1974. In this workshop,
David Gutmann and Joan Israel strongly disagreed
with each other's point of view. Gutmann (see No.
319 of this Bibliography) stated that the self-
fulfillment of parents must take second place to
the emotional development of their young children,
that the life cycle guarantees an "inner liberation"
to men and women, and that while each sex must repress
in parenthood qualities potentially lethal to children,
one may re-affirm the self when children are grown.
He believes the younger woman in our society should
be educated to help prepare for later periods of
the life cycle: she should plan in her first period
of freedom (pre-child) for her second period of
freedom (post-child). He stated that older women
feel they have earned the right to be more aggressive.
Israel's position was entirely different. She stated
that having only pre-child and post-child freedom
is not tenable to today's women, and that a new
choice of roles allowing for a more aggressive sense
of self does not need to interfere with the child-
rearing years. It is very late to make changes in a
woman's self concept at 40 or 50; by then she is
caught up in stereotypes; it is often only in widowhood that opportunities for self-development emerge.
But society is changing, and widows of the future,
less bound by tradition, will be more militant, more
aware, and have more "savvy" about getting things done.
In her later years, a woman can be her own locus of
control, as she should have been all her life.

347. Weg, Ruth. "More Than Wrinkles." In *Looking Ahead: A
Woman's Guide to the Problems and Joys of Growing
Older*, pp. 22-42, Lillian E. Troll, Joan Israel and
Kenneth Israel, eds. Englewood Cliffs, New Jersey:
Prentice-Hall, Inc., 1977. Aging is not disease
but part of the developmental process from birth
to death. Topics are: the double standard of aging,
physiological age changes, the importance of nutrition for both appearance and physiology of older
persons, the benefits of exercise, "Insult and
Injury" (oral health, cigarette smoking, hypertension,
stress, osteoporosis, arthritis), Procreation and
Recreation--reproductive decline in the later years
(few changes with age appear to be as threatening
to ego, identity and sense of well-being as changes

in sexuality, but human sexuality is flexible and
covers a wide range of human behavior, and the need
to express it is continuous throughout life),
"interest and capacity" (these remain relatively
high in older women, but lack of opportunity and
early stereotyped sex education frustrate healthy
involvement), the climacteric, older women as sexual
partners, dysfunction, estrogen therapy, and "Not
by Body Alone: The Human Dimension" (the present
and the future).

348.   Willemsen, Eleanor Walker.   "Terman's Gifted Women:
       Work and the Way They See Their Lives."   In *Life
       Course: Integrative Theories and Exemplary Popula-
       tions*, pp. 121-32, Kurt W. Back, ed.   (AAAS Selected
       Symposium 41.)   Boulder, Colorado: Westview Press,
       Inc., 1980.   This paper is concerned with the responses
       of those women in the Terman sample of gifted children
       (a study begun in 1922) who returned their 1977
       questionnaires by 1978 and who wrote of at least
       one critically significant event in their lives.
       General findings show the experience of work has been
       positive for those who engaged in it, that working
       women were as positive about their lives as other
       Terman subjects, and that their marriages and family
       lives have as much importance to them as to those
       women who worked little or not at all.   The women
       who worked experience their lives as their own
       creation; for those who are married, this creation
       is perceived as having improved the marriage.   Many
       of these gifted women, although from a generation
       for whom work outside the home was definitely not
       the expected pattern, did work for substantial
       portions of their lives, albeit at traditionally
       feminine occupations.   Their work experience may
       have enabled them to look back over their lives with
       a greater subjective sense of accomplishment than
       they would experience without it.   Today's intelligent
       and educated working woman may have higher expecta-
       tions from a lifetime of work, and may not view her
       life as positively as these women unless these
       expectations are fulfilled.

See also: 123, 127, 129, 163, 267, 388, 389, 556, 570, 583, 595,
601, 622, 640, 642, 657, 659, 661, 745.

A. General

*349. Berdes, Celia. "Winter Tales: Fiction About Aging."
      The Gerontologist (April 1981) 21(2):121-5.

 350. Blue, Gladys F. "The Aging as Portrayed in Realistic
      Fiction for Children 1945-1975." *The Gerontologist*
      (April 1978) 18(2):187-92. A report from findings
      from a sample comprised of 125 realistic fiction
      trade books, including picture books, published in
      the U.S. from 1945 to 1975. Topics: demographic
      portrayals; physical characteristics; state of
      health; personality traits; activities; aspects of
      choice, dependency and change; conveyance of the
      concept of aging or old; relationships and patterns
      of social interaction. Concludes that character
      development was generally multidimensional (the
      aging were presented in situations judged both to
      be accurate and adequate depictions from the stand-
      point of realistic presentation, and the literature
      seemed to suggest both the needs and assets of
      elderly persons), that portrayals were *not*
      disparaging, derogatory or otherwise negative,
      nor were they stereotypic; and that the literature
      indicated a general humanistic concern for under-
      standing the elderly as individuals in diverse styles
      of life and circumstance. Compares these research
      findings with those of others; suggests implications
      for further research.

*351. Clark, Martha. "The Poetry of Aging: Views of Old
      Age in Contemporary American Poetry." *The
      Gerontologist* (April 1980) 20(2):188-91.

 352. *Expanding Horizons.* 93-05 68th Avenue, Forest Hills,
      New York 11375. "The grass roots voice of people of

retirement age for people of all ages." Sponsored by
Adelphi University Center on Aging, Garden City, New
York 11530.

353. Freedman, Richard. "Sufficiently Decayed: Gerontophobia
      in English Literature." In *Aging and the Elderly:
      Humanistic Perspectives in Gerontology*, pp. 49-61,
      Stuart F. Spicker, Kathleen M. Woodward and David
      D. Van Tassel, eds. Atlantic Highlands, New Jersey:
      Humanities Press, Inc., 1978. The intention of this
      paper is to confront Western society's hostile
      treatment of the aged in some of its more eloquent
      and enduring literary manifestations. This could
      counter glibly optimistic views of the role of the
      humanities and point the way to further research
      into the large body of literary opprobrium to which
      the aged have been subjected. Examples of modes of
      literary gerontophobia include Congreve's *The Way of
      the World*, Swift's *Gulliver's Travels* and "Verses
      on the Death of Dr. Swift," Frances Burney's *Evelina*,
      Gilbert and Sullivan's light operas and Arnold
      Bennett's *The Old Wives' Tale*. Freedman argues that
      literature helps us to identify even the areas in
      our psyches we would least like to contemplate, and
      that in this way it helps rid us of cant and of
      guilt so that we may be able to address the genuine
      problems of the aging with free intelligences and
      with clear consciences.

*354. Loughman, Celeste. "Eros and the Elderly: A Literary
       View." *The Gerontologist* (April 1980) 20(2):182-7.

355. Loughman, Celeste. "Novels of Senescence: A New
      Naturalism." *The Gerontologist* (February 1977)
      17(1):79-84. Since *Memento Mori*, many novels have
      appeared on the subject of what it is like to be
      old, but they focus on degeneration and decay.
      Sexuality is a recurring form of self-assertiveness
      in Bellow's *Mr. Sammler's Planet*, Sparks's *Memento
      Mori*, Amis's *Ending Up* and Tanizaki's *Diary of a
      Mad Old Man*, but all four authors "offer little to
      mitigate their naturalistic treatment of old age"
      in depicting its isolation and impotence and decay.
      "The impulse is to resist such unrelieved bleakness;
      yet the dramatic force of these novels makes the
      vision ring frighteningly true."

356. Lyell, Ruth Granetz, ed. *Middle Age, Old Age: Short
      Stories, Poems, Plays, and Essays on Aging*. New

York: Harcourt Brace Jovanovich, Inc., 1980.
Selections from literature on the themes of generational relationships; disappointment, the life review,
and unresolved conflicts; old age as wisdom and peace;
loss; dying and death; alone and with peers; and
the life cycle.

357. *Nimrod.* (Spring/Summer 1976) 20(2), 175 pp. The
entire issue is on "Old People: A Season of the
Mind." Over 60 contributors.

358. Olsen, Tillie. *Silences.* New York: Delacorte Press/
Seymour Lawrence, 1978. Explorations of the ways
literary creativity is silenced because of sex,
age, class, color, or for other reasons--which include
excerpts from letters, diaries, notebooks and other
personal documents, and an essay on Rebecca Harding
Davis. Olsen writes that where gifted women or men
have remained mute or have never attained their full
capacity, this is because of inner or outer circumstances that oppose the needs of creation. She
concludes from a survey of achievement as measured
by appearance in 20th-century literature courses,
required reading lists, texts, anthologies, and
works that are critically acclaimed that only one
of twelve writers is a woman. In youth, women's
aspirations are reduced; in adulthood, writing is
not first in their lives, and hence women are made
"mediocre caretakers of their talent." Although
there are more women writers who are assuming fullness
of work *and* family life as their right in society
today, Olsen fears that their work may be lessened
or impeded or only partial, because the essential
situation has not changed.

359. *Parabola: Myth and the Quest for Meaning.* (February
1980) V(1), 128 pp. The entire issue is on "The
Old Ones," and includes poetry and prose on aging:
"Time Stands Still" by Keith Critchlow on new
visions of ancient places; Epicycle by Tokahe;
Coming Back Slow by Agnes Vanderburg ("A Flathead
American Indian teaches the old ways"); "Living
Ancestors" by Frederick Franck on Japan's aged
artists; Epicycles, Ah! (from Chuang tse, retold by
P.L. Trovers) and Pilgrimage (from an old Persian
story, retold by P.L. Trovers); Cycles of Time by
J. Stephen Lansing on being old in Bali; "The
Object, The Ritual," a poem by Joy Elvey Bannerman;

"The Old People Give You Life" by Megan Bisele on
the Kung Bushmen; "Arcs: Legacy," on the wisdom of
our Native American grandfathers; The Transmission
of Blessings: An interview with Deshung Rinpoche,
a Tibetan *tulku*; "Gatherer of Glorious Virtues" by
Lobsang Lhalungpa, a portrait of Tibet's great woman
saint; "Elders and Guides," a conversation with
Joseph Campbell, on remembering Heinrich Zimmer;
Epicycle: The Old Man of the Sea (retold from
classical sources by D.M. Dooling); "Old Oaks and
Ancient Sages" by Jonathan Cahves; "Re-membered
Lives" by Barbara G. Myerhoff; Four Poems by Robert
Bly and Rolf Jacobsen; and "Where We Are" by Gary
Snyder on how knowledge of place helps us to know
ourselves.

*360.   Seltzer, Mildred M.   "Changing Concept of and Attitude
        Toward the Old as Found in Children's Literature
        1870-1960." Diss., Department of Sociology, Miami
        University, 1969.

361.   Sohngen, Mary.   "The Experience of Old Age as Depicted
        in Contemporary Novels." *The Gerontologist* (February
        1977) 17(1):70-8.   Sohngen found 87 titles, in
        compiling a listing of commercial novels published
        between 1950 and 1975, each with a protagonist aged
        60 or more and with a narrative point of view
        essentially that of the protagonist.   She suggests
        three uses for her list: these novels can broaden
        students' personal vision of aging beyond the usual
        field experience and field assignments (they can
        "look sensitively at their youthful enthusiasm for
        intervention"); discussing fictional characters
        "can open the way toward sensitized consciousness
        and mutual support" for mature students in adult
        education courses; and the list is a valuable
        supplement to novels about adolescence or early
        maturity in continuing education courses on the
        contemporary novel or social problems.

362.   Sohngen, Mary.   "Humanities Approaches to Gerontological
        Education in the Colleges." *The Gerontologist*
        (December 1978) 18(6):577-8.   Sohngen discusses the
        various ways a humanities approach can offer the
        perspective of time.   She states that related materials
        providing this perspective are part of her course
        entitled "Old Age Depicted in Literature."   In
        reading fiction and sharing responses to it, students

can develop an awareness and insight into the
infinite varieties of humankind and an understanding
of our common humanity, seeing old age in terms of
"we" and not "they." This paper is one of a symposium
on the role of the humanities in gerontology, which
includes an Introduction by David D. Van Tassel,
and other papers by Susan J. Kleinberg, Stuart F.
Spicker and Walter G. Moss.

363. Sohngen, Mary, and Robert J. Smith. "Images of Old
Age in Poetry." *The Gerontologist* (April 1978)
18(2):181-6. It is commonly assumed that mass
culture, especially television and the popular
press, are responsible for the continuation of
negative stereotypes of old age. This study--with
the bibliography--of 127 poems listed under "old
age" in *Granger's Index to Poetry*, raises the
disturbing possibility that the very process of
acquiring a liberal education, which it is assumed
could help counteract these stereotypes, may be in
part responsible for the persistence of negative
attitudes. The portrait of old age in most of the
poems was negative, with only minor differences
between the internal or external narrative point
of view. A composite of the physical characteristics
is almost without exception negative; many of the
losses borne in old age relate to these physical
attributes. Social and emotional losses were
generally thought to be at least as great as physical
and mental decline. The overall picture is one of
great loss, although not everything is diminished
and old age does have some gains. Metaphors for
old age reflect the poet's emphasis on decline and
loss; positive metaphors are few. This study could
help "scientists" become aware of a previously
neglected source of negative attitudes toward old
age and encourage "humanists" to consider old age
as an area of study that can benefit from the
application of their knowledge and skills.
Recommendations are made for studies in poetry.

364. Somerville, Rose M. "The Future of Family Relationships
in the Middle and Older Years: Clues in Fiction."
The Family Coordinator (October 1972) 21(4):487-98.
Insights from fiction into present and future functioning of families and parafamilies, of necessity
from a middle-class perspective. Topics: defining
the middle and older years; early and advanced middle

age; the future for the middle aged: divorce, delayed
marriage, consensual unions; the older years;
institutions; communes; retirement villages and
other age groupings. Somerville thinks current
efforts to change the family or to substitute other
groups for traditional family forms are likely to
accelerate in the next decade or two, and that the
future middle-aged and elderly will carry the effects
of experimentation into their new age groups.
Fictional works selected for the clues they provide
to new role definitions include short stories about
older women by Joan Merrill Gerber in *Stop Here,
My Friend* (1965).

See also: 189, 199, 233, 236, 603, 871, 873, 876.

B. Older Women

365.   Auerbach, Nina. *Communities of Women: An Idea in
        Fiction.* Cambridge, Massachusetts: Harvard Univer-
        sity Press, 1978. Auerbach explores changing visions
        of communities of women, drawing from fiction and
        from social commentary. Her literary texts are
        Pride and Prejudice, *Little Women*, *Cranford*,
        Villette, *The Bostonians*, *The Odd Woman* (see No.
        468 of this Bibliography) and *The Prime of Miss
        Jean Brodie*.

366.   Bahr, Howard M., Marcia Cebulski, Laura Kemp, Dorothy
        Frost and Susan Rutherford Muller. Appendix D,
        Reactions to Disaffiliation among Aged Women: The
        Novelists' View. In *Women Alone: The Disaffiliation
        of Urban Females*, pp. 185-99, Howard M. Bahr and
        Gerald R. Garrett, eds. Lexington, Massachusetts:
        D.C. Heath and Co., 1976. Selected aspects of
        disaffiliation, drawing upon selected works of fiction
        (19 novels) published between 1950 and 1970 dealing
        with women's isolation and loneliness. The research
        objective is to identify hypotheses to serve as
        sensitizing devices or to illuminate and illustrate
        findings of this study. The aged woman has three
        alternatives in "choice" of residence--living alone,
        living with surviving kin, or living in a nursing
        home. Disaffiliation in old age may be the continua-
        tion of a lifelong pattern; more often, it follows

bereavement or forced retirement. It is enhanced by
loss of physical health. Women's reactions to disaffiliation vary, but all present a bleak and gloomy
picture--living in the past; resistance to change;
search for a substitute, human or animal; fantasy;
a return to religion; superficial social involvement;
clinging to status; an urgent need for communication;
preoccupation with the affairs of others; self-pity;
unrealistic fears.

367. Cather, Willa. Preface. In *The Best Stories of Sarah
Orne Jewett*, The Mayflower Edition, pp. ix-xix,
Sarah Orne Jewett. Gloucester, Massachusetts: Peter
Smith, 1965. In her appreciation of Jewett's work,
the very best of which she has tried to gather here,
Cather observes that her stories "have much to do
with fisher-folk and seaside villages; with juniper
pastures and lonely farms, neat gray country houses
and delightful, well-seasoned old men and women."
She recalls that an English actor said that he had
supposed Americans kill the aged in some merciful
fashion, until he had made a motor trip through New
England, because he did not see any old people in
the cities where he performed. Jewett once told
Cather "that her head was full of dear old houses and
dear old women, and that when an old house and an old
woman came together in her brain with a click, she
knew that a story was under way."

368. Gardiner, Judith Kegan. "A Wake for Mother: The Maternal
Deathbed in Women's Fiction." *Feminist Studies*
(June 1978) 4(2):146-65. Gardiner analyzes five
women's novels currently popular with Women's Studies
courses which have remarkably similar maternal
deathbed scenes that dramatize the central struggle
on the part of the heroine for identity--Agnes Smedley's *Daughter of Earth*, 1927; Jean Rhys's *After
Leaving Mr. Mackenzie*, 1931; Margaret Drabble's
Jerusalem the Golden, 1967; Marge Piercy's *Small
Changes*, 1972; and Lisa Alther's *Kinflicks*, 1975
(see No. 491 of this Bibliography). She then discusses Tillie Olsen's story "Tell Me a Riddle," 1960,
which "transforms the generational conflict by
expanding it." (See No. 692 of this Bibliography.)
Here, the death of the older woman heals and transcends
the polarities described in the five novels because
the older woman is a grandmother and the narrative
point of view allows us to see both older and younger
women as persons--i.e., as heroines.

369. Goodman, Charlotte. "Despair in Elderly Women:
      Katherine Anne Porter's 'The Jilting of Granny
      Weatherall' and Tillie Olsen's 'Tell Me a Riddle.'"
      Paper presented at MLA Special Session-Perspectives
      on Aging, New York, December 1978. Goodman stated
      that Beauvoir's observation that few works explore
      women's experience of aging was borne out by her
      search for literary works dealing with elderly
      female characters for a humanities course on the
      stages of life. Porter's and Olsen's stories (see
      Nos. 692 and 697 of this Bibliography) read in
      conjunction with Mann's "Death in Venice" and
      Tolstoi's "The Death of Ivan Ilych" provided her
      students with insights into the differing experience
      of aging males and females in a patriarchal society.
      Using Erikson's conceptual framework, she stated that
      the final moments of Porter's Granny and Olsen's Eva
      are marked by despair rather than by ego integrity.
      In her view, these two women, wives and mothers, put
      their families first and spent their lives in
      service to others. She found that both stories
      celebrate the self-abnegating dedication of these
      women to their families and are probing examinations
      of personal anguish. Whereas Mann's and Tolstoi's
      male protagonists regret their own past actions and
      choices, Granny and Eva regret the ways males acted
      towards them and determined the course of their lives.

370. Hamblen, Abigail Ann. *Ruth Suckow*. Boise State University
      Western Writers Series, No. 34. Boise: Boise State
      University, 1978. A literary biography of Ruth
      Suckow (1892-1960), daughter of a clergyman, who
      wrote in her *Memoir* of her childhood, her parents,
      and her intellectual and emotional coming of age.
      Suckow's fictions examine the problems of individual
      isolation (*The Bonney Family*), of passionate devotion
      ("Mrs. Vogel and Ollie") and of old age (in *The
      Folks*, "her masterpiece," where "she achieves a
      perfectly realized picture of Iowa," "The Uprooted,"
      "Wanderers," *Country People* and "The Resurrection,"
      a story that goes beyond old age to deal with
      death). Suckow's fiction is notable for its
      portrayals of women. Her viewpoint is "almost always
      feminine." She sees women as victims (*Cora*), yet
      she has created "portraits of women who are happy
      because they are content to live on the bright
      surface of life" ("Auntie Bissel," "Mid-Western
      Primitive"). Hamblen states that Suckow perceives

life as an ordeal, that she does not believe anyone
can escape suffering, and that every relationship,
no matter how beautiful and satisfying, has "its
inner core of discontent, of bitterness, and of
disappointment." A regional writer who has portrayed
Midwestern life and people, Suckow has gone beyond
this to give us universals (see Nos. 492, 611 and
704 of this Bibliography).

371. Hemenway, Robert. *Zora Neale Hurston: A Literary
      Biography*. Urbana: University of Illinois Press,
      1977. Hurston, an artist--novelist, dramatist and
      essayist--and social scientist--folklorist and
      anthropologist--was the author of four novels, two
      books of folklore, one of which, *Mules and Men*, was
      "the first popular book about Afro-American folklore
      ever written by a black scholar," an autobiography,
      and over 50 short stories and essays. Born in
      Eatonville, Florida, a self-governing, all-black
      town, she was the daughter of Reverend John Hurston,
      Mayor of Eatonville for three terms and codifier of
      its laws, and "special child" of her mother, Lucy,
      whose death when Hurston may have been only nine
      was traumatic. In Eatonville, the child listened
      to the "lying sessions" on the front porch of Joe
      Clarke's general store; her initial contribution to
      the Harlem Renaissance, "Drenched in Light," was
      the story of her experience in Eatonville, to which
      she returned in 1927 to see again through the "spy
      glass" of Anthropology. Hurston collected folklore
      in the American South and conjure lore through
      participation in hoodoo rites in New Orleans; in
      1936, she went to Jamaica, and afterwards to Haiti,
      where in seven weeks she wrote *Their Eyes Were
      Watching God* (see No. 476 of this Bibliography). A
      participant in the Federal Writers' Project for the
      state of Florida, she wrote *Moses, Man of the Mountain*.
      She went to Honduras in 1947, where she began writing
      Seraph on the Suwanee (see No. 475 of this Bibliography).
      In her last years, Hurston lived in Florida with
      "toughness of spirit," despite being often ill and
      alone and without money. Like Janie Crawford in
      Their Eyes Were Watching God, she married in 1939 a
      man much younger than herself. This second marriage
      failed; the age difference, "a positive force for
      Janie and Tea Cake, ... divided Albert and Zora."
      Hurston was deceptive about her birth date throughout
      her life; she "always thought of herself as a young
      woman." Foreword by Alice Walker; Appendix of a
      Checklist of Hurston's writings.

372.   Howard, Maureen, ed. *Seven American Women Writers of
       the Twentieth Century: An Introduction*. Minneapolis:
       University of Minnesota Press, 1977. The seven essays
       in this book, first published separately in the series
       of University of Minnesota Pamphlets on American
       Writers, include Louis Auchincloss on Ellen Glasgow,
       Dorothy Van Ghent on Willa Cather, Ray B. West, Jr.
       on Katherine Anne Porter, J.A. Bryant, Jr. on
       Eudora Welty, Irvin Stock on Mary McCarthy, Lawrence
       Graver on Carson McCullers and Stanley Edgar Hyman
       on Flannery O'Connor. Howard contributes an Intro-
       duction and an Editor's Note on Edith Wharton and
       Gertrude Stein. In her Introduction, she discusses
       the fiction by these writers, paying particular
       attention to their creation of female characters,
       and points to the desire for a real identity "in
       these self-portraits or fragments of the self turned
       into character."

373.   Kates, George N. "Willa Cather's Unfinished Avignon
       Story." In *Five Stories*, pp. 175-214, Willa Cather.
       New York: Vintage Books, 1956. Cather directed that
       her manuscript *Hard Punishments*, a story set in
       medieval Avignon, be destroyed after her death;
       Edith Lewis provides a brief account of it from
       memory, although reluctantly, "for it is like the
       story of an opera without the music." Kates quotes
       Lewis's account, and writes that in this *nouvelle*,
       Cather wanted to deal with youth again; the longer
       novels had to do with the end of life and the gloom
       and decline of old age. Cather had written in
       "Before Breakfast" that "Plucky youth is more bracing
       than enduring age." In Kates's judgment, Cather,
       who had turned away from America and had become
       almost a recluse, and who had worked for over seven
       years on her Avignon story while "facing the
       adamant combination of old age, illness, and the
       slow approach of death," worked with material in her
       last years that presented the same problems with
       which her earliest characters had been absorbed.

374.   Klein, Marcus. Introduction. In *My Mortal Enemy*, pp.
       v-xxii, Willa Cather. New York: Vintage Books, 1926,
       1954. In form, *My Mortal Enemy* is "the most severe
       and in its implications the most furious of Willa
       Cather's novels" (see No. 459 of this Bibliography).
       Cather wrote in her essay on Mansfield's fiction that
       "human relationships are the tragic necessity of

human life ... they can never be wholly satisfactory,
... every ego is half the time greedily seeking them,
and half the time pulling away from them." Klein
writes that the secret history of all Cather's
novels is the struggle to get beyond the necessity
of human relationships, that in every novel after
My Antonia, the enemy, successively, is a more intimate
part of the hero, and that in *My Mortal Enemy*, "it
is friendship and love, human relationship itself."

375. Lawrence, Margaret. *The School of Femininity: A Book
      For and About Women As They Are Interpreted Through
      Feminine Writers of Yesterday and Today*. New York:
      Frederick A. Stokes Co., 1936. Strong literary and
      social criticism of (Part I), The 19th Century School
      of Femininity and (Part II), The 20th Century School
      of Femininity. Lawrence's book is neither "an all-
      inclusive resumé of women's writing, nor an academic
      study of finest writing" but "a pattern of thought,
      vaguely resembling a theory...." Selection was made
      only on the basis of the appearance of the feminist
      pattern in these women's works. Among the 20th-
      century American writers are Anita Loos and Dorothy
      Parker (Little Girl Pals), Edna Ferber and Fannie
      Hurst (Go-Getters), Dorothy Canfield, Evelyn Scott
      and Ruth Suckow (Matriarchs), Edith Wharton and Kay
      Boyle (Helpmeets), Ellen Glasgow (Sophisticated
      Ladies), Pearl Buck (Priestesses), and Willa
      Cather (*Artistes*).

376. Lewis, R.W.B. *Edith Wharton: A Biography*. New York:
      Harper and Row, 1975. Older women in Wharton's life
      were drawn into her fictions--her "formidable,
      benevolent" Aunt Mary (Mrs. Mason Jones) who was
      "one of the great ladies of the still older New
      York, and a magnificent wreck of a survival in
      Edith's youth," was the model for Mrs. Manson
      Mingott, and Wharton's own mother, in middle age,
      for Mrs. Welland, in *The Age of Innocence*. Wharton,
      who in "The Fullness of Life" wrote of a woman's
      nature as resembling a great house full of rooms,
      where "in the innermost room" the soul "sits alone
      and waits for a footstep that never comes," said
      she excessively hated to be 40. She believed the
      denial of life to be the true "unpardonable sin."
      After her divorce, and when the First World War was
      over, she turned to the theme of the relationships
      between the generations. Like many older people, she

could recall very clearly the events of her early
life, but her memory was less dependable in recalling
the later periods. In her late 60s, she took a
genuine interest in the Church of Rome. Lewis states
that in this decade she attained full human maturity
of a rather rare kind. She "entered into a new mood
of sensuality" in her early 70s, and in her last
years, she "moved gradually into a new state of
being." At the last, Wharton "had arrived at a
deep harmony with her own life history" and could
calmly confront the whole truth about herself.

377.   Lewis, R.W.B. Introduction. In *The Age of Innocence*,
        pp. v-xiv, Edith Wharton. New York: Charles Scribner's
        Sons, 1968. Lewis suggests that in this novel, the
        58-year-old Wharton can be seen looking back upon
        herself when she was in her early 20s, reconsidering
        a part of herself in the character of Newland Archer,
        and imagining what her life might have become if,
        like Newland, she had "accepted defeat at the hands
        of the implacable 'tribe.'"

378.   McClure, Charlotte S. *Gertrude Atherton*. Boise State
        University Western Writers Series, No. 23. Boise:
        Boise State University, 1976. Atherton, more of an
        observer than an analyst, created a story-chronicle
        of old Spanish and new American California throughout
        her 60-year-long career. "Eighteen of her thirty-
        four novels, three of her four collections of short
        stories, and all three of her histories drew their
        inspiration from California." Her California was
        a "fool's paradise" and her favorite character "lacked
        self-knowledge and depended upon the illusions of
        society to determine her fate." Atherton left
        California in 1888, and moved between New York and
        Europe and New York and California until 1931. She
        took the Viennese (Steinach) rejuvenation treatment,
        and her novel *Black Oxen* (1923), which became the
        best seller of the year, was about the rejuvenation
        of an older woman (see No. 452 of this Bibliography).
        In the 1930s, when she was in her 70s, she returned
        to California to live. In the 1940s, she was named
        first among California's most distinguished women,
        and she became the first living author to contribute
        manuscripts and memorabilia to the Library of Congress
        (1943). In the character of Helena Belmont of *A
        Whirl Asunder*, and in an essay in *Yale Review* (April
        1913), Atherton wrote of the "intermediate sex" who

would be a "woman of tomorrow." In essays in
Harper's Bazaar (January 1926), she stated that those
men and women who developed common interests before
they were married would have a better and a more
lasting union "and a better chance for a fulfilling
independence of purpose for women after the children
were grown." In *The House of Lee*, she recounted the
lives of three generations of Southern women as they
adapted to the changing times, structuring her story
on her idea of "Time's cycles" and the metamorphosis
from a life purpose formed on the basis of inherited
family position to one formed on the basis of financial and emotional self-reliance for women.

379. Moers, Ellen. *Literary Women: The Great Writers*. Garden
City, New York: Anchor Press/Doubleday, 1977. Over
70 20th-century American women are listed in the
Notes, with birth and death dates, the genre for
which it is thought that the literary name of each
will be remembered, a selected listing of literary
works, and secondary sources. Some are also cited
in the text.

380. Patraka, Vivian M., Recorder. "Literature and Myths."
In *No Longer Young: The Older Woman in America, Work
Group Reports*, pp. 39-42. Ann Arbor, Michigan: The
Institute of Gerontology, The University of Michigan-
Wayne State University, 1974. The few older women
in 19th-century British fiction can be divided into
three categories--the witch, who is almost wholly
evil, and the petulant, irritating older woman; the
"good mothers"; and the spinsters. Eliot's Mrs.
Transom in *Felix Holt, the Radical* is an exceptionally
sympathetic portrayal of an older woman from an
interior point of view. Older people became more
numerous in 19th-century America; hence the realities
of the aged became more apparent. With the rise of
the urban proletariat, there was a shift in fiction
to the realistic novel. But 19th-century fiction
was dominated by men. Jewett, in *The Country of
the Pointed Firs*, is an example of a 19th-century
woman writer who treated older women quite successfully. Western literature has a long tradition of
treating older women negatively, or neglecting them.
In contrast, the Chinese tradition of honor combined
with the concept of societal roles as ends in themselves has created more positive, albeit generalized,
portraits of older women. Western culture emphasizes

the individual's active fulfillment of destiny and contributing to the creation of the new. In a male-dominated culture, older women are seen as inferior and prevented from doing what is thought to be significant. Thus they were never conceived of as major characters in the literature unless they were excessively evil, and they were not suitable characters for novels that emphasized action and had external points of view. 20th-century literature tends to concentrate on an interior point of view, and therefore older women characters have become more numerous. Also, literature is no longer written almost exclusively by white males. It is to be hoped that the new concern with aging will ultimately express itself in literary works that honestly confront the experience of growing old.

381.   Sohngen, Mary. "The Selfhood of Aging Women in the Contemporary Novel." Paper presented at MLA Session on Women: Aging and Death in Literature, Chicago, December 1977. Fictional representations of old women in fairy tales and on television and in films evince negative images and subject us to sexism and ageism. These are external views. In *written* fiction, the writer can adopt a narrative point of view that makes the reader a participant, rather than a spectator. Many studies in Gerontology indicate that the self-image of old people differs markedly from the image society has, and even from the image of the trained observer. Except for pathological cases, the self-image of the old person is more positive than the external view. The narrative point of view is crucial in discussing old women as they are portrayed in literature. Of her briefly annotated bibliography of novels published since 1950, Sohngen selects two--Margaret Laurence's *The Stone Angel* and Lael Wertenbaker's *Perilous Voyage*--to show how novels written from the point of view of the aged protagonist are positive affirmations of extreme old age. "We can know different old women and can gain insight into many different life experiences and responses to life through fictional representations."

382.   Sohngen, Mary. "The Writer as an Old Woman." *The Gerontologist* (December 1975) 15(6):493-8. An "unabashedly statistical" paper about the current works of 19 British and American women writers born before 1910. Sohngen found only four examples

available of novels by contemporary older women who
present a developed protagonist who is herself an
older woman--Margaret Culkin Banning's *The Will of
Magda Townsend*, Daphne du Maurier's *Rule Britannia*,
Margery Sharp's *The Innocents*--all three are light,
entertaining novels--and Ellen Douglas's *The Apostles
of Light*, which "stands alone in its seriousness, its
artistry, and its significance for the relationship
between literature and gerontology" (see Nos. 453
and 461 of this Bibliography). In general, these 19
living authors presented here, who have in common
both age and activity, started late--the median age
for first publication is 31--and experienced success
late. These women have written in their lives the
recipe for successful aging: interest in the world
around, flexibility in facing daily reality, and
continued active work.

383. Spacks, Patricia Meyer. *The Female Imagination*. New
York: Alfred A. Knopf, Inc., 1975. An examination
of the nature and uses of women's creativity from
many different points of view--autobiographical,
fictional and theoretical--in Anglo-American
literature of the past three centuries. Explicitly
antihistorical, the work is organized around certain
recurrent problems emerging from the texts, and
includes observations made by students that were
tape-recorded during class meetings of the colloquium
"Women Writers and Woman's Problems." In this
exploration of the continuities of the special point
of view of women and of the patterns in the stories
they tell, Spacks discusses the autobiographical and
fictional works of a number of 20th-century American
women writers--Margaret Anderson, Kate Chopin,
Isadora Duncan, Charlotte Perkins Gilman, Ellen
Glasgow, Lillian Hellman, Mabel Dodge Luhan, Betty
MacDonald, Mary MacLane, Mary McCarthy, Kate Millett,
Anaïs Nin, Sylvia Plath, Gertrude Stein, Eudora
Welty and Edith Wharton.

384. Washbourn, Penelope, ed. *Seasons of Woman: Song, Poetry,
Ritual, Prayer, Myth, Story*. San Francisco: Harper
and Row, 1979. Chapter 8, The Changing Seasons,
includes poetry by Adrienne Rich, Charlotte Brontë,
Dorothy Livesay, Mary Oliver, Tu Fu, Homer, Irene
Claremont de Castillejo, Muriel Rukeyser, and Anne
Finch; and A traditional Chinese lady's reflections;
An Indian folksong; the unhappy relationships of

woman; The words of an old woman of New Mexico; A
lamentation for her dead relatives, sung by the
weaver in the Osage tribe of American Indians;
Colette's memories of her mother; An Apache com-
memoration of middle age and old age; Folksongs of
India; An old woman's song, from the Caribou Eskimos;
Song of the Old Woman, From the Netsilik Eskimos;
"An old woman remembers"; "The Mountain Spirits and
the Old Woman," a myth of the Chiricahua Indians;
The song of a woman abandoned by the tribe because
she is too old to keep up with their migration, from
the southern Shoshone Indians; "The Origin of Death,"
a folk tale of the Salishan and Sahaptin tribes of
the American Indians; and The lament of the dying
mother of a Maori chief.

385. Welty, Eudora. "Is Phoenix Jackson's Grandson Really
      Dead?" In *The Eye of the Story: Selected Essays
      and Reviews*, pp. 159-62, Eudora Welty. New York:
      Random House, 1978. The question in the title of this
      essay refers to Welty's story "A Worn Path" (see No.
      709 of this Bibliography), which is told through
      Phoenix's mind as she goes on her errand. The
      journey, the carrying out of the errand of love,
      is the story, and whether or not her grandson is
      dead cannot affect this in any way. Welty writes
      that her best answer to this question is that "*Phoenix*
      is alive," that one day she saw a solitary old woman
      like Phoenix and she made up an errand for her
      journey. The "deep-grained habit of love" is the
      subject of the story, in which what Welty hoped would
      come through is that the worn path is the only
      certain thing there is.

386. Wolff, Cynthia Griffin. "Edith Wharton and the
      'Visionary' Imagination." *Frontiers* (Fall 1977)
      II(3):24-30. For many years, the "strange region"
      of Wharton's fictional worlds was too dangerous for
      her to explore for any protracted time period: she
      "did not have the stamina to write a full length
      novel until she was forty." Her full maturity both
      as a novelist and a woman is revealed by a greater
      trust and confidence in the visionary capacity.
      Wolff writes that Edith Wharton was more heroic than
      were any of her characters, in that she "confronted
      all that was potentially destructive in her own
      nature and transformed it into strength."

387. Wolff, Cynthia Griffin. *A Feast of Words: The Triumph
      of Edith Wharton*. New York: Oxford University Press,
      Inc., 1977. Wolff draws upon Erik Erikson's insights
      in her critical study. Edith Wharton, whose literary
      talents were discouraged in adolescence and who was
      deeply ambivalent about writing, "started late." She
      did not publish a novel until she was almost 40, and
      thus might have had both a family and a literary
      life. She was 45 when she first experienced sexual
      intimacy; the affair was symbolized by the witch
      hazel, the "old woman's flower," exchanged between
      her and her lover. In "Diptych--Youth and Age,"
      Wolff observes a shift in Wharton's later fictions
      to the subject of families--parents and children,
      and youth and age--in which Wharton's imaginative
      sympathies are shown, for the most part, for the
      older generation. Wharton saw incest from the per-
      spective of the parent, not the child. The exclusion
      and estrangement that are the sorrows of old age
      "gave rise to the theme of the would-be parent" in
      the later fictions. The passage of time is the
      structure of *The Mother's Recompense* (see No. 495
      of this Bibliography); *The Children*, the "saddest
      novel" she ever wrote, is a story "of the chance
      encounter between age and youth." The death of
      Walter Berry, her closest friend, occurred while
      Wharton was writing *The Children*, and affected the
      ending, which she changed from that planned in her
      original outline. Wharton's "ineradicable sorrow
      was that she discovered and accepted her time only
      after it had passed her by." She called her fictions
      her children; she affirmed the value of the family,
      yet, childless, she had no family of her own. Her
      last challenge was to find a way to confront the
      losses of her life. She was most plagued by old age
      because she still felt eager for life and new
      experience. But it was a season with its own
      distinctive pleasures, and in her last years she
      was more at peace than she had ever been.

388. Woodward, Kathleen. "Aging and Disengagement: May
      Sarton's *As We Are Now* and *Journal of a Solitude*."
      Paper presented at MLA Session on Women: Aging and
      Death in Literature, Chicago, December 1977.
      Woodward stated that although sociological theories
      of aging and works of the literary imagination are
      incommensurable, they do have common ground: the
      tension between them could clarify and illuminate

new questions. She discussed *As We Are Now* and
the *Journal* in the light of the activity and disengagement theories of aging (see Nos. 484 and 600
of this Bibliography). Both Sarton's books were
published in 1973, and up to then, aging gracefully
had been a persistent, even obsessive theme in her
work. Woodward showed how Sarton's feminist theory
of art corresponds to her conception of aging and
the life cycle. In her analysis of the novel and the
Journal, she found these two books mirror one another
in important ways, and that the novel is the
(Jungian) shadow of the *Journal*. She concluded
that in Sarton's view, it is the *activity* theory
which could lead to the oppression and fragmentation
of the human soul. She found that Sarton offers a
model for successful aging, the Jungian theory of
the development of the psyche, which appears at
this time in history in conjunction with a theory
of feminist disengagement. Woodward suggested that
it may be that sensitive women, who live closer to
the cycles of life, age with more grace and vigor
than do men, who typically devote themselves to
the public sphere.

389.   Woodward, Kathleen. "May Sarton and Fictions of Old
       Age." In *Gender and Literary Voice*, pp. 108-27,
       Janet Todd, ed. New York: Holmes and Meier Publishers,
       Inc., 1980. Woodward observes that May Sarton's
       portrayal of old age "is a welcome departure from
       the Western literary tradition of gerontophobia"
       and that a developmental theory of age, time and
       work is implicit in Sarton's point of view. Sarton,
       whose theory of aging is primarily Jungian, believes
       that old age offers the possibility of special
       growth, that the threshold of old age is marked
       by the passage from eros to agape, and that the
       last phase of life is ideally devoted to the composing
       of the self. Woodward's paper discusses the ideal
       of graceful aging as it appears in Sarton's work
       prior to 1973, focusing on *Kinds of Love* and *Plant
       Dreaming Deep*--in which it is seen that Sarton's
       view is essentially romantic; relates this ideal
       to the writer's theory of art, which is feminist;
       and shows how in *Journal of a Solitude* and *As
       We Are Now*, Sarton's depiction of aging and the
       single woman becomes more complex, and her ideal
       of graceful aging "yields to guerilla warfare" (see
       Nos. 484, 486, 600 and 601 of this Bibliography).

See also: 68, 79, 80, 81, 82, 84, 85, 86, 87, 90, 91, 93, 245, 452, 453, 459, 461, 475, 476, 484, 485, 486, 487, 488, 489, 491, 492, 495, 496, 497, 548, 600, 601, 611, 692, 697, 704, 709, 861, 885.

IX. MIDDLE AGE

A. General

*390. Artson, Barbara Friedman. "Mid-Life Women: Homemakers, Volunteers, Professionals." Diss., School of Professional Psychology, University of California at Berkeley, 1978.

*391. Bardwick, Judith M. "Middle Age and a Sense of the Future." Paper presented at American Sociological Association, San Francisco, California, 1975.

392. Barnett, Rosalind C., and Grace K. Baruch. "Women in the Middle Years: A Critique of Research and Theory." *Psychology of Women Quarterly* (Winter 1978) 3(2):187-97. Little is known about the middle years, and the need for this knowledge is especially urgent in the case of women, for whom social changes have made much previous research and theory obsolete. There is conflicting evidence on the life satisfaction of adult women. Erikson's and Levinson's theoretical models are concerned with male experience. Chrono-logical age cannot be a central variable in view of the reality and diversity of women's lives. The concept of stage is not used with sufficient rigor. Empirical studies have many limitations and biases, among them the assumption of biological determinism of feminine behavior. Although 90% of women work for pay at some time in their lives, paid employment has not been seen as central to women's lives. When working women are included in studies, distinctions in terms of level of occupation and commitment are rarely made. Two potentially useful conceptual areas for future theory are: locus of control and attributions; support systems and social networks.

393.   Bart. Pauline B.   "Depression in Middle-Aged Women."
       In *Woman in Sexist Society: Studies in Power and
       Powerlessness*, pp. 163-86, Vivian Gornick and Barbara
       K. Moran, eds. New York: Basic Books, Inc., 1971.
       A study of how, given the traditional female role,
       the actions of her children can result in a mother's
       neurosis or psychosis. Mrs. Gold's case is typical
       of the pre-illness personality of involutional
       depressives: she shows a history of martyrdom with
       no rewards for her sacrifices; inability to cope
       with aggressive feelings; rigidity; a need to be
       useful so as to feel worthwhile; obsessive, compulsive
       supermother and superhousewife behavior; and generally
       conventional attitudes. There are few clear norms
       guiding the relationship of a mother to her grown
       children in our society, and no rites of passage
       for menopause. Depressed women are over-committed
       to the maternal role; Jewish women had the highest
       rate of depression. Bart found that depressed middle-
       aged women view as important just the roles that
       are contracted as women grow older, and do not
       consider as important the roles that could be ex-
       panded at middle age. She sees these women as
       casualties of our culture, and recommends ways
       the women's liberation movement can aid in the
       development of personhood for both women and men.

*394.   Bart, Pauline B.   "Depression in Middle-Aged Women:
       Some Sociocultural Factors." Diss., Department of
       Sociology, University of California at Los Angeles,
       1967.

395.   Bart, Pauline.   "The Loneliness of the Long-Distance
       Mother." In *Women: A Feminist Perspective*, pp.
       156-70, Jo Freeman, ed. Palo Alto, California:
       Mayfield Publishing Co., 1975. A cross-cultural
       survey indicates that middle age is not usually
       considered to be an especially stressful period for
       women, but in most cultures a major buffer against
       problems of mid-life women is the kinship group.
       The case study of Sara, "the martyr mother," who
       is typical in many ways of the 20 middle-aged women
       Bart interviewed in mental hospitals, exemplifies
       the depression of women who were over-involved in
       motherhood when the maternal role is lost. Bart's
       findings are that women who play the traditional
       feminine role are most vulnerable to depression
       when their children leave home. She recommends that

society be changed--that the entire system of sex
roles be altered so that women can remain in the
labor force after childbearing if they choose to
do so.

396. Bart, Pauline B. "Why Women's Status Changes in Middle
Age: The Turns of the Social Ferris Wheel." *Sociological Symposium* (Fall 1969) 3:1-18. Status changes
throughout the life cycle. Bart reports findings
from information about six post-child-rearing roles
open to women (grandmother; mother or mother-in-law;
economic producer; participant in government;
performer of religious or magical rites; daughter
of aged parents) in 30 societies representative of
the eight culture areas of the world, selected from
the Human Relations Area Files. In addition, six
selected societies were studied directly from the
ethnographic material. She found that in every
respect, with the exception of the mother-child bond
which is strong but not reciprocal in our society,
our own culture has the characteristics of those in
which the woman's status declines at middle age.
Rather than a return to an extended family system,
Bart recommends that occupations with intrinsic
satisfaction be open on a non-discriminatory basis
to women at middle age, in order that significant
roles be available for them.

397. Benedek, Theresa. *Psychosexual Functions in Women*
(Volume II of Studies in Psychosomatic Medicine).
New York: The Ronald Press Co., 1952. Chapter 13
(pp. 352-72) of this collection of studies in female
sexuality, based on psychoanalytic investigation and
conducted in conjunction with physiologic observation,
is entitled "Climacterium: A Developmental Phase."
Here, Benedek points out that in many cultures,
women about to lose their propagative powers and
sexual attractiveness enjoy enhanced power and
prestige, and she states that much of the exaggerated
fear of menopause seems to be culturally determined.
She also states that the lack of understanding of
the physiology and psychology of the sexual cycle
accounts for much of the confusion about the
climacterium. She believes that motherhood plays
an important role in women's development, and that
the personality will be sustained during "change of
life" by the accomplishments of the reproductive
period, which means not only propagation but also

the total developmental achievement of the personality.
The climacterium is described as a period of intrapersonal reorganization in women. In comparing it
with the oedipal phase, Benedek states that the
cessation of biological growth affects further
intrapersonal integration--a transmutation of growth
--and it releases new impetus for both socialization
and learning.

398. Bergquist, Laura. "Recycling Lives." *Ms.* (August 1973)
      II(2):58-61, 105. The author, who has been talking
      with women from their late 20s through their 50s who
      feel it is time to change their lives "after umpteen
      years as somebody's wife and/or mother," discusses
      women's lack of confidence in their ability, and
      their need for peer support in coping with "that
      common saboteur, Guilt," quotes from women's
      experiences in re-entry to the labor force, and
      states that it is frightening for women in midlife
      to "make a move" because, having lived traditional
      roles, they find "the old rules have changed."

*399. Boedecker, Anne Louise. "Women's Life Patterns, Role
       Involvements, and Satisfaction at Mid-Life." Diss.,
       Pennsylvania State University, 1978.

400. Clay, Vidal S. *Women: Menopause and Middle Age.*
      Pittsburgh: Know, Inc., 1977. Chapters: Introduction
      to the Problem of Menopause (menopause is defined
      as a normal developmental phase in the life of a
      woman; a woman's feelings about it reflect society's
      notions about women growing older; the climacteric
      is only one of many other changes a woman faces at
      this time in her life); The Physical Side (changes
      are the end of menstruation, but not the end of
      estrogen; the change in hormonal balance can lead
      to distressing effects in some women; the only two
      physical effects directly attributable to menopause
      are hot flashes and sweats, and genital atrophy);
      The Social Side (lesbian women and middle age, the
      postparental phase, the socialization of women, the
      attitude of the medical profession, and ageism in
      America); The Psychological Side (feelings about the
      changes of middle age, menopause and sexuality, the
      end of mothering, facing middle age, facing old age
      and changing social roles--responsibility for aging
      parents, becoming widowed or divorced, making friends
      with women, and facing your own death); Estrogen

Replacement Therapy; Menopause: Health or Disease?
Clay shows that hot flashes and vaginal atrophy are
the only *symptoms* of menopause that are helped by
ERT, and that menopause is not the trauma it is often
made out to be. Stating why it is difficult to
evaluate it, she presents the benefits vs. the
risks (medical opinions vary widely; the risks
are grave; a chart shows that the contra-indications
for taking ERT are similar to those for the birth
control pill), and presents medical and non-medical
therapies for the problems of menopause and aging,
together with the advantages and risks of each.
Clay writes that menopause is not a disease, but
an opportunity for growth. Appendices, on a pilot
study on menopause and on three pencil and paper
exercises--on drawing your own life-line, drawing
your personal sociogram, and analyzing the uses of
time to find possibilities for enjoyment and fulfillment. Bibliography.

401. Cohen, Dr. Stephen Z., and Bruce Michael Gans. *The
      Other Generation Gap: The Middle-aged and Their Aging
      Parents*. Chicago: Follett Publishing Co., 1978.
      Addressing their book to the "beleaguered, overlooked
      group" of middle-aged sons and daughters of elderly
      parents, Cohen and Gans draw from a wide range of
      sources to present fresh personal standards and
      approaches to the problems and inner conflicts they
      face in their relationship with the older generation.
      The topics of the physical, emotional and social
      needs of the elderly are discussed within the context
      of common reactions and misinterpretations of middle-
      aged children so as to enhance their understanding
      and assist them in their efforts to prolong their
      parents' independence, and to strike a balance
      between the aging parent's needs for care and
      attention and their own needs for living "with minimal
      guilt and maximum peace of mind." The seriousness
      of the physical and emotional changes experienced
      by middle-aged people are under-estimated in our
      culture, and although their aging parents' problems
      fall at their doorstep at the worst possible time,
      they must still take the initiative in meeting them
      --until such time as social programs and the public
      attitude in the U.S. become more accepting of and
      responsive to the elderly. Middle-aged children
      should prepare for their own old age as well as for
      their parents'. They should sort out and face up

to their complicated feelings about their parents so
they can prepare ahead of time for what the scope
of their involvement can comfortably be. Part Four,
The Waning of Independence, includes a discussion
of the problems of relocation and a nursing-home
checklist. "A Healthy Frame of Reference" lists
nine principles--a distillation of the overall
approach of this book--recommended as a guide in
relationships with elderly parents, and endorses
the concept of minimal intervention. The authors
state that a distinction should be maintained between
parental and filial duty. They believe the guidelines
presented here must inevitably be applied on a
national scale because of the growing numbers and
proportion of the elderly in the U.S.

402. Datan, Nancy, Aaron Antonovsky and Benjamin Maoz. *A
      Time to Reap: The Middle Age of Women in Five Israeli
      Subcultures*. Baltimore: The Johns Hopkins University
      Press, 1981. Comparative study of middle-aged women
      of five ethnic groups, in Israel; the groups are
      seen as points on a continuum ranging from tradi-
      tionalism to modernity. The "modern" are the Central
      Europeans, the "traditional" the Moslem Arab villagers;
      the "transitional" are the Turkish, Persian and North
      African. Born 1915-1924, these women were in their
      childbearing years during World War II and the Israel
      War of Independence, yet made different decisions
      about family size. Their life histories show the
      interaction between culture, the biological life
      cycle, and history. Each theme--the new freedoms
      of the modern women, the generational continuity
      of the traditional women, and the dislocations of
      the transitional women--is part of the experience
      of the transition to middle age, differently ex-
      pressed in various cultures, but potentially present
      in all. The most remarkable finding is that of the
      similarity of feelings among women from all five
      subcultures about menopause and the loss of fertility
      --menopause did not signify a "closing of the gates";
      it was welcomed by all, whether they had borne one
      or two children, or fifteen. This affirms a natural
      rhythm in the life cycle, and thus the wisdom of
      the passage in Ecclesiastes. Phases are: a pilot
      study, a broad-scale (interview) survey, medical
      examinations, and follow-up psychiatric interviews.
      The major finding is that this phase of the life
      cycle, like all others, is marked not by loss or

liberation but by *transition*. Other findings:
involutional depression is an extremely infrequent
response in any culture; the balance of joy and
sorrow was most positive for Central Europeans and
Arabs, the most modern and most traditional women
in the study; there is no evidence that provision
for equal rights threatens family stability or that
the experience of having abortions in an accepting
culture leaves emotional scars; the process of
transition is costly and painful. Cultural differences
converge around a common theme--the liberation of
women from the constraints of traditional roles. It
is an error to equate tradition with passivity--the
traditional woman has a pivotal position in the
household economy. Transition brings change, and
with change comes the unknown. But in a larger
sense, all middle-aged women today are in transition.
A major contribution of the study is the material
provided for study of the effect of modernization
and changing sex roles on the lives of women.
Appendices on methods and findings. Bibliography.

403. Deutsch, Helene. "The Climacterium," Epilogue. In
The Psychology of Women, A Psychoanalytic Interpre-
tation, Volume II: Motherhood, pp. 456-87, Helene
Deutsch. New York: Grune and Stratton, 1945. One
aim of this book is the effort to understand the
nature of motherliness, not only in the direct
exercise of the reproductive function, but as a
principle that radiates into every field of life and
that is innate in women. This principle outlasts
the capacity of the generative organs. It is possible
for the motherly woman to richly repossess her children
if she has given them their freedom, and old age has
added a fourth phase to woman's life--grandmotherhood.
Deutsch describes good and bad grandmothers, and
writes that whatever course any woman's life has
taken, she believes as a grandmother that she has
fulfilled herself only if she has been rich in those
experiences that make up the essence of motherhood.
Mastering the psychological reactions to the organic
decline is one of the most difficult tasks of woman's
life. In the preclimacterial life period, woman is
engaged in the struggle for preservation of her
femininity. Many feel a strong urge to become
pregnant again, but those who had been completely
absorbed by the reproductive function turn to
creative activities that had been lost in the

conflicts of puberty. The urge to intellectual and
artistic creativity and the productivity of motherhood spring from common sources, and it seems natural
that one can replace the other. Deutsch describes
types of climacterial women, notes that woman's
relation to her own sex often undergoes change in
the climacterium, and discusses parallels between
puberty and the climacterium. She observes that
feminine-loving women have a milder climacterium
than masculine-aggressive ones, that feminine-
erotic women, experienced in love, accept the inevitable
with greater dignity and calm than spinsterish, frigid,
ever-frustrated women, and that women who are keen
observers of themselves say that in this phase of
life they experience a kind of depersonalization, a
split in which they feel both young and old. She
concludes with the hope that woman will become man's
social equal, and states the experiences presented
here show that the achievement of full social equality
will benefit her and all humanity only if at the
same time woman achieves ample opportunity to develop
her femininity and motherliness.

404.   Eckstein, Alice Raphael. "The Problem of the Woman of
       Forty." *Psychoanalytic Review* (January 1933)
       XX(1):19-37. Eckstein begins her paper by quoting
       from *The White Peacock* by D.H. Lawrence a passage
       about the abnegation of self being a woman's resource
       for escaping the responsibilities for her own
       development. Remarking that every end is also a
       beginning, she states that with the approach of the
       40th year a conflict breaks out between the biological
       libido, which is nearing completion, and that part
       of the libido invested in cultural tasks, which is
       involved with the responsibility for individuation.
       She presents the case of a woman nearing 40 who has
       been neither physically nor economically favorably
       endowed, and states that although circumstances may
       favor a fortunate woman in the first half of life,
       the problem of individuation is exactly the same for
       each person--privileged or not, female or male--in
       approaching the task of the second half of life and
       becoming responsible for the good progress of her or
       his life. This is the task not of women or men,
       but of the *individuated being*. The case is of a
       woman, not privileged in any way, who keeps house
       for her widowed father and motherless siblings,
       and who became depressed in her late 30s. Responsive

to therapy with Eckstein, the patient was able to
undertake the process of individuation. Eckstein
concludes with the close of the Helena episode in
Faust, Part II, observing that Panthalis "voices
what so many women discover to their sorrow, that
unless a step is taken towards the goal of individuation nothing is created to sustain them during
the second half of life...."

405. Fuchs, Estelle. *The Second Season: Life, Love and Sex
      --Women in the Middle Years*. Garden City, New York:
      Doubleday Anchor Press, 1977. As a woman, and as a
      professional anthropologist and educator, Fuchs
      became convinced of the need for this study because
      so little is known about menopause, and because the
      highly variable social roles played by mature women
      in various cultures and periods of time contrast
      sharply with the constricted view of female middle
      age prevalent in the U.S. In "Middle Age--Where
      It's At," she discusses the relativity of views of
      age and sexual vigor, and states that for the modern
      woman, midlife can encompass a quarter of a century.
      In "Women and Sex--Here to Stay," she shows the
      cultural diversity of attitudes toward age and
      sexual attraction, presents evidence that the
      menopause in the healthy woman with opportunity
      for continuing sexual activity does not mean an
      end to female sexuality, and observes that it is
      only in our era that hundreds of millions of women
      can look forward to living one third of their lives
      beyond menopause, and thus that it is illogical to
      connect sex only with childbearing. Includes
      chapters on Men and the Middle Years; The Beauty
      Industry--Friend or Enemy?; A Social "Change of
      Life"; The Many Roles of Women--Motherhood: Mothers
      and Sons, Sons-in-law, Daughters, Daughters-in-law;
      Roles as Grandmother, Daughter, Wife and Housewife;
      Magic and Religious Roles (in many societies, these
      are not available to women until after menopause);
      Women in Government (in many traditional societies,
      women take on the role of governor at menopause);
      Menopause--When; Menopause--a Biological "Change of
      Life"--The Physiological Facts; Menopause--Is It
      Necessary?--The Search for Immortality and the
      Estrogen Controversy; Pregnancy and Babies; You
      Don't Go Crazy at Menopause; Middle Age and Health--
      Women are Mortal; Hysterectomy--The Chances Are You
      Won't Need One; Divorce and Widowhood--on Being Alone;

Growing Older Is in Style. Fuchs believes this
generation must consider what to do with this period
of life since their experiences will set the stage
for their daughters, that other societies have shown
there is nothing inevitable about demise with aging,
and that women ought to grasp the opportunity for
enriched contact with life through friendships,
activities and new social roles in midlife and after.
Includes an Appendix, "A Shopper's Guide to Surgery."

*406.   Goodman, Madeleine J., Cynthia J. Stewart and Fred
        Gilbert, Jr. "Patterns of Menopause: A Study of
        Certain Medical and Physiological Variables Among
        Caucasian and Japanese Women Living in Hawaii."
        Journal of Gerontology (May 1977) 32(3):291-8.

407.   Gorney, Sondra, and Claire Cox. *After Forty: How Women
        Can Achieve Fulfillment*. New York: The Dial Press,
        1973. A "guide to feminine fulfillment in the second
        forty years of life," focusing on middle age, with
        chapters on middle age and women's potential; the
        menopause; sexuality after 40; physical aging; marriage
        and family life; Women Alone: The Widowed, Divorced
        and Unmarried; work; retirement; and "The Best Is Yet
        to Come."

408.   Graber, Edward A., and Hugh R.K. Barber. "The Case For
        and Against Estrogen Therapy." In *The Older Woman:
        Lavender Rose or Gray Panther*, pp. 99-108, Marie
        Marschall Fuller and Cora Ann Martin, eds. Spring-
        field, Illinois: Charles C. Thomas, 1980. The authors
        make the important point that many women still have
        adequate endogenous estrogen for many years after the
        cessation of menstruation, and that routine replace-
        ment may do a little good at the risk of doing much
        harm. Topics discussed are arteriosclerosis, hyper-
        tension, osteoporosis, cancer, the usefulness of the
        vaginal smear in following the therapeutic response
        to estrogens, psychiatric disorders, and "When Do
        Estrogens Help?" The authors state they are not
        opposed to the use of estrogen, that it is an excellent
        drug to be used on indication, but that some of the
        indications for which it is generally advocated are,
        in the opinion of many competent gynecologists,
        borderline. They conclude that what is needed to
        address the question of postmenopausal estrogen
        therapy is "less passion, fewer theoretical hypotheses,
        and more facts."

*409.   Griffen, Joyce.   "A Cross-Cultural Investigation of
        Behavioral Changes at Menopause."   *The Social Science
        Journal* (April 1977) 14(2):49-55. Using data from the
        Human Relations Area Files on "Senescence," two linked
        hypotheses were explored--(1) anthropologists who
        have detailed rituals performed at menarche would
        also have recorded rituals at menopause, and (2)
        cultures lacking these ceremonies will in some other
        way indicate acceptable behavioral changes during and
        after menopause. No instances of rituals specifically
        for menopausal women were found, and changed behavior
        has been recorded for very few cultures: one type is
        withdrawal from previous social activities, and
        another is treating menopause as a disorder of one's
        social or supernatural world. In several cultures,
        greater freedom in behavior is permitted, especially
        in regard to participation in ceremonial life.

410.   Gross, Irma H., ed. *Potentialities of Women in the
        Middle Years*. East Lansing: Michigan State University
        Press, 1956. Papers presented at the conference
        convened by the School of Home Economics during the
        (1955) Centennial Year at Michigan State University.
        Section I is comprised of papers by Robert Havig-
        hurst on middle-aged women's changing roles, and
        reports of pertinent research in progress by Esther
        Lloyd-Jones, The Commission on the Education of
        Women of the American Council on Education, Pauline
        Park Wilson Knapp, Director of the Merrill-Palmer
        School, and Bernice L. Neugarten of the University
        Of Chicago. Havighurst claims there is evidence
        that after the age of 45 or 50, women surpass men
        in health and intellectual vigor. He contrasts
        women's roles in 1850 and 1950, and states that the
        middle years are potentially the best years of their
        lives for women who are able to use their freedom,
        and that the major task of middle age is emotional
        and intellectual expansion. Neugarten presents a
        report on the Kansas City Study of Adult Life, an
        analysis of responses to a TAT stimulus picture,
        and a discussion of the implications of the finding
        that middle-aged women see the older woman in the
        TAT picture in a positive light. Section II includes
        papers on physiological changes and adjustments by
        a physician and a nutritionist; papers focusing on
        psychological aspects of personal adjustment,
        interpersonal and social aspects of problems and
        opportunities in the maturation of women, and the

economic role of women aged 45 to 65. Section III
has papers on The Middle-Aged Woman in Contemporary
Society, Employment Opportunities in the Woman's
Service Exchange Program of Madison, Wisconsin, and
How Home Economics Can Contribute to Meeting These
Problems. Appendix: program, participants, discussion
leaders, discussion group reports.

411. Hendricks, Jon A. "Women and Leisure." In *Looking
      Ahead: A Woman's Guide to the Problems and Joys of
      Growing Older*, pp. 114-20, Lillian E. Troll, Joan
      Israel and Kenneth Israel, eds. Englewood Cliffs,
      New Jersey: Prentice-Hall, Inc., 1977. Due to the
      compression of the family life cycle, growing numbers
      of women are at the end of what they were taught was
      their life's work when they are just entering middle
      age. Very little is known about older women's life
      and leisure. The available evidence suggests a
      continuity of earlier patterns. In a study of time
      budgets in twelve countries, it was found that house-
      wives without outside jobs had the greatest amount of
      free time, employed men ranked second and employed
      married women last, although this pattern varies
      according to the day of the week. A marked similarity
      in the broad use of free time is evident from the
      data. It is significant that many forms of leisure
      occur simultaneously. Studies indicate that the
      feeling of *deprivation* of free time reaches a peak
      between ages 46 and 55 for women. Most women do
      not attribute emptiness to middle age. At this time
      in life, there is a change in the *locale* and *focus*
      of their leisure activities. Women with grown
      children become more involved in community-based
      leisure and "self-enriching" forms of leisure. There
      is a tendency to increase the time given to social-
      izing activities. Until middle age, men watch more
      TV than women, but during their late 40s and 50s,
      women spend more time watching TV than their male
      counterparts. During midlife, women also extend
      their involvement in hobbies, volunteer work and
      club activities. Women must redistribute work and
      leisure two decades before this is demanded of men,
      and their "retirement years" are twice as long as
      men's; without adequate preparation, they will not
      automatically become leisure years. Today's midlife
      women are an advance guard, whose leisure may portend
      what the future will hold.

412. Israel, Joan. "Confessions of a 45-Year-Old Feminist."
      In *Looking Ahead: A Woman's Guide to the Problems
      and Joys of Growing Older*, pp. 65-9, Lillian E.
      Troll, Joan Israel and Kenneth Israel, eds.
      Englewood Cliffs, New Jersey: Prentice-Hall, Inc.,
      1977. Until shortly after her 45th birthday, Israel
      had believed in "mind over matter" and also thought
      she would not mind growing older because she did not
      look her age. A feminist therapist, helping other
      women explore new facets of themselves so they would
      not depend upon youth and beauty for a positive
      self-image and security, she was upset to see
      sagging and wrinkling of the skin under her chin
      and neck, and wondered why she was distressed. She
      asked feminist friends and clients about their
      attitudes towards aging, and reports their and her
      own positive and negative feelings and concerns.
      She believes "rap groups" on aging are helpful.

*413. Kraines, Ruth J. "The Menopause and Evaluations of
      the Self: A Study of Middle-Aged Women." Diss.,
      University of Chicago, 1963.

414. LeShan, Eda J. *The Wonderful Crisis of Middle Age:
      Some Personal Reflections*. New York: David McKay
      Co., Inc., 1973. LeShan, who dedicates her book to
      Maslow, believes the challenges of middle age present
      an opportunity to become most truly alive and
      individual. Her central concern is the developmental
      task of middle age, and the ways one can move
      creatively and courageously into "middlescence,"
      to find a new balance and fill in what has been
      missing. Chapters: What's So Wonderful?, Caught in
      the Middle, The Feminine Mistake, The Oppression
      of Men--By Themselves, We Are a Generation of Re-
      markable Parents: So Why Are We Hurting?, Erich
      Segal Was a Coward (she believes the greatest
      challenge of the middle years has to do with love
      and marriage), The Heavy Burden of Our Masks, Can
      There Be a Renaissance in Our Middle Ages? (her
      answer is in the affirmative, and she suggests that,
      since each of us is alone, we ought to find pleasure
      in the "inner companion"), A Last Testament of Will,
      and Today Is the First Day of the Rest of Our Lives.
      In her view, many women who do find joy in the
      traditional tasks of womanhood need the encouragement
      and self-respect that will lead them to find new
      outlets for their talents in middle age, and LeShan

affirms the need for opportunities in jobs,
education and training for middle-aged people.

415. Livson, Florine B.   "Coming Out of the Closet: Marriage
       and Other Crises of Middle Age."   In *Looking Ahead:
       A Woman's Guide to the Problems and Joys of Growing
       Older*, pp. 81-92, Lillian E. Troll, Joan Israel and
       Kenneth Israel, eds.   Englewood Cliffs, New Jersey:
       Prentice-Hall, Inc., 1977.   Do Noel Coward's film
       Brief Encounter and Ingmar Bergman's film *Scenes
       from a Marriage* reflect a shift in the values of
       our society and in the institution of marriage since
       the end of World War Two?   Women who are divorced or
       widowed in later life may be confronted at that time
       with the same issues--developing independence and
       an identity apart from the family--confronting
       adolescents.   The middle years of marriage are often
       stressful.   Today's middle-aged women bear the brunt
       of the shift in social values, and the emergence of
       the new morality emphasizing individual achievement,
       which are a reversal of that to which they were
       socialized as young adults.   The "fit" between a
       woman's personality and her social roles may be the
       key factor influencing her experience of the transi-
       tional middle years.   Livson's study of middle-aged
       "traditionals" and "independents" (see No. 339 of
       this Bibliography) suggests that "women would do
       well to wear the roles that fit them."   Today's
       middle-aged woman has more alternatives available
       to her and more social pressure to change than the
       woman of an earlier generation; she is offered "a
       second chance."   The young women of the next generation
       may fare even better.

*416. Livson, Florine B.   "Evolution of Self: Patterns of
       Personality Development in Middle-Aged Women."
       Diss., The Wright Institute, Berkeley, California,
       1974.

*417. Mitteness, Linda S.   "The Social Definition of Bodily
       State Changes: The Menopause."   Diss., Pennsylvania
       State University, 1979.

*418. Morgan, Leslie Ann.   "Widowhood and Change: A
       Longitudinal Analysis of Middle-aged Women."   Diss.,
       University of Southern California, 1979.

419. Neugarten, Bernice L.   "The Awareness of Middle Age."
      In *Middle Age and Aging: A Reader in Social
      Psychology*, pp. 93-8, Bernice L. Neugarten, ed.
      Chicago: The University of Chicago Press, 1968.
      Some psychological issues of middle age, derived
      primarily from interviews with 100 well-placed middle-
      aged men and women are: middle age is perceived as a
      distinctive period in the life cycle in which people
      refer to positions in various contexts--body, career,
      family--to clock themselves; the self-perception of
      the middle-aged is as a bridge between the generations
      within contexts of work, family and community; most
      are acutely aware of their responsibility to the
      younger generation; there is greater projection of
      the self in interaction with older people.   Sex
      differences are that women define their age status
      more in terms of events within the family cycle, that
      men perceive a close relationship between life-line
      and career-line, that the most dramatic cues for the
      male are often biological, that health changes are
      more of an age-marker for men than for women, that
      women are more concerned over the body-monitoring of
      their husbands than their own, and that women saw
      the most conspicuous aspect of middle age as the
      sense of heightened freedom.   Both sexes have a new
      perspective on time as time-left-to-live when they
      reach middle age, and this is a time of central
      importance for the executive processes of personality,
      a time for reflection, and a time of awareness of
      increased control over impulse life.

420. Neugarten, Bernice L., Vivian Wood, Ruth J. Kraines
      and Barbara Loomis.   "Women's Attitudes Toward the
      Menopause."   In *Middle Age and Aging: A Reader in
      Social Psychology*, pp. 195-200, Bernice L. Neugarten,
      ed.   Chicago: The University of Chicago Press, 1968.
      Preliminary interviews revealed a wide variation in
      women's attitudes toward and experiences of menopause;
      however, middle-aged women were eager to discuss the
      issue and many were aware of "old wives' tales"
      about it.   A checklist of statements culled from
      these interviews and from published material on the
      subject was administered to a sample of 100 women
      aged 45 to 55--the C group--and comparisons were
      made of these responses with those of two age groups
      under 45 and one group aged 55 to 65.   Differences
      in responses are attributed both to age and experience
      with menopause.   The loss of reproductive capacity is

not an important concern of these middle-aged women.
Most younger women have generally more negative views
about it, perhaps because menopause is too far
removed in time from them and is regarded as part
of the process of aging.

421.   Nowak, Carol A.   "Does Youthfulness Equal Attractiveness?"
       In *Looking Ahead: A Woman's Guide to the Problems and
       Joys of Growing Older*, pp. 59-64, Lillian E. Troll,
       Joan Israel and Kenneth Israel, eds.   Englewood
       Cliffs, New Jersey: Prentice-Hall, Inc., 1977.   Nowak
       found no support for her expectations that *old* women
       lament their age or their looks: looking old and
       unattractive is among the least of their concerns.
       She speculates that it is the *anticipation* of lost
       youth and beauty on the part of the middle-aged
       woman that "is far more distressing than the actual
       extent of such 'damages' in old age."   Her preliminary
       research suggests that a woman's concern with facial
       attractiveness is highest during middle age; women,
       especially those between 45 and 55, are unable to
       separate appearance from feelings.   A test of 240
       men and women of young, middle and late adulthood
       showed that to the middle-aged women, "the younger
       one looks, the better one looks, and the more
       youthful ... one is presumed to be" and that a
       middle-aged woman cannot look truly attractive nor
       youthful to another middle-aged woman.   Nowak concludes
       that a middle-aged woman "will have to accept her own
       aging before she can once more perceive herself as
       attractive" and that "The sooner the midlife transi-
       tion is passed, then, the better."

422.   Ravenscroft, Catherine, Recorder.   "Biological Realities
       and Myths."   In *No Longer Young: The Older Woman in
       America--Work Group Reports*, pp. 15-22.   Ann Arbor,
       Michigan: The Institute of Gerontology, The University
       of Michigan-Wayne State University, 1974.   Current
       menopausal myths give a mockingly unsympathetic view
       of the older woman or make unrealistic promises of
       fulfillment in later life.   Accurate, easily accessible
       information about biological matters is lacking, even
       from expected sources.   Few doctors offer their
       patients more than what is given in misleading
       popular articles.   Menopause has not received much
       research interest or money.   Little is known about
       women's feelings about and reactions to it and to
       the medical care they receive.   The physical reality

of menopause and the menopausal syndrome were
described. It was noted that many hysterectomies
are not justified but are performed by "over-treaters."
Myths about menopausal women, a physician's definition
of aging, and the needs of older persons were discussed.
Special attention was given to malignancies often
found among older women. Chronic ailments common
among older persons and their treatment were discussed, and doctors' attitudes toward elderly patients
assessed. It was pointed out that biological
illiteracy is responsible for creating many of
the myths that become problematic in old age, that
the medical self-help movement is one approach taken
to correct this illiteracy, and that dispersion of
medical myths is one of the significant goals of
NOW. Some myths that need to be replaced by realities
are that women's sexuality ends at age 30, that women
can be equated with their reproductive capacity, that
"pills cure all ills," and that women's thinking
capacity is distinctive from that of men--which implies
that women need to be protected from making decisions
about their own health.

423.   Rubin, Lillian B. *Women of a Certain Age: The Midlife
       Search for Self*. New York: Harper and Row, 1979.
       Problems and prospects of 160 women interviewees
       aged 35 to 54. Topics discussed in interviews
       include: the empty nest, identity, sexuality, marriage
       and family relationships, planning for the future,
       and the menopause. Extensive bibliography.

424.   Ruddick, Sara, and Pamela Daniels, eds. *Working It
       Out: 23 Women Writers, Artists, Scientists and
       Scholars Talk About Their Lives and Work*. New
       York: Pantheon Books, 1977. A collection of auto-
       biographical essays by 23 women who report "from
       mid-life on the dilemmas and pleasures their work
       has afforded them." Almost all are near age 40.
       They were educated in the 1950s "at the height of
       the feminine mystique" and are therefore a "pivotal"
       generation. Their stories provide evidence that
       significant changes can and do occur in adulthood.
       Contributors: Kay Keeshan Hamod, Alice Atlinson
       Lyndon, Amelie Oksenberg Rorty, Pamela Daniels,
       Catharine R. Stimpson, Evelyn Fox Keller, Alice
       Walker, May Stevens, Joann Green, Sara Ruddick, Diana
       Michener, Virginia Valian, Connie Young Yu, Anne
       Lasoff, Marilyn Young, Naomi Thornton, Naomi Weisstein,

Cynthia Lovelace Sears, Nanette Vonnegut Mengel,
Miriam Schapiro, Celia Gilbert and Tillie Olsen.
Foreword by Adrienne Rich.

425. Sicher, Lydia. "'Change of Life': A Psychosomatic
      Problem." *American Journal of Psychotherapy* (July
      1949) III(3):399-409. Sicher observes that, as in
      many conflict situations, the person experiencing
      the physical effects of the clash between reality
      and personal desires is not aware of the psychic
      background of the "panic of the closing door."
      The medical diagnosis "change of life" has done much
      to obscure the psychic factors involved in the period
      of endocrine disequilibrium. She recommends the
      psychosomatic approach: "change of life" is a change
      of glandular function, but also a postulate to change
      from a life that, in the opinion of the person, had
      meaning and value to one that appears to be devoid
      of both. Saying farewell to youth and youthfulness
      may create the idea that the time after middle age
      is a time of decline, and this morbid anticipation
      induces hypochondriacal depression. The fear of
      death is also a powerful factor in generating nervous
      symptoms. Sicher presents clinical material on the
      change of life of both women and men, and says that
      ideally, training for this period should begin in
      early childhood. The door that seems to *close
      behind* the person who is psychically unprepared is
      a door that *opens onto new vistas* for those who are
      ready to meet new experiences.

426. Smith-Rosenberg, Carroll. "Puberty to Menopause: The
      Cycle of Femininity in Nineteenth-Century America."
      In *Clio's Consciousness Raised: New Perspectives
      on the History of Women,* pp. 23-37, Mary S. Hartman
      and Lois Banner, eds. New York: Harper and Row
      Publishers, Inc., 1974. This study of Victorian-
      American attitudes toward puberty and menopause from
      the perspective of the medical profession cites
      evidence of marked hostility and even contempt on
      the part of male physicians in their discussions of
      menopausal women, and evidence from diaries, letters
      and the medical literature that women viewed menopause
      with ambivalence. An extremely positive view was
      expressed by social reformer and suffrage advocate
      Eliza Farnham, who wrote that menopause could become
      woman's golden age.

427. Stern, Karl, M.D., and Miguel Prados, M.D. "Personality
      Studies in Menopausal Women." *American Journal of
      Psychiatry* (November 1946) 103(3):358-68. The authors
      review the literature on this subject, and state that
      with one exception (Merson, 1876), distinct types of
      reactions are identifiable only in this century.
      While involutional melancholia is the only well-
      defined type, it is not directly associated with the
      gonadal changes in the climacterium. They report on
      results of interviews with and examinations of 50
      patients, aged 33 to 58, all from "a poor or marginal
      economic class" and found that in 23 cases there were
      marked emotional symptoms. Reports are on physical
      symptoms; emotional pattern (41 stated they were
      depressed, but the intensity of depression varied);
      heredity and childhood history; "causes" of depressive
      reaction; artificial menopause and emotional dis-
      turbance; relation between emotional pattern and physical
      symptoms; arterial hypertension; relation between
      emotional reaction and estrogenic level; sexual
      adjustment; previous breakdowns; Rorschach results
      (all but five women took this test). Findings were
      that the clinical picture is surprisingly uniform.
      The overt psychiatric disturbance is one of a reactive
      depression which is rooted in a maladjustment usually
      preceding the menopause. "Menopausal depression,"
      therefore, is a characteristic disturbance, different
      from other breakdowns occurring during the climacteric
      period, and no more than an accentuation of a
      previously existing maladjustment.

428. Stieglitz, Edward J. "Sex and Age." In *The Second
      Forty Years*, pp. 192-212, Edward J. Stieglitz.
      Philadelphia and New York: J.B. Lippincott Co.,
      1946. In this work, published at the end of World
      War II, it is stated that nine women of every ten
      experience an "essentially symptomless" menopause, and
      that the 10% actually distressed do not have difficulties
      much greater than those experienced during puberty
      and adolescence. At least half the difficulties of
      the change of life are stated to have an *emotional*
      source. Women are advised to take pride in continuing
      maturation and to replace physical attractiveness
      with spiritual and intellectual beauty. Note that
      as long ago as 1946 it is stated that "The menopause
      has for long been a convenient diagnostic catchall,
      glibly presented to explain almost any symptoms
      which may arise between forty and fifty years," that,

more often than not, for maturing women menopause
means freedom, that during the climacteric there is
often renewed enthusiasm for the development of
neglected talents that may have lain dormant for
many years, and that the administration of female
sex hormones is justified only for severe cases; it
is pointed out that serious hazards accompany these
"potent substances." Stieglitz also states that
years of experience with the problems of aging men
and women have shown him that "the commonest source
of marital rupture in later years is an asymmetric
maturation of one or the other partner."

*429. U.S. Congress. House. Select Committee on Aging.
       National Policy Proposals Affecting Midlife Women.
       Hearings before the Subcommittee on Retirement Income
       and Employment, House of Representatives, Comm. Pub.
       No. 96-195, 96th Congress, 1st Session, 1979.

*430. U.S. Congress. House. Select Committee on Aging and
       the Subcommittee on Retirement Income and Employment.
       Women in Midlife--Security and Fulfillment. Wash-
       ington, D.C.: Government Printing Office Publications
       95-170 and 95-171.

431.   Vincent, Carl E. "An Open Letter to the 'Caught
       Generation.'" *The Family Coordinator* (April 1972)
       21(2):143-50. Those between ages 35 and 55 are
       "caught" between the demands of youth and the
       expectations of the elderly and caught *up* in the
       side-effects of change, of a combination of historical
       factors that may never be repeated. Born and reared
       during the restrictive "parents' era" of 1915-1935,
       strongly influenced by the Depression and the work-
       and-save ethics of the 1930s, they were parents during
       the permissive "children-youth" era of 1945-1965,
       and, moreover, were far outnumbered by the generation
       succeeding them. Vincent predicts that those aged
       23 to 35 in 1980 will usher in a highly restrictive
       child-rearing era, and a period of political
       conservatism and international isolationism,
       as well.

432.   Wax, Ann, Recorder. "Continuing Education and Second
       Careers." In *No Longer Young: The Older Woman in
       America,* Work Group Reports, pp. 63-7. Ann Arbor:
       The Institute of Gerontology, The University of
       Michigan-Wayne State University, 1974. There are

both social and psychological aspects of the problems facing today's older woman if she opts for additional schooling, a new career, or a return to a previous role in the work force. Counselors should not assume that all women ought to return either to school or to the work force. Female members of "poverty groups" are less likely than middle-class women to have career options in middle age. Women over 40 of all socioeconomic groups are likely to be caught within the conflicts of three generations--the young, age peers, and the elderly--and a major determinant for equilibrium is the woman's ability to mediate among all these needs. The major emotional concern of the woman over 45 is lack of self-esteem. The services of The Center for Continuing Education of Women at the University of Michigan are described: it was found that the major barriers for older women were attitudinal and financial. Individual counseling is essential; group techniques are also being used. A summary of the discussion identified open access to a variety of forms of assistance as a necessity for the woman returnee. Various forms of counseling, from information-giving to help in personal and family adjustment, should be available, and an increasing recognition of the older woman's need for financial assistance is paramount.

*433. Wax, Judith. *Starting in the Middle*. New York: Holt, Rinehart and Winston, 1979.

434. Winokur, George. "Depression in the Menopause," Brief Communications. *American Journal of Psychiatry* (January 1973) 130(1):92-3. Winokur studied 71 women who had an affective disorder either before or after the menopause to determine if they were at greater risk for depression at this time, and found a 7.1% risk of developing an affective disorder during the menopause compared with a 6% risk during other times. Thus, menopause does not seem to be an important factor in precipitating an episode of affective disorder on the basis of these data. In his discussion, Winokur notes possible sources of error in his methodology.

See also: 111, 119, 121, 141, 254, 346, 347, 629, 657, 658, 659, 786.

184   *Middle Age*

B. Displaced Homemakers

435. Baker, Nancy C. *New Lives for Former Wives: Displaced
      Homemakers*. Garden City, New York: Anchor Press/
      Doubleday, 1980. The messages that displaced
      homemakers across the country interviewed by Baker
      for this book have for their "sisters in crisis" are,
      "There is hope" and "You are not alone" and "You
      can profit from the experience of being displaced."
      Baker's topics are: being alone; the need for self-
      esteem; the importance of finding a network of sup-
      porting persons; altered relationships with friends,
      with children, with the former spouse and with other
      kin after widowhood or divorce; "growing up middle-
      aged"; creating new friendships with women and men;
      money management, and ways to combat discrimination
      and inflation; entry and re-entry to the job market.
      Includes references to helpful publications and
      organizations, and an extensive bibliography. Baker's
      focus is on "the journey to self-sufficiency."

*436. Burke, Yvonne Braithwaite. "Displaced Homemakers Act."
      Congressional Record, December 7, 1977.

*437. McCarthy, Abigail. "The Displaced Homemaker."
      Commonweal (January 16, 1976) C111(2):38, 63.

*438. Older Women's League. *Displaced Homemakers: Program
      Options ... an Evolving Guide*. Baltimore: Older
      Women's League Educational Fund, 1978.

*439. Scheele, Adele M., and Beverly Kaye. "Designs for
      Transition: An Assessment of Life Planning for Women
      Seeking Change." Unpublished paper for UCLA
      project, 1974.

*440. Seal, Karen L. "No-Fault Divorce: A Financial Disaster
      for California Women." Diss., U.S. International
      University, 1978.

441. Shields, Laurie. *Displaced Homemakers: Organizing for
      a New Life*. New York: McGraw-Hill Book Co., 1981.
      A displaced homemaker, a term coined in 1974 by Tish
      Sommers, founder of the first national Task Force
      on Older Women in NOW, is a person who has for a
      substantial number of years provided unpaid service
      to her family, and who has been dependent on her

spouse for her income but who loses that income
through death, divorce, separation, desertion or
the disablement of her husband. Shields intended
this book to be of use to professionals serving
displaced homemakers and to be a source of encouragement to older women in their efforts to secure new
and gratifying work using their experience as
homemakers as a foundation for their future. In
this book, she provides an account of the genesis
of this grassroots movement which began in 1975,
documents the extensive discrimination against older
women in our society, stresses the importance of
peer counseling and of job creation (which she sees
as "the crux of the problem"), and forcefully makes
the point that aging is a woman's issue. Includes
an Epilogue by Sommers, and five appendices--A
Volunteer Contract; California Senate Bill No. 825;
Resources; Displaced Homemakers Program Directory;
Helpful Publications (an annotated bibliography of
recent publications of particular relevance to
older women).

*442. U.S. Congress. House. Hearing Before the Subcommittee
on Employment Opportunities of the Committee on
Education and Labor, House of Representatives,
Ninety-fifth Congress, First Session on H.R. 28
(The Displaced Homemakers Act), Washington, D.C.,
July 14, 1977. Washington, D.C.: U.S. Government
Printing Office, 1977.

*443. U.S. Congress. House. Hearings Before the Subcommittee
on Equal Opportunities of the Committee on Education
and Labor, House of Representatives, Ninety-fourth
Congress, Second Session on H.R. 10272 (The Equal
Opportunity for Displaced Homemakers Act), Los
Angeles, California, November 18, 1976. Washington,
D.C.: U.S. Government Printing Office, 1976.

*444. U.S. Congress. Senate. Hearings Before the Subcommittee
on Employment, Poverty, and Migratory Labor of the
Committee on Human Resources, U.S. Senate, Ninety-
fifth Congress, First Session on S. 418 (Displaced
Homemakers Act, 1977), September 12 and 13, 1977.
Washington, D.C.: U.S. Government Printing Office,
1977.

*445. U.S. Department of Labor. *Displaced Homemakers: A
CETA Program Model, Fitchburg, Massachusetts*. Washington,
D.C.: U.S. Government Printing Office, 1978.

*446.   U.S. Department of Labor. Women's Bureau. *A Guide
        to Coordinating CETA/Vocational Education Legislation
        Affecting Displaced Homemaker Programs.* Washington,
        D.C.: U.S. Government Printing Office, 1979.

*447.   Vinick, Barbara H., and Ruth H. Jacobs. *The Displaced
        Homemaker: A State-of-the-Arts Review.* Wellesley,
        Massachusetts: Wellesley College Center for Research
        on Women, 1979.

*448.   Women's Equity Action League, Greater Los Angeles
        Chapter. "Project Wider Horizons: A Study of Job-
        Related Problems of Women 40+." Unpublished report
        of a project, 1978.

See also: 30, 33, 250, 251, 720, 725, 754.

X. NOVELS AND NOVELLAS
BY AND ABOUT OLDER WOMEN

449. Adams, Alice. *Listening to Billie*. New York: Alfred
     A. Knopf, Inc., 1978. This novel about a woman's
     changing relationships to her mother, sister, daughter,
     lovers and friends, and about her growth as a poet,
     moves through time--from 1950, when young and pregnant
     Eliza is listening to Billie Holiday singing in a
     night club in New York, wondering if she should
     marry Evan Quarles, to the late 1970s, when her
     daughter has made her into a grandmother three
     times over--and from the West Coast to the East,
     from California to Maine, where Eliza's mother, a
     successful writer, still lives in the house where
     her two daughters were born and came of age.

450. Anderson, Barbara Tunnel. *Southbound*. New York:
     Farrar, Straus and Co., 1949. The love and courage
     and strength of two older women--her grandmother,
     Laura, and her great-grandmother, Persy--are the
     guiding forces in the life of Amanda Crane, the
     musically gifted child of a black woman (Arlene,
     Laura's daughter) and the son of a prosperous and
     respected white family in Alabama. The novel tells
     the story of Amanda's odyssey from Alabama to Ohio
     to France, and, on the eve of World War Two, home
     to the South again.

451. Arnold, June. *Sister Gin*. Plainfield, Vermont:
     Daughters, Inc., 1975. Sister Gin is 50, and has
     been living with her 46-year-old lover Bettina for 20
     years when her life changes again. Through her love
     for 77-year-old Mamie Carter, Sister Gin (Su) enters
     the country of old women and discovers their power.
     Gin is the witch's brew. Mamie Carter tells Su
     that she who can be old at any age is the one who
     is truly free.

452.   Atherton, Gertrude. *Black Oxen*. New York: Boni and
       Liveright, 1923. The protagonist of this novel,
       which was a best seller in 1923, is a 58-year-old
       woman who has been rejuvenated, and who comes to terms
       with the meaning of romantic love and the purpose
       of life for the older woman.

453.   Banning, Margaret Culkin. *The Will of Magda Townsend*.
       New York: Harper and Row, 1974. At age 81, successful
       writer Magda Townsend revises her will, which was
       drawn up 28 years before, in 1944. The task is an
       occasion for her life review, and the new document
       is accompanied by a letter to her family about her
       attitude toward wills.

454.   Barrett, Mary Ellin. *American Beauty*. New York: E.P.
       Dutton and Co., Inc., 1980. In 1975, while dressing
       for her 75th birthday party, famous soprano Mary Gay
       opens the door of her home to an armed burglar,
       posing as a florist, who has come for the ruby
       necklace her husband gave her in 1925 when their
       first child, a son, was born. The life review of
       the Chicago-born singer, whose career was launched
       when she was the star of Broadway's 1922 production
       American Beauty, begins with her refusal to give
       up this family jewel that is the symbol of her
       "good young days."

455.   Beresford-Howe, Constance. *The Book of Eve*. Toronto:
       Macmillan of Canada, 1973. Eve Carroll, coming up
       to her 70th year, receives her first old-age pension
       cheque and leaves her confining, loveless marriage
       of 40 years to find a life of her own in a basement
       apartment she rents in Montreal. She had nursed her
       irascible arthritic husband for the past 18 years.
       Now she has decided to leave all she had, "and
       go underground."

*456. Buck, Pearl S. *Pavilion of Women*. New York: The John
       Day Co., 1946. A woman's search for self set in
       pre-war China.

457.   Carroll, Gladys Hasty. *Unless You Die Young*. New
       York: W.W. Norton and Co., Inc., 1977. 70-year-old
       Alice, who was widowed ten years before, after
       nearly 50 years of marriage, is visited by her son
       and daughter and their families on an island off the
       New England coast where she is spending the summer.

Her reflections on their growing and changing
relationships lead to reflections on the phases of
life and the experience of aging. She has discovered
that one who has lived 70 years has the gift of
re-living the ecstatic moments in all their original
intensity, and that her dead husband, Harley, was
with her--not the memory of Harley, or the occasional
re-living of some experience they had shared, but
Harley himself.

458. Cather, Willa. *A Lost Lady*. New York: Alfred A. Knopf,
1923. Beautiful Mrs. Forrester, the second wife of
Captain Daniel Forrester, a contractor whose house
had been famous from Omaha to Denver for its charm
and hospitality to the Burlington railroad aristocracy
of that time, is 25 years younger than her husband.
She is seen through the eyes of young Niel Herbert;
as a boy, he admired her, for she represented one
of the most beautiful things in his life. As a
young adult, Niel discovers that Mrs. Forrester was
unfaithful to the Captain some years before, and it
was not a moral scruple, but an aesthetic ideal she
had outraged: Niel becomes aware that he had been a
witness to the end of an era, the era of the Old West,
and that the generations who came after would plunder
and destroy the old way of life. Captain Forrester
dies, and an age dies with him. But his widow was
not willing to fade with the pioneer period to which
she belonged. Niel feels contempt for her because
she would rather have life on any terms.

459. Cather, Willa. *My Mortal Enemy*. New York: Vintage
Books, 1926, 1954. Young Nellie Birdseye is the
narrator of this story of a proud and passionate
woman, Myra Driscoll Henshawe, who became almost a
legend in Parthia, Illinois, where she was raised
by her uncle John Driscoll, when she eloped with
Oswald Henshawe against her uncle's wishes. Nellie
sees Myra at age 45, in New York City, and again
ten years later when she is teaching out West and
finds the Henshawes, like herself, had met hard
times. Oswald is aged beyond his 60 years, now,
and Myra is crippled and fatally ill. Shortly before
she dies, Myra confides to Nellie that she bitterly
regrets having defied her uncle. She speaks of
what cannot be known when one is young, and she
dies seeking absolution for her willfulness.

460. Chase, Mary Ellen. *The Plum Tree*. New York: The
      Macmillan Co., 1949. When it becomes necessary to
      have three elderly ladies, long-time residents of a
      Home for Aged Women, "committed" to a mental insti-
      tution, Miss Emma Davis, the nurse at the Home who
      is devoted to them, finds a way to fulfill this
      unhappy responsibility with creativity and compassion.

461. Douglas, Ellen. *Apostles of Light*. Boston: Houghton
      Mifflin Co., 1973. Martha Clarke and Elizabeth
      Griswold are sisters who had raised the widowed
      Elizabeth's two children and their two nephews who
      had been orphaned at an early age. When Elizabeth
      dies at age 80, Martha is persuaded by her nephews,
      and a politically ambitious grand-nephew, to rent a
      room in her big house to a cousin, Howie Snyder.
      Before too long, Howie converts the house into
      "Golden Age Acres," a nursing home for well-to-do
      old people. One of the boarders is 76-year-old
      Martha's lifelong lover, Dr. Lucas Alexander. Lucas,
      Martha and the aging black servant Harper discover
      the venality and avarice of Howie, who keeps the
      residents drugged and confined, and who intends to
      expand his profiteering in the nursing home industry.
      Set in the deep South, this story of the cruel
      exploitation of the elderly has a tragic dénouement.

462. French, Marilyn. *The Women's Room (a novel)*. New York:
      Summit Books, 1977. The story of what it is like to
      be a woman in the U.S. in the mid-20th century told
      through a narrator split in half--into Marilyn and
      Mira, her alter ego and the heroine of the novel.
      The book spans three decades and a generation of
      middle-class housewives of the 1950s in the suburbs
      who changed into the women of the 1970s.

463. Glasgow, Ellen. *Barren Ground*. New York: The Modern
      Library, 1936. In her youth, Dorinda Oakley's love
      for Jason Greylock is betrayed, and she resolves she
      will not allow any man to spoil her life as her
      great-aunts had done. In her 30s, she accepts
      Nathan's proposal of marriage--although she does
      not love him, she respects him, and she feels that
      the marriage might be a refuge from loneliness, which
      she fears more than poverty or death. In this novel,
      first published in 1925, Dorinda is avenged by time.
      The story is divided into three parts--Broomsedge,
      Pine and Life-Everlasting. By the time she is 50,

Dorinda's mother and Nathan are dead and she is left
alone. Standing at Jason's grave, she mourns the love
she never had; she envies the suffering of her youth,
for "the passive despair of maturity" and "the end
of expectancy" are the heaviest burdens to bear.
Yet the spirit of the land flows into her own,
strengthening and refreshing it so that it flows
out again toward life. In her middle age, facing
the future with integrity of vision, Dorinda feels
that the best of life is ahead of her.

464. Glasgow, Ellen. *The Sheltered Life.* Garden City, New
York: Doubleday, Doran and Co., Inc., 1932. In this
novel, thought by many critics to be Glasgow's finest
work of art, Eva Birdsong, who was famed for her
beauty in her youth in the 1890s, and who suffers
what she says is the most terrible fate that can
befall a woman--to be loved for her beauty--is seen
from the perspectives of Jenny Blair Archbald at
ages 9 and then 17, and Jenny's grandfather, at ages
75 and then 83. In early middle age, Eva undergoes
a "maiming" operation, and afterwards discovers the
17-year-old Jenny in her husband's arms. The novel
ends with a shocking dénouement. In aging, Jenny's
grandfather, General Archbald, searches for a pattern
to his life and for a lost sense of wholeness; memory
is a means of recovery of the past. Glasgow wrote
in a letter to Signe Toksvig (see No. 596 of this
Bibliography) that the reflective vision of the
middle section, "The Deep Past," contains the
writing she should wish to be remembered by in
the future. General Archbald was profoundly real
to her, she wrote Toksvig, and she found in him the
inner poetry or rhythm of life. She stated that
she liked to write of old people even when she was
still very young, "because the old had attained a
kind of finality."

465. Glasgow, Ellen. *They Stooped to Folly, A Comedy of
Morals.* Garden City, New York: Doubleday, Doran and
Co., Inc., 1929. Victoria Littlepage, who in failing
health underwent an "inward isolation," and her
friend, Louisa, who loved Victoria all her life, are
vivid, contrasting portraits of older women in
Glasgow's post-World War One comedy of morals.
Other older women characters are Mrs. Burden, whose
daughter had been in love with the man the Little-
pages' daughter married, Mrs. Dalrymple, to whom

Mr. Littlepage is strongly attracted, and Aunt
Agatha, who had "reached the age when a woman,
however piquant her reputation, has ceased to be
an object of wonder to men...."

466. Glasgow, Ellen. *Vein of Iron*. New York: Harcourt,
      Brace and Co., 1935. The "vein of iron," Glasgow
      wrote in a letter (to a Miss Forbes, who is not
      identified except by name--see No. 596 of this
      Bibliography) is that which enables people to survive
      and endure in the struggle for life. In the novel,
      Ada Fincastle, later Ada McBride, grows from child-
      hood into full maturity, moving through time from
      the early years of this century through World War
      One to the Depression, and moving from the family
      home at Ironside to Queenborough. In the latter
      part of the novel, Ada is seen as an older woman
      during the Depression years. Other older women who
      are strong characters in the novel are Grandmother
      Fincastle and Aunt Meggie and Ada's mother, Mary
      Evelyn. Love, the doctrine of predestination and
      the future of civilization are seen from the per-
      spectives of these women and of Ada's father and her
      lover/husband, Ralph McBride. At the end of the novel,
      Ada's father, John Fincastle, a minister who became
      a philosopher, returns to Ironside to die, sinking
      "into changeless beatitude."

467. Glaspell, Susan. *Brook Evans*. New York: Frederick A.
      Stokes Co., 1928. Brook Evans is the child conceived
      in love between Naomi Kellogg and Joe Copeland in
      1881 in the American Midwest. Joe is killed in an
      accident, and Naomi's family, learning that she is
      pregnant, insist that she accept Caleb Evans's proposal
      of marriage and go to Colorado to live with him.
      When Brook is a young woman and Caleb forbids her to
      go on seeing Tony, the young man she loves, Naomi
      contacts Tony, tells him of her past, and helps him
      plan to persuade Brook to elope and go with him to
      California. Brook discovers her mother's complicity
      in Tony's proposal and, rejecting them both, she
      joins a woman missionary in the Near East. In 1927,
      now the mother of an 18-year-old son, the widowed
      Brook chooses Life over Duty, as her mother had
      wanted her to do when she was young. This is the
      story of the continuity of love over three generations,
      and of the estrangement and reconciliation--after
      death--of a mother and her grown daughter.

468. Godwin, Gail. *The Odd Woman.* New York: Alfred A.
Knopf, 1974. Jane Clifford, aged 32, who teaches
literature at a Midwestern university, is nearing
the end of her second year of a love affair with
Gabriel Weeks, a married man and a professor of
Art. Jane's goal is to become her own woman and to
find her own best life; unlike women who, in marrying
and having children, postpone the day when they must
face the truth of their individual life, she "faces
the void" now. Jane's beloved grandmother Edith, who
is in her 80s, dies, and Jane flies South for the
funeral. Afterwards, when she and her mother Kitty
go to Edith's apartment to pack up her possessions,
both weep at saying farewell to certain roles. Kitty
is not a daughter any longer, and Jane is no one's
grandchild anymore and is not, and perhaps never
will be, anyone's mother; she feels "exposed at both
ends of her life." Edith had told Kitty and Jane
over and over again a "cautionary tale" about Jane's
great-aunt Cleva. After Jane leaves the South, she
meets Gabriel in New York. Tired of being patient,
she decides to try to break off their relationship.
She researches her great-aunt Cleva's past, tracking
down the man she believes was Cleva's long-ago lover;
it is a way of "researching her [own] salvation."
On the way back from New York, she stops overnight
at the apartment of a friend from her college days.
While there, Jane perceives a connection between
something her own mother had revealed about her
relationship with Edith and the feelings expressed
by an older woman in Gerda's apartment whose husband
had deserted her for a younger woman. Jane finds
that for "daughters" to tell "mothers" that all is
still possible is futile and unkind--an act of
cruelty "to shine these too bright might-have-beens
upon the tired countenances of older women who had
lived by other lights."

469. Grumbach, Doris. *Chamber Music.* New York: E.P. Dutton
and Co., Inc., 1979. This novel about love and the
calamities of love takes the form of an aging woman's
autobiography, "this lengthy statement" she reads
over at the end, discovering that too few facts have
been included in it, then asking if facts are anything
more than "the catafalque upon which one hangs all
the memories of an emotional life," which leave only
that which seems real and at the last, for all of
us, "the omnipresent aloneness of our lives."

470. Hailey, Elizabeth Forsythe. *A Woman of Independent Means*. New York: Viking, 1978. A novel in letters spanning three-quarters of the 20th century, written by a woman who lost her husband and a child when still quite young. In these letters, the protagonist reflects on widowhood and remarriage, on an older woman's relationship to her grown children and grandchildren, and on aging. Hailey dedicates this book to her grandmother "whose life inspired these letters," and to her husband "who inspired me."

471. Hardwick, Elizabeth. *Sleepless Nights*. New York: Random House, Inc., 1979. "It is June," this novel of memory begins, and the writer intends to "do this work of transformed and even distorted memory" and to lead the life she is leading today. She remembers places—in Kentucky, in New York ("a woman's city"), in New England—and writes that she does not believe that it is true "that it doesn't matter where you live" or "that all are linked naturally to their regions." She remembers her mother; she remembers Billie Holiday; she remembers spinsters, bag ladies, her old neighbor Miss Cramer, and an old lady of 87 whose "last year of life was a marvel"; she remembers Josette and her disasters, and Ida, to whom she returns in the present summer, and the women in the rooming houses near Columbia University.

472. Herbst, Josephine. "Hunter of Doves." In *Botteghe Oscure* (1954) 13:310-44. Mrs. Heath, a painter, is visited by a young man who asks her to tell him what she remembers about a writer who had been her friend and her husband's friend in the 1930s. "She was no filing cabinet, neatly documented, but a living soul, who had been abandoned in Arcadia by the two of them."

473. Howe, Helen. *The Fires of Autumn*. New York: Harper and Brothers, 1959. In the 1950s, the middle-aged narrator, Little Beatrice, returns to the village of Cranford, Maine, to spend the "little season" with her Aunt Bee and her aunt's friends, the widows who had spent more than twenty summers together watching their children grow up. Older women—summer people and a year-round resident, Emma Fogg—are the main characters in this novel about Aunt Bee's search for (and her namesake's discovery of) the meaning of her life.

474. Hunter, Kristin. *God Bless the Child*. New York:
Charles Scribner's Sons, 1964. A tragic story of
the struggle for survival of three generations of
black women--Granny (Mrs. Lourinda Baxter Huggs),
who works "in a white palace with marble stairs and
crystal fountains" and who lives every other week-
end and every Thursday in a poor neighborhood with
her daughter, Queenie (named Queen Victoria Regina
"out of some magazine"), and her granddaughter,
Rosie. Queenie once told Rosie she would always
spite herself to spite her mother and that Granny
had spoiled her so much that Queenie had to be twice
as rough on her. In the passage of time, Rosie is
consumed with--and destroyed by--the desire to trans-
form the lives of her grandmother and her mother.

475. Hurston, Zora Neale. *Seraph on the Suwanee*. New York:
Charles Scribner's Sons, 1948. Hurston's novel
about white Southerners is the story of the marriage
between Arvay and Jim Meserve, told from Arvay's
point of view, as they move from place to place,
from northwest Florida to the citrus country, and
through time--from their courtship at the turn of
the century to 1930, when they are middle-aged.
Their first-born son, Earl, is retarded, and is
killed when in his teens after he attacks a neighbor's
daughter. When their daughter Angie is grown and
married and their second son Kenny is working as a
musician in New York, Arvay does not know what to do
with her time. One day, Jim captures a diamond-back
and calls to Arvay to show her his virility in holding
it. When the snake begins to coil itself around his
body, Jim asks Arvay to help him, but she is unable
to move. After this, Jim decides to leave her and go
to the coast. He says they are not truly married
because they do not have the same point of view.
Arvay is left desolate. Her mother dies, and she
returns to her old home. She burns down the old
house, and tells her neighbor that she intends to
have a play- and pleasure-park built on the property.
Some time later, she goes to the coast to be with
Jim; eventually, they are reconciled. Arvay believes
that inside Jim is still a little boy who needs her
to mother him, and that, "Her job was mothering....
She was serving and meant to serve."

476. Hurston, Zora Neale. *Their Eyes Were Watching God*.
New York: Negro Universities Press, 1969, originally

published by The J.B. Lippincott Co., Philadelphia,
1937. A story of the love between an older woman,
Janie Crawford, and a younger man, Tea Cake, a migrant
laborer whom she meets after two failed marriages.
Janie was raised by her grandmother, who was born
into slavery, as was Janie's own mother, and Nanny
chooses Logan Killicks as Janie's husband, because he
represents security and Nanny "loved to deal in
scraps." It is a marriage without love; later,
Janie meets Joe Starks, who "spoke for change and
chance," and leaves with him for Eatonville, Florida
(Hurston's birthplace), where "thought pictures"
are passed around on Joe's store porch, always like
"crayon enlargements of life." Love leaves this
marriage; Joe wants Janie to be submissive, and when
she is nearly 40, and he nearly 50, he begins talking
about her age. After Joe dies, Janie meets Tea Cake
who is twelve years younger than she, and travels
with him as a migrant worker. During a hurricane,
Tea Cake is bitten by a rabid dog, tries to kill
Janie, and is killed by her in self-defense. Later,
a white jury acquits her of the shooting. Tea Cake
had told Janie that age has nothing to do with love,
and that she was a little girl baby in his eyes.

*477.   Irwin, Hadley. *The Lilith Summer*. Old Westbury, New
        York: The Feminist Press, 1979. Ellen, aged twelve,
        reluctantly agrees to spend the summer as a companion
        to 77-year-old Lilith Adams, and the experience
        leads to a lasting friendship between the two.

478.   Janeway, Elizabeth. *The Third Choice*. Garden City,
        New York: Doubleday and Co., Inc., 1959. At age 61,
        Mrs. Diana Belchamber begins writing her life review
        while confined to a nursing home because of a broken
        hip (both to amuse herself and to pass the time "in
        limbo") just at the time when her niece, Mrs. Lorraine
        de Koning, reaches a moment of truth in her own life..
        The novel alternates between chapters of the aunt's
        memoir, with a vivid account of World War One (she
        was in London when it began and in Paris when it
        ended) and the coming crisis in Lorraine's marriage.
        Mrs. Belchamber closes her life story, which she then
        sends to her niece, by writing that old people all
        want to offer the next generation their experiences--
        their wisdom--and that it is a mean excuse for one
        generation not trying to reach the other, to claim
        that the young can never learn from the old. She

has appointed Lorraine to the task of reading her
life story and of judging her, since she does not
believe that anyone can judge herself or himself.
She writes that in spite of everything she would live
her life over again, and tells her niece, who is all
the child she has in her old age, to trust herself
to go on with her life.

*479. Katzenbach, Maria. *The Grab*. New York: Pocket Books,
1977. After their mother's death, Barbara, Louisa
and Sadie are called upon to follow family tradition
--to meet in her home in Georgetown and "grab" at
the pieces of inheritance their mother has left them.

480. Kumin, Maxine. *The Designated Heir*. New York: The
Viking Press, Inc., 1974. Robin Parks, who was
brought up by Gran and Tante, her grandmother and
great-aunt (sisters-in-law for 50 years, who disliked
one another but cherished the same child), comes into
her inheritance.

481. Lawrence, Josephine. *,Years Are So Long*. New York:
Frederick A. Stokes Co., 1934. 73-year-old Barkley
Cooper and his 72-year-old wife, Lucy, have only
their five children as insurance in old age. When
Bark loses his job, and asks which one of them wants
to take their aging parents in to live with them,
the children make it clear that their parents are an
unwanted burden. Four of them (the fifth daughter
has moved to California) decide to separate their
parents and have the father and mother each take
turns living with each of them. The novel is a
searing portrayal of the conflict between the
generations, the rejection of the elderly by the
middle-aged and the young, and the dereliction that
was the fate of so many older people in the United
States at that time. The film "Make Way for
Tomorrow" was based on this novel.

482. Markus, Julia. "A Patron of the Arts." In *Two Novellas*,
pp. 9-31, Julia Markus and Barbara Reid. Cambridge,
Massachusetts: Apple-wood Press, 1977. Gert Scholtz
loves beauty; her 55-year-old daughter Cookie and
Cookie's husband, Hersh, are practical people who
have no aesthetic sense. Conflict erupts twice over
the grandchildren's futures. Gert encouraged her
grandson, Richard, when at thirteen he wanted to
study at Juilliard. But after a bitter family

argument over this issue, Richard smashed his violin;
in time, he became a dentist like his father. Now
Gert opposes the middle generation again, when she
decides to give her granddaughter, an artist, and
her granddaughter's husband, a philosopher, money
to go to Europe for two years. Gert would say to
them, "Paint your pictures and read your books....
Fly away, if you can, over those unreal valleys
toward a different sun. Blow yourself to life."

483.   Rex, Barbara. *I Want To Be in Love Again*. New York:
       W.W. Norton and Co., Inc., 1977. At the age of 69,
       an independent and vibrant woman, Jessica Gosse, is
       confronted with the challenges of aging and with her
       overpowering need for reconciliation with her estranged
       younger daughter, 38-year-old Molly.

484.   Sarton, May. *As We Are Now*. New York: W.W. Norton and
       Co., Inc., 1973. Former math teacher Caroline Spencer
       is 76 when her 80-year-old brother John brings her
       to the Twin Elms Nursing Home. Caro had to close her
       home after suffering a heart attack, and she is not
       getting along with John and his younger wife. Twin
       Elms is "a concentration camp for the old, a place
       where people dump their parents or relatives exactly
       as though it were an ash can." To maintain her
       sanity in the face of the threat of a failing memory,
       Caro keeps a journal, which she entitles The Book of
       the Dead. She needs to think of the Hell that is
       Twin Elms as the House of Gathering, where she can
       make herself whole and find her redemption. Her final
       resolution is to end everything in a purifying fire.
       Her copybook is found in the ashes of the fire that
       destroys Twin Elms.

485.   Sarton, May. *Crucial Conversations*. New York: W.W.
       Norton and Co., Inc., 1975. At age 50, a woman leaves
       her husband of 27 years to explore the meaning of
       her life and the possibilities of her creativity as
       a sculptor. The novel is narrated by Philip Somers-
       worth, a lifelong friend of the couple and their
       three grown children.

*486. Sarton, May. *Kinds of Love*. New York: W.W. Norton and
       Co., Inc., 1970. An elderly couple, Christina Chapman
       and her ailing husband, Cornelius, spend the winter
       for the first time in a small town in New Hampshire
       where they have been summer people for many years.

487. Sarton, May. *Mrs. Stevens Hears the Mermaids Singing.*
      New York: W.W. Norton and Co., Inc., 1975. 70-year-
      old F. Hilary Stevens, poet and novelist, reflects
      on love, the sources of woman's creativity--for women
      artists, the Muse is "she"--on memory, and on aging.
      The occasion for her self-examination is an interview
      by two young reporters in which she reviews her past.
      Stevens sees life as "a picaresque novel ... in which
      the episodes are all inward." She tells her inter-
      viewers that the one thing forbidden to poets is
      power, and that when an artist is a woman, she
      fulfills the need for wholeness at the expense
      of herself as a woman.

488. Sarton, May. *A Reckoning.* New York: W.W. Norton and
      Co., Inc., 1978. In dying, 60-year-old Laura Spelman
      wants to use the time she has left to reckon up her
      life. She discovers that the journey towards death
      takes her deeper and deeper into what it is to be
      a woman, that images of *women* haunt her, chiefly
      those of her mother, Sybille, and her English friend,
      Ella.

489. Sarton, May. *The Small Room.* New York: W.W. Norton
      and Co., Inc., 1961. This novel is the story, told
      from the point of view of a young teacher at a New
      England women's college, of the discovery of plagiarism
      on the part of a brilliant senior, a protogée of an
      accomplished professor and scholar, and the conse-
      quences of the discovery. Sarton probes the
      complexity, variousness and unpredictability of
      the student-teacher relationship, and the love
      between two older women. The theme of the novel
      is the moral responsibility of the teacher, and the
      nature both of the vocation of teaching and the
      daimon of the "keeper of the sacred fire" dedicated
      to the "care of souls."

*490. Schneider, Nina. *The Woman Who Lived in a Prologue.*
      Boston: Houghton Mifflin Co., 1980. The protagonist
      of Schneider's first novel is in her 70s.

491. Smedley, Agnes. *Daughter of Earth.* Old Westbury,
      New York: The Feminist Press, 1973. The author's
      mother and her father's elder sister, "Aunt Mary,"
      are unforgettable older women characters in this
      autobiographical novel by Smedley (1890-1950),
      political activist, writer and teacher, about the

suffering, poverty and bitter struggles of the first
30 years of her life. Afterword by Paul Lauter.

492. Suckow, Ruth. *The Folks*. New York: The Literary Guild,
      1934. (Drawings by Robert Ward Johnson.) "The folks"
      are Annie and Fred Ferguson, whose four children--
      Carl, Dorothy, Margaret and Bun--grow up one by one
      and leave home. Afterwards, their mother reflects
      that her children were at the center of her life,
      that her home was nothing without them, and that,
      although her marriage had been happy, her own separate
      life had gone down beneath it, and now when she needed
      it again she was no longer able to find it.

493. Welty, Eudora. *Losing Battles*. New York: Random House,
      Inc., 1970. Granny, who can still take very good
      care of herself, is celebrating her 90th birthday--
      the occasion for the reunion of the Beecham family.

494. Welty, Eudora. *The Optimist's Daughter*. New York:
      Vintage Books, 1978. Aged 45, Laurel McKelva comes
      back South from Chicago to be with her father during
      his last illness, and sees him and her stepmother
      of one and one-half years, the insensitive and shallow
      Fay, for the first time since her widowed father's
      remarriage. After the Judge's death, Laurel returns
      with Fay to her old home in Mount Salus, Mississippi,
      for the funeral, and there she journeys into the past.

495. Wharton, Edith. *The Mother's Recompense*. New York:
      D. Appleton and Co., 1925. After nearly 20 years of
      self-imposed separation, Kate Clephane receives a
      telegram from her daughter Anne, asking her to come
      home and live with her now that Kate's mother-in-law
      (Anne's paternal grandmother) is dead. Soon after
      her return, Kate discovers that Anne is engaged to
      marry Chris Fenno, who had once been Kate's lover.
      At first, she feels that the agony, instead of
      aging her, "seemed to have plunged her into a very
      Fountain of Youth." But later, after she resolves
      it is better not to tell Anne about the past, Kate
      feels she "must put the world" between herself and
      the couple, and therefore she must give up her
      daughter for a second time.

496. Wharton, Edith. *Old New York: The Old Maid (The
      'Fifties)*. New York: D. Appleton and Co., 1924.
      Widowed when still young, Delia Ralston took her

cousin Charlotte to live with her and help her raise
her young son and daughter. Delia took Charlotte's
"ward" into her home, also, and raised the child,
called Tina Lovell, as her own daughter. Tina is
really Charlotte's illegitimate daughter, and the
child's father is a man Delia loved and lost before
her marriage to Jim Ralston. Delia decides to adopt
Tina so that the girl can marry the man she loves.
The night before Tina's wedding, Charlotte claims
the right to go to Tina to give her the customary
mother's counsel. Delia accepts this, but in the end
Charlotte cannot go through with it, and tells her
cousin to go, acknowledging, "You're her real mother."

497. Wharton, Edith. *Twilight Sleep*. New York: D. Appleton
     and Co., 1927. In this novel of American life after
     the Great War, middle-aged Pauline Manford uses
     rest-cures, mental uplift, meditation and exercises
     as armament against suffering. To suffer is to sin;
     she does not permit herself to worry because it
     leaves wrinkles around the eyelids and lips. Pauline
     seeks a Twilight Sleep, an anodyne, for the pain of
     consciousness--and aging. Her grown daughter, Nona,
     perceives the "beaming determination" of her mother's
     generation--"bright-complexioned white-haired
     mothers mailed in massage and optimism"--to think
     sorrow and evil away, and she assumes the moral
     responsibility for awareness of wickedness, suffering,
     and death.

See also: 370, 371, 372, 373, 374, 375, 376, 377, 378, 382,
383, 386, 387, 388, 389.

XI. ORAL HISTORIES

A. First-Person Stories

498. Banks, Ann, ed. *First-Person America*. New York:
      Alfred A. Knopf, Inc., 1980. Banks selected the 80
      life histories in this book from some ten thousand
      because they "communicated an unmistakable vitality
      that made itself felt across forty years." Among
      these narratives from the Thirties, collected by the
      Federal Writers' Project between 1938 and 1942 and
      published here for the first time, are the life
      stories of women--young, middle-aged and elderly
      (one woman was 90 at the time of her interview).
      Some chapters focus on a particular industry--"The
      Yards," "Monumental Stone," "Tobacco People,"
      Troupers and Pitchmen, The Jazz Language; the
      remaining--Old Times, Immigrant Lives, Industrial
      Lore, Rank and File, Testifying--include one entitled
      Women on Work, with life histories of a millworker,
      a Bahamian midwife from the small Conch fishing
      village of Riviera, Florida, an Irish domestic and
      others; Monumental Stone, Barre, Vermont, 1939 and
      1940, ends with the narratives of three widows of
      stonecutters who were victims of silicosis. Intro-
      duction and Afterword by Ann Banks on the Federal
      Writers' Project; Notes; List of Interviews; Bibliography.

*499. Botkin, Benjamin A., ed. *Lay My Burden Down: A Folk
       History of Slavery*. Chicago: The University of
       Chicago Press, 1945. Anthology of Federal Writers'
       Project material, culled from thousands of inter-
       views with former slaves.

*500. Coles, Robert, and Jane Hallowell Coles. *Women of
       Crisis: Lives of Struggle and Hope*. New York:
       Delacorte Press/Seymour Lawrence, 1978. The lives
       of five relatives or associates of the children Coles

wrote about in the "Children of Crisis" series--
Ruth James, a migrant worker from Florida; Hannah
Morgan, a Harlan County, Kentucky, woman who moves
to Chicago and Dayton, Ohio, with her daughter;
Teresa Torres Cardenas, a Chicana of San Antonio;
Lorna, an Alaskan Eskimo; and Helen, a white maid
from Somerville, Massachusetts.

501.   Cooper, Patricia, and Norma Bradley Buferd. *The*
        Quilters: Women and Domestic Art, An Oral History.
        Garden City, New York: Anchor Press/Doubleday, 1978.
        A record of the art of quilting and the lives of the
        quilters in Texas and New Mexico, whose average age
        was 73. Most of these women were pioneer-settlers
        of the land or had come as children with their
        parents to homestead in the last quarter of the
        19th century. The stories are of childhood, youth,
        the middle years, and old age. The quilts represent
        an all-inclusive portrait of the quilters, and are
        an artistic expression of their selves and their
        whole experience. In exploring the relationship of
        quilting to the lives of the quilters, Cooper and
        Buferd thought of the quilts as a record of family
        and community history and a repository of American
        design and textiles, and understood the quilts as
        art coming directly out of family life. The home
        served as studio, art school, and gallery. The
        direct speech of the quilters is presented with
        photographs of the artists, their art, and the
        landscape in which they work. Includes a quilt
        index. A 1977 Selection by the Notable Books Council.

*502.   Couch, William T., ed. *These Are Our Lives.* Chapel
        Hill: University of North Carolina Press, 1939,
        1967; Norton Library, 1975. Anthology of Federal
        Writers' Project material consisting of life-history
        narratives of black and white Southerners.

503.   Ebner, Marion. "About the Life and Death of Rae Edith
        Rose." In *The New Old: Struggling for Decent Aging,*
        pp. 166-7, Ronald Gross, Beatrice Gross and Sylvia
        Seidman, eds. Garden City, New York: Anchor Press/
        Doubleday, 1978. The story of 102-year-old Rae Edith
        Rose, a fiercely independent woman who was able to
        live and die on her own terms--with dignity--because
        of the Home Care Program at Bellevue Hospital.

*504. Elsasser, Nan, Kyle MacKenzie and Yvonne Tixier y
Vigil. *Las Mujeres: Conversations from an Hispanic
Community.* Old Westbury, New York: The Feminist
Press, 1981. Oral histories of four generations of
New Mexico Hispanic women.

505. Foley, Eileen. "The Way It Was." In *Looking Ahead:
A Woman's Guide to the Problems and Joys of Growing
Older*, pp. 14-20, Lillian E. Troll, Joan Israel and
Kenneth Israel, eds. Englewood Cliffs, New Jersey:
Prentice-Hall, Inc., 1977. Descriptive statements
about "the way it was" for older women--"To be a
retired woman in 1975 is to be just under to well
over 70, to have grown up in Peter Thompson middy
dresses, and to have absorbed a host of catechetical
definitions of 'ladylike' behavior." Today's older
woman in retirement grew up in a less populous
America, without radio, TV or telephones, and with
many more older people around her than do young
people today--are followed by three older women's
narratives about their past and present lives.

506. Gladney, Margaret Rose. "If It Was Anything for
Justice." *Southern Exposure* (Winter 1977) 4(4):19-23.
Story of 56-year-old community leader and civil
rights activist Sallie Mae Hadnott from Prattville,
Alabama. Mrs. Hadnott organized the Autauga County
NAACP in the mid-1960s, planned voter registration
campaigns, and raised eight children, two of whom
were among the first black students to integrate
Autauga County High School.

507. Green, Rayna. "Magnolias Grow in Dirt: The Bawdy Lore
of Southern Women." *Southern Exposure* (Winter 1977)
4(4):29-33. Most scholars of pornography, obscenity
and bawdry are men, and most collected their lore
from men. Green heard her first bawdy stories from
Southern women, among them her grandmother and other
kin. Many women who tell vile tales are "gloriously
and affirmatively old." As in many traditional cultures, their age gives them license, and many delight
in presenting themselves as wicked old ladies.
Repertories include stories about preachers, old
men, and country boys and strangers. Through bawdy
lore, women see themselves as comic story-tellers
and comic artists. Bawdry, a vehicle for social
criticism, is a means of socialization of young women
and of providing sex education. Green writes of it
as participation in fun, rebellion and knowledge-giving.

*508.   Kahn, Kathy. *Hillbilly Women*. (With photographs by
        Al Clayton; Migrant photographs by Frank Blechman,
        Jr.) Garden City, New York: Doubleday and Co.,
        Inc., 1973.

 509.   Kramer, Sydelle, and Jenny Masur, eds. *Jewish Grand-
        mothers*. Boston: Beacon Press, 1976. Oral histories
        of ten Eastern European Jewish women who emigrated
        to the U.S. in the first quarter of this century and
        who now live in Chicago, presented in three sections:
        why they came to America; how they came; how they
        fared. In the Introduction: Breaking Stereotypes,
        the authors observe that the Jewish woman has been
        caricatured as saint, sacrificial stepmother or
        aggressive female Shylock, in literature from Sholom
        Aleichem's *Tevye's Five Daughters* to Roth's *Portnoy's
        Complaint*, and that every chapter in this book is a
        refutation of stereotypes, for none of these women is
        ignorant, passive or weak. In the Afterword,
        acknowledging they, too, had been surprised by what
        these women told them, they affirm their belief that
        these stories "flow together to form a portrait of
        a generation's experience." Photographs; Background
        notes on customs and events; Glossary; Bibliography.

 510.   Krause, Corinne Azen. *Grandmothers, Mothers and Daughters:
        An Oral History Study of Ethnicity, Mental Health,
        and Continuity of Three Generations of Jewish, Italian,
        and Slavic-American Women*. New York: The Institute
        on Pluralism and Group Identity of the American
        Jewish Committee, 1978. Study of ethnic women in
        America. Data are derived from oral histories of
        225 women of the Pittsburgh area, equally divided
        among three generations of the three ethnic groups.
        Topics include age at marriage, average number of
        children, levels of education, attitudes towards
        ethnicity, sex-specific experiences, work histories,
        attitudes toward male and female roles, careers and
        sexual behavior (a feminist index was developed for
        the study), specific mental health issues, mobility,
        and inter-generational relationships. Documents the
        salience of ethnicity in the lives of these women.
        Identifies special problems of elderly ethnic women.
        Tables and bibliography.

 511.   Krause, Corinne Azen. "Italian, Jewish, and Slavic
        Grandmothers in Pittsburgh: Their Economic Roles."
        Frontiers (Summer 1977) II(2):18-28. Oral histories

of working grandmothers of Italian, Jewish and Slavic
ethnic backgrounds illustrate the active economic
roles of the older women included in the sample of
Krause's Pittsburgh study of ethnicity, mental health
and continuity. The oral histories document a wide
variety of work done by married women that is wholly
absent from the census data. Differences between
the ethnic groups were primarily in attitudes toward
work and values placed upon work, rather than in the
nature of the jobs performed. The primary motivation
for work in any breadwinning capacity was concern for
the family. Women of all three ethnic groups exhibit
characteristics of dignity, pragmatism, a sense of
responsibility, and enhanced self-esteem from contributing to the welfare of their families.

512. Le Sueur, Meridel. *Women on the Breadlines*. Cambridge,
      Massachusetts: West End Press, Worker Writers Pamphlet
      1, 1977. Four women's stories from the 1930s--the
      title story and "Sequel to Love," "They Follow Us
      Girls," and "Salvation Home," recorded by Meridel
      Le Sueur.

513. Linderman, Frank B. *Pretty-shield, Medicine Woman of
      the Crows (as told to Frank B. Linderman)*. Nebraska:
      University of Nebraska Press, 1932, 1972. Tribal
      history and myths, and "grandmother tales" told by
      Pretty-shield, a "Wise-one," or medicine woman of
      the Crow tribe, to "Sign-talker" Linderman through
      an interpreter who translated Crow thoughts into
      English words. Of all the old Indian women, Linderman
      writes, she was the ideal informant, because her age
      meant that she knew the natural life of her people
      on the Plains, because of her keen mentality, and
      because of her willingness to talk freely with him.
      Pretty-shield's narrative offers many insights into
      aging.

514. MacKenzie, Kyle, Yvonne Tixier y Vigil and Nan Elsasser.
      "Grandmothers' Stories." *Frontiers* (Summer 1977)
      II(2):56-8. At age 85, Grandma Vigil gives her
      granddaughter the first threads to be woven with the
      lives of other Grandmas, *madres* and *hijas* into an
      Hispanic story of mothering.

515. Mead, Margaret. "Growing Old in America," Margaret
      Mead interviewed by Grace Hechinger. In *The New
      Old: Struggling for Decent Aging*, pp. 267-72, Ronald

Gross, Beatrice Gross and Sylvia Seidman, eds. Garden
City, New York: Anchor Press/Doubleday, 1978. At age
75, Mead was interviewed by Hechinger for *Family
Circle* magazine. The anthropologist observed that
as a nation of immigrants, America has always put a
great premium on youth. But in the past, older
people stayed in the family, and families lived close
together in communities. The flight to age- and class-
segregated suburbs has separated the old from the
young. Few early societies treated old people as
badly as civilized societies do, in her opinion.
Our treatment of the old reflects the high value we
place on independence and autonomy. Americans have
little sense of *interdependence*. Communities that
welcome old people ought to be built in the U.S.
Early retirement is a very wasteful practice--men
suffer from this more than women. There is much old
people can teach the young. Mead also said that
Americans fear aging and fear the aged, and that it
is very important to prepare onself for old age. She
often has her students interview old people, and
write an autobiography for their as-yet-unborn
grandchildren.

516.   Morse, Dean W.   "Aging in the Ghetto." In *The New Old:
Struggling for Decent Aging*, pp. 16-27, Ronald Gross,
Beatrice Gross and Sylvia Seidman, eds. Garden City,
New York: Anchor Press/Doubleday, 1978. Among the
major themes of life stories told by 100 elderly
blacks living in a Northeast urban area, many of whom
lead lonely lives, are "self-pride," manifest in
self-reliance and giving and receiving charity on a
personal, not public basis; the absence of the illusion
that work should be pleasurable or fulfilling; the
searing memory of the Great Depression; a profound
respect for education (and parents' desire to provide
their children with the education they did not have);
and the pervasiveness of discriminatory practices
in our society. In contrast to older men, many
older women were eager to remain active after full-
time employment ended. Also, many older black men
who attended school in the South had a sense of
lifelong handicap because of a lack of education,
whereas many older women educated in the South told
stories of extraordinary efforts made to extend
formal education into college or nurses' training.

517. Murray, Pauli. "The Fourth Generation of Proud Shoes."
     Southern Exposure (Winter 1977) 4(4):4-9. This story,
     selected and edited by Lee Kessler, is from the rough
     draft of a chapter from Murray's new book of this
     title. The story is about her Aunt Pauline, who
     adopted Murray at the age of three after her own
     mother's death, in 1914. Distinguished civil-rights
     attorney, feminist leader, writer and poet, in 1977
     Murray became the first Negro woman ordained as a
     priest in the history of the Protestant Episcopal
     Church.

518. O'Farrell, M. Brigid, and Lydia Kleiner. "Anna
     Sullivan: Trade Union Organizer." *Frontiers*
     (Summer 1977) II(2):29-36. Description of the
     collaborative model of the oral history project,
     "The Twentieth Century Trade Union Woman: Vehicle
     for Social Change," with excerpts from an interview
     with Anna Sullivan, born in 1904, a union organizer.

519. Rousseau, Ann Marie. *Shopping Bag Ladies: Homeless
     Women Speak About Their Lives*. New York: The Pilgrim
     Press, 1981. First-person stories, with over 100
     photographs. In the notes to her Preface, Alix Kates
     Shulman writes that she knows of only two serious
     book-length studies of this subject--Bahr and
     Garrett's *Women Alone* (see No. 276 of this Bibliography)
     and a study in progress by Stephanie Golden, *The
     Women Outside*, to be published by St. Martin's
     Press. Shulman states that homeless women remain,
     as they have always been, essentially invisible
     for most people, and that they have received far less
     care and attention than homeless men. She suggests
     that "Historically, homeless men have been romanti-
     cized in American consciousness in a way that women
     have not." Rousseau's book is the outcome of her
     experiences teaching a recreational art class at the
     Shelter Care Center for Women in New York City, and
     the many hours she spent sitting in train stations
     and other places that shopping bag ladies make their
     homes, meeting and talking with these women about
     their lives.

520. Seifer, Nancy. *Nobody Speaks for Me: Self-Portraits
     of American Working Class Women*. New York: Simon
     and Schuster, 1976. Oral histories of ten working-
     class women, with a Preface and Introduction by
     Seifer, who states that these women had "one common

denominator: each of their lives had changed rather
significantly over the course of the last six to eight
years and illustrated the transition from fairly
traditional housewife to activist." These women
are not "typical," yet they are representative of
millions of women in their world-views and life-
styles. Their ethnic and religious backgrounds
include Irish, Italian, Jewish, Black, Chicana,
English, white Southern Baptist, French, Norwegian,
and German. They live in all four regions of the
country, and in cities, suburbs, small towns and rural
areas; their ages ranged from 24 to 58 (in 1974).
One factor that had no bearing on the selection of
these women was their attitude toward the Women's
Movement. They seemed much more likely to become
activists on behalf of others facing similar problems
than feminists seeking their own personal fulfillment
in life. Contents: Taking Care of the Neighborhood--
Mary Sansone and Janice Bernstein; Women Helping
Women--Dorothy Bolden and Betty Gagne; Joining the
Ranks: Unionism and Feminism--Cathy Tuley and Bonnie
Halascsak; Practical Politics--Rosalinda Rodriguez
and Anita Cupps; Listening to Each Other Across
Class Lines--Ann Winans and Terry Dezso.

521. Seskin, Jane. *More Than Mere Survival: Conversations
     with Women Over 65*. New York: Newsweek Books, 1980.
     Transcripts of interviews with 22 women over the age
     of 65 and of varying ethnic and religious backgrounds
     and lifestyles.

522. Seskin, Jane, and Bette Ziegler. *Older Women/Younger
     Men*. Garden City, New York: Doubleday and Co., Inc.,
     1979. Stories told by the women and men in older
     woman-younger man relationships, about 10% of which
     crossed racial lines and more than 60% of which
     crossed religious or ethnic barriers. Includes a
     chapter on "What the Experts Say," and a brief listing
     of plays, a filmography, and bibliography of current
     books on this subject. The authors state that their
     focus is on what might become a new major sociosexual
     trend, and suggest that the sign of progress will
     be that this relationship is no longer considered
     to be newsworthy.

523. Silverman, Eliane. "In Their Own Words: Mothers and
     Daughters on the Alberta Frontier, 1890-1929."
     Frontiers (Summer 1977) II(2):37-44. A discussion,

with excerpts from Silverman's interviews with women
who arrived in Alberta (where the last land rush in
North America took place) before 1929, of the theme
of daughters' perceptions of their mothers. These
frontier women came from a variety of social classes
and of ethnic, religious and regional backgrounds.
In some cases, the strong bond between mothers and
daughters documented in their narratives formed the
basis of their strength and courage.

*524. Terrill, Tom, and Jerrold Hirsch, eds. *Such As Us:
Southern Voices of the Thirties*. Chapel Hill:
University of North Carolina Press, 1978. An
anthology of Federal Writers' Project life-history
materials culled from the Southern Historical Collection
at the University of North Carolina.

*525. Thomas, Sherry. *We Didn't Have Much, But We Sure Had
Plenty: Stories of Rural Women*. (Illustrated by
Judith Brown.) New York: Doubleday Anchor Press,
1981. Oral histories of twelve older women farmers
in the U.S., among them a field hand on a Georgia
farm, co-partners on a family homestead ranch in
New Mexico, and a dairy farmer in Vermont.

526. Toussie, Carol-Grace. "Mabel, You Don't Belong Here."
In *The Older Woman: Lavender Rose or Gray Panther*,
pp. 50-2, Marie Marschall Fuller and Cora Ann Martin,
eds. Springfield, Illinois: Charles C. Thomas, 1980.
A tribute to 91-year-old Ms. Mabel Maye Harrison,
who has managed 30 years of perfect attendance at
the race track, who came to the hospital from a hotel
she has called home for 40 years, and who, refusing
to accept the recommendation to move to a senior
citizens apartment complex, was ready to be discharged
to her hotel--and to go back to her beloved horse
races--five days after admission to the hospital.
In contrast to her 60-year-old roommate who is too
timid to go for a walk, Mabel is a living symbol
of strength, independence and beauty in old age.

527. Watriss, Wendy. "It's Something Inside You." *Southern
Exposure* (Winter 1977) 4(4):76-81. Story of the
survival and family and community service of Anna
Mae Dickson, a 55-year-old black woman, a maid, born
in a rural county in East Texas. Includes an historical
overview of Grimes County. Mrs. Dickson discovered
her organizing skills through her work with the Baptist

missionary society. She has directed home demonstra-
tion projects for black girls, served as president
of PTAs at three schools, helped establish a county
club to raise funds to support school athletics,
and worked in numerous other community programs,
and is regarded as a leader by those in both the
black and white communities.

*528.   Wershaw, H.J. "Days Beyond Recall: Subsistence Home-
        steading in the Rural South, Circa 1920." *The
        International Journal of Aging and Human Development*
        (1975) 6(1):1-5.

529.   Westin, Jeane. *Making Do: How Women Survived the 30s.*
        Chicago: Follett Publishing Co., 1976. Recollections
        of the Great Depression by women of various ethnic,
        nationality, racial and religious affiliations from
        every social class and region in the country. *Making
        Do* is subdivided into four sections--women at home,
        women growing up, women at work and women influencing
        the world about them--each preceded by a sketch of
        social conditions prevailing in the 1930s. Westin,
        who spent a year interviewing 160 women whose ages
        ranged from 47 to 91 (most were in their 60s and
        70s) sought to put daughters of the Depression in
        touch with their foremothers through this book--"to
        build clear, simple, strong bridges of human experience
        between us."

530.   Wigginton, Eliot, ed. *The Foxfire Book*, ed. and with
        an introduction by Eliot Wigginton. New York: Anchor
        Press, Doubleday, 1972. Foxfire materials are gathered
        by students at Rabun Gap-Nacoochee School in the
        Appalachians. This first *Foxfire* book includes oral
        histories of Mrs. Marvin Watts ("this is the way I
        was raised up"), and Aunt Arie, who, although widowed
        several years before, and although one side of her
        body was later paralyzed as the result of a stroke,
        refuses to leave her log cabin; and appearances of
        elderly women in features on Rope, Straw, and Feathers
        Are to Sleep On; A Quilt is Something Human; Soap-
        making; Cooking on a Fireplace, Dutch Oven, and
        Wood Stove; Mountain Recipes; Preserving Vegetables;
        Preserving Fruit; Churning Your Own Butter; Curing and
        Smoking Hog; Planting By the Signs; Home Remedies;
        Dressing and Cooking Wild Animal Foods; Faith
        Healing.

531. Wigginton, Eliot, ed. *Foxfire* 2, ed. and with an
       introduction by Eliot Wigginton. New York: Anchor
       Press, Doubleday, 1973. Includes oral histories of
       Maude Shope, who at age 76 "hasn't slowed down much,"
       and Anna Howard, who at 93 is "a long way from
       surrendering," and a feature on Midwives and Granny
       Women. Appearances of older women in features on:
       Spring Wild Plant Foods; Happy Dowdle; From Raising
       Sheep to Weaving Cloth; How to Wash Clothes in an
       Iron Pot; Old-Time Burials; Boogers, Witches, and
       Haints; "Corn Shuckin's, House Raisin's, Quiltin's,
       Pea Thrashin's, Singin's, Log Rollin's, Candy Pullin's
       and...."

532. Wigginton, Eliot, ed. *Foxfire* 3, ed. and with an
       introduction by Eliot Wigginton. New York: Anchor
       Press, Doubleday, 1975. Includes oral histories of
       80-year-old Beulah Perry ("Her belief in God and the
       Bible are the main forces in her life") and Aunt Nora
       Garland, faith healer for many years, who lives in
       a stone house north of Clayton, Georgia, next to a
       building she and her husband owned and in which they
       operated a grocery store for many years. Appearances
       of elderly women in features on: Animal Care;
       Florence and Lawton Brooks; Summer and Fall Wild
       Plant Foods; Apple Butter; Cornshuck Mops, Dolls
       and Hats.

533. Wigginton, Eliot, ed. *Foxfire* 4, ed. and with an
       introduction by Eliot Wigginton. New York: Anchor
       Press/Doubleday, 1977. Includes oral histories of
       Annie Perry, "a lively 83-year-old lady who lives in
       a home that her ancestors built before the Civil War,"
       and Aunt Lola Cannon, born March 26, 1894, whose
       great-niece Anita Jenkins says of her, "A very
       generous and gentle-natured person, I have never
       heard her say a harsh word to or about any other
       person." Appearances of older women in: Etta and
       Charlie Ross Hartley; Gardening; Logging; Cheese
       Making; Update.

534. Wigginton, Eliot, ed. *Foxfire* 5, ed. and with an
       introduction by Eliot Wigginton. Garden City, New
       York: Anchor Press/Doubleday, 1979. An oral history
       of--from interviews with--Mrs. Carrie Stewart, who
       celebrated her 100th birthday in November 1978, and
       who still sews and quilts, works in her garden, keeps
       house, and attends the dinners sponsored by the Macon

County senior citizens' groups "without the aid of a walking cane." Mrs. Stewart is the first-born of ten children; her father was born a slave, and her mother's mother was a "bound girl." This issue also includes the oral history of Will and Magaline Zoellner.

*535. Wigginton, Eliot, ed. *Foxfire* 6, ed. and with an introduction by Eliot Wigginton. Garden City, New York: Anchor Press/Doubleday, 1980.

See also: 133, 134, 167, 169, 182, 423, 874, 875, 882.

B. Memory, Reminiscence
and the Life Review;
The Uses of Oral History

*536. Adams, Eleanor B. "Reminiscence and Life Review in the Aged: A Guide for the Elderly, Their Families, Friends, and Service Providers." Denton, Texas: Center for Studies in Aging, North Texas State University, 1979.

 537. Addams, Jane. *The Long Road of Woman's Memory*. New York: The Macmillan Co., 1916. The rumor that a mythical Devil Baby was visiting Hull-House brought a procession of old women there to see him, and the first two chapters of Addams's book are a record of this six-week period which revealed Memory's "important rôle in interpreting and appeasing life for the individual." Certain elderly women's reminiscences revealed another function of Memory-- "its activity as a selective agency in social re-organization," impelling Addams to write the next two chapters, on the functions of reminiscence. Chapter V is composed of conversations Addams had in Europe in 1915 with "desolated women, stripped by war of all their warm domestic interests and of children long cherished" who "sat shelterless in the devastating glare of Memory." These experiences showed Addams that Memory insists upon "the great essentials," even sacrificing the inherent power it has to appease. Chapter VI is "A Personal Experience in Interpretative Memory," in which, after a winter she spent in Egypt, visiting its tombs and temples, Addams reflects on the powers of Memory, and our obligations to it.

*538. Baum, Willa. "The Therapeutic Value of Oral History."
      *The International Journal of Aging and Human
      Development* (1980-81) 12(1):49-53.

 539. Butler, Robert N. "The Life Review: An Interpretation
      of Reminiscence in the Aged." In *Middle Age and
      Aging: A Reader in Social Psychology*, pp. 486-96,
      Bernice L. Neugarten, ed. Chicago: The University
      of Chicago Press, 1968. This paper postulates the
      universal occurrence in older people of a mental
      process of reviewing one's life. Butler proposes
      that this process helps account for the increased
      reminiscence in people as they age, that it contributes
      to the occurrence of certain late-life disorders,
      especially depression, and that it also participates
      in the evolution of candor, serenity, and wisdom
      among certain of the aged. The more usual view of
      reminiscence is negative; the prevailing tendency is
      to identify reminiscence in the aged with psychological
      dysfunction, and thus to regard it as a symptom.
      But the life review, which includes reminiscence,
      although it is not synonymous with it, is a possible
      response to death, may play a significant role in
      the psychology and psycho-pathology of the aged, and
      potentially proceeds toward personality reorganization.
      Persons who seem especially prone to anxiety, despair,
      depression and other psychopathological manifestations
      are those who always tended to avoid the present and
      to emphasize the future, those who have consciously
      exercised the human capacity to injure others, and
      those who are characterologically arrogant and
      prideful. Butler provides case materials and literary
      and social scientific references to illustrate his
      themes, and emphasizes the importance of observing
      the positive, affirmative changes reported by the
      aged as part of their life experience, and of finding
      constructive alterations in character which may be
      a consequence of the life review.

*540. Butler, Robert N. "The Life Review: An Unrecognized
      Bonanza." *The International Journal of Aging and
      Human Development* (1980-81) 12(1):35-8.

*541. Falk, Jacqueline M. "The Organization of Remembered
      Life Experience in Old Age: Its Relation to Antici-
      pated Stress, to Subsequent Adaptive Capacity and
      to Age." Diss., Committee on Human Development,
      University of Chicago, 1970.

542.   George, Diana Hume.   "Community and Creativity, an
       Approach to Teaching the Subject of Aging."   Paper
       presented at MLA Special Session-Perspectives on
       Aging, New York, December 1978.   George discussed a
       work experience that integrated the humanistic and
       social sciences approaches--her job as a CETA worker
       for the Chautauqua County Office for the Aging--which
       formed her own perspective on aging.   Noting that this
       is the first generation of old people who are living
       and dying with TV in the background, she suggested
       that old age needs a productive kind of mythologizing
       in our society.   She affirmed the need for an inter-
       disciplinary emphasis in humanities courses, and
       suggested community involvement and field work should
       be assigned to students, that aging should be made
       the subject of art, poetry, fiction and drama in the
       humanities classroom, and that a creative writing
       approach to teaching aging as a theme in humanities
       should be adopted (this could be easily integrated
       with field work).   She stated that taped conversations
       with old people are superb raw material for poetry,
       fiction, songs and drama.   Her major point was that
       a humanities perspective on aging should contribute
       to keeping this generation of the elderly alive in
       creative ways.

543.   Gluck, Sherna.   "What's So Special About Women?   Women's
       Oral History."   *Frontiers* (Summer 1977) II(2):3-17.
       Women are reconstructing our own past; using our own
       voices and experiences, we are creating a new history.
       The political base of women's oral history differs
       from the Nevins model.   Also, the content is special,
       and for this reason it was decided to devote an
       entire issue to this subject.   Prominent women are
       included.   But most women did not lead public lives,
       and the pieces in this issue indicate the unique
       potential of oral history to move beyond the written
       record to document the lives of all kinds of women.
       Women's oral history is a feminist encounter, even
       if the interviewee is not herself a feminist.   It
       creates a new kind of material about women, validates
       women's experiences, represents the communication
       among women of different generations and the discovery
       of our own roots and the development of a continuity
       heretofore denied us.   The three types of interviews--
       topical, biographical and autobiographical--overlap;
       the autobiographical is a strange hybrid, and repre-
       sents a collaborative effort of the archivist or

historian and the source or history. The best
interviewer encourages spontaneity and self-direction.
But it is intellectually dishonest to discount the
interviewer's role in creating oral history. There
are also drawbacks to the collaborative reconstruction
of the interviewee's life. Oral historians must
work to maintain a balance between what we, as
feminist historians, think is important, and what
the women we are interviewing think was important
about their own lives. Oral history allows for the
creation of a new literature. It is not the province
of experts. Reading about interviewing technique and
actual practice at "mock" interviews are helpful in
developing technique. Ideas based upon Gluck's own
experience in gathering oral histories of elderly
women are offered. Methods of making contact, adopting
an interviewing style (Gluck sees the interview as a
transaction between interviewer and interviewee) and
processing the interview (including ways of making
the tape accessible to others) are discussed. Includes
appendices on choosing equipment, and summarizing
and indexing the tape, with a sample tape summary and
a sample index page.

*544.　Gorney, James E.　"Experiencing and Age: Patterns of
Reminiscence Among the Elderly."　Diss., Committee
on Human Development, University of Chicago, 1968.

*545.　Harris, Raymond, and Sara Harris.　"Therapeutic Uses
of Oral History Techniques in Medicine."　*The
International Journal of Aging and Human Development*
(1980-81) 12(1):27-34.

546.　Jensen, Joan, Beverly Baca and Barbara Bolin.　"Family
History and Oral History."　*Frontiers* (Summer 1977)
II(2):93-7.　A report, with excerpts from a Chicana
and an Anglo family history, of the uses of family
history in women's history classes and the enthusiastic
responses of students to these projects.

*547.　Lo Gerfo, Marianne.　"Three Ways of Reminiscence in
Theory and Practice."　*The International Journal of
Aging and Human Development* (1980-81) 12(1):39-48.

548.　Meese, Elizabeth A.　"Telling It All: Literary Standards
and Narratives by Southern Women."　*Frontiers*
(Summer 1977) II(2):63-7.　A broad definition of
literature that includes literary and non-literary

documents and oral as well as written testimonies
would enfranchise the works of women, blacks, and
others unfairly excluded. Criteria for inclusion
ought to be revised. Feminist critics "must insist
on the embodiment of certain values and attitudes
because ours is a revolutionary activity." Feminist
scholarship needs reliable studies on female ontology
and on female epistemology. Meese states that there
is a sense in which a woman "owns" the space in which
she lives, and makes this space the very ground of
her being. She suggests that the movement of
women's fiction often tends to be vertical rather
than horizontal, and that it favors spatialized
interruption. "Only by expanding our sense of
history and literature to accommodate oral narrative
can we begin to establish the whole truth of our
national consciousness, and perhaps then begin to
understand art in its most inclusive and holistic
sense."

*549.   Revere, Virginia, and Sheldon S. Tobin. "Myth and
        Reality: The Older Person's Relationship to His
        Past." *The International Journal of Aging and Human
        Development* (1980-81) 12(1):15-26.

550.   Ryant, Carl. "Comment: Oral History and Gerontology."
        The Gerontologist (February 1981) 21(1):104-5. Ryant
        discusses the values and dangers of oral history in
        gerontology research, and provides information on
        the location of the national Oral History Association
        and a list of useful references.

551.   Spicker, Stuart F. "Gerontogenetic Mentation: Memory,
        Dementia and Medicine in the Penultimate Years."
        In *Aging and the Elderly: Humanistic Perspectives
        in Gerontology*, pp. 153-80, Stuart F. Spicker, Kathleen
        M. Woodward and David D. Van Tassel, eds. Atlantic
        Highlands, New Jersey: Humanities Press, Inc., 1978.
        Spicker believes the contributions philosophers can
        make to the domain of aging and the mentation of
        the aged are considerable. He states that research
        into the structure of memorial consciousness in
        senectitude must abandon the model of time as linear
        and objectified, and identifies the difficulties
        inherent in accurate assessment of mentation, the
        limitations of the M.S.Q. and the impreciseness of
        the concept of "dementia." Variables studied in
        inquiries into mentation must be kept conceptually

and operationally distinct. Piaget's successful
approach should be taken as an analogue for a study
of mentation of the aged. Spicker calls for the
establishment of a center for gerontogenetic mentation.

552. Wagner, Sally Roesch. "Oral History as a Biographical
Tool." *Frontiers* (Summer 1977) II(2):87-92. This
subject is discussed within the context of Wagner's
working relationship with 91-year-old Matilda Jewell
Gage, the only living grandchild and namesake of
Matilda Joslyn Gage, an important but overlooked
theoretician and activist in the radical wing of the
19th-century woman's movement. Gage is an old
family friend with whom Wagner has worked for four
summers reconstructing her grandmother's life from
the documents and family stories Gage gathered over
the years.

553. Wrye, Harriet, and Jacqueline Churilla. "Looking Inward,
Looking Backward: Reminiscence and the Life Review."
Frontiers (Summer 1977) II(2):98-105. Life review
has value for the older person who reminisces, and
for the immediate audience and those in the broader
culture as well. Reminiscence is positively associated
with good morale, and this suggests that it serves
a positive adaptive function for the aging. It is
a means of achieving what Erikson calls "ego integrity."
The integration of both positive and negative experiences is therapeutic for the elderly. Life
reviews in the form of oral histories can lead
historians and others to develop important insights
for further research. Taking life histories of the
aged benefits clinicians and social workers as
well as those working in the growing field of
Gerontology.

See also: 298, 577, 626, 710.

XII. PERSONAL DOCUMENTS OF OLDER WOMEN--
DIARIES, ESSAYS, JOURNALS, LETTERS, MEMOIRS;
WOMEN'S REFLECTIONS ON AGING;
WORD-PORTRAITS OF OLDER WOMEN

554. Addams, Jane. *The Second Twenty Years at Hull-House,
With a Record of a Growing World Consciousness.*
New York: The Macmillan Co., 1930.

555. Atherton, Gertrude. "Are Women Born Liars?" In *Can
Women Be Gentlemen?*, pp. 3-24, Gertrude Atherton.
Boston: Houghton Mifflin Co., 1938. Although it will
be some time before men realize this, the "long era
of male dominance" is coming to an end, and women
are moving toward complete equality. The writer
finds it amusing that political and economic affairs
excite the imagination, while this revolution--which
is all but unseen--gathers strength and momentum
with every passing year.

556. Atherton, Gertrude. "A Course in Life and Human Nature."
In *Can Women Be Gentlemen?*, pp. 86-91, Gertrude
Atherton. Boston: Houghton Mifflin Co., 1938. Girls,
especially, should have it pounded into them that
human emotions are even more transitory than life:
Tout lasse, tout casse, tout passe. Perhaps, if
girls were convinced that all Stepmother Nature wants
is the continuance of the race, and that youthful
passion is brewed by "that old harridan" to victimize
the young and fruitful, they might want to thwart
her. And again, perhaps not. A course in Life and
Human Nature might neutralize the influence of the
popular culture. In time, girls become middle-aged
women, and would demand love and sex as but two of
the major interests life has to offer.

557. Atherton, Gertrude. "Defeating Old Age." In *Can
Women Be Gentlemen?*, pp. 58-65, Gertrude Atherton.
Boston: Houghton Mifflin Co., 1938. The most

interesting single expression of human personality
is the attitude taken toward life when middle age
begins. Intelligent men and women of today no
longer accept the notion that the normal life span
is three score and ten and the latter part brings an
inevitable decline; they know that the end result of
too much routine is death in life; and they have a
far better chance of fruition and adjustment than
those of earlier generations. Between the Steinach
reactivation treatment, beauty parlors, cosmetic
surgeons and cosmetics, no woman has any excuse not
to look and feel twenty or even thirty years younger
than her actual age. The loss of friends is in-
escapable, and a tragedy. Old age can be defeated by
making new friends and by making Life yield many
interests: those who are engaged in artistic endeavor
or organizational activity are very fortunate. Anyone
with spirit fights the enemy. "And Life is the most
persistent and pitiless of man's enemies. To fight
and confound her is the antidote for all ills."

558.   Atherton, Gertrude.   "Superwomen."   In *Can Women Be
       Gentlemen?*, pp. 112-5, Gertrude Atherton.   Boston:
       Houghton Mifflin Co., 1938.   Today, no one seems to
       care how old a woman is, once her first youth has
       passed, and marital status has little to do with her
       position in life; the term "old maid" is obsolete.
       This is one of the most interesting periods in world
       history, and a Godsend to women. For the first time
       in modern history, moreover, women are independent
       of men. Intelligent women enjoy men's companionship,
       but if they do not find husbands, life is full of
       other resources. Millions of alert, modern women
       know the psychological as well as business value of
       keeping their looks. After middle age, they have
       outgrown the folly of wanting to look young, but
       they are determined to look *well*. The intelligent
       woman is attentive to diet, exercise and moderation
       in every sort of indulgence, and watches the behavior
       of her organs and glands. The most important gland
       is the thyroid. Life is harsher for men than for
       women, who seem to have developed a tougher fiber.
       Men's moral as well as physical resistance wears
       thin, often. Atherton writes that she feels sorry
       for them, and that this would have sounded quaint
       fifty, or even thirty years earlier.

559. Atherton, Gertrude. "Why Do Women Hate One Another?" In *Can Women Be Gentlemen?*, pp. 38-49, Gertrude Atherton. Boston: Houghton Mifflin Co., 1938. In this essay, Atherton observes that American women must take refuge in one another's society once the "mating season has run its initial course." Most of the more intelligent women would make excellent companions for men. But since that is rarely possible, "the result will be a solidarity of women, too experienced to quarrel and hate one another, that will increasingly threaten the supremacy of the male, although he is still too blind or too arrogant to suspect it."

560. Baldwin, Faith. "My Crabbèd Age." In *The Older Woman: Lavender Rose or Gray Panther*, pp. 75-8, Marie Marschall Fuller and Cora Ann Martin, eds. Springfield, Illinois: Charles C. Thomas, 1980. The occasion for this essay is the presentation of a lightweight cane to the writer by her daughter. Baldwin takes exception to Browning's invitation to grow old along with him, which she remarks that the poet extended when he was only 29 himself, and she states that she is weary of books advising how to grow old gracefully, of articles extolling old age, and of the admonitions of physicians. She observes that the years have brought her knowledge rather than wisdom, that she has not been serene since she was a toddler, and that she is not grateful to have all her buttons, since she never had a "buttoned-down mind." She keeps up with the times as best she can, and has not lost her hopes for the world and for the young. She does not mind her age, but she *does* mind the insistence that all is sweetness and light, and also the disabilities and prohibitions that come with age. She salutes old people who are adventurous, and remarks she has an inner self who stubbornly refuses to grow up.

*561. Barr, Amelia E. *Three Score and Ten*. New York: D. Appleton, 1915.

562. Beard, Mary R., ed. *America Through Women's Eyes*. New York: Greenwood Press, Inc., 1976. A collection of writings first published in 1933. Women of all ages are represented in these personal documents and publications dating from the time of "Opening Up the Wilderness" and "Making the Revolution" to "World War and World Peace" and "Taking New Bearings." In

her Introduction, Beard hails the tendency of
contemporary (early 1930s) thought towards integration, which she finds to be striking and significant,
and the revelation of the limitations and relativity
of the feminism of an earlier age made possible by
this broadening of social thought to include all of
culture, and woman as primordial force in history
(the thesis of her book, *Woman As Force in History*,
published in 1947).

563.   Benary-Isbert, Margot. *These Vintage Years*. New York:
       Abingdon Press, 1968. Widowed after thirty-eight
       years of marriage, an elderly woman reflects on the
       possibilities of later life for solitude, creativity,
       freedom and ripening. She writes that this last
       challenge can be accepted or rejected just as chal-
       lenges of earlier years, and that, "Adventure never
       ends."

564.   Bevington, Helen. *The House Was Quiet and the World
       Was Calm*. New York: Harcourt Brace Jovanovich, Inc.,
       1971. In her memoir, poet Bevington vividly recalls
       life in post-World War Two America, and the years of
       the "witch hunt."

565.   Bogan, Louise. "From the Journals of a Poet." (Ruth
       Limmer, ed.) *The New Yorker* (January 30, 1978)
       LIII(50):39-70. The poet meditates on childhood,
       on looking backward, on how she had imagined her old
       age would be, on music, on flowers, on her memories
       of her mother, on the workings of memory, on aging,
       death and dreams.

566.   Bowen, Catherine Drinker. *Adventures of a Biographer*.
       Boston: Atlantic Monthly Press, 1959. Reflections
       on the artistic task of recreating the past.

567.   Buck, Pearl S. *A Bridge for Passing*. New York: The
       John Day Co., 1962. Novelist, short story writer and
       translator Pearl Buck (1892-1973) writes an auto-
       biographical account of her experience of widowhood.
       In Japan for the filming of her book *The Big Wave,*
       she received a call from her daughter, telling her
       that her husband, who had been ill for seven years,
       had died. "The day I had dreaded had come. The
       final loneliness was here."

568.   Burns, Edward, ed. *Staying on Alone: Letters of Alice
       B. Toklas*, edited by Edward Burns with an Introduction

by Gilbert A. Harrison. New York: Liveright, 1973.
Toklas (1877-1967) was nurse, secretary, chef and
confidante of Gertrude Stein.

569. Cather, Willa. "A Chance Meeting." In *Not Under
      Forty*, pp. 3-42, Willa Cather. New York: Alfred A.
      Knopf, 1936. Cather has a chance meeting with
      Madame Franklin-Grout, who she later discovers is
      Flaubert's niece Caroline, at Aix-les-Bains in
      August 1930. Madame Grout is 84 at the time, yet
      is "contemptuously intolerant of the limitations
      of old age." She often goes sketching in the morning,
      and attends concerts and operas in the wilting heat,
      listening to the music with attentiveness and appre-
      ciation. Cather was especially astonished by Madame
      Grout's keen and sympathetic interest in modern music.
      This essay is a portrait of an utterly self-disciplined
      lady whose character impressed Cather as profoundly
      as did her devotion to great art.

570. Conover, Charlotte (Reeve). *On Being Eighty and Other
      Digressions*. Yellow Springs, Ohio: Antioch Bookplate
      Co., 1938. A collection of four humorous and life-
      affirming essays, "On Being Eighty," "Grow Old and
      Like It" (both originally written for *The Dayton
      News* in 1935 and 1937), "Signposts in the Dark,"
      and "The Pools Are Filled With Water." Conover, a
      "humble octogenarian," was blind in later life. She
      counsels younger people to cultivate imagination and
      appreciation, and to begin to prepare for old age
      when still in youth. Blindness is a challenge to
      "be grasped like a nettle," and every challenge is
      "a hope, and hope means growth, and growth brings
      freedom of the soul."

571. "A Crabbit Old Woman Wrote This." In *The Older Woman:
      Lavender Rose or Gray Panther*, pp. 71-2, Marie
      Marschall Fuller and Cora Ann Martin, eds. Springfield,
      Illinois: Charles C. Thomas, 1980. A poem found among
      the possessions of an elderly lady who died in the
      geriatric ward of Ashludie Hospital, near Dundee,
      that so impressed the staff that copies were duplicated
      and distributed to all the nurses in the hospital.
      In the poem, which has since been published in a
      magazine and newspaper, the unknown author writes
      that "inside this old carcass a young girl still
      dwells...."

572. De Mille, Agnes. *And Promenade Home*. Boston: Little,
      Brown and Co., 1958. De Mille's (1905-) Story of
      love and marriage during World War II.

573. De Mille, Agnes. *Where the Wings Grow (a Memoir of
      Childhood)*. New York: Doubleday and Co., Inc., 1978.
      De Mille's last summer in Merriewold in 1914.

*574. An Elderly Woman. "The Land of Old Age." *Harper's
      Bazaar* (August, Sept., Dec., 1906) 40:675, 777,
      1149-50.

575. Fisher, Dorothy Canfield. Prologue, "What My Mother
      Taught Me." In *A Harvest of Stories: From a Half
      Century of Writing by Dorothy Canfield*, pp. xi-xxix.
      New York: Harcourt, Brace and Co., Inc., 1956. At
      the age of 77, the writer remembers being with her
      artist-mother at the Prado nearly a half-century
      before, and the illumination she had then--expressed
      in one of her earliest stories, "The Bedquilt"--that
      brought her to change her calling from scholarship
      to writing fiction (see No. 674 of this Bibliography).

576. Hahn, Aloyse. "It's Tough to Be Old." In *The Older
      Woman: Lavender Rose or Gray Panther*, pp. 317-9,
      Marie Marschall Fuller and Cora Ann Martin, eds.
      Springfield, Illinois: Charles C. Thomas, 1980. A
      94-year-old woman placed in a nursing home six years
      before by her family longs to be taken home, and asks
      how she can trust the strangers upon whom she is now
      dependent. Not knowing the inner workings of her
      memory, the nurses say she is "confused" and "dis-
      oriented." She wishes the nurses would not write
      her off as being "not in touch," and she appreciates
      how one particular nurse who is very kind to her shows
      that she understands her. She needs this understanding,
      as well as a sense of security, hope and respect;
      most of all, she needs love.

577. Hellman, Lillian. Introduction. In *Three*, with new
      commentaries by the author, pp. i-xxv. Boston: Little,
      Brown and Co., Inc., 1979. In her introductory note
      to this one-volume edition of *An Unfinished Woman*,
      Pentimento and *Scoundrel Time*, Hellman says she fights
      going back to anything she has written, and even
      though these books are made up of selective memories,
      she has no love for the past, whether written or
      remembered. She has believed for a long time that
      few people grow wiser with the years. Parts of these

three books seem to have been written by a woman she
does not know very well. She tried to tell the truth
in them. "What a word is truth. Slippery, tricky,
unreliable."

*578.   Jacoby, Susan. "What Do I Do with the Next Twenty Years?"
        The New York Times Magazine, June 17, 1973, pp. 10-11,
        39-40, 42-3, 49.

*579.   Jastrow, Marie. *A Time to Remember: Growing Up in New
        York Before the Great War*. New York: W.W. Norton and
        Co., Inc., 1979. Jastrow's father, an Austrian Jew,
        came to America in the immigration wave of the 1900s,
        penniless and in search of the legendary gold that
        was to provide for his wife and child, who were left
        behind in Serbia, for the rest of their lives.
        Jastrow's book is a memoir of these early years in
        New York, of the ordeals of the immigrants, and of
        the closely-knit neighborhood of Jews and Germans
        in Yorkville where the family later settled.

580.   Johnson, Josephine. *Seven Houses: A Memoir of Time and
        Places*. New York: Simon and Schuster, 1973. Poet
        and novelist Johnson (1910-) recalls her childhood,
        youth and mature years through this memoir of time
        and places.

581.   Kamp, Irene Kittle. "Facing a New Face." *The New York
        Times Magazine*, September 9, 1979, pp. 116-9, 130.
        Kamp, a former magazine editor, playwright and
        screenwriter, had cancer, and as a result she had
        to have her nose surgically removed. She writes
        that she loves to be old, that mentally she is better
        than ever, but that it is a struggle to cope with the
        physical problems of aging. Older people feel accep-
        tance and affection and forgiveness, but they do not
        always have the strength "to put it to work."

582.   Laird, Carobeth. *Limbo: A memoir about life in a
        nursing home by a survivor*. Novato, California:
        Chandler and Sharp Publishers, Inc., 1979. A memoir
        about experiences in a nursing home in Arizona. In
        her "Epilogue--Before and After *Limbo*," Anne Buffington-
        Jennings writes that Carobeth Laird (1895-) was,
        at the time she was rescued from "Limbo" in 1974 by
        the Michelson family, beginning "an eighth life."
        Laird's *Encounter with an Angry God* and *The
        Chemehuevis* (both published by Malki Museum Press)

had been accepted for publication by then, and Laird, who had been writing all her life, but whose first book was not published until her 80th birthday, looked forward to writing still more books--one of which is *Limbo*. Laird's other "seven lives" are outlined in the Epilogue, as well as in her other books. In one of these lives she was the wife of George Laird, a Chemehuevi tribesman, and for years she collected lore on Chemehuevi language, customs and beliefs.

583. L'Engle, Madeleine. *A Circle of Quiet*. New York: Farrar, Straus and Giroux, 1972. Writer L'Engle's (1918-) "circle of quiet" is her special place for meditation in solitude, a little brook in a glade near Crosswicks, the family's New England farmhouse. This book, which she thinks of as her "letter from Crosswicks," is comprised of pages from her journals and the writing she did during the summer of her 51st year when four generations of the family were gathered under one roof. She believes, with Jung, that middle age is the time for finding the meaning of our par- ticular lives. Together with the subjects of youth, middle age and old age, and the relationships between the generations, she reflects on the responsibilities of parents, teachers and writers, and on the nature of reality and the imagination, and creativity and compassion.

584. L'Engle, Madeleine. *The Summer of the Great-Grandmother*. New York: Farrar, Straus and Giroux, 1974. The writer has promised her mother that she will never put her in a nursing home. In the summer of 1970, the 90-year-old Great-Grandmother comes to Crosswicks suffering from atherosclerosis and begins her "swift descent" into senility. L'Engle writes of the mother she knew and the mother she did not know, of her mother's irascibility and of her loss of memory and of all sense of time, of her own sorrow and guilt, of family history, of the dilemma she faces because of the promise she made to her mother, and of her confrontation with her own mortality, in this, the fourth and last summer when four generations are gathered together at Crosswicks.

585. Limmer, Ruth, ed. *What the Woman Lived: Selected Letters of Louise Bogan 1920-1970*. New York: Harcourt Brace Jovanovich, Inc., 1973.

*586. Lindbergh, Anne Morrow. *War Within and Without,
       Diaries and Letters of Anne Morrow Lindbergh, 1939-
       1944.* New York: Harcourt Brace Jovanovich, 1980.

587.   MacDougall, Allan Ross, ed. *Letters of Edna St. Vincent
       Millay.* New York: Harper and Brothers, 1952.

588.   Mead, Margaret. *Ruth Benedict (1887-1948).* New York:
       Columbia University Press, 1974. Topics: Ruth Benedict,
       A Humanist in Anthropology; Selected Papers by Ruth
       Benedict; Selected Bibliography of the Writings of
       Ruth Benedict.

589.   Moffat, Mary Jane, and Charlotte Painter, eds.
       Revelations: Diaries of Women. New York: Random
       House, 1974. Samples from the work of women diarists
       who, with the exception of Sei-Shonagon, are from the
       19th and 20th centuries. Excerpts are arranged under
       three broad headings--Love, Work, and Power--from
       youth to old age. The authors propose that Love,
       Work, and Power be redefined. The book includes a
       Foreword, excerpts "On Keeping a Diary," and an
       Afterword, "Psychic Bisexuality" by Painter.

590.   Nies, Judith. *Seven Women: Portraits from the American
       Radical Tradition.* New York: Penguin Books, 1977.
       In Nies's Introduction, The Tradition of American
       Radical Women, she states that the difficult choice
       of these seven women was made with the hope that
       each represented a specific problem in the inter-
       pretation of women as radicals. Portraits are of:
       Sarah Moore Grimké (1792-1873), Harriet Tubman
       (1820-1913), Elizabeth Cady Stanton (1815-1902),
       Mother Jones (1830-1930), Charlotte Perkins Gilman
       (1860-1935), Anna Louise Strong (1885-1970), and
       Dorothy Day (1897-1980). Epilogue: The Legacy of
       the Radical Tradition.

591.   Nin, Anaïs. Letter. *Ms.* (July 1974) III(1):7. In
       this letter, Nin expresses her surprise that *Ms.*
       printed an old photograph of her that was taken in
       1967, rather than selecting an untouched photograph
       from those sent to them by her agent. Nin stated
       that she expected the magazine to publish one of
       her more recent photographs (which they did, along
       with this letter), writing that it was not a question
       of vanity that was involved, but a matter that is
       vital to other women. "I have spent much of my time

seeking to help women overcome the fear of aging.
I have made myself an example of how one could work,
live, act, and look at 70."

592. "An Old Woman Speaks." Prologue in *Aging in America*,
      pp. 1-4, Bert Kruger Smith, ed. Boston: Beacon Press,
      1973. The narrator's *cri de coeur* is that she is a
      living, sentient being, that she exists although no
      one affirms her existence or responds to her as a
      person. "I am an island, barren, surrounded by the
      waters of my life, my own shores drouth-pounded, des-
      sicated."

593. Paine, Harriet E. *Old People*. Boston: Houghton Mifflin
      Co., 1910. In Alice Brown's Introduction--a memoir
      of Paine--she says that the author was not yet 60
      when she wrote this book, and that for Paine (1845-
      1909), age "seemed to be her blossoming time," even
      though she was deaf, her sight was dimming, and she
      had always been frail. In this book, stories about
      old people she knew are interwoven with Paine's own
      meditations on "greeting old age" (with valor), on
      change and breadth in late life, on the decline of the
      senses, on work ("Much of the best work of the world
      is done by men and women past sixty"), on the problem
      of earning a living in old age, on keeping young, on
      beauty in old age, on "Darkness" (blindness) and
      "silence" (deafness), on weakness and dependency,
      the inner life of the old, the relationship between
      old and young, "After Fourscore" (here she writes
      about garrulousness, "the discipline of loneliness,"
      and "fads"), on the renewal of emotions (the years
      when the old think over the past "have a great part
      to play in the unfolding of the character"), "A
      Last Lesson in Friendship," "Last Lessons in Char-
      acter" (the lesson of humility and the conquest of
      envy and pride), the privileges of old age, and
      "Sunset," in which Paine writes that she wonders
      "if anybody reads *De Senectute* in modern days without
      a feeling of sadness that, with all its noble
      thought, it is so little touched by the ideal."
      She refers frequently to Helen Keller. Note her
      observation that most people experience more struggle
      and suffering at the age of 50 than at any other
      time: with responsibilities to both older and younger
      generations, 50-year-olds "are in the thickest of
      the fight of life."

594. Parker, Dorothy. "The Middle or Blue Period." In
      The Portable Dorothy Parker, pp. 594-7. New York
      and Harmondsworth, Middlesex, England: Penguin Books
      Ltd., 1976. Parker awakens on her birthday, knowing
      there was something terrible she had to remember--
      "Not just plain terrible" but "fancy terrible; this
      was terrible with raisins in it." She has bade
      farewell to her 30s for the tenth and last time.

595. Robinson, Anna Hope Gould. *The Evolution of an Idea,*
      a personal research project in Analytical Psychology.
      Unpublished mss., 2 volumes, Copyright Rosamond
      Robinson Jaqua, Kristine Mann Library, C.G. Jung
      Foundation for Analytical Psychology, New York City.
      The personal story, written in the 1950s, of a 60-
      year-old woman, an "aging grandmother," who, in working
      out her relationship with her husband, undertakes
      the "inner journey" of individuation. Her Jungian
      analyst believes that people have a potentiality
      that is best developed after the years normally
      devoted to natural ego-development are over, that
      Life has breadth and depth as well as mere length,
      and that because people change continually, we need
      to prepare for the future. Robinson writes that to
      live decades beyond the child-bearing period is a
      threat and not a promise if one lacks purpose. She
      believes that for an old woman, life's bitterest
      tragedy is not to be needed. She suggests that when
      woman finishes her work in the home, she may emerge
      into her larger home--the world with its problems,
      and that whatever personal problems a woman has not
      resolved, she carries with her and adds to the burden
      of the world. Robinson writes that it is demanded
      by Life that woman accept her responsibility in the
      human venture in consciousness.

596. Rouse, Blair, ed. *Letters of Ellen Glasgow*. New York:
      Harcourt, Brace and Co., 1958.

597. Russ, Lavinia. *A High Old Time or How to Enjoy Being a*
      Woman Over Sixty. New York: Saturday Review Press,
      1972. A humorous and spirited inside view of being
      60, and a "how-to" book on aging. Chapters: The
      Best Is Yet to Be, My Foot; Boring from Within;
      I'm Glad I Wasn't Born Beautiful; That Dress Is *You*;
      Dresses for Breakfasts, and Dinners, and Balls; Red
      Does Something for You; Well-Suited for the Sixties;
      Free and Easy; Accessories to the Crime; You Don't

Have to Break Your Hip; Mothers-in-Law Are No Joke;
There's Always Money for the Movies; Whistling in
the Dark; Time on Your Hands; Off to See the Wizard.

*598. Sarton, May. *The House By the Sea: A Journal*. New
       York: W.W. Norton and Co., Inc., 1977.

*599. Sarton, May. *I Knew a Phoenix: Sketches for an Auto-
       biography*. New York: Rinehart, 1959.

 600. Sarton, May. *Journal of a Solitude*. New York: W.W.
       Norton and Co., Inc., 1977. Sarton writes that one
       reason she wanted to keep this journal of a year at
       Nelson was because she thinks that her *Plant Dreaming
       Deep* has created the myth of a false Paradise, and
       she wants to destroy that myth. She reflects on
       solitude, on nature, on writing and on growing older.
       For Sarton, Anne Thorp--whom she visits every year on
       Greenings Island--is a good example of the values an
       unmarried woman may sometimes represent, for her
       capacity for experience is immense, yet does not
       ever seem burdened by all her relationships. Anne
       Thorp "lives each moment of the day as if it were
       the first and the last, with the whole of herself."

 601. Sarton, May. *Plant Dreaming Deep*. New York: W.W.
       Norton and Co., Inc., 1968. In this book written
       in praise of Nelson, Sarton reflects on the
       presences in her home--chiefly those of her dead
       parents--and on Perley and other neighbors and
       friends, on middle age, on gardening, on writing and
       teaching, and on solitude. In her last chapter, she
       reflects that full awareness of mortality comes only
       when one is "past the meridian" of 50, that there
       are "late joys" in life, that in aging we become
       contemporaries of those who once seemed much older,
       and we also become more available to and depended
       upon by the young. She writes of having come recently
       to value the inward-turning of the adventure of
       life more and more.

*602. Sarton, May. *Recovering*. New York: W.W. Norton and
       Co., Inc., 1980. "A journal of hope after pain."

 603. Saul, Shura. *Aging: An Album of People Growing Old*.
       New York: John Wiley and Sons, Inc., 1974. Literary
       presentations in the form of vignettes of real
       stories about older people "presented as highlights

of a spectrum of circumstances that may be faced by any aging person in modern times." Selections are based on the recommendations of 54 students, professionals and elderly people serving as readers and judges of 40 vignettes submitted to them to be evaluated for their reality, emotional appeal, and instructional value. Three major sections--"Picture Frames," a philosophic perspective, humanistic and optimistic, for the circumstances and emotions depicted in the vignettes; "An Album," including fiction, letters, poetry, journalistic accounts and conversations and contributions of both younger and older people sharing their ideas and feelings, for creative use by teachers and students; and "Background Discussions," suggesting implications for service in an interdisciplinary context, and education combining cognitive with emotional elements. In "Picture Frames," Saul observes that the "learning process involves experience plus interpretations within an emotional climate conducive to growth and change," and sets forth the premises of the album, among which is the idea that patterns of aging are very diverse. She also discusses the challenge presented to society to revise the current view of senescence and the world of the aging person (her topics are the work ethic, retirement, widowhood, change, urban living and family life, and the concept of interdependence), a variety of myths and stereotypes about the aging person, and the problems and tasks of the person in senescence. Themes of Album vignettes are: "Life, Work and Death," "Love, Loneliness and Loss," "Change, Hope and Struggle," "Young People Write of Aging," and "Old People Write of Aging." The "Background Discussion" includes annotations about the vignettes.

604. Scott-Maxwell, Florida. *The Measure of My Days*. New York: Alfred A. Knopf, Inc., 1969. In this personal journal about being old, 82-year-old Scott-Maxwell writes that she is puzzled by age, that she found her seventies to be interesting and to be fairly serene, but that her "eighties are passionate." She finds that she grows more intense as she ages. She thinks that, "The crucial task of age is balance," that old age is "a time of discovery," that the experience of old age is intense and varied, and that "The last years may matter most."

605.   Scott-Maxwell, Florida.   "We Are the Sum of Our Days."
       Epilogue in *Culture and Aging: An Anthropological
       Study of Older Americans*, pp. 434-8, Margaret Clark
       and Barbara Gallatin Anderson.   Springfield, Illinois:
       Charles C. Thomas, 1967.   A meditation on the inner
       life of old people, of the experience of anonymity
       and invisibility, the buoyant feeling of freshness,
       and the freedom and storminess and sense of immortality
       of old age, by a Jungian analyst.   This paper is
       slightly abridged from the text of a radio talk
       delivered on the Third Programme of the BBC, and
       printed in *The Listener* (LII: 1337, October 14,
       1954, pp. 627-9), and later in *Harper's Bazaar*.

606.   Scudder, Vida.   "The Privilege of Age."   *Atlantic
       Monthly* (February 1933) 151(2):205-11.   At age 70,
       Scudder meditates on old age.   She states that she is
       writing this essay because she believes that the
       experience is social as well as private, that old
       people need to confer in order to discover how to
       make the later years "the climax of the fine art of
       living."   She enjoys being old far more than she
       ever enjoyed being young.   She feels more alive
       (although not in her body) because she is free to
       enjoy the sensory impressions she receives.   She
       can at last be forgetful of the tyranny of time.
       In old age, limitations are transmuted into privilege.
       And age brings the renunciation of greed--the lust
       for possession and the lust for achievement.   She
       finds the escape from responsibility to be delightful.
       But the gradual cessation of responsibility and action
       must mean not less life, but more.   An energetic
       middle life is the only safe precursor of a vitally
       happy old age.   All old people, when they withdraw
       from active life, should take up at once some interest
       remote from any they had before.   In old age, one
       is at last free from the demand to specialize.   The
       loss of memory does not necessarily portend the loss
       of one's very being.   There is reason to believe
       that memory is suspended, rather than gone: in two
       cases known to Scudder, a mind apparently reduced
       to puerile futility was restored to radiant clarity:
       each detail of the past and present shone clear before
       the approach of death.   To her, this was convincing
       proof of immortality.   The old, when lonely, can find
       fellowship in good books and affections which make
       no personal claims.   The bereaved become awesomely
       aware that the dead are present, that the beloved

dead can be possessed and cherished in a sense
peculiar and blessed, "for death holds a unique
revelation of personality." Old age gives us the
opportunity to understand how the eternity awaiting
us is even now our home.

607. Smith, Ethel Sabin. *Passports at Seventy*. New York:
      W.W. Norton and Co., Inc., 1961. In her account of
      her journey around the world by ocean freighter at
      the age of 70 after her retirement from college
      teaching, psychologist Ethel Sabin Smith writes with
      an awareness of the likenesses between the journey
      by ship and the journey that is human life. In the
      chapter "Letters to Write," she contemplates the
      relationship between the writer and the reader of the
      letters of the traveller. Throughout her world
      tour, she reflects on the lives of older people,
      both those she sees in her travels and those who
      are her fellow passengers, and on aging itself.

608. Stuhlmann, Gunther, ed. *The Diary of Anaïs Nin*, Vol.
      4, 1944-1947. New York: Harcourt Brace Jovanovich,
      1971.

609. Stuhlmann, Gunther, ed. *The Diary of Anaïs Nin*, Vol.
      5, 1947-1955. New York: Harcourt Brace Jovanovich,
      1974.

610. Stuhlmann, Gunther, ed. *The Diary of Anaïs Nin*, Vol.
      6, 1955-1966. New York: Harcourt Brace Jovanovich,
      1976.

611. Suckow, Ruth. "A Memoir." In *Some Others and Myself:
      Seven Stories and a Memoir*, pp. 169-281, Ruth Suckow.
      New York: Rinehart and Co., Inc., 1952. In her
      reflections on the meaning that art and religion
      and the First World War came to have in her life,
      Suckow, who grew up as a minister's daughter, recalls
      reading over her father's writings and recognizing
      how close they both were in literary composition,
      and how much she owed to his sermons, which she
      came to see were a foundation for her fiction.

612. Tacha, Athena. "The Process of Aging." *The Village
      Voice* (February 26, 1979) XXIV(9):57. Sculptor and
      Professor of Sculpture at Oberlin College, Athena
      Tacha writes with precision of the signs of aging
      on her face and body, which she has been observing
      since she was a teen-ager.

613. Vining, Elizabeth Gray. *Being Seventy: The Measure of
      a Year*. New York: The Viking Press, 1978. The
      journal of Vining's 70th year, during which the writer
      made a trip to Japan, stayed for a time in the
      writers' colony on Ossabaw Island, Georgia, completed
      her book *Mr. Whittier*, and reached a difficult
      decision about moving to a Quaker retirement com-
      munity. She recalls that in her 30s, she and a
      friend classified old ladies into four categories--
      Whiny, Bossy, Fussy and Batty; she resolved to become
      a Batty Old Lady. In this book, Vining also writes
      about models of aging and the growing interest in
      aging on the part of the young. She reflects on
      widowhood from the perspective of one who was bereaved
      40 years ago, and on death, on the meaning of
      loneliness, on acceptance and memory and pain in
      age, on all the moves she has made during her life,
      and on the relationship between the generations.

614. West, Jessamyn. *The Woman Said Yes: Encounters with
      Life and Death (Memoirs)*. Greenwich, Connecticut:
      Fawcett Publications, Inc., 1976. Two women said
      "yes"--the author's mother, Grace (the subject of
      Part One), who gave birth to Jessamyn West three
      times over, the second time when she would not accept
      that her daughter, at age 28, would die of tuber-
      culosis, and the third time when she gave birth to
      West as a writer of fiction that was fashioned of
      her own memories and musings and anecdotes; and
      Carmen (the subject of Part Two), West's younger
      sister, who said "yes" to death with the same
      courage with which their mother had affirmed life.

615. Wharton, Edith. *Quaderno Dello Studente*, Wharton
      Archives, Beinecke Library, Yale University, New
      Haven, Connecticut. Begun in 1924, when Wharton was
      62 years old, her few entries here include reflections
      about loss and solitude, quotations from Traherne,
      Goethe, *Ecclesiastes* and St. Bernard, and a lullaby
      she composed, together with her plan for *The
      Buccaneers*.

616. White, Whitney. "A Lamp at Dusk: Adjusting Puts Peace
      into Growing Old." In *The New Old: Struggling for
      Decent Aging*, pp. 200-4, Ronald Gross, Beatrice
      Gross and Sylvia Seidman, eds. Garden City, New
      York: Anchor Press/Doubleday, 1978. A letter from
      Mary Whitney White, great-grandmother of four, to her

daughter, who had asked her to write down some
thoughts about old age. She writes about her attach-
ment to her homestead of 50 years, her enjoyment of
solitude, the need to adjust to physical changes as
one ages, and the loss of friends, and also the
alternative ways of meeting old age--resignation, or
adjustment with the effort to remain as active as
possible.

617. Williams, Nancy. "'I Want To Go Home': A Very Old
     Lady Dies in Style." In *The New Old: Struggling
     for Decent Aging*, pp. 161-5, Ronald Gross, Beatrice
     Gross and Sylvia Seidman, eds. Garden City, New
     York: Anchor Press/Doubleday, 1978. A letter from
     Nancy Williams to her daughter about the brief
     final illness and death of Williams's 96-year-old
     mother. "She did it exactly the way she had lived,
     with style and humor and incredible courage."

*618. "A Word for the Modern Old Lady." *Atlantic Monthly*
     (July 1907) 100:283-4.

See also: 41, 43, 52, 55, 59, 63, 64, 65, 67, 69, 70, 72, 73,
74, 76, 77, 89, 378, 383, 388, 389, 452, 463, 464, 465, 466,
470, 526, 537, 674, 885.

XIII. PSYCHOLOGICAL PERSPECTIVES ON AGING

A. General

*619. Beckman, Alan C. "Role-Loss, Powerlessness and
       Depression Among Older Men and Women." Diss.,
       Social Work, Case Western Reserve University, 1972.

620.   Butler, Robert N., and Myrna I. Lewis. *Aging and
       Mental Health: Positive Psychosocial Approaches*.
       St. Louis: The C.V. Mosley Co., 1973, 1977. Part
       One: The nature and problems of old age, includes
       chapters on: Who are the elderly?; Healthy,
       successful old age; Common emotional problems;
       Functional disorders; Organic brain disorders;
       Special concerns (racism, sexism, sexuality, etc.);
       Older people and their families. Part Two, Evaluation,
       and treatment, and prevention, includes chapters on
       General treatment principles; Diagnostic evaluation:
       how to do a work-up; How to keep people at home;
       Proper institutional care; Psychotherapy and
       environmental therapy; Drug and electroshock therapy;
       Treatment of specific conditions; Old age and the
       future. Appendices on Sources of gerontological and
       geriatric literature; Organizations pertaining to the
       elderly; Government programs for the elderly; Grant
       programs and social services; Training and education
       in gerontology and geriatrics; Staff inservice
       education material for work with older people.
       "Special Concerns" includes a "Profile of the elderly
       woman," with information on income, employment,
       marriage, living arrangements, health, and emotional
       results of prejudice against older women, and concludes
       with a section on, "What's good about being an older
       woman?" Here, the authors state that "Older women
       today have unexplored potential in terms of personal
       expression." They note that "Older women by example
       could give younger women confidence to resist the

                          239

mania to remain young, with the knowledge that a
rich life can await them as they age."

*621.   Giesen, Carol Boellhoff.   "Problems and Coping
        Strategies: A Comparison Between Younger and
        Older Individuals." Unpublished ms., West Virginia
        University, 1978.

622.   Gutmann, David, Jerome Grunes and Brian Griffin.   "The
        Clinical Psychology of Later Life: Developmental
        Paradigms." In *Transitions of Aging*, pp. 119-31,
        Nancy Datan and Nancy Lohmann, eds. New York:
        Academic Press, Inc., 1980. Recent life-cycle
        developmental research, particularly in Chicago,
        suggests that the post-parental years, rather than
        being a prelude to death, are a complex set of life
        periods, each with specific potentialities, as
        well as risks and losses. This paper reports on
        findings by those working in the Older Adult Program
        of Northwestern University Medical School from studies
        of patients who sought psychiatric treatment for the
        first time in mid- or later life. The transition
        to the post-parental phase is a process of undergoing
        a universal "return of the repressed": there is an
        internal re-establishing by each sex of the sexual
        bimodality that was earlier parcelled out externally
        between the self and the mate for the purposes of
        active parenting, and both sexes move toward the
        normal androgyny of later life. But potentialities
        can engender psychopathologies as well as growth.
        In some cases, mostly for those in their 40s or 50s,
        the onset of symptoms reflects the intersection of
        midlife developmental potentialities with lesions
        of the personality structure that had been latent.
        In other cases, mainly in patients in their late
        60s and 70s, the problem is "existential stress"--
        the person has been shocked by the threat of death or
        the awareness of the life-cycle, or by the loss of
        a significant person. This paper also discusses
        (1) Men: The Masculine Protesters and (2) Threats to
        the Older Woman. It states here that for women in
        their late 40s and 50s the real losses are, as with
        men, internal rather than external: they are based
        on a loss of self-esteem. It finds the externalized
        "victim" hypothesis to be simple-minded, and states
        that these women may be afraid of the energy and the
        capacity for autonomy which their fantasies reveal--
        that they may be enduring their own anger in the form

of depression before they can possess it and enjoy
it and make use of it. These men and women are seen
to be victims of their own growth potential when this
potential is experienced as a threat. The older
patients suffer from *real* depletions. One conclusion
is that clinical studies of women who are patients
for the first time in their 60s suggest that parenthood is a pivotal developmental period of the human
life cycle. While these women have childlessness
in common, they may be divided into two major
categories, the *aging tomboys* and the *perpetual
daughters*. It is stated that maternity may protect
women against the psychoses of later life.

623. Jung, Carl G. *Modern Man in Search of a Soul*, trans.
      W.S. Dell and Cary F. Baynes. New York: Harcourt,
      Brace and World, Inc., 1933. Jung states that only
      after their 40th year do many women awaken to social
      responsibility and to social consciousness. In his
      essay on "The Stages of Life," he states that middle
      life (two-thirds of his patients were past middle-
      age) begins between ages 35 and 40, when "a significant
      change in the human psyche is in preparation." There
      is a transformation in the physical, but even more in
      the psychic, realm at the "noon of life," when our
      values and even our bodies "undergo a reversal into
      the opposite." Catastrophes in marriage often
      accompany this reversal. Jung states that life's
      afternoon must "have a significance of its own and
      cannot be merely a pitiful appendage to life's
      morning." Wisdom is a return to the primordial
      images--symbols older than human history that make
      up the groundwork of the human psyche. This book
      also contains chapters on the uses of dream analysis,
      problems and aims of psychotherapy, Jung's theory
      of types, contrasts between Freudian and Jungian
      perspectives, archaic man, psychology and literature,
      the basic postulates of Analytical Psychology,
      modern spiritual problems, and psychotherapy and
      religion.

624. Knopf, Olga, M.D. *Successful Aging*. New York: The
      Viking Press, 1975. Psychological and social aspects
      of aging, with chapters on: "A New 'Minority'?"
      and aging (of the sense organs, aging and illness,
      and aging and stress and emotional responses to stress);
      self-acceptance; "Making a New Start"; retirement;
      the use of leisure time; volunteer work; sexual

adaptation in later life; "Making Life Easier and
Keeping Fit"; "The Aged Parent and His Family";
"Living Arrangements"; "Putting the House in Order";
"The Summing Up." Appendices on facilities;
bibliography.

*625.   Kuypers, Joseph Andrew. "Elderly Persons En Route to
Institutions: A Study of Changing Perceptions of
Self and Interpersonal Relations." Diss., Univer-
sity of Chicago, 1968.

626.   Labouvie-Vief, Gisela. "Adaptive Dimensions of Adult
Cognition." In *Transitions of Aging*, pp. 3-26,
Nancy Datan and Nancy Lohmann, eds. New York:
Academic Press, Inc., 1980. Labouvie-Vief challenges
the prevailing definition of cognitive aging which is
stated chiefly in terms of regression and decrement.
She proposes that interpretations of increments and
decrements are inherently relative. The first section
of this paper presents an overview of some interpretive
tensions that have arisen in psychogerontology as a
result of the juxtaposition of notions of growth and
aging. The second (and principal) section proposes
an outline of a life-span model that integrates these
dualistic tensions. The third section indicates
several areas of research that are integrated within
this model. In testing a working model from evidence
that there are qualitative changes in the processing
of information with adulthood, Labouvie-Vief reports:
"We believe that in the study of aging and cognition,
one must look simultaneously at the integration of
information at several levels. Thus one may find
evidence of deficit when focusing on one level, only
to find that deficit is made up at another level."
The trade-off situation that develops may be a useful
strategy for adaptation. She states that the mature,
older adult has undergone the experience of the
limitations of his or her memory and has "learned
to attend to those codes that are less likely to be
transitory, thus more permanent and stable."

*627.   Lieberman, Morton A. "Adaptive Processes in Late Life."
In *Life-Span Developmental Psychology: Normative
Life Crises*, pp. 135-59, Nancy Datan and Leon H.
Ginsberg, eds. New York: Academic Press, Inc., 1975.
Lieberman presents a model for predicting adaptational
success or failure of the elderly under crises, which
is used to explore the reasons why some persons adapt
better than others to the crises associated with old age.

628. Lohmann, Nancy. "Life Satisfaction Research in Aging:
      Implications for Policy Development." In *Transitions
      of Aging*, pp. 27-40, Nancy Datan and Nancy Lohmann,
      eds. New York: Academic Press, Inc., 1980. Research
      on life satisfaction reflects the pursuit of knowledge
      for its own sake, represents the pursuit of peer
      approval, and, most importantly, has potential for
      improving the lives of the aged by contributing to
      the formation of public policy. Lohmann reviews
      research findings on five variables--marital status,
      retirement, health, housing and the physical environ-
      ment, and social activity--and concludes that 40
      years of research on the relationship between these
      variables and life satisfaction has not contributed
      to a more informed public policy, in part because
      the findings are often contradictory. She suggests
      that future research should focus on substantive
      areas, as retirement, housing and social activity,
      which lend themselves to manipulation by public
      policy, that it should focus on causal rather than
      on correlational relationships, and that methodological
      sophistication, especially in the area of measurement,
      should be further refined. Extensive bibliography.

629. Neugarten, Bernice L., and David L. Gutmann. "Age-Sex
      Roles and Personality in Middle Age: A Thematic
      Apperception Study." In *Middle Age and Aging: A
      Reader in Social Psychology*, pp. 58-71, Bernice L.
      Neugarten, ed. Chicago: The University of Chicago
      Press, 1968. Adult age-sex roles in the family were
      studied by analysis of responses of men and women aged
      40 to 54 and 55 to 70 to a TAT picture with four
      figures--Young Man, Young Woman, Old Man and Old
      Woman. The Old Man seemed to symbolize the ego
      qualities, and the Old Woman the impulsive, self-
      centered qualities, of the personality. The most
      striking finding was that, with increasing age of
      respondents, the Old Man and Old Woman reversed roles
      in regard to authority in the family, the Old Woman
      becoming more dominant and the Old Man more submissive.
      Personality changes from age 40 to age 70 are implied:
      women appear to become more tolerant of their aggres-
      sive, egocentric impulses, and men of their nurturant,
      affiliative impulses, as they age. Ego qualities of
      the personality appear to become more constricted
      with aging.

630. Oberleder, Muriel. "Psychotherapy with the Aging."
      In *The Later Years: Social Applications of Gerontology*,
      pp. 327-32, Richard A. Kalish, ed. Monterey,
      California: Brooks/Cole Publishing Co., 1977. The
      "old age" syndrome of fear, frustration, anger and
      depression may manifest itself at *any* life stress
      period. But an illness-oriented approach with
      institutionalization as the goal still prevails in
      treatment of mental and emotional problems of the
      aging. Therapists hold many erroneous and stereo-
      typed attitudes toward aging persons. The psycho-
      therapeutic viewpoint has not yet been appreciably
      influenced by research findings which suggest that
      full mental ability may be retained in old age, and
      that many of the "senile" symptoms are remediable.
      Most behavioral and emotional problems of the elderly
      are within the province of psychotherapy. Promising
      results have been obtained in group and individual
      therapy (usually in institutional settings), using
      directive, supportive and activity-oriented approaches.
      Therapy with the elderly has two main goals--the
      alleviation of anxiety, and the maintenance of
      adequate psychological functioning. In therapy,
      a tolerance for loss must be developed because loss
      is the reality of old age. The therapist should
      prevent the deterioration which results from with-
      drawal and disuse. The personal feelings of the
      therapist about aging and the old are usually greater
      obstacles to the successful course of therapy than
      the feelings of the patient.

631. Puner, Morton. "What It's Like to Be Old." In *To the
      Good Long Life: What We Know About Growing Old*, pp.
      105-24, Morton Puner. New York: Universe Books,
      1974. Six types of response--the most successful,
      the saddest, the most acid, the most bittersweet,
      the most ordinary and the most eloquent--to this
      question suggest the range of people's expressions
      of feelings about being old. Includes observations
      about the difficulty of eliciting self-portraiture
      that has depth and clarity, and about the meanings
      of loneliness ("one of the blights of old age, far
      worse than it is for youth or middle age"), together
      with guidelines explicitly drawn in the Administra-
      tion on Aging report, *Let's End Isolation*, for
      confronting the problems of social isolation.

*632. Sabatini, P., and Labouvie-Vief, Gisela. "Age and
Professional Specialization in Formal Reasoning."
Paper presented at the Gerontological Society,
Washington, D.C., November 1979.

633. Smith, Ethel Sabin. *The Dynamics of Aging.* New York:
W.W. Norton and Co., Inc., 1956. After writing this
book, Smith observed, she found to her chagrin that
it is a "how-to-grow-old" book, but she suggests
that this may have been inevitable. She believes
that every person has undeveloped aptitudes, and she
discusses ways these could be discovered early in
life and developed in youth so as to be an asset in
old age. It is her conviction that art, more than
any other experience, enhances life. In her view,
many old people "are neither emotionally mature nor
educated in the proper use of power." In her concern
for the potential significance of later life, she
argues for the importance of aspiration for *old*
people as well as for the young. *"Old people
must care."*

*634. Turner, Barbara Formaniak. "Psychological Predictors
of Adaptation to the Stress of Institutionalization
in the Aged." Diss., University of Chicago, 1968.

635. Waters, Elinor, and Betty White. "Helping Each Other."
In *Looking Ahead: A Woman's Guide to the Problems
and Joys of Growing Older*, pp. 184-93, Lillian E.
Troll, Joan Israel and Kenneth Israel, eds.
Englewood Cliffs, New Jersey: Prentice-Hall, Inc.,
1977. Older people receive a disproportionately
small share of psychotherapeutic services. This
paper is a description of the program of group
counseling offered since 1972 by the Continuum Center
for older persons who are affiliated with various
community centers in the metropolitan Detroit area.
About 80% of the clientele are women. The program,
which is primarily preventive, trains older people
(peers) to work as paraprofessional counselors.
The general response of participants is positive,
and the program has had positive effects outside
the counseling group. One unexpected development
was the participation of handicapped persons.

*636. Woodard, R. "Selected Aspects of Personal Adjustments
of Aged Persons Among an Older Population of Greeley,
Colorado." Diss., Colorado State College, 1969.

*637.   Zibbell, R.   "Activity Level, Future Time Perspective
        and Life Satisfaction in Old Age."   Diss., Boston
        University Graduate School, 1972.

See also: 137, 536, 538, 539, 541, 545, 551, 553, 733, 800,
844.

                        B. Older Women

*638.   Aldredge, Gwendolyn W.   "The Self-Concept of Elderly
        Women."   Diss., Home Economics, Florida State
        University, 1973.

 639.   Berry, Jane.   "Do Special Folks Need Special Strokes?
        Counseling Older Women: A Perspective."   In *The
        Older Woman: Lavender Rose or Gray Panther*, pp. 45-9,
        Marie Marschall Fuller and Cora Ann Martin, eds.
        Springfield, Illinois: Charles C. Thomas, 1980.
        Major problems of older women who are seeking new
        careers in midlife and of those who are facing the
        additional pressures of feeling really "over the hill"
        are discussed under the subheadings Old is Ugly
        (many employers are caught up with the "youth is
        beautiful" syndrome, and an additional problem for
        older women is that the new educational and employment
        opportunities for younger women that have been
        fostered by the women's movement often arouse re-
        sentment on the part of older women who are unhappy
        about what they have missed); The Retirement Blues;
        Partners and Families; and Counselors and Older
        Women, in which it is stated that priorities are
        specialization, sensitivity, empathy, and examination
        of the counselor's own perceptions of and attitudes
        toward aging.

 640.   Bradway, Katherine.   "Hestia and Athena in the Analysis
        of Women."   *Inward Light* (Spring 1978) XLI(91):28-42.
        The Hestia and Athena personifications provided a
        means of identifying two contrasting groups of
        women in the author's practice in the early 1970s:
        18 married women in the Hestia group and 12 unmarried
        women in the Athena group.   In analysis, these women
        worked toward recognizing and respecting their own
        uniqueness.   Once this had been achieved, each could
        explore the side that had been neglected--the woman

in the home could develop her achieving or logos
side, and the professional woman could more fully
actualize her relating or eros side. A common plaint
in both groups related to fears of being like their
mothers, that is, of feeling inadequate, being
critical of self and others and being unable to
give. Women of this generation live at a significant
time in history, when the chain of socially inherited
feelings of inferiority is being broken. Coming
generations are destined to be more free of the
struggle against their mothers' negative self image,
while mothers will be ever more able to contribute
to a daughter's positive self image. Peer women are
also helping one another to achieve esteem. Most
of the women in these two groups were born or grew
up in the 1930s and 1940s, and came into analysis
in the 1960s and early 1970s; thus, they had been
subjected to societal changes in expectations for
women. The women in the two groups have shown
increasing balance between Hestia and Athena sides,
and women who have presented themselves for analysis
since these two groups were distinguished show more
equal development of the two sides at the time of
entering analysis. Although this is a selected
sample, it probably reflects what is happening
culturally. In the 1980s, there will probably be
more comfortable variations in life style. Women
are beginning to aim toward individual goals, rather
than trying to live out collective expectations.

*641.   Cassetts, Rhondda, D.S. Newell and Mary Lou Parlagreco.
        "Morale Changes in Women During Aging." Paper
        presented at the Midwest Sociological Society, St.
        Louis, April 1960.

642.   Castillejo, Irene Claremont de. "The Older Woman."
        In *Knowing Woman: A Feminine Psychology*, pp. 149-64,
        Irene Claremont de Castillejo. New York: Harper
        and Row, 1973. A woman's life curve, unlike that of
        a man, is not a slow rising to the zenith of power
        followed by a gradual decline in the later years,
        but follows more nearly the pattern of the seasons.
        The autumn of a woman's life can be far richer than
        the spring. Far too many women feel their life is
        finished at 50 and that vibrant loving ends with the
        menopause. A woman's most profound and meaningful
        sex life often occurs after 50 when she is wholly
        free of fear of conception. The menopause is a

change of direction, an enormous release of energy
for some new venture. The crucial moment in the life
of any wife and mother is when her children are
grown. Both she and society lose if, when she is
no longer vitally needed by her family, she does not
find this new direction. Society should provide
outlets for this new energy, and a woman should find
in which direction her newly released libido wants
to flow. The possibilities are manifold; all have
a very personal love at their center. The author
quotes her poem, "The Last Years," which expresses
the feelings of an old woman. She believes that the
old need to gather up the past, to grieve, to review
their lives and to tell their life stories, and that
this creative act initiates further creativity.
In her view, it is imperative that an old person
have a positive attitude towards death. One needs
to be as complete a person as possible, and therefore
to be as fully conscious as possible. The old need
solitude; old age is a time of reckoning. Old
people are too much shielded, often by middle-aged
women whose own life makes its claims. Mistakes
that were made should be brought out, so that
forgiveness is made possible. Our last task may be
forgiveness of the self.

643. Chesler, Phyllis. *Women and Madness*. New York:
      Avon Books, 1972. Chesler presents a feminist
      critique of female psychology--of the various fortunes
      of 20th-century incarnations of Demeter and her
      four daughters, Persephone, Psyche, Athena and
      Artemis, and of their interpretations and treatments
      in psychiatric settings. Interweaving social
      scientific with literary and philosophical/mytho-
      logical perspectives, she perceives women in
      contemporary Judeo-Christian societies as motherless,
      infantilized or driven mad by an unmet need for
      maternal nurturance. She argues that almost all
      women in our culture have experienced the Demeter-
      Persephone myth in their own lives, and that self-
      actualization is impossible for women so long as men
      control the means of production and reproduction.
      In Section One, Madness, she discusses women in
      asylums (Elizabeth Packard, Ellen West, Zelda
      Fitzgerald and Sylvia Plath Hughes); the mythological
      dimensions of the mother-daughter relationship and
      Heroines and Madness: Joan of Arc and the Virgin
      Mary; Asylums; Clinicians; The Female Career as a

Psychiatric Patient. In Section Two, Women, she
discusses sex between patient and therapist,
psychiatrically institutionalized women, lesbians,
third world women, feminists and the past, present
and future of female psychology, which includes a
description of the ideal woman's group and of
Amazon societies where women had power by virtue
of their biology. Appendix on The Female Career As
a Psychiatric Patient, with data on the sex, class,
race and marital status of America's psychiatrically
involved population from 1950 to 1969.

644.   Christ, Carol P. "Why Women Need the Goddess:
        Phenomenological, Psychological, and Political
        Reflections." In *Womanspirit Rising: A Feminist
        Reader in Religion*, pp. 273-87, Carol P. Christ and
        Judith Plaskow, eds. San Francisco: Harper and Row,
        Inc., 1979. Christ states that Western culture
        "gives little dignity to the postmenopausal or aging
        woman. It is no secret that our culture is based on
        a denial of aging and death, and that women suffer
        more severely from this denial than men." Old women
        are pitied and shunned in age, whereas some men are
        perceived to be wise and authoritative. This cultural
        attitude towards aging women is supported by religious
        iconography, in which Mary and the women saints are
        expressed in the convention of perpetual youth.
        "Religious mythology associates aging women with
        evil in the symbol of the wicked old witch."
        Feminists have shown that the "power" of the young
        woman is illusory, and "have urged women to reject
        patriarchal beauty standards and to celebrate the
        distinctive beauty of women of all ages."

645.   Christ, Carol P., and Judith Plaskow, eds. *Womanspirit
        Rising: A Feminist Reader in Religion*. San
        Francisco: Harper and Row, Inc., 1979. This book
        has four sections--The Essential Challenge: Does
        Theology Speak to Women's Experience?, The Past:
        Does it Hold a Future for Women?, Reconstructing
        Tradition, and Creating New Traditions. Chapters:
        I: The Human Situation: A Feminine View; Motherearth
        and the Megamachine; After the Death of God the
        Father. II: Reflections on the Meaning of Herstory;
        Eve and Adam: Genesis 2-3 Reread; Women in the
        Early Christian Movement; The Christian Past: Does
        It Hold a Future for Women?; What Became of God the
        Mother; When God Was a Woman. III: Feminist

Spirituality, Christian Identity, and Catholic
Vision; Theology in the Politics of Appalachian
Women; The Dilemma of Celebration; Female God
Language in a Jewish Context; Sabbath Prayers for
Women; Bringing a Daughter into the Covenant; A
Jewish Woman's Haggadah. IV: The Coming of Lilith:
Toward a Feminist Theology; Why Speak about God?;
Dreams and Fantasies as Sources of Revelation:
Feminist Appropriation of Jung; Spiritual Quest and
Women's Experience; Becoming Woman: Menstruation as
Spiritual Experience; Witchcraft and Women's Culture;
Self-Blessing Ritual; Why Women Need the Goddess:
Phenomenological, Psychological, and Political
Reflections.

*646.   Cooper, Pamela Elaine. "Spatial and Communicative
        Egocentrism Among Middle-aged and Elderly Women."
        Diss., Pennsylvania State University, 1978.

647.   Flax, Jane. "The Conflict Between Nurturance and
        Autonomy in Mother-Daughter Relationships and Within
        Feminism." *Feminist Studies* (June 1978) 4(2):171-89.
        Flax discusses conflicts that make it difficult for
        the mother to be as emotionally available as her
        infant daughter needs her to be, and the inadequacies
        of the symbiotic phase, as a consequence of which the
        process of separation and individuation that follows
        is more difficult for the female infant. She states
        that only through relationships with other women
        can women heal the hurts suffered during their
        psychological development. In her view, the
        feminist analysis of women's rage or depression
        that blames it all on external society overlooks
        this internal struggle. The character of mother-
        daughter relationships results in major difficulties
        in relationships between adult women. Flax believes
        that the psychic roots of the unrealistic expectations
        aroused early in the women's movement are also the
        source of some women's opposition to feminism.
        While the women's movement has yet to develop adequate
        methods for mediating profound differences among
        women, it has made it possible for many women to
        develop strong one-to-one intimate relationships
        with other women, some of them for the first time
        in their lives. The impasse will remain until the
        wishes and longings the movement evoked can be brought
        out and analyzed. But "Women may be forgiven a
        temporary failure of nerve" in the face of the immensity
        and variety of the tasks ahead in transforming society.

*648. Giesen, Carol Boellhoff. "Stress and Coping Among the Wives of West Virginia Coal Miners." M.A. thesis, West Virginia University, 1978.

649. Goldenberg, Naomi R. "A Feminist Critique of Jung." *Signs* (Winter 1976) 2(2):443-9. Goldenberg believes that Jungian psychology especially warrants a feminist critique because it has become a form of patriarchal religion itself. A feminist critique begins by questioning the veneration of Jung himself. Feminist scholars must confront the sexism of Jung's theories, in her view: there is overt sexism in Jung's concept of the feminine, and in the inequity of the anima-animus model of the psyche. She argues in favor of postulating a similar psychic force for both sexes, and for a critical examination of the concept of the archetype. Goldenberg believes that the separa-tion of the absolute from experience lies at the basis of all patriarchal religion, and that archetypes ought to be understood as referring to the imaginal or religious process itself rather than to past documents of that process.

650. Gove, Walter R. "The Relationship Between Sex Roles, Marital Status, and Mental Illness." *Social Forces* (September 1972) 51(1):34-44. In modern, industrial societies, women have higher rates of mental illness than men. Gove states this is probably due not to biological susceptibility nor to some characteristic of women's generalized sex role, but to the role of *married* women, which has become more tenuous since World War Two. He discusses the major characteristics of the married woman's role as compared with that of married men, compares the role of single women and men, and cites evidence from recent studies of sex, marital status and mental illness showing that married women have higher rates of mental disorder than married men--but that if there is a difference between men and women who are single, divorced and widowed, it appears that women in these categories have lower rates than men. All these differences correspond with the pattern associated with residency in mental hospitals, and there is tentative evidence that the rates of mental illness of married men and women are more alike after retirement age. The married of both sexes have lower rates of mental illness than the unmarried, but differences between the sexes in this regard suggest that being married

is much more advantageous to men than it is to women,
while being single is slightly more disadvantageous
to men.

651. Israel, Kenneth. "Is There a Psychiatrist in the
      House?" In *Looking Ahead: A Woman's Guide to the
      Problems and Joys of Growing Older*, pp. 178-83,
      Lillian E. Troll, Joan Israel and Kenneth Israel,
      eds. Englewood Cliffs, New Jersey: Prentice-Hall,
      Inc., 1977. Many older women seen in Israel's
      practice talk about their feelings of emptiness or
      profound doubts about how they can fill this void.
      Not all problems of older women are related to
      loneliness. But a growing feeling of self-doubt may
      make it ever more difficult to function, to enjoy
      life and to want to go on living. Two cases are
      presented to show how psychotherapy can help older
      women address questions about their identity and
      the meaning of their lives, and to see the possibil-
      ities for change. "Life at all ages is a process of
      change, not a state of immutable being." Psychotherapy
      can be a means of inspiring a sense of individuality
      for those who derived their sense of worth from
      another person.

652. Lantero, Erminie Huntress. *Feminine Aspects of Divinity*.
      (Pendle Hill Pamphlet 191.) Wallingford, Pennsylvania:
      Pendle Hill Publications, 1973. Lantero discusses
      the recognition of the androgyneity of the divine
      image in a number of religions and philosophies,
      archaeological, mythological and historical indica-
      tions of the feminine component of "the contrasexual
      balance," Sophia ("Wisdom"), the Friend of Man, in
      scripture and in philosophical and theological
      writings, "The Holy Spirit as Mother," Mary as
      Mediator, The Shekinah as Presence in Exile, and,
      in "Comfort, Life, and Fire of Love," how "Sophia,
      Spirit and Shekinah may be seen as somewhat different
      but overlapping bands of the total spectrum of
      Divinity as immanent in the universe and in man."

653. Neumann, Erich. *The Great Mother: An Analysis of the
      Archetype*, trans. Ralph Manheim. (Bollingen Series
      XLVII.) Princeton: Princeton University Press, 1963.
      Neumann's comprehensive structural analysis of the
      primordial image of the Great Mother, with illustra-
      tions of both the elementary and the transformative
      character of the timeless archetype drawn from the

myth, religion, art and dreams of all historical
epochs and human cultures, and correlated with the
stages in the development of the human psyche.

654. Pearlin, Leonard I. "Sex Roles and Depression." In
      *Life-Span Developmental Psychology: Normative Life
      Crises*, pp. 191-207, Nancy Datan and Leon H. Ginsberg,
      eds. New York: Academic Press, Inc., 1975. Women
      are more susceptible to symptoms of depression than
      men. Some conditions contributing to this sex
      difference are examined through analysis of inter-
      viewing data from a sample of 2300 people representative
      of an urban population. No differences were found
      between employed women and full-time homemakers with
      regard to depression. The chances of women being
      depressed increase with the degree of role disenchant-
      ment that they feel. Coping responses must be taken
      into account in predicting psychological distress
      directly from role strains. Some factors associated
      with differential reactions to homemaking are (1)
      stage of the family life cycle, which, in turn, is
      related to the age of the homemaker, and (2) presence
      or absence of a network of social relations. Some
      factors associated with differential reactions to
      employment are (1) the degree of integration of the
      job with family roles and (2) stage of the family
      life cycle, which again is related to the age of the
      employed woman. Older women who are at a later stage
      of the family life cycle are for that reason less
      vulnerable to disaffection with homemaking or conflict
      between work and maternal roles than their younger
      counterparts.

655. Query, Joy M.N., and Meriel Steines. "Disillusionment,
      Health Status and Age: A Study of Value Differences
      of Midwestern Women." *The International Journal of
      Aging and Human Development* (Summer 1974) 5(3):245-56.
      Disillusionment theory, which suggests that as people
      encounter health and other problems in aging, they
      will express disillusionment with the American values
      of youth, work and activity, success and achievement,
      and a belief in progress and the mastery of science
      over nature, was supported in Ludwig's study of male
      Midwestern farmers. This paper reports a test of the
      theory through interviews with women aged 40 to 54,
      55 to 69, and 70 and over in a metropolitan community
      on the North Central Plains. It was found, as
      hypothesized, that religious optimism decreases with

advancing age (belief in a benevolent God declines with
age), and that the work-activity orientation does not.
But the hypothesis that belief in science and technology decreases with age was not supported; differences
in education, rural background, income and employment
history may account for this. This sample did not
permit control for health by age, but the influence
of health status as an intervening variable is
discussed. Poor health was not related to disillusionment with the medical profession. Fair or
poor health appears to be related to a decline in
religious optimism, but this may reflect a generational
difference. Adherence to the work ethic remains of
great importance to those in fair or poor health.
Disillusionment theory clarifies the inadequacy of
the American value system for promoting adjustment
to the aging experience.

*656.   Reakes, Juliann T. Casey. "The Effects of Two Approaches
        to Assertive Training on Self-esteem, Assertiveness,
        Locus of Control, and Life Satisfaction with Women
        Sixty Years of Age or Over." Diss., East Texas
        State University, 1979.

657.   Rickles, Nathan K., M.D.   "The Discarded Generation:
        The Woman Past Fifty." *Geriatrics* (October 1968)
        XXIII:112-6. Recommends a frank dialogue between
        doctor and patient about the unnecessary fears
        attached to sex and death; also recommends useful
        and rewarding work outside the home, older women's
        participation in continuing education programs,
        and preparation for the entire life course from the
        teen years on.

658.   Sarnat, Joan, Recorder. "Psychotherapy and Counseling."
        In *No Longer Young: The Older Woman in America,
        Work Group Reports*, pp. 9-13. Ann Arbor, Michigan:
        The Institute of Gerontology, The University of
        Michigan-Wayne State University, 1974. The workshop
        opened with a focus on the problem of the middle-
        aged woman who is suddenly abandoned by her successful
        husband. It was stated that fear of being abandoned
        is now becoming as common as fear of widowhood was
        in the past. During a divorce, a woman's initial
        feelings of shock and self-revulsion are coupled with
        panic at having to assume many responsibilities
        formerly assumed by her spouse. Topics of the workshop
        included considerations in working with older women--

factors affecting prognosis in psychotherapy (it
was pointed out that the person over age 50 can be
an excellent candidate for long-term therapy)--the
effects of no-fault divorce; the negative effects of
ageism on the helping professions; the normal
physiological aspects of aging as they relate to
sexuality; and the distinctions between the feminist
position and the way that psychotherapists define
their responsibility to individual clients.

659.   Scarf, Maggie. *Unfinished Business: Pressure Points in
       the Lives of Women.* Garden City, New York: Doubleday
       and Co., Inc., 1980. A study of depression and women
       from the life course perspective. Scarf found that
       depressive disorders, which are more common among
       women than men, and which have everything to do with
       life stage, appear to be failures in adaptation to
       changes in inner and outer life. She presents case
       studies and research findings in chapters on each
       decade of life from the teens through the sixties,
       and identifies the *context* of most depressions in
       women--both housewives and employed women, including
       professionals--as "the loss of emotional relatedness."
       In Scarf's view, the loss of a love-bond is the
       catalyst of depressive episodes in women, who are more
       vulnerable than men to depression because the female's
       nature is inherently affiliative. Women are not
       prepared to be alone, yet most will have to learn to
       live alone at some point in their lives. Scarf has
       encountered women in late life who are still engaged
       in the work of separation of Self from parents. She
       believes that individuation is crucial for a woman.
       In "Middlescence," she writes that women confront
       the problem of creating an identity of their own much
       later in life than most men do, and that this phase
       of life has many more discontinuities for women than
       for men. Throughout the book, Scarf discusses the
       properties and effects of a number of antidepressant
       compounds. In the chapter "In the Fifties," she
       states there is no scientific evidence to support the
       idea that the hormonal decline of the middle years is
       the cause of the depressions of the female climacteric,
       and that there is no proof that female hormones are
       effective anti-aging agents. She suggests that those
       who feel great shock or deep grief or fear because of
       physical aging may not only be mourning the lost
       former self but may be limited in their capacity to
       relate to others. In the chapter "In the Sixties,"

she describes electroconvulsive therapy, which, as
it is used at the present time, can be a life-saving
procedure. She states that ECT remains one of the
most effective treatments available, especially for
those in middle and later life whose severe depressions
are accompanied by endogenous ("neuro-vegetative")
symptomatology. The problem with using anti-
depressant drugs to treat those aged sixty and older
"is that of getting the person up to a therapeutic
dosage level without having devastated her or him
with a range of side effects along the way."
Appendices on Signs That You May Be Suffering from
Depression; Do Numbers Lie?; Critical Periods.

660.   Singer, June. "Androgyny Experienced in Widowhood, the
       Creative Life and Old Age." In *Androgyny: Toward a
       new theory of sexuality*, pp. 310-21, June Singer.
       Garden City, New York: Anchor Press/Doubleday, 1976.
       Jungian psychoanalyst June Singer discusses the
       special potentiality of the older woman living alone
       to live out her true androgynous nature. If a woman
       cherishes the inner child, the man-child, throughout
       wifehood and motherhood, she will have the inner
       Masculine principle ready to provide, in a cultivated
       way, the counterpoint to her Feminine side. The
       conscious presence of the inner opposite makes a
       woman aware that she has within herself the basis
       for living alone. If she has found and developed
       her own creativity during the years of family life,
       she will be able to express it in widowhood. If
       she has prepared herself during her lifetime by
       undergoing all the necessary rites of passage, she
       will be able to live the way of the androgyne--"able
       to carry the image of the Sophia-wisdom, the
       companion of the soul."

661.   Starhawk (Simos, Miriam). "Witchcraft and Women's
       Culture." In *Womanspirit Rising: A Feminist Reader
       in Religion*, pp. 259-68, Carol P. Christ and Judith
       Plaskow, eds. San Francisco: Harper and Row, Inc.,
       1979. "Witchcraft, 'the craft of the wise,' is the
       last remnant in the west of the time of women's
       strength and power," and a living tradition of
       Goddess-centered worship that extends far back in
       time before the triumph of patriarchy. The
       mythology, rituals and knowledge of the ancient
       matricentric times were preserved in the covens of
       Europe. Before Christianity came, witchcraft was an

earth-centered and nature-oriented worship venerating
the Goddess, the source of life, and her son-lover-
consort, the Horned God of the hunt and animal life.
Today, women are re-awakening to our ancient power.
The feminist movement is now opening to a spiritual
dimension. The moon is our great symbol for the
Goddess. Her three aspects reflect the three stages
in women's lives. As waning moon, "she is the old
woman, past menopause, the hag or crone that is
ripe with wisdom, patroness of secrets, prophecy,
divination, inspiration, power--Hecate, Ceridwen,
Kali, Anna." Starhawk sees the next few years "as
being crucial in the transformation of our culture
away from the patriarchal death cults and toward
the love of life, of nature, of the female principle."

662. Ulanov, Ann Belford. *The Feminine in Jungian Psychology
      and in Christian Theology*. Evanston: Northwestern
      University Press, 1971. Jung's view is that the
      feminine is a distinct category of being and a mode
      of perception inherent in all men as well as all women,
      and in all culture. The Jungians describe the
      feminine in the language of symbol and of myth so
      as to meet it on its own ground. This approach is
      based on the idea that psychic wholeness--a demand
      issued from the psyche itself--can only be achieved
      by a full awareness of contrasexuality. The psyche
      has a religious function, that is, to relate the
      personal self to the transpersonal source of the
      power and meaning of being. Integration has more
      and more to do with recovering an inner value than
      with establishing outer adaptation, as one grows
      older, and Jung calls this ongoing process individu-
      ation. It is the process of the ego finding and
      establishing a relationship to the objective
      psyche, and successful individuation leads to the
      self replacing the ego as the center of personality.

663. Van Coevering, Virginia G.R. "An Exploratory Study
      of Middle-Aged and Older Widows to Investigate Those
      Variables Which Differentiate High and Low Life
      Satisfaction." Diss., Guidance and Counseling,
      Wayne State University, 1973.

See also: 84, 283, 284, 388, 389, 393, 394, 395, 397, 403, 404,
415, 416, 425, 427, 434, 537, 592, 595, 738, 752, 840.

XIV. SHORT STORIES BY AND ABOUT
OLDER WOMEN

664. Bambara, Toni Cade. "My Man Bovanne." In *Bitches and
      Sad Ladies: An Anthology of Fiction By and About
      Women*, pp. 382-8, Pat Rotter, ed. New York: Dell
      Publishing Co., Inc., 1975. Mama's grown children
      object to the way she is dancing with Bovanne. Mama
      takes blind Bovanne away from the "benefit" for her
      niece's cousin, who was running for office in a
      Black party. She is going to buy him some sunglasses,
      and then take him home and bathe and massage him and
      give him a good dinner. "'Cause old folks is the
      nation."

665. Borenstein, Audrey. "On the Rites of Separation."
      In *Womanblood: Portraits of Women in Poetry and
      Prose*, pp. 148-56, Aline O'Brien, Chrys Rasmussen
      and Catherine Costello, eds. San Francisco:
      Continuing SAGA Press, 1981. The narrator, in
      writing of the divestiture of her possessions by her
      aging mother-in-law, remembers an old wound of
      sibling rivalry between daughters who could not
      share a mother.

666. Calisher, Hortense. "A Box of Ginger." In *The
      Collected Stories of Hortense Calisher*, pp. 204-13.
      New York: Arbor House Publishing Co., Inc., 1975.
      On the day of the funeral of young Kinny Elkins's
      Uncle Aaron, the second of his father's brothers to
      die that year, the boy offers to read a letter "from
      Aaron" to his paternal grandmother. Kinny's father
      had been writing these letters and having them
      mailed to her. It was thought that the old woman,
      now in her 90s, would not be able to withstand the
      shock of the news of the death of her son.

667. Calisher, Hortense. "The Scream on Fifty-seventh
      Street." In *The Collected Stories of Hortense*

259

Calisher, pp. 479-502. New York: Arbor House
Publishing Co., Inc., 1975. Eight months after
her husband, Sam, her companion of 20 years, died,
Mrs. Hazlitt subleased an apartment in New York City
that belonged to a woman who, widowed almost as
recently as she had been, had gone to London. It
was there in that apartment that Mrs. Hazlitt heard
"the scream on Fifty-seventh Street."

668. Calisher, Hortense. "A Wreath for Miss Totten." In
      The Collected Stories of Hortense Calisher, pp. 152-62.
      New York: Arbor House Publishing Co., Inc., 1975.
      Memory lays its wreath on Miss Totten, who had been
      in the school system for 40 years at the time of
      her death, who was ignored by the teachers as well
      as by the students of P.S. 146, and who, during her
      last term, dedicated herself to correcting the severe
      speech impairment of a girl who had been ridiculed
      for it by her classmates.

      CANFIELD: See Fisher, Dorothy Canfield

669. Cather, Willa. "The Old Beauty." In *The Old Beauty
      and Others*, pp. 3-72, Willa Cather. New York:
      Alfred A. Knopf, Inc., 1948. The last days of an
      old woman who had been famous for her beauty in the
      closing years of Queen Victoria's reign, narrated
      by a 55-year-old man who meets her by chance at
      the Hotel Splendide at Aix-les-Bains.

670. Cather, Willa. "Old Mrs. Harris." In *Obscure Destinies
      and Literary Encounters*, pp. 65-158, Willa Cather.
      Boston: Houghton Mifflin Co., 1938. Old Mrs. Harris
      sold her home in Tennessee to go to Colorado with
      her daughter Victoria Templeton, and Victoria's
      husband and children. Grandmother Harris sacrifices
      herself completely for her daughter's family. This
      was expected of widows of the middle-class and
      country-folk in Tennessee, but the townspeople in
      Skyline, Colorado, are critical of the old woman's
      serving as her married daughter's housekeeper. The
      kindly neighbor, Mrs. Rosen, takes a strong interest
      in the welfare of *de old Lady Harris*. Mrs. Rosen
      is happy to help when old Mrs. Harris prevails upon
      her to ask Mr. Rosen to borrow money to pay towards
      granddaughter Vickie's college tuition. Old Mrs.
      Harris's health is failing. Her only prayer--that
      she not become a burden to the family--is answered.

671. Ferber, Edna. "Old Lady Mandle." In *One Basket:
      Thirty-One Short Stories by Edna Ferber*, pp. 145-61.
      New York: Simon and Schuster, Inc., 1947. Ma
      Mandle's 40-year-old son Hugo marries, and at age 70
      she must come to terms with the "law of life" that
      decrees that, where there had once just been herself
      and Hugo, there now had to be Hugo and his wife and
      the child about to be born to them.

672. Ferber, Edna. "The Sudden Sixties." In *One Basket:
      Thirty-One Short Stories by Edna Ferber*, pp. 198-214.
      New York: Simon and Schuster, Inc., 1947. Widowed
      Hannah Winter, who has been enslaved by her married
      daughter, arrives at her 60s quite suddenly, and hears
      an inner voice shouting, *Threescore, and ten to go.*

673. Fisher, Dorothy Canfield. "Almera Hawley Canfield."
      In *A Harvest of Stories: From a Half Century of
      Writing by Dorothy Canfield*, pp. 61-75. New York:
      Harcourt, Brace and Co., Inc., 1956. A portrait of
      Dorothy Canfield Fisher's great-grandmother, who
      had died in 1874, years before Fisher was born,
      which is drawn by the stories various people told
      the old woman's great-granddaughter over the years.

674. Fisher, Dorothy Canfield. "The Bedquilt." In *A
      Harvest of Stories: From a Half Century of Writing
      by Dorothy Canfield*, pp. 52-60. New York: Harcourt,
      Brace and Co., Inc., 1956. At the age of 68, Aunt
      Mehetabel, who was an "old-maid dependent" in the
      Elwell family, and who performed the lowliest and
      most tedious tasks of the household, reveals herself
      to be a creative artist.

675. Freeman, Mary Wilkins. "A Village Singer." In *Middle
      Age, Old Age: Short Stories, Poems, Plays, and Essays
      on Aging*, pp. 10-20, Ruth Granetz Lyell, ed. New
      York: Harcourt Brace Jovanovich, Inc., 1980. Candace
      Whitcomb, leading soprano in the choir of the village
      church for 40 years, is dismissed because it is
      thought that "her voice had grown too cracked and
      uncertain on the upper notes." Candace is insulted
      by her forced retirement and replacement by a younger
      singer, and she decides to fight back. This story
      was first published in 1891.

676. Hale, Nancy. "The Great-Grandmother." In *Short Stories
      from the New Yorker, 1925 to 1940*, pp. 402-7. New

York: Simon and Schuster, Inc., 1940. The August
before she died, old Mrs. West--who has lived with
her daughter, Mrs. Cambridge, for 20 years, and with
her great-grandson Robert, for whom Mrs. Cambridge
has been caring since he was born--cries out for
help to people who had been dead for 50 years.

677.   Highsmith, Patricia. "The Cries of Love." In *Middle
       Age, Old Age: Short Stories, Poems, Plays, and Essays
       on Aging*, pp. 339-44, Ruth Granetz Lyell, ed. New
       York: Harcourt Brace Jovanovich, Inc., 1980. Hattie
       and Alice have been sharing the same room in a hotel
       for seven years. Unable to live with one another,
       each torments the other unmercifully. But they find
       that they are also unable to live *without* one another,
       and go on with their relationship of inflicting
       cruelties upon each other.

678.   Howland, Bette. "Golden Age." In *Blue in Chicago*,
       pp. 119-47, Bette Howland. New York: Harper and Row,
       Inc., 1978. Images of aging in Chicago: old people
       from the hotels, sitting on the park benches by the
       underpass during Indian Summer; the Woodlawn Nursing
       Home; lunchtime at the Golden Diners Club, where the
       author's mother works; the old elevator building and
       neighborhood in Uptown, where her grandmother now
       lives; and the hospital, where her grandmother is
       recuperating from a fall.

679.   Howland, Bette. "How We Got the Old Woman to Go." In
       Blue in Chicago, pp. 149-83, Bette Howland. New
       York: Harper and Row, Inc., 1978. The story of the
       death of the author's grandmother. After the
       funeral, the family gathers to say prayers for
       the dead. The author reflects, "And now I see that
       this squalid little tale is a love story."

680.   Howland, Bette. "Public Facilities." In *Blue in
       Chicago*, pp. 67-94, Bette Howland. New York:
       Harper and Row, Inc., 1978. Scenes from the Borglum
       Branch Library in Chicago's Uptown, with portraits
       of the older women librarians and the elderly who
       are among the "regulars" and the "cranks."

681.   Jackson, Shirley. "The Bus." In *Come Along with Me*,
       pp. 180-92, Shirley Jackson. New York: The Viking
       Press, Inc., 1968. Elderly Miss Harper, returning
       home on a rainy, nasty night from a visit to a

relative, has to ride a bus she dislikes because it
is uncomfortable and dirty and has a surly driver.
During this ride, she takes a sleeping pill, and has
a strange experience.

682. Jackson, Shirley. "Island." In *Come Along with Me*,
pp. 79-90, Shirley Jackson. New York: The Viking
Press, Inc., 1968. Mrs. Montague, who has lost her
mind, and whose devoted son and guardian sees to it
that she is well provided for in her apartment in
New York, leads "a life of placid regularity" with
her middle-aged companion, Miss Oakes.

683. Jackson, Shirley. "The Summer People." In *Come Along
with Me*, pp. 66-78, Shirley Jackson. New York: The
Viking Press, Inc., 1968. Mrs. Allison, aged 58,
and Mr. Allison, aged 60, had come to their summer
house for 17 years. Their children are grown and
married and their friends have lives of their own;
their relatives are "vague." So they decide for the
first time to stay on after Labor Day. They cannot
get fuel, their car does not start, the telephone
goes dead--and then they discover that someone has
been tampering with their car.

684. Jewett, Sarah Orne. "Aunt Cynthy Dallett." In *The
Best Stories of Sarah Orne Jewett*, The Mayflower
Edition, pp. 279-306. Gloucester, Massachusetts:
Peter Smith, 1965. Abby Pendexter, Aunt Cynthy's
niece, has fallen into financial difficulty. On
New Year's Day, Abby and her friend Mrs. Hand walk
up the mountain to visit Aunt Cynthy, who is 85
years old now, and lame. During this visit, Aunt
Cynthy confesses that she feels more lonely than
she did when younger. Abby invites her aunt to come
down to the village and spend the winter with her.
Aunt Cynthy wonders if her niece would be willing to
come up there and stay until spring instead, and
"the great question was settled."

685. Jewett, Sarah Orne. "The Flight of Betsey Lane." In
The Best Stories of Sarah Orne Jewett, The Mayflower
Edition, pp. 22-63. Gloucester, Massachusetts:
Peter Smith, 1965. When the granddaughter from a
household where 69-year-old Betsey Lane had worked
for most of her life came calling at the Byfleet
Poorhouse, she left Betsey a gift of money. Soon
after, Betsey disappeared. Her friends, the "upsighted"

Miss Peggy, well on in her 70s, and Lavinia Dow,
a good ten years older than that, feared the worst.
Later that summer, Miss Peggy and Aunt Lavinia looked
for Betsey, who they feared had drowned in the
Byfield pond. They were overjoyed to meet their
friend, who had taken the short way back from the
railroad, and to hear of her great adventure at
the Centennial in Philadelphia. Betsey "had always
known that there was an amazing world outside the
boundaries of Byfleet."

686.   Jewett, Sarah Orne. "Going to Shrewsbury." In *The
       Best Stories of Sarah Orne Jewett*, The Mayflower
       Edition, pp. 90-108. Gloucester, Massachusetts:
       Peter Smith, 1965. At age 76, Mrs. Peet had lost
       her farm to a perfidious nephew. She could have
       remained there as a dependent, but that would have
       hurt her pride. Widowed and childless, she means
       to "airn" her living in Shrewsbury. She hopes to
       be of some use to one of her nieces in the town,
       and had written ahead that she would be moving
       there. Uprooted from her home and friends, her
       prospects in a town 22 miles away are uncertain. The
       narrator, her traveling companion, is moved by the
       elderly lady with her cat basket and her bundle
       handkerchief filled with "a touching collection of
       the last odds and ends" of her housekeeping.

687.   Lamb, Margaret. "Management." In *Solo: Women on
       Woman Alone*, pp. 25-40, Linda Hamalian and Leo
       Hamalian, eds. New York: Dell Publishing Co., Inc.,
       1977. Robbed twice of her welfare checks, old Bitsy
       Larkin is warned by her hostile landlady that she
       will be transferred soon to a nursing home. Bitsy
       finds a way to outsmart a man who swindles her of
       her next check, and to keep her independence for
       a while longer.

688.   Lavin, Mary. "Senility." In *The Shrine and Other
       Stories*, pp. 114-37, Mary Lavin. Boston: Houghton
       Mifflin Co., 1977. An elderly woman who has sold
       her house and "joined forces" with her married
       daughter and son-in-law begins to have episodes of
       bed-wetting. The word "senile" is spoken--a word
       that had been a source of friction between mother
       and grown daughter since the death of the elderly
       woman's own mother, who was put into a home for the
       aged because of physical debility when in her late 80s.

689. Le Sueur, Meridel. *Harvest: Collected Stories*.
     Cambridge, Massachusetts: West End Press, 1977.
     This publication of Le Sueur's early writings, from
     her first story, "Harvest," written in 1929, to
     "We'll Make Your Bed," from *The New Masses*, 1946,
     appeared in her 77th year, and consists of two
     pieces of reportage, "What Happens in a Strike"
     and "Women on the Breadlines," four short stories--
     "Harvest," "Fudge," "Autumnal Village," and "God
     Made Little Apples"--and two humorous works, "To
     Hell with You, Mr. Blue!" and "We'll Make Your Bed."

690. Neville, Susan Schaefer. "Banquet." *Ascent* (1978)
     4(1):26-32. Alma sits alone at the table at the
     Oktoberfest banquet among her children, grand-
     children and great-grandchildren, watching, thinking.
     "All of the grandchildren standing unaware of the
     things that have come from her, a gift." She wants
     to tell her children that she did not *will* her
     cancer, and that she does not want it to happen to
     them, but that if it does, they will be able to
     stand it. She wants to tell them "that things
     change form with ease, that they should remember
     the family." But she knows that every one of them
     is certain "they'll be the one human being in the
     history of the earth that will never ever die."

691. Olsen, Tillie. "I Stand Here Ironing." In *Tell Me
     a Riddle*, pp. 9-21, Tillie Olsen. New York: Dell
     Publishing Co., Inc., 1976. The narrator speaks of
     her love for her daughter, the eldest of five
     children, now aged nineteen, who was born during the
     Depression and who came of age during the war years
     --a child of a time when it was impossible for a
     mother to give the care and attention children need
     for "easy growth."

692. Olsen, Tillie. "Tell Me a Riddle." In *Tell Me a
     Riddle*, pp. 72-125, Tillie Olsen. New York: Dell
     Publishing Co., Inc., 1976. For Eva, dying is taking
     leave of her husband, her children and her grand-
     children, and making a last journey to her self.

693. Parker, Dorothy. "Big Blonde." In *The Portable Dorothy
     Parker*, pp. 187-210. New York and Harmondsworth,
     Middlesex, England: Penguin Books Ltd., 1976.
     Depressed by a failed marriage and the parade of
     drinking companions moving through her life, Hazel
     Morse tries to put herself out of her misery with
     veronal.

694. Parker, Dorothy. "Clothe the Naked." In *The Portable
      Dorothy Parker*, pp. 360-9. New York and Harmondsworth,
      Middlesex, England: Penguin Books Ltd., 1976. Raymond,
      who is blind, is Big Lannie's only living kin, a
      grandson who "was all her children to her." One
      winter, when he has outgrown all his clothes and
      has nothing to wear when he goes down to the street,
      Big Lannie asks her employer, Mrs. Ewing, to give
      her some of Mr. Ewing's old clothes for Raymond.

695. Parker, Dorothy. "Lolita." In *The Portable Dorothy
      Parker*, pp. 384-93. New York and Harmondsworth,
      Middlesex, England: Penguin Books Ltd., 1976.
      Everyone in her Southern town, including Mrs. Ewing
      herself, "a soft little widow" widely known "for
      causing the hearts of gentlemen to beat warm and
      fast," is amazed when her plain daughter Lolita is
      chosen by the supremely eligible bachelor John
      Marble to be his wife.

696. Parker, Dorothy. "The Wonderful Old Gentleman." In
      The Portable Dorothy Parker, pp. 52-64. New York and
      Harmondsworth, Middlesex, England: Penguin Books,
      Ltd., 1976. Two married sisters, Allie Bains and
      Hattie Whittaker, wait with Allie's husband in the
      Bains's living room, as their 84-year-old father lies
      upstairs dying. Hattie, who had been "Cordelia-like
      to her father during his declining years," assures
      her sister it was best that "the wonderful old
      gentleman" had gone to live with the Bainses, who
      are poor, rather than with the much wealthier
      Whittakers five years before, best that the Bains's
      son should have left home after his grandfather moved
      in, best that their black sheep brother should not
      be told about their father's death until after the
      funeral, and best that the old man had willed all
      his money to the Whittakers and his furniture to
      the Bainses.

697. Porter, Katherine Anne. "The Jilting of Granny
      Weatherall." In *The Collected Stories of Katherine
      Anne Porter*, pp. 80-9. New York: New American Library,
      1970. In dying, Granny sees Dr. Harry as a brat who
      belongs in knee breeches, and her daughter Cornelia
      as under the illusion that her mother cannot hear or
      see or speak. Granny wishes the old days were back
      again "with the children young and everything to be
      done over." Nothing had been too much for her, not

even digging post holes for the fencing in of a
hundred acres that she had done by herself once.
For sixty years, she had prayed against remembering
George, who had jilted her on their wedding day.
She wanted one thing, for those around her bed to
find him "and be sure to tell him I forgot him."
For she had had her husband and her children and her
home just like any other woman. And now, "for the
second time there was no sign. Again no bridegroom
and the priest in the house."

698. Porter, Katherine Anne. "The Journey," *The Old Order*.
In *The Collected Stories of Katherine Anne Porter*,
pp. 326-40. New York: New American Library, 1970.
The "journey" is into the past, for in their old age,
Grandmother and old Nannie often sat together for
some hours every day over their sewing, and talked
about the past. They talked about God and heaven and
planting a new hedge of rose bushes, about religion
and the changes in the world, and about the younger
generation--a subject which had an endless fascination
for them--and, often, "about how strangely things come
out in this life."

699. Porter, Katherine Anne. "The Last Leaf," *The Old
Order*. In *The Collected Stories of Katherine Anne
Porter*, pp. 348-51. New York: New American Library,
1970. After Grandmother's death, old Nannie asked
to have the little cabin across the creek as a place
of her very own (the entire family was a little
wounded by her request), and there she transformed
herself from the faithful old servant, Nannie, a
freed slave, to "an aged Bantu woman of independent
means."

700. Porter, Katherine Anne. "The Source," *The Old Order*.
In *The Collected Stories of Katherine Anne Porter*,
pp. 321-5. New York: New American Library, 1970.
Once a year, in early summer, Grandmother took the
three grandchildren to the country, to visit her
third son and his family. There she went into a
frenzy of restoration, and just before leaving she
called her old saddle horse, Fiddler, to take her
on her yearly gallop.

701. Rosenberg, Carol Weiss. "Someone Else's Life." In
Womanblood: Portraits of Women in Poetry and Prose,
pp. 160-84, Aline O'Brien, Chrys Rasmussen and

Catherine Costello, eds. San Francisco: Continuing
SAGA Press, 1981. The last days of Susan Blank, who
began her life in 1920 as "Sarale," Sara Grunbaum--
who had always awakened to the sound of birds in the
villa on the outskirts of Berlin, who came to
America in 1934 to live with her Aunt Yetta and
Uncle Schmuel until her parents would come (they
never did), who married "Harry Blank" (Chaim
Abramiewicz) in 1946, when she was 26 years old,
and who shared first good fortune and then hard
times with Harry, until his death three years before
her own.

702. Stafford, Jean. "The Children's Game." In *The Collected
      Stories of Jean Stafford*, pp. 19-33. New York: Farrar,
      Straus and Giroux, 1969. Abby Reynolds, widowed in
      her early forties, lives for nearly a year in Europe
      after her husband's death. She was so stricken by
      his wholly unexpected death that she had become one
      of the forlorn, brave orphans she and her husband
      used to see whenever they traveled abroad. While
      in Europe, she meets Hugh Nicholson, a man she and
      her husband had known for many years, who has a
      periodic hankering to play roulette. (This story
      was originally published as "The Reluctant Gambler"
      in the *Saturday Evening Post*.)

703. Stafford, Jean. "Life Is No Abyss." In *The Collected
      Stories of Jean Stafford*, pp. 93-112. New York:
      Farrar, Straus and Giroux, 1969. 20-year-old Lily,
      Cousin Will's ward and secretary, visits the poor-
      house to which old Cousin Isobel Carpenter had taken
      herself in reproach to the whole family after she
      had turned over her fortune to Cousin Will, the
      worst investment broker who had ever lived, who
      brought her to destitution. Lily is visiting Cousin
      Isobel in place of Cousin Will, who is sick with
      bronchitis. While there, she sees the wickedness
      of the old woman, who loves every minute of her
      hardship, and the pathos of Isobel's blind room-mate
      Viola and of the old women in the adjoining large
      ward.

704. Suckow, Ruth. "Mrs. Vogel and Ollie." In *Some Others
      and Myself: Seven Stories and a Memoir*, pp. 35-65,
      Ruth Suckow. New York: Rinehart and Co., Inc., 1952.
      Whenever young Susie visited her Aunt Grace, she
      would run over to the Vogels' kitchen, where Mrs.

Vogel's cronies began drifting by from three o'clock
on, when their work was done. Ollie's child-mother,
now past 70, even invited the neighborhood bachelors
to bring Ollie their laundry. Everyone was welcome
to come in for coffee and some of Ollie's freshly
baked cakes or cookies. Ollie's farmer friend LeRoy
never joined the kitchen crowd, preferring to have
his refreshments outside; he, too, had a mother.
Susie returned years later and visited Ollie. Mrs.
Vogel had died three years before, and LeRoy's mother,
too, had died. But Ollie told Susie she and LeRoy
were grownups who had spoiled their two old children,
and now they could not get together themselves.

705. Suckow, Ruth. "Sunset Camp." In *Children and Older
People*, pp. 218-31, Ruth Suckow. New York: Alfred
A. Knopf, Inc., 1931. "Sunset Camp" seems an out-
landish place to Mrs. Grobaty, who is on a trip with
"Mister," her ailing husband, Henry, but then she
remembers that "Ioway," which is "back home," now,
was once a strange place to her when she came there
as a bride from Pennsylvania. She thinks that now
they didn't have to think about the children or the
weather or anything but themselves, for as long as
they were there together.

706. Walker, Alice. "Everyday Use." In *In Love and Trouble:
Stories of Black Women*, pp. 47-59, Alice Walker.
New York: Harcourt Brace Jovanovich, 1973. A mother
of two grown daughters, one of whom has "made it"
in the world, chooses which of them shall have the
quilts pieced by their grandmother.

707. Walker, Alice. "The Welcome Table." In *In Love and
Trouble: Stories of Black Women*, pp. 81-7, Alice
Walker. New York: Harcourt Brace Jovanovich, 1973.
An old woman, thrown out of a white church, meets
Jesus coming down the highway and walks on with
him, not stopping.

708. Welty, Eudora. "A Visit of Charity." In *A Curtain of
Green*, pp. 219-27, Eudora Welty. New York: Doubleday,
Doran and Co., Inc., 1943. 14-year-old Marian is a
Campfire Girl who brings a potted plant to the Old
Ladies' Home (she will get only three points to her
score from this visit), and pays her visit of charity
to two old women in one of the rooms.

709. Welty, Eudora. "A Worn Path." In *A Curtain of Green*,
      pp. 273-85, Eudora Welty. New York: Doubleday, Doran
      and Co., Inc., 1943. Old Phoenix Jackson walks to
      Natchez on an errand of love for her ailing grandson.

710. Wharton, Edith. "After Holbein." In *Certain People*,
      pp. 63-101, Edith Wharton. New York: D. Appleton and
      Co., 1930. Evalina Jaspar, once a leading hostess
      of New York, is now "gently dying of softening of
      the brain," and still orders terrapin, champagne and
      orchids to be served in her now shrouded dining-room
      to imaginary guests. Anson Warley, who recently
      became aware that "he had reached the time of life
      when Alps and cathedrals become as transient as
      flowers," finds himself on Fifth Avenue dressed in
      evening clothes, forgetting where he was invited to
      dine. He decides his invitation was from Mrs. Jaspar,
      rings her bell, and is received as though he were
      expected. Together, the two older people partake of
      a repast that they imagine is quite elegant, in the
      midst of an imagined company, while the old maid and
      the nurse watch them through cracks in the Coromandel
      screen in the dining-room.

711. Wharton, Edith. "Mrs. Manstey's View." In *The Collected
      Short Stories of Edith Wharton*, Vol. 1, pp. 3-11,
      ed. and with an introduction by R.W.B. Lewis. New
      York: Charles Scribner's Sons, 1968. The story of an
      elderly widow living alone in a New York boarding-
      house, who discovers that, after seventeen years
      during which the view from her window has become the
      whole of her life, a neighbor intends to build an
      extension to her house.

712. Winslow, Thyra Samter. "Grandma." In *Middle Age, Old
      Age: Short Stories, Poems, Plays, and Essays on Aging*,
      pp. 35-49, Ruth Granetz Lyell, ed. New York: Harcourt
      Brace Jovanovich, Inc., 1980. At age 73, Grandma
      spends a third of every year with each of her children,
      a daughter and two sons, but it is while traveling
      from one to the other on the train, and in telling
      her fellow passengers romantic stories about her life,
      that she comes most fully into a life of her own.

713. Winslow, Thyra Samter. "The Odd Old Lady." In *Middle
      Age, Old Age: Short Stories, Poems, Plays, and Essays
      on Aging*, pp. 298-307, Ruth Granetz Lyell, ed.
      New York: Harcourt Brace Jovanovich, Inc., 1980.

Past, present and future flow together for old Mrs.
Quillan, who lives with her daughter, Julia, and
Julia's family. Those around her think her clair-
voyance is a sign of senility. By the time they
discover otherwise, old Mrs. Quillan is preparing
for her own future.

714. Winslow, Thyra Samter. "The Old Lady." In *Short
Stories from the New Yorker, 1925 to 1940*, pp. 203-6.
New York: Simon and Schuster, Inc., 1940. Mrs.
Schellingheim lives with her daughter, Mrs. Zwill,
and her son-in-law, who are said to do everything
in the world for the old lady.

715. Yezierska, Anzia. "The Open Cage." In *The Open Cage:
An Anzia Yezierska Collection*, pp. 245-51, Alice
Kessler-Harris, ed. New York: Persea Books, 1979.
A bird flies into the window that an old woman keeps
open in the dingy, furnished room in an apartment
house where she lives--a place where the roomers hate
one another because of self-hatred "for being trapped
in this house that's not a home, but a prison where
the soul dies long before the body is dead."

716. Yezierska, Anzia. "Take Up Your Bed and Walk." In
The Open Cage: An Anzia Yezierska Collection, pp.
237-44, Alice Kessler-Harris, ed. New York: Persea
Books, 1979. At the age of 89, the author is invited
to speak to seminary students who read her recently
published story, "A Window Full of Sky," about growing
old in New York. When a young student visits her to
schedule her speech, she feels reborn; when the
student returns to visit her again with his girl
friend, the writer remembers her own youthful literary
ambitions, and she tells her visitors that a new
generation of writers has taken the place of the old,
and have no need of them.

717. Yezierska, Anzia. "A Window Full of Sky." In *The Open
Cage: An Anzia Yezierska Collection*, pp. 230-6,
Alice Kessler-Harris, ed. New York: Persea Books,
1979. An elderly woman suffering from neuritis
seeks admission to an old people's home because she
feels she can no longer function alone in the rooming
house where she now lives.

718. Zugsmith, Leane. "The Three Veterans." In *Short
      Stories from the New Yorker, 1925 to 1940*, pp.
      167-70. New York: Simon and Schuster, Inc., 1940.
      Twice a week, Mrs. Farrell, Mrs. Gaffney and Mrs.
      Betz appeared at the clinic. They never saw one
      another outside the dispensary, but once they were
      there, "they formed a sisterhood."

See also: 349, 370, 372, 373, 375, 376, 383, 385, 387.

719. Allan, Virginia R.   "Economic and Legal Status of the
     Older Woman." In *No Longer Young: The Older Woman
     in America*, pp. 23-30. Ann Arbor, Michigan: The
     Institute of Gerontology, The University of
     Michigan-Wayne State University, 1975. The financial
     fortunes of today's older woman are greatly affected
     by international economic forces of the devalued
     dollar and inflation, by a socialization which led
     her to believe a husband would provide everlasting
     security, by the necessity for the two-income family,
     by her lack of experience, opportunity and equal
     pay in the labor market, by overt and covert dis-
     crimination which denied her training and upward
     mobility, by society's failure to recognize her
     contribution as a housewife, and by the lack of
     far-sightedness in the legislative process that would
     make a quality of life to which she is entitled in
     her later years possible for her. Mature women workers
     are, for the most part, economically disadvantaged.
     Discrepancies between median income of men and women
     are largely due to the kinds of jobs mature women
     hold, and reflect the difficulties they face when
     they enter or re-enter the labor force. A woman
     worker's educational attainment makes a considerable
     difference in the income she receives. Mature women
     workers should be provided with more and better
     counseling, and with the education and training to
     qualify for the jobs that are available. In this
     paper, existing programs and services are identified;
     prejudices and stereotypes about older women on the
     part of employers are shown to be unfounded; legal
     protections against age and sex discrimination are
     delineated; and the inherent inequities of the Social

Security system are discussed. Recommendations are
made for concrete action that would improve the
economic and legal status of mature women.

*720. Antoniak, Helen, M.L. Scott and N. Worcester. *Alone:
       Emotional, Legal and Financial Help for the Widowed
       or Divorced Woman.* Millbrae, California: Les
       Femmes Publishing Co., 1979.

 721. Atchley, Robert C. "Respondents vs. Refusers in an
       Interview Study of Retired Women: An Analysis of
       Selected Characteristics." *Journal of Gerontology*
       (January 1969) 24(1):42-7. Refusals of older people
       represent a source of bias in gerontology research
       results. After 41% of an original sample of 153
       retired women telephone company employees refused to
       be interviewed, a questionnaire was mailed, and the
       high return rate (93%) allowed an assessment of the
       non-response bias. Variables compared were age,
       health, income, job deprivation, years worked, job
       commitment, contacts with friends, mobility, self-
       esteem, stability of self-concept, leisure activity,
       education, and perceived age. No difference was found
       between respondents and refusers in total number of
       years worked, mobility, self-stability and education.
       Significant differences were found on the basis of
       all the other criteria. Poor health, low job
       deprivation, low job commitment (these two appeared
       to be mutually reinforcing), reporting of low
       contacts with friends, self-assessment of having
       insufficient incomes, high self-esteem, preference
       for solitary leisure activities and resistance to
       identification with being old, all had a significantly
       positive correlation with predisposition to refuse an
       interview. Atchley distinguishes between background
       factors, interest in the subject of the research,
       and personality traits of those predisposed to refuse
       an interview. He observes that the only factor the
       researcher can do much about is that of interest in
       the subject being studied, but suggests that the
       operation of the other two may outweigh that of
       motivation, and continue to contribute to a high
       refusal rate.

*722. Atchley, Robert C. "Retired Women: A Study of Self
       and Role." Diss., University of Michigan, 1967.

723. Atchley, Robert C. "Selected Social and Psychological Differences Between Men and Women in Later Life." *Journal of Gerontology* (March 1976) 31(2):204-11. In many research studies, the effects of marital status, age, education, and adequacy of income are confounded with the effects of sex differences. This paper reports sex differences that have been controlled for these four variables. Attitudes toward work and retirement, self-concept, psychological well-being, self-reported health, perceived income adequacy and perceived social participation are explored through study of survey questionnaire returns of 3630 retired teachers and telephone company employees. Data indicate that both men and women seriously embrace job success as a life goal, and that women are less likely than men to make a quick adjustment to giving up their jobs; that older women are more often lonely, anxious, unstable in self-concept, highly sensitive to criticism and highly depressed than are older men, and that older women are much more likely than older men to report their incomes as inadequate--a tendency especially marked among telephone company retirees. These data challenge the assumptions of marked differences by sex in attitudes toward work and retirement and of widespread psychological problems among older people. They suggest that men often respond to aging in terms of how it affects their relation to the social system, and that women respond to aging with high levels of psychological stress. This paper includes theoretical implications of the data and alternative hypotheses.

724. Atchley, Robert C., and Sherry L. Corbett. "Older Women and Jobs." In *Looking Ahead: A Woman's Guide to the Problems and Joys of Growing Older*, pp. 121-5, Lillian E. Troll, Joan Israel and Kenneth Israel, eds. Englewood Cliffs, New Jersey: Prentice-Hall, Inc., 1977. Because of the paucity of research in this area, much of this paper is stated to be speculative. Contrary to popular belief, a job may be just as important to a woman as to a man. Jobs may be central in the lives of older women because of the effects of the "empty nest" and of widowhood. Women who have a late career start may not have enough time to advance along customary career mile-stones, and retirement is likely to come before job goals are achieved. To assume that women can easily refocus after retirement is to ignore the fact that

it was partly because of role loss in the home in
middle age that they became involved in jobs. Thus,
women tend to take longer than men to adjust to
retirement. As women's relations to their jobs come
to resemble those of men, retirement could become an
easier transition for them than it is at the present
time.

*725. Barker, Susan R., and Julia Loughlin. "Implications of
the Present Economic Position of Middle-Aged,
Divorced and Widowed Women." Paper presented at
the American Sociological Association, Syracuse
University, September 1979.

*726. Berman, Eleanor. *Re-Entering: Successful Back-to-Work
Strategies for Women Seeking a Fresh Start*. New
York: Crown Publishers, Inc., 1980.

727. Bernstein, Merton C. "Forecast of Women's Retirement
Income: Cloudy and Colder; 25 Percent Chance of
Poverty." *Industrial Gerontology* (Spring 1974)
1(2):1-13. What women need from retirement programs
are higher benefits from Social Security and assured
eligibility and widows' benefits from private pension
plans. Social Security has made steady improvements;
private pensions remain unreliable for men and
seriously inadequate for women. The outlook for
meaningful pension reform is cloudy, at best. In
contrast, Social Security already contains a cost-of-
living escalator provision, and any improvements
in the system can become effective in a matter of
months, or at most a year. There is no effective
lobby to back pension reform, but organized labor
and some retiree groups do work effectively for
Social Security improvements.

728. Cohen, Wilbur J. "Social Security: Next Steps." In
No Longer Young: The Older Woman in America, pp.
95-102. Ann Arbor, Michigan: The Institute of
Gerontology, The University of Michigan-Wayne State
University, 1975. Cohen describes the Social Security
program as the largest life, disability and health
insurance program as well as the largest retirement
program in the nation, and discusses important aspects
and major accomplishments of the system. He proposes
a number of changes which would remove inequities a-
gainst women and make the system more responsive to
their needs. These are changes in the method of com-
puting retirement benefits, the recognition of household employment as covered employment under the system,

and the elimination of the dependency provisions in the
law. It is also recommended that the Medicare system be
expanded to include prescription drugs, hearing aids
and eyeglasses for those aged 65 and over, that a
major medical insurance program be provided for
everyone in society by the SSA, and that a complete
program of prenatal and postnatal care be provided
for every woman and child. Cash maternity benefits,
and more generous deductions or tax credits on
income taxes for children are also recommended,
with these benefits limited to three children per
family. Higher taxes are required to fund these
proposals. It is recommended that the tax structure
be changed so that the Social Security payroll tax
does not become burdensome to low- and middle-income
workers, and that the minimum Social Security benefit
be raised to the poverty line, with funds for the
difference being paid from the general revenues. For
the longer term, Congress might appoint a national
commission on the quality of life to receive and
analyze proposals for the improvement of domestic
welfare, and make recommendations as to how this
would be accomplished.

*729. Data Resources, Inc. *Inflation and the Elderly.*
       Washington, D.C.: National Retired Teachers
       Association/American Association for Retired
       Persons, 1980.

*730. Flaim, Paul O., and Howard N. Fullerton, Jr. *Labor
       Force Projections to 1990: Three Possible Paths.*
       U.S. Department of Labor, Bureau of Labor Statistics.
       Washington, D.C.: U.S. Government Printing Office,
       1979.

*731. Fowles, Donald G. *Income and Poverty Among the Elderly:
       1975.* U.S. Department of Health, Education and
       Welfare, Statistical Reports on Older Americans,
       No. 2. Washington, D.C.: U.S. Department of Health,
       Education and Welfare, 1977.

 732. Fox, Judith. "Effects of Retirement and Former Work
       Life on Women's Adaptation in Old Age." *Journal of
       Gerontology* (March 1977) 32(2):196-202. Study sample
       consists of 212 white, middle-class women interviewed
       in 1970-72 as participants in the second Duke
       Longitudinal Study of Aging, reporting themselves

as retirees, workers or housewives. Mean age is 61
years. The paper questions prevailing assumptions
about the relationship between women and work, and
demonstrates that the work role is salient for many
women. Findings are that retirement negatively
affects psychological well-being in that it reduces
income and perceived general level of social contact. Data indicate that, compared to women still
working, retirees have a lower *perceived* level of
social contact, but are more involved in informal
interaction with friends and neighbors. Retirees
have a less positive balance of affect than workers,
but this may be attributed to the fact that retirees
are lower in income, subjective health state and
perceived level of social contact. Only income
discrepancies begin to explain the fact that retirees'
affect balance is much lower than that of housewives.
Social contact is much more highly related to psychological well-being for retirees than for workers or
housewives. It is hypothesized that retirees are
more dependent than housewives on extra-familial
social contact, and that failure to maintain a
sufficient level of interaction accounts for their
less positive affect balance.

*733.   Githens, Grace G. "A Study of the Effects of Income,
        Physical Health, Sex and Marital Status on the
        Life Satisfaction of Aged Individuals." Diss.,
        Adult Education, University of Oklahoma, 1975.

*734.   Gordon, Nancy M. *The Treatment of Women Under Social
        Security*. Consultation on Discrimination Against
        Minorities and Women in Pensions and Health, Life
        and Disability Insurance, No. 3. Washington, D.C.:
        U.S. Commission on Civil Rights, 1978.

 735.   Haberkorn, Susan B., Recorder. "Low Pay/Low Status."
        In *No Longer Young: The Older Woman in America,
        Work Group Reports*, pp. 23-6. Ann Arbor, Michigan:
        The Institute of Gerontology, The University of
        Michigan-Wayne State University, 1974. Women are
        very disproportionately represented in the full-time,
        low-income work force. The work force of older
        women, in contrast to that of younger women, is
        stable. Public awareness of laws prohibiting sex
        and age discrimination must be increased. Affirmative
        action also might be directed toward modifying the
        stereotypes of "men's" and "women's" work. Local

job counseling centers should be established, and
these centers could assume an advocacy role in
opposition to discrimination in employment. A
major objective of community service employment
programs will be to provide part-time jobs for low-
income older people. Solutions to the problem of
women's low retirement income include equalization
of the Social Security system.

*736. Irelan, L.M., D.K. Motley, K. Schwab, S.R. Sherman and
J. Murray. *Almost 65: Baseline Data from the
Retirement History Study*. Research Report No. 49.
Washington, D.C.: Social Security Administration,
1976. Report from a ten-year (1969 to 1979) national
sample longitudinal panel study of the retirement
process on over 11,000 members of the 1905-1911
birth cohort, who represent the American retirees of
the 1970s. Note that these three sub-samples do
not include the married women; they represent
4,117,000 married men with spouses present in the
household, 729,000 men with no spouses present, and
1,954,000 women living with no spouses present in
the household; at the first interviewing, all were
between 58 and 63 years old.

*737. Jaffe, A.J., and Jeanne C. Ridley. "The Extent of
Lifetime Employment of Women in the U.S." *Industrial
Gerontology* (Winter 1976) 3:25-35.

738. Jaslow, Philip. "Employment, Retirement, and Morale
Among Older Women." *Journal of Gerontology* (March
1976) 31(2):212-8. Cross-sectional data are used to
test the hypothesis that older working women have
better morale than those who do not work. Data
were originally gathered in 1968 from a multi-stage
area probability sample of 3,996 non-institutionalized
persons aged 65 and over in the U.S., and the analysis
here is restricted to 2,398 women in the sample:
6.3% were classified as employed (now working),
54.1% as retired (worked at least five years since
age 21), and 39.6% as never having worked. Employed
women had higher morale than the retirees, with the
exception of those with incomes of $5,000 or more,
among whom morale was higher than that of the workers.
Women who "never worked" had the lowest morale as
a group. Small but statistically significant
differences remained when the intervening effects
of age, income and health were simultaneously isolated,

indicating that the group differences in morale
stemmed in part (but not entirely) from the fact that
the employed women tended to be the youngest, healthiest
and most affluent of the three groups, while women
who had never worked tended to be the oldest, poorest,
and in the worst health. Jaslow urges that women
be included in future research studies focusing on
social or psychological dimensions of work and
retirement.

*739. Jewson, Ruth Hathaway. "After Retirement: An Explora-
       tory Study of the Professional Woman." Diss.,
       University of Minnesota, 1978.

 740. Kreps, Juanita M. "Career Options After Fifty:
       Suggested Research." *The Gerontologist* (Spring
       1971) 11(2):4-8. Affinity to work seems to be
       related to the nature of the work more than to age.
       We now know very little about how people would like
       to divide their time between work and non-work
       activity, about the quality of retirement leisure,
       about industry's capacity to accommodate workers'
       preferences, and about the possibilities for broadening
       options as to career patterns in middle and later
       work life. Kreps identifies some career preferences
       (among them, second careers, which are necessarily
       applicable to certain groups, such as middle-aged
       women re-entering the labor force), and institutional
       constraints; she suggests ways of researching these
       issues. We need to make continuous evaluations of
       the institutional arrangements which control most of
       adult life, i.e., of the forces that govern labor
       force activity. A very important question is whether
       leisure time becomes more or less valuable as one
       grows older.

 741. Kreps, Juanita. *Sex in the Marketplace: American
       Women at Work*. Baltimore: The Johns Hopkins University
       Press, 1971. In the Preface, Kreps remarks the
       significance of the impact of work discontinuity on
       a woman's career, and finds it curious that public
       interest in manpower training has paid so little
       attention to the needs of middle-aged women. Her
       chapters, "intended to serve as a brief review of
       the literature on the subject of women's labor force
       activity, and to examine when women work, at what
       jobs, and under what arrangements," are: Introduction:
       Some Things We Know About Women; The Demand for and

> Supply of Women Workers; A Case in Point: Women in
> the Academic Profession; The Values of Women's Work;
> Home and Market Work in Lifetime Perspective; The
> Future: Some Things We Don't Know About Women. In
> her book, she explores many aspects of women's work,
> both market and nonmarket, and points out in the
> chapter on the future that women's increased labor
> force activity raises interesting questions about the
> future allocation of time among market work, home
> work, and leisure.

742. Kreps, Juanita, and Robert Clark. *Sex, Age, and Work:*
      The Changing Composition of the Labor Force.
      Baltimore: The Johns Hopkins University Press, 1975.
      In "The Allocation of Work and Free Time," it is
      predicted that, if educational levels continue to
      rise and if fertility continues to decline, the
      worklife pattern for married women will come to
      resemble more closely than previously those of men
      and single women, but that "the cumulative effect
      of these changes in women's worklives has not been
      fully recognized in the literature nor integrated
      into public policy." Chapters on: Worklife Changes
      of Married Men and Women; One-Adult Families and
      Labor Force Activity; Worklives in Transition: Some
      Implications. In the latter, it is noted that market
      work has been becoming more evenly distributed
      between the *sexes*, but that in the case of *age*,
      the re-allocation has been toward concentrating
      work in the middle years. Both industry practice
      and government policy bias the worker's decision
      about allocation of time toward working continuously
      until the mid-sixties and then consuming leisure
      full time for her or his remaining years. Kreps
      and Clark suggest means by which these constraints
      might be removed.

*743. Lobsenz, Johanna. *The Older Woman in Industry*. New
      York: Scribner's Sons, 1929. This early study, which
      provides valuable historical information on the
      subject, includes data on older women engaged in
      clerical work, general office work, selling and
      domestic labor, but does not include material on
      older women in the professions.

744. Lopata, Helen Znaniecki. *Occupation: Housewife*. New
      York: Oxford University Press, 1971. White and black
      women are included in the sample of this interview

study of the social roles of 268 suburban housewives,
200 urban housewives, and 100 working women, all
living in the Chicago area. It was found that the
more trained and educated among these women "are
solving the problems of 'retirement' by becoming
competent in new areas of life and by enjoying their
expanding horizons." Those in their late 50s, many
of whom are first- or second-generation Americans,
"tend to describe the roles of women in an almost
matriarchal manner" and women aged 60 and over, unless
they are members of the upper social classes and
involved in societally active roles, focus on the
role of housewife. Many older women, both widows
and wives of retired men with a limited pension,
perceive themselves to be limited by scarce financial
resources. On the whole, this research challenges
the stereotype of the housewife as a woman who is
passive, uninterested in the world beyond the walls
of her home, and unimaginative. It also challenges
the current view of the life cycle of the American
woman as a sequence of definite and irreversible
states with the last stage seen as the least functional.
It identifies a broad range of styles in performing
the housewife and related roles, extending "from the
very restricted to the highly competent, from the
ritualistic to the creative, from the task- to the
relation-oriented." Lopata's basic conclusion from
her studies is that women today are becoming ever
more competent and creative in performing the social
role of housewife and in the way in which they combine
various roles throughout the life course.

745. Lopata, Helena Znaniecki, and Frank Steinhart. "Work
      Histories of American Urban Women." *The Gerontologist*
      (Winter 1971) 11(1, Part II):27-36. Few older women,
      especially white women, were adequately prepared for
      effective engagement in today's work world. This
      article presents research evidence and statistical
      data supporting the conclusion that most young women
      of past generations were trained for passive work
      roles and had erratic work histories limited to
      minimal level jobs. It also discusses case studies
      of the work histories of a sample of older urban
      (Chicago-area) women who did have work experience,
      strongly recommends that young women be made aware
      of the gulf between the traditional value system
      and their actual work needs over the life course,
      and suggests building flexible career expectations

into American education and training. Re-training
of people at the end of each "natural cycle" of
work in any given occupation is also strongly
recommended.

*746.   Mallan, Lucy B.   "Women Born in the Early 1900s:
        Employment, Earnings, and Benefit Levels." *Social
        Security Bulletin* (March 1974), second reprint,
        37(3):3-24.

 747.   Mueller, Charles W., and Blair G. Campbell.   "Female
        Occupational Achievement and Marital Status: A
        Research Note." *Journal of Marriage and the Family*
        (August 1977) 39(3):587-93.   A representative
        national sample of white and black native-born
        U.S females, aged 30 to 44, surveyed in 1967 as part
        of the "longitudinal study of labor market experience
        of women," initiated and directed by Herbert S.
        Parnes, was used to test the hypothesis that single
        and never-married females who experience high
        occupational achievements are more likely to
        remain single than comparable females who do not
        experience high occupational achievements.   The
        data indicate support for the hypothesis for the
        white population; for black females, the overall
        pattern is not as convincing.

 748.   O'Neil, Kate, Recorder.   "Economic and Legal Status."
        In *No Longer Young: The Older Woman in America,
        Work Group Reports*, pp. 57-61.   Ann Arbor, Michigan:
        The Institute of Gerontology, The University of
        Michigan-Wayne State University, 1974.   One word--
        poor--describes the economic and legal status of older
        women.   The single poorest category of people in
        America consists of 7½ million widows and single
        women, half of whom exist on an income of less than
        $1,888 a year.   Topics: labor force participation
        on the part of older women, their earnings, and the
        effect of fewer years of service and lower pay on
        their retirement income.   Old age, especially for
        women living alone, usually means living in poverty.
        Discrimination in the marketplace was discussed; it
        was stated that the magnitude of the problem has
        hardly begun to be appreciated.   The administrative
        tools needed to carry out the concepts of the new
        laws are clearly still lacking.   The concept of
        equal pay for equal work is only now beginning to
        be enforced.   Inequities in compensation for work

are matched by inequities in retirement income.
Older women who have followed society's dictates
to become wives and mothers are made economically
and legally helpless. They must be provided with
some form of unemployment compensation, either as a
chance for re-training or as a means to live at a
dignified level. Wives' vested interest in the
family income should be recognized. "Divorce
insurance" for married couples is a possibility;
another is Social Security coverage for household
work. The need to find some way to redistribute
societal income to women who have contributed to the
family--and to redistribute it in these women's own
names--is compelling.

*749.   Quinn, Jane Bryant. "Women and Social Security," "Money
        Facts." *Woman's Day* (August 7, 1978) Vol. 13, 41st
        year, 13th issue:32.

 750.   Redmond, Rosemary. "Legal Issues Involving the Older
        Woman." In *The Older Woman: Lavender Rose or Gray
        Panther*, pp. 228-33, Marie Marschall Fuller and Cora
        Ann Martin, eds. Springfield, Illinois: Charles C.
        Thomas, 1980. Special legal problems of older
        citizens include discrimination in employment,
        reduction of employment benefits, high costs for
        health insurance, and difficulties encountered in
        the financial exploitation, neglect, and physical
        abuse of older persons. Redmond discusses the in-
        adequacy of elderly women's retirement income and
        Congresswoman Barbara Jordan's legislative plan for
        giving earned Social Security credits for homemaker
        service, the higher cost of health insurance that is
        borne by women, and the problems of financial
        exploitation, neglect and physical abuse of the
        elderly. The Legal Protective Services for Adults
        Component of the Older Americans Legal Action Center
        investigates cases of financial exploitation involving
        older persons, and since 1976, about 78% of the
        clientele in this category have been women. The
        fear of trusting outsiders may encourage an older
        person to become reclusive. News of financial
        exploitation by a neighbor's family or friends can
        lead to paranoia, which in some cases results in
        extreme self-neglect. Prevention and protective
        services legislation are needed to prevent adult
        abuse and neglect. With women's increased life
        expectancy, greater numbers of the elderly may

continue to be part of the average household. Skills
must be taught to families to assure the older
individual of a dignified and safe environment
with the family.

*751.   Rix, Sara E. Paper on the labor force participation
        of women, presented to a briefing sponsored by the
        Congresswomen's Caucus, Washington, D.C., October
        30, 1979.

*752.   Schneider, Clement. "Adjustment of Employed Women to
        Retirement." Diss., Sociology, Cornell University,
        1964. A longitudinal study of 603 retired working
        women aged 63 to 65 which focuses on their adjustment
        to retirement; a major finding was that single employed
        women adjust best to retirement, that widows make
        the poorest adjustment, and that married women's
        adjustment is midway between these groups.

753.   Sheppard, Harold L. "The Status of Women, 1993-1998:
        Financial Aspects." In *No Longer Young: The Older
        Woman in America*, pp. 107-10. Ann Arbor, Michigan:
        The Institute of Gerontology, The University of
        Michigan-Wayne State University, 1975. These
        projections are contingent upon the supply of
        technological and natural resources to sustain or
        raise the current status of people in the labor
        force, political decisions about funding "social
        programs," the supply of day care centers, educational
        opportunities for women, the enforcement of age and
        sex discrimination laws, and the changes in the
        general culture, in life styles and sources of
        identity. It is likely that work will be a signifi-
        cant source of identity for women, who are more and
        more becoming attached to the labor force and who
        will be more reluctant than men to retire early.
        Working women aged 45 to 64 will have increased by
        63% by 1990 over the year 1960, and women aged 65
        and over by 46% in these years. The comparable
        figures for men are 14% and *minus* 12% respectively.
        Women are increasingly becoming year-round, full-time
        members of the labor force. Some studies show that
        as women increase their earnings, the odds are great
        that they will remain single or become divorced. It
        has also been found that there is less resentment
        and discontent as a result of the wife's having to
        go to work to keep the family together in the
        professional group of men than in the blue-collar

working class. It is projected that this will be
less the case in 1990 than at the present time:
younger male workers appear to be much less author-
itarian than their older counterparts, and there are
indications this will be the case in the future.

754.   Sommers, Tish. "On Growing Older Female: An Interview
       with Tish Sommers." In *The Older Woman: Lavender
       Rose or Gray Panther*, pp. 31-4, Marie Marschall
       Fuller and Cora Ann Martin, eds. Springfield,
       Illinois: Charles C. Thomas, 1980. The displaced
       homemaker is a woman who has experienced a sudden
       personal and economic dislocation because of divorce
       or widowhood and departure of children from the
       home. The empty nest syndrome, widowhood or divorce
       are forms of forced retirement from the homemaker
       status, and in a tight job market only the exceptional
       woman will break through the combined barrier of
       age and sex. Because sexism is compounded by ageism,
       older women are more vulnerable--especially economically
       --than older men. Legislative reforms are needed,
       and they represent *preventive* care, because the
       middle years are crucial in a woman's life cycle
       and a situation in which displaced homemakers
       are left either to sink or swim, and are paid
       exploitative wages at exploitative jobs, simply
       lays the basis for more costly welfare and services
       later on.

755.   Sommers, Tish. "Social Security: A Woman's Viewpoint."
       In *The Older Woman: Lavender Rose or Gray Panther*,
       pp. 247-61, Marie Marschall Fuller and Cora Ann
       Martin, eds. Springfield, Illinois: Charles C.
       Thomas, 1980. Social Security, as it now stands,
       presents a "classic syndrome of institutionalized
       sexism." Based upon the "archaic" assumption that
       men are breadwinners and women are homemakers-
       dependents, features of the system highly discriminatory
       against women include benefits calculated on earnings
       rates, penalizing of motherhood by averaging earnings,
       failure to provide credits for homemaking, making
       dependents' benefits tied to the breadwinner,
       actuarial deductions, and regressive tax rates.
       Sommers presents a feminist critique of Social
       Security, shows the plight of the widow caught in
       the "widow's gap," of the displaced homemaker, and
       of very old women caught in the inflationary spiral,
       and makes a number of recommendations for change.

In her view, the system should be improved, rather than
eliminated. She discusses legislative proposals for
change, and emphasizes the need for provision of
adequate and varied employment opportunities for those
of all ages. This paper first appeared in *Industrial
Gerontology*, Fall 1975.

*756.   Sommers, Tish, and Laurie Shields. *Older Women and
         Health Care: Strategy for Survival*. Gray Paper #3,
         Oakland, California: Older Women's League Educational
         Fund, 1980.

*757.   Sommers, Tish, and Laurie Shields. *Older Women and
         Pensions: Catch 22*. Gray Paper #4, Oakland, California:
         Older Women's League Educational Fund, 1979.

*758.   Sommers, Tish, and Laurie Shields. *Older Women and
         Public Policy*. Gray Paper #1, Oakland, California:
         Older Women's League Educational Fund, 1979. OWLEF
         testimony before the Senate Committee on Human
         Resources.

 759.   Sommers, Tish, and Laurie Shields. *Social Security:
         Adequacy* and *Equity For Older Women*. Gray Paper #2,
         Oakland, California: Older Women's League Educational
         Fund, 1979. Topics: Poverty and Older Women; Why
         Are Older Women So Poor?; How Does Social Security
         Contribute to the Poverty of Older Women?; The HEW
         Report: A Critique From the Viewpoint of Older
         Women, positive features and negative features;
         Administration Budget Proposals (eliminating the
         lump sum death benefit of $255, phasing out Social
         Security benefits for post-secondary students, elim-
         inating the minimum benefit for low-wage workers,
         limiting the number of work years that may be
         disregarded in computing benefits, and eliminating
         benefits to a surviving parent when a minor child
         reaches age sixteen); New Myths and Their Dangers
         (that women are going into the workforce in such
         numbers that dependency is only a transitional
         problem, that women want equality and should not have
         special privileges, that women should not depend
         upon men and, if necessary, ought to be pushed into
         the labor market, that as women move into non-
         traditional jobs, they will have supplementary income
         from pensions and other sources, and that "It won't
         happen to me!"); What Should Be Our Current Strategy?

*760.   Sommers, Tish, and Laurie Shields. *Welfare: End of
        the Line for Women*. Gray Paper #5, Oakland,
        California: Older Women's League Educational Fund,
        1980.

 761.   Thompson, Gayle B.   "Economic Status of Late Middle-
        Aged Widows."   In *Transitions of Aging*, pp. 133-49,
        Nancy Datan and Nancy Lohmann, eds.   New York: Academic
        Press, Inc., 1980.   The income, labor force and
        demographic characteristics of late middle-aged
        widows, the impact of employment on their economic
        status, and the labor force determinants of economic
        status among employed widows.   Data are derived from
        the Retirement History Study (Irelan, et al., 1976).
        They suggest that education and work decisions made
        early in life have an impact on economic status among
        women widowed prior to their eligibility for Social
        Security aged widows' benefits at age 60: they affect
        the probability of employment, and, among the employed,
        they affect job characteristics and ultimately the
        level of earnings.

*762.   U.S. Commission on Civil Rights. *Women Still in Poverty*.
        Clearinghouse Publication 60.   Washington, D.C.:
        U.S. Government Printing Office, 1979.

*763.   U.S. Congress.   House.   Select Committee on Aging.
        Pension Problems of Older Women.   Hearings before
        the Subcommittee on Retirement Income and Employment
        of the Select Committee on Aging, House of Representa-
        tives, 94th Congress, 1st Session, 1975.

*764.   U.S. Congress.   House.   Select Committee on Aging.
        *Women and Retirement Income Programs: Current Issues
        of Equity and Adequacy*.   Report prepared by the
        Congressional Research Service of the Library of
        Congress, House of Representatives, Comm. Pub. No.
        96-190, 96th Congress, 1st Session, 1979.

*765.   U.S. Department of Commerce.   Bureau of the Census.
        *Social and Economic Characteristics of the Older
        Population: 1978*.   Washington, D.C.: U.S. Government
        Printing Office, 1979.

 766.   U.S. Department of Commerce.   Bureau of the Census.
        A Statistical Portrait of Women in the U.S., Special
        Studies Series P23, No. 58.   Washington, D.C.: U.S.
        Government Printing Office, 1976.   Data, with charts

and tables, on the changing social and economic
status of women in the U.S., compiled by the Bureau
of the Census in recognition of International Women's
Year. Topics include population growth and composition;
longevity, mortality and health; residence and
migration; marital and family status; fertility;
education; labor force participation; occupation and
industry; work experience; income and poverty status;
voting and public office holding; crime and victimization; Black women; Spanish women,

*767. U.S. Department of Commerce. Bureau of the Census.
A Statistical Portrait of Women in the U.S., 1978,
Current Population Reports, Series P23, No. 100.
Washington, D.C.: U.S. Government Printing Office,
1980. A statistical overview of the changing status
of women in American society during the 1970s. Data
were compiled from U.S. Government sources, including
surveys, decennial censuses, vital statistics, and
administrative records. Includes a separate discussion
of comparisons of black women with white women, and
recent data for women of Spanish origin as well as
data for American Indian and Asian-American women.

768. U.S. Department of Health, Education, and Welfare.
*Social Security and the Changing Roles of Men and
Women.* Washington, D.C.: U.S. Department of Health,
Education, and Welfare, February 1979. Chapters:
Issues; Comprehensive Options; Limited Options;
Gender-based Distinctions; Offset Provision;
Conclusion. Appendices.

*769. U.S. Department of Justice. Civil Rights Division.
Task Force on Sex Discrimination. *The Pension Game:
American Pension System from the Viewpoint of the
Average Woman.* Washington, D.C.: U.S. Government
Printing Office, 1979.

*770. U.S. Department of Labor. *Employment and Economic
Issues of Low-Income Women: Report of a Project.*
Washington, D.C.: U.S. Government Printing Office,
1978.

*771. U.S. Department of Labor. *Women with Low Incomes.*
Washington, D.C.: U.S. Government Printing Office,
1977.

*772.   U.S. Department of Labor. Bureau of Labor Statistics.
        Women in the Labor Force: Some New Data Series.
        Report No. 575. Washington, D.C.: U.S. Government
        Printing Office, 1979.

*773.   U.S. Department of Labor. Employment and Training
        Administration. *Women and Work.* R and D Monograph
        46. Washington, D.C.: U.S. Government Printing
        Office, 1977.

*774.   U.S. Department of Labor. Women's Bureau. *The
        Earnings Gap Between Women and Men.* Washington,
        D.C.: U.S. Government Printing Office, 1979.

*775.   U.S. Department of Labor. Women's Bureau. *Facts
        About Women Heads of Households and Heads of Families.*
        Washington, D.C.: U.S. Government Printing Office,
        1979.

776.   U.S. Department of Labor. Women's Bureau. *Mature
        Women Workers: A Profile.* Washington, D.C.: U.S.
        Government Printing Office, 1976. Provides data for
        women and minority women aged 45 and over on labor
        force participation rates, unemployment, earnings,
        average annual income, living arrangements, level
        of educational attainment, and marital status.

777.   Westerman, Marcine P., Recorder. "Volunteerism." In
        *No Longer Young: The Older Woman in America, Work
        Group Reports*, pp. 53-6. Ann Arbor, Michigan: The
        Institute of Gerontology, The University of Michigan-
        Wayne State University, 1974. The stereotyped role
        of the older woman as the mainstay of community
        voluntary associations is a peculiarly American
        phenomenon of perhaps the past 125 years. It was in
        the latter half of the 19th century that the major
        social movements in the U.S. developed a significant
        female component. The stereotype of the volunteer
        as an older women is almost dangerous; these stereo-
        types can diminish the impact of voluntary associations,
        seen as "women's work" rather than as business. We
        should be clear as to the difference between the
        volunteer's act of consent and the activity. Also,
        there is no essential difference between the act of
        the volunteer and the act of the "professional."
        Last, we must recognize that it is not the volunteer-
        ing, but rather the covenant, which makes the nation
        survive. The effectiveness of volunteer organizations

was a topic of discussion in this workshop; differences
of opinion regarding the value to society of volunteer
services were expressed. It was pointed out that
problems can be minimized when roles are carefully
defined, so that volunteers serve appropriate
functions. Characteristics of a good volunteer
program were delineated, and several suggestions
were offered in regard to the social dynamics that
motivate volunteers.

778. Zanar, Eileen. "Reentry Ripoff: One Housewife's Exposé."
      Ms. (October 1977) VI(4):83-6. An account, based
      upon personal experience, of how older women can
      be exploited by re-entry programs.

See also: 18, 19, 25, 27, 36, 37, 119, 257, 428, 429, 430,
432, 435, 436, 437, 438, 439, 440, 441, 442, 443, 444, 445,
446, 447, 448, 506, 512, 518, 519, 520, 529, 590, 687, 689,
836, 843.

A. Love and Sexuality;
Marriage and Family Relationships;
Friendship; Older Women's
Neighborhood and Community Relationships;
Older Women Alone

779.   Adams, Bert N.   "The Middle-Class Adult and His
       Widowed or Still-Married Mother." *Social Problems*
       (Summer 1968) 16(1):50-9.   This study comparing two
       samples of married men and women in their 30s in
       terms of their relations with their mother (118 have
       a widowed mother, and 145 have both parents still
       living) is one portion of a kinship study conducted
       in Greensboro, North Carolina in the 1960s.   Five
       types of contact with widowed mothers or still-married
       parents are delineated.   Findings are that for sons,
       contact with widowed mothers tends to be restricted
       to giving aid and home visiting; for daughters,
       mutual aid with the widowed mother is common, and
       contact with the mother is increased after her
       widowhood.   Concludes that the most satisfactory
       relations between a grown middle-class son and his
       widowed mother are those characterized by the mother's
       independence, whereas for daughters, they result
       from balanced help and a variety of other contact
       patterns.   Non-independence and a one-way aid pattern,
       which often occurs for widowed mothers and their
       middle-class sons, make for a relationship based
       upon filial piety and a weak affectional tie.

780.   Alston, Letitia T., and Jon P. Alston.   "Religion and
       the Older Woman." In *The Older Woman: Lavender Rose
       or Gray Panther*, pp. 262-78, Marie Marschall Fuller
       and Cora Ann Martin, eds.   Springfield, Illinois:
       Charles C. Thomas, 1980.   Data presented here are
       derived from six national annual surveys of the

American population from 1972 to 1977 conducted by
the National Opinion Research Center. Findings are
reported for church attendance, marital status, work
status, perceptions of health, and self-ratings of
strength of religious identity. Data indicate that
today's older woman is far more likely to attend
church often than are young women or older men, that
effects of marital status, presence or absence of
children, and work status on attendance patterns of
women are not as great as might be expected, and
thus that age is a more important variable for
predicting church attendance levels of women today
than their involvement in other roles. Data are
cross-sectional; therefore the question of age vs.
generational effect cannot be addressed directly.
The age of 30 appears to be a significant watershed;
this means that some age differences may be due to
differences between generations of women born before
and after World War Two. But there do appear to
be indications that the changes inherent in the aging
process may have important effects on religious
identification and participation; also, the data
show that at all ages, women are more active in
religion than are men.

*781.   Angres, Salma B.   "Intergenerational Relations and
        Value Congruence Between Young Adults and Their
        Mothers." Diss., University of Chicago, 1974.

*782.   Antonucci, T., and Bornstein, J.   "Changes in Informal
        Social Support Networks." Paper presented to
        American Psychological Association, 1978.

 783.   Ballweg, John A.   "Resolution of Conjugal Role Adjustment
        After Retirement." *Journal of Marriage and the
        Family* (May 1967) 29(2):277-81. Married women over
        age 65, whose spouses were either retired or still
        employed, were interviewed about the distribution of
        household tasks by sex, and their attitudes toward
        their spouses' behavior in this regard. Findings
        were that retired husbands engaged in joint household
        tasks more extensively than those still working, and
        that they assumed full responsibility for tasks which
        the employed husbands avoided.

 784.   Berardo, Felix M.   "The Family and Aging: An Editorial
        Comment." *The Family Coordinator* (October 1972)
        21(4):3-4. In this paper, introducing the special

issue on Aging and the Family, Berardo notes the
changes that have taken place since the essay, "Are
the Aged Ex-Family?" appeared in *Social Forces*
nearly 25 years before, the growing interest in
the elderly, and the diversity of the aged population
--a major theme in the papers in this issue. Prepared several months before the convening of the
1971 White House Conference on Aging, the papers
are: "Older Families and Their Troubles" by Gordon
F. Streib; "Marital Life Among Aging Blacks" by
Jacquelyne Johnson Jackson; "The Impact of Health
on the Aged Family" by Donald P. Kent and Margaret
B. Matson; "The Housing Patterns of Older Families"
by James E. Montgomery; "Religion and the Aging
Family" by David O. Moberg; "A New Look at Older
Marriages" by Walter C. McKain; "Aging and Suicide"
by E. Wilbur Bock; "Of Social Values and the Dying"
by Richard A. Kalish; "Widowhood and Preventive
Intervention" by Phyllis R. Silverman; "Social Work
and the Aging Family" by Martin Bloom and Alexander
Monro (see Nos. 146, 813 and 854 of this Bibliography).

*785.   Berkman, Lisa F.   "Social Networks, Host Resistance
        and Mortality: A Follow-Up Study of Alameda County
        Residents." Diss., School of Public Health,
        Department of Epidemiology, University of California,
        Berkeley, 1977.

786.   Bernard, Jessie. *Remarriage: A Study of Marriage.*
        New York: Russell and Russell, 1971. First published
        in 1956, Bernard's book presented evidence that in
        any sample of the remarried, most are as successful
        in their remarriages as are those in their first
        marriages. In her Preface here, she cites data
        for 1967 corroborating this conclusion. Data used
        in this study are: census-type statistical material;
        case material from interviews, from reports and
        from popular, fictional and technical literature;
        and questionnaire data on 2,009 cases of remarriage
        gathered from people who were intimately acquainted
        with the remarried families. These remarried
        families were conceived of as the total remarried
        population of an imaginary community, "Utopolis."
        This book contains a section on the potential for
        love in the middle and later years. Methodological
        appendices.

787. Blood, Robert O., Jr., and Donald M. Wolfe. *Husbands*
      and Wives: The Dynamics of Married Living. New
      York: The Free Press, 1960. A "wife's-eye view of
      marriage" from interviews with 731 urban and suburban
      wives and 178 farm wives in 1955. The data are
      derived from a systematic probability-sample survey
      of families in the Detroit metropolitan area and
      from a comparable survey of farm families in
      southeastern Michigan. The book reports on decision-
      making; the division of labor; family functions--
      economic; having children; companionship; understanding
      and emotional well-being; love; and an evaluation
      of the stresses and strengths of American marriage,
      all from the honeymoon to the post-parental and
      retirement stages of the family-life cycle. The
      authors conclude that "corrosion is not too harsh
      a term for what happens to the average marriage in
      the course of time." Appendices include research
      methods and the questionnaire.

788. Cameron, Marcia, Recorder. "Family Relationships."
      In *No Longer Young: The Older Woman in America,*
      Work Group Reports, pp. 47-51. Ann Arbor, Michigan:
      The Institute of Gerontology, The University of
      Michigan-Wayne State University, 1974. The two
      afternoons of discussion centered on three subjects,
      the socialized roles of women and the consequences
      of these roles, marital satisfaction over the life
      course, and measures to reduce the stereotyping of
      older people. Lillian E. Troll spoke on women's
      roles, and Harold Feldman on marital satisfaction.
      The entire life course, not just the child-rearing
      period, should be encompassed in discussions about
      family relationships. What happens to a woman at
      age 50 who has been socialized only to be a wife and
      mother? Often there are strong relationships between
      family members, including older members, all through
      life. Anticipatory socialization--preparing for
      life without children or without a spouse--is
      recommended. Feldman's studies of marital satisfac-
      tion over the life course disclose a U-shaped pattern;
      marital satisfaction in the later stages is not
      significantly lower than that in the beginning,
      although the same marriage involves a different
      kind of relationship at these two points in time.
      Decision-making by women changes over the life
      cycle. Troll reported a study of career women that
      showed that the women like their husbands more,

although the husbands did not like their wives as
much, after their wives began their careers.
Alternatives to family relationships for older
women, the positive aspects of being alone, and the
need to break down age stereotyping were also
discussed.

789. Candy, Sandra E. Gibbs. "What Do Women Use Friends
For?" In *Looking Ahead: A Woman's Guide to the
Problems and Joys of Growing Older*, pp. 106-11,
Lillian E. Troll, Joan Israel and Kenneth Israel,
eds. Englewood Cliffs, New Jersey: Prentice-Hall,
Inc., 1977. Women between ages 14 and 80, who were
high school students, teachers or retired teachers,
were asked to describe their relationships with their
five closest friends. All had at least five closest
friends--people they had known for a long period of
time. Over 80% of these friends were women. Few
considered kin to be "best" friends, although among
women over age 60, one third of friends who *were*
kin were daughters who lived nearby. All close
friends were depended upon to give intimacy and
help. Retired teachers used their friends more
for status-giving purposes than any other age group.
The third major use of friends by women is for the
purpose of "power"--of having influence over friends,
or of being influenced by them.

790. Cath, Stanley H., M.D. "The Institutionalization of a
Parent--A Nadir of Life." *Journal of Geriatric
Psychiatry* (1972) 5:25-46. At this critical time
in family life, the character structure of the
family unit is revealed, and the conflicts created
by the need for a decision on this question can be
catalytic or paralytic. Thus, any label of a family
group is an oversimplification. There are three
stages of the crisis, the periods before institutionalization, the time during which it occurs, and the
period afterwards. Cath discusses each at length--
the grief and denial and guilt of the first stage,
the depression and despair of decision-making, when
grief and mourning *can* represent a step in growth,
the complexities added when a consultant-caretaker is
sought by family members, the "transplantation shock"
of the second stage, when the grown child must
become the protector and parent of the parent (Cath
points out that most institutionalizations *are* justified), and the third stage, the one period we have

not been able to generalize about in a useful way,
which he illustrates by presenting a poignant and
dramatic case--a case reminiscent of Shakespeare's
King Lear.

791.   Christenson, Cornelia V., and John H. Gagnon. "Sexual
        Behavior in a Group of Older Women." *Journal of
        Gerontology* (July 1965) 20(3):351-6. This report is
        based upon the non-institutionalized portion of the
        case history files of the Institute for Sex Research.
        Data were derived from interviews with a non-
        representative sample of 241 white females aged
        50 or older, all of whom had been married. Incidences
        and frequencies of sexual behavior were calculated
        for ages 50, 55 and 60; data are reported for coitus,
        masturbation and nocturnal sex dreams to orgasm;
        comparisons are reported between marital and post-
        marital subjects, and between subjects assigned to
        one of three groups--low, intermediate or high--
        according to the amount or extent of early sexual
        experience. An aging effect on sexual behavior after
        age 50 was apparent, and this varied according to
        marital status and type of sexual activity. Except
        for masturbation rates, of the group classified as
        high, sexual levels of the women before age 30 were
        not strongly related to later marital sexual patterns.
        The "high" group before age 30 also had higher inci-
        dences of postmarital coitus. The capacity to have
        orgasms appears to be a strong factor in the desire
        of the woman to continue coitus after marriage ends.
        A major factor in the rates of coitus during marriage
        was the age of the husband. These data indicate
        that sexual behavior does continue later in life,
        and should serve to aid in making more realistic
        appraisals of sexuality among older persons.

792.   Christenson, Cornelia V., and Alan Blaine Johnson.
        "Sexual Patterns in a Group of Older Never-Married
        Women." *Journal of Geriatric Psychiatry* (1973)
        6(1):80-98. This sample of 71 never-married white
        women aged 50 and over were interviewed as part of
        the larger program of the Institute for Sex Research.
        Of the 71, most born between 1890 and 1899, 84% had
        gone on to college, and most had studied at the
        graduate level. A wide range of individual differences
        was found. Almost one third gave little evidence
        of the development of erotic interests, so the aging
        factor could not be traced; the rest reported active

sexual behavior of varying types and levels, and
both incidence and frequency of sexual activity
showed aging effects by age 55. Comparison with the
1965 Christenson and Gagnon study shows lower levels
of sexual activity in this (1973) group, but similar
patterns of sexual aging. Both studies re-affirm
the predictive value of early sex behavior.

*793. Davidoff, Ida F., and May E. Markeiwich. "Post-parental
Phase in the Life Cycle of Fifty College Educated
Women." Diss., Teachers College, Columbia University,
1961. (a joint project)

794. Deutscher, Irwin. "The Quality of Postparental Life."
In *Middle Age and Aging: A Reader in Social
Psychology*, pp. 263-8, Bernice L. Neugarten, ed.
Chicago: The University of Chicago Press, 1968.
Findings from interviews with 49 spouses in 31
households in two socio-economic areas of Kansas
City are: 22 persons saw this stage of life as
"better" than earlier stages of the family cycle,
and only three gave equally clear negative evaluations;
for the former, postparental life is seen as a time
of freedom, leading to a re-defining of the self
and the marital partnership; the advent of menopause,
the judgment of the self as a "failure," and the
inability to fill the space left empty by departure
of the children account for the (rare) unfavorable
evaluations; more wives evaluate this life stage
both more favorably and more unfavorably than do
husbands (who were not as communicative in the
interviews); the upper-middle-class spouses have a
much more favorable outlook on postparental life
than do their lower-middle-class counterparts.

795. Duvall, Evelyn Millis. *In-Laws, Pro and Con: An
Original Study of Inter-Personal Relations*. New
York: Association Press, 1954. What a sample of
5,020 men and women feel about in-laws, and how they
work out their relationships with them. The sample,
drawn from all states and regions in the U.S., and
from those married from a few weeks to 40 years or
more, has a larger representation of women than men,
of those married 10 years or less, and of those less
privileged. Methods included interviews and content
analysis of response to a national network radio
contest soliciting letters on "Why I Think Mothers-
in-Law Are Wonderful People." Includes chapters on

the mother-in-law--on mother-in-law jokes; Is the
Mother-in-Law Stereotype Being Renounced?; Mother-
in-Law Roles in Mixed Marriages; the mother-in-law
as a mother, as a person, and as a grandmother; How
It Feels to Be a Mother-in-Law; Mother-in-Law is the
Most Difficult; and How To Be a Good Mother-in-Law.
Also includes a chapter on the sister-in-law ("the
Number Two hazard among in-laws"), and chapters on
male in-laws, in-laws in general, and Parents and
Courting Couples. Bibliographies on: You and Your
Aging Relatives; Identification and Emancipation;
In-Law Relations in Various Cultures; In-Laws in
Biographies.

796. Fengler, Alfred P. "Attitudinal Orientation of Wives
Toward Their Husband's Retirement." In *The Older
Woman: Lavender Rose or Gray Panther*, pp. 137-50,
Marie Marschall Fuller and Cora Ann Martin, eds.
Springfield, Illinois: Charles C. Thomas, 1980. A
review of studies is followed by a report of
research findings derived from a broader study
concerned with changing marital relationships at
various stages of the life cycle. Three major
categories of responses to an open-ended interview
question about the effect of retirement on the
marital relationship are identified among the
subsample of 73 women married to men aged 50 and
over: the Optimists (39%), most of whom look forward
to retirement so they can spend more time with their
husbands; the Pessimists (32%), who are concerned
that their husbands will have too much time on their
hands or who fear their husbands will intrude on
their domestic domains; and the Neutralists (29%),
the least diversified of the three groups, whose
responses were usually quite brief and gave no
information about perceived changes or adjustments
related to retirement. The Neutralists had the
largest number of poorly educated husbands and
wives. Many more Pessimists than Optimists emphasized role segregation in the home. With more
educated cohorts entering the older age brackets,
and with greater emphasis on role equality and
companionship in marriage, the Pessimists' concerns
about task segregation may become a thing of the
past. But closer, more intense companionate relationships between spouses whose wider social network
is loosely knit may mean that the loss sustained by
widowhood may be devastating.

797. Fengler, Alfred P., and Nancy Goodrich. "Wives of
      Elderly Disabled Men: The Hidden Patients." *The
      Gerontologist* (April 1979) 19(2):175-83. The impact
      of the husband's disability on the wife's morale and
      life-style emerged from an evaluation study of a
      volunteer workshop in a setting for older handicapped
      males in a northern New England city in 1976-77.
      Wives' ages varied from 59 to 81, and their husbands'
      from 65 to 86. The study indicated there is
      greater likelihood of institutionalization if there
      is no alternative source of support, and that the
      wife-as-caregiver is one such source. Findings were
      that perhaps two-thirds of the married men would be
      institutionalized if they did not have wives serving
      as caregivers, and that there was an association
      between the morale scores of husbands and wives.
      In general, morale scores of this sample were low
      compared with those in a national sample, but wives
      were divided into higher and lower morale groups
      for comparison. Problems of wives with lower morale
      scores were: perceived financial inadequacy, role
      overload (excessive responsibilities), marital
      relationships in which spouses were not confidantes
      or companions, isolation and loneliness (heightened
      by the long, cold, snowy New England winters), and
      relative lack of support from kin and friends. The
      tasks of the caretakers of the elderly and disabled
      are often as complex and needy as those of their
      patients. "Many of these wives need help and support
      as much as their husbands do."

798. Foner, Anne. "Age Stratification and the Changing
      Family." In *Turning Points: Historical and
      Sociological Essays on the Family*, pp. S340-S365,
      John Demos and Sarane Spence Boocock, eds. Chicago:
      The University of Chicago Press, 1978. An inquiry
      into how varying age-related patterns of life events
      affect the family. The analysis uses three themes
      derived from the age stratification model--the
      importance of the age structure of a family at a given
      period; changing family patterns over the life cycle;
      and the impact of the succession of cohorts of
      families; all these suggest unexpected strengths
      in 20th-century family life. Consideration of the
      dynamic features of the age stratification perspective
      reveals that, since the society and age structure
      change continually, no two cohorts age in exactly
      the same way. Among the important differences

between modal families of the 19th and 20th
centuries are the age range of nuclear family
members and the size of the household and age
composition of household members. Living alone
appears to be a modern development. The 19th- and
20th-century families at the stage where parents are
middle-aged and children are in their teens or early
20s are compared in terms of potential sources of
age-related cohesion and conflict. Varying patterns
in the family cycle of the 19th and 20th centuries
are discussed in terms of their impact on family
life. In the 19th century, there was continuity
in the *individual's* life course; discontinuities
were most evident at the *family* level. In the 20th
century, the reverse seems to be the case. Empty-
nest or retirement-stage families today may be quite
different from families at these stages decades
ago; today there are role models, social supports
and role structures, all of which were absent in
the past. Relations between family and society are
reciprocal; thus, age strata relationships within
the family and youth-age relationships outside the
family may be reciprocal, also.

*799.   Friedeman, Joyce Sutkamp. "Relationships of Selected
        Variables to Sexual Knowledge in a Group of Older
        Women." Diss., University of Cincinnati, 1978.

*800.   Glenn, N.D. "Psychological Well-Being in the Post-
        parental Stage: Some Evidence from National
        Surveys." *Journal of Marriage and the Family*
        (1975) 37(1):105-10.

 801.   Greenfield, Sidney M. "Industrialization and the
        Family in Sociological Theory." In *Marriage and
        the Family: A Comparative Analysis of Contemporary
        Problems*, pp. 9-27, Meyer Barash and Alice Scourby,
        eds. New York: Random House, Inc., 1970. The small
        nuclear family of Western European and North American
        society is generally viewed in sociological theory as
        a consequence of the urban-industrial revolution.
        The industrial revolution, beginning in the 19th
        century, is seen as the force that changed the farm
        family and gave rise to the modern family form in the
        U.S. Citing Johnson's research on the stable stem
        family in modern Japan, Garigue's finding of extensive
        kinship networks among urbanized, industrialized
        French-Canadians in Montreal, and Wagley's reports

on the Luso-Brazilian kinship patterns, Greenfield
presents further evidence that questions the hypothesis
of functional interdependence and implied causality
between urban-industrial technology and the small
nuclear family. This evidence challenges that part
of the hypothesis in which the diachronic formulation
of sociocultural events is used. It is provided
by Greenfield's analysis of the family on the island
of Barbados, where the small nuclear family and
fragmented kindred are present in the same form, and
functionally articulated with the larger society in
the same way, as in industrialized Western society,
but without urbanization and industrialization.
Greenfield thinks the small nuclear family, Le
Play's *famille particulariste*, probably antedates
both urbanism and machine technology in England and
the U.S., and that it was reworked in the U.S., as
it had been several centuries before in England, to
provide the foundation for the new system of social
organization that developed and spread with the
industrial revolution. Thus, it was not the industrial
revolution that produced the small nuclear family;
indeed, it may have been the other way around.

*802.   Hagestad, G. "Patterns of Communication and Influence
Between Grandparents and Grandchildren in a Changing
Society." Paper presented at the World Conference
of Sociology, Uppsala, Sweden, August 1978.

*803.   Heyman, Dorothy K. "Does a Wife Retire?" *The
Gerontologist* (Spring 1970) 10(1, Part 2):54-6.
A wife has "retired" three times by the time her
husband retires--from the job she had before she
was married, from child-rearing, and upon the
occasion of her husband's retirement. This paper
also discusses characteristics of couples who make
a good adjustment to retirement.

804.   Heyman, Dorothy K., and Frances C. Jeffers. "Wives
and Retirement: a Pilot Study." *Journal of
Gerontology* (October 1968) 23(4):488-96. A bi-racial
group of 33 wives (age range 66 to 92) of retired
manual and non-manual workers were divided into two
groups--those who were glad (15) and those who were
sorry or undecided (18) about their husbands'
retirement. These women were participants in a
longitudinal research program on aging underway
at Duke University Medical Center since 1954. The

wives who were sorry their husbands had retired
tended to be older, in the manual occupational
category, and in poorer physical health, as well
as to have lower ratings in activities and attitudes
and to say they were more unhappy during their
lifetime and in their present marriage. More of
the early retiring husbands had wives in this group,
and these retirements were due to the man's poor
health. More men who had been retired longer than
ten years had wives who were sorry they had retired.
Although most couples had congruent attitudes
towards retirement, more were sorry than glad
about it.

805. Huyck, Margaret Hellie. "Sex and the Older Woman."
In *Looking Ahead: A Woman's Guide to the Problems
and Joys of Growing Older*, pp. 43-58, Lillian E.
Troll, Joan Israel and Kenneth Israel, eds.
Englewood Cliffs, New Jersey: Prentice-Hall, Inc.,
1977. Even within age and social class groups,
female sexuality patterns are highly variable.
Huyck discusses patterns of sexuality in the later
years, the significance of changing age norms for
older women, incentives for behaving sexually (older
women were not socialized to define their sexuality
in terms of biological need; physical contact is
often denied those no longer young; touching
contact is tabooed in our culture except as a
prelude to sexual activity), and options for sexual
expression--self-pleasuring, about which most older
women feel guilty because of early socialization,
and sex in a legally sanctioned, loving relationship
(however, the chances increase with every decade
of age that older women will not be in a legally
recognized marriage). All sexual encounters involve
risk, and older women who believe they are not
sexually desirable risk rejection in a sexual
encounter. Thus, older single women may have a
difficult time finding a partner and negotiating
an acceptable relationship. There are problems
also for those who do have a sexual partner in
later life: some women are in marriages that are
not warm, comfortable, and gratifying. Although
most women seek affirmation or denial of their
sexuality in relationships with men, some "have long
shared love, companionship, and sexuality with other
women." Sexual deprivation is a harsh reality for
many older women, but there are some who have very
positive feelings about their past and present lives.

806. Johnson, Elizabeth S., and Barbara J. Bursk. "Re-
      lationships Between the Elderly and Their Adult
      Children." In *The Older Woman: Lavender Rose or
      Gray Panther*, pp. 158-69, Marie Marschall Fuller
      and Cora Ann Martin, eds. Springfield, Illinois:
      Charles C. Thomas, 1980. Overview of research
      findings and report on interviews with 54 pairs of
      elderly parents and adult children, hypothesizing
      that health, living environments, finances, and
      attitude toward aging would be associated with the
      affective quality of their relationships. This
      study found a significant association between a
      positive elderly parent-adult child relationship,
      and health and attitude toward aging factors
      associated with the elderly parent. The association
      between good health and good relationships indicates
      not only that intervention strategies for elderly
      in poor health should be developed, but that they
      should be seen as essential. These should be directed
      toward ameliorating the relationship between poor
      health and a poor elderly parent-adult child
      relationship. Supportive services should be
      developed for the elderly of *all* income groups.
      In taking away some of the burden from adult
      children, they may promote good relationships
      between the generations, and facilitate more
      involvement between the elderly parent and adult
      children if and when more serious problems develop.
      Future studies should take into consideration the
      possible effects of the interview process itself;
      resources should be made available to interviewees
      who wish further assistance.

807. Kassel, Victor. "Polygyny after 60." *Geriatrics*
      (April 1966) 21(4):214-8. Kassel observes that since
      1950, the attitude of many geriatric patients has
      changed. Previously, they felt a greater personal
      responsibility for working out solutions to their
      problems. Now they are more passive, and use
      their disabilities to win attention from others and
      to control their families. He recommends polygyny
      after age 60, which has the advantages of providing
      a chance to re-establish a family group; improving
      the diet because mealtime would again have a
      social atmosphere; providing a means of sharing
      care during illness, thus reducing the need for
      institutionalization; providing sexual opportunities
      for older women, and a means for men to express

their innate proclivity for polygyny; and providing
an incentive for good grooming. Suggests that group
health insurance should include polygynous families
in its coverage, and charge less expensive premiums.

808. Kerckhoff, Alan C. "Husband-Wife Expectations and
      Reactions to Retirement." *Journal of Gerontology*
      (October 1964) 19(4):510-6. Spouses in this sample
      of 90 white married couples with the husband within
      five years of retirement, and 108 in which the
      husband was retired, living in the Piedmont region
      of North Carolina and Virginia, were interviewed
      separately and simultaneously. Findings were that
      very few couples had made any retirement plans, that
      pre-retirement men felt a greater sense of improvement
      and satisfaction in retirement than did their wives,
      that men who had been retired less than five years
      were the most satisfied, and that the wife was much
      less deeply involved than her husband in both
      expectations about and reactions to retirement.
      Upper-level couples did not welcome retirement, but
      their experience was favorable and their reactions
      positive; middle-level couples welcomed it and had
      good experiences, but did not respond as favorably
      as upper-level couples. Lower-level couples
      exhibited much more role tension, were more passive
      in anticipating retirement, did not find it pleasant,
      and responded more negatively than the others.

*809. Kornhaber, Arthur, M.D., and Kenneth Woodward.
      Grandparents/Grandchildren: The Vital Connection.
      New York: Doubleday Anchor Press, 1981. Taking the
      viewpoint that children are the best barometer of
      family life, the authors present children's percep-
      tions of the relationship, using their comments
      about their grandparents and their drawings as a
      source of information about this. Also presents a
      profile of the world of the older generation and
      advice to grandparents on how best to fulfill their
      important role.

810. Laslett, Barbara. "The Family as a Public and Private
      Institution: An Historical Perspective." *Journal
      of Marriage and the Family* (August 1973) 35(3):480-92.
      The hypothesis studied here is that the private
      family--an institution characterized by relatively
      limited access to and greater control over the
      observability of behavior--is a modern development

which has occurred only in the 20th century in the U.S. Recent research has shown that the dominant structure of the family in the pre-industrial household, both in England and in the American colonies, was nuclear. Available evidence for the period after the early colonial experience continues to support the conclusion that an extended kinship structure was in no way characteristic of a large proportion of American households. Evidence for the change of the family from a more public to a more private institution includes the decline in the number of children born per family and the removal of young adults from their parental households, both of which contribute to privacy. Apprentices and other people's children may have declined as sources of non-kindred household members early in the 19th century, and servants decreased steadily as industrialization advanced; however, boarders seem to have replaced these groups as non-kin household residents. Boarding continued to be a widespread practice until well into this century. Thus, only in the middle 20th century did household composition become restricted to the nuclear kin group. Evidence is presented here that privacy continues to be a 20th-century ideal for home design, and that the home economics movement emphasized the traditional views of woman's place in the home and reinforced the privacy of the individual family. Laslett thinks it is possible that an increase in alternative family styles does not necessarily herald the death of the nuclear family, but rather a variability, in which several types of family organization will exist simultaneously.

811. Lipman, Aaron. "Role Conceptions and Morale in Couples in Retirement." *Journal of Gerontology* (July 1961) 16(3):267-71. Interviews of 100 retired couples over age 60 residing in Miami showed that the man who, after retirement, views his role as primarily instrumental is twice as likely to have low morale as the man who views his marital role as primarily expressive, and that because of emergent new male roles relating to housework after retirement, women must alter their instrumental role conception as "good housewife and homemaker" or experience a decline in morale. Wives who adhered to the traditional sentiment of the woman's role had the largest percentage of those with low morale.

812.   Lowenthal, Marjorie Fiske, and Clayton Haven.
       "Interaction and Adaptation: Intimacy as a Critical
       Variable." In *Middle Age and Aging: A Reader in
       Social Psychology*, pp. 390-400, Bernice L. Neugarten,
       ed. Chicago: The University of Chicago Press, 1968.
       Analysis of detailed life histories of a small
       group of people in samples for previous studies
       indicated that the happiest and healthiest among
       them often were--or had been--involved in close
       personal relationships. It seemed that the existence
       of such relationships might serve as a buffer against
       age-linked social losses. This paper reports on
       a study of the role of the confidant as an inter-
       vening variable between social resources and
       deprivation and adaptation. Parent sample and
       possible sources of bias are described. The maintenance
       of a stable, intimate relationship is more closely
       associated with good mental health and high morale
       than is high social interaction or role status, or
       stability in interaction and role. The loss of a
       confidant has a more deleterious effect on morale,
       although not on mental health status, than does a
       reduction in either of the other two social measures.
       The impact on adjustment of a decrease in social
       interaction, or a loss of social roles, is considerably
       softened if the person has a close personal relationship.
       The presence of a confidant also cushions the age-
       linked losses of widowhood and retirement, but not
       physical illness. It was found that women are more
       likely than men to have an intimate relationship
       at all age levels. The differences between the
       sexes are especially pronounced in those under age
       65. The married are more likely to have a confidant
       than the unmarried. The three identities of
       confidant most often mentioned were spouse, child
       and friend. Among women in general, husbands are
       least often mentioned, whereas wives are the most
       important confidant for men. This holds true for
       both the widowed and the married. Having a confidant
       is also positively correlated with higher socio-
       economic status. It is suggested that women's
       greater adaptability for survival may be causally
       connected with their greater sensitivity to, and
       versatility in choice of, close relationships.

813.   McKain, Walter. "A New Look at Older Marriages."
       The Family Coordinator (January 1972) 21(1):61-9.
       Research results from a survey of 100 remarried

elderly couples suggest that older marriages are
generally successful. The majority of these people
gave the desire for companionship as their major
reason for remarrying. Widows and widowers who
knew one another well, whose remarriages had the
approval of friends and relatives, who had been
able to adjust satisfactorily to the role changes
accompanying aging, who owned a house but did not
live in it after remarriage, and who had an adequate
income were those most likely to have successful
remarriages.

814. Masters, William H., and Virginia E. Johnson. "Human
Sexual Response: The Aging Female and the Aging
Male." In *Middle Age and Aging: A Reader in Social
Psychology*, pp. 269-79, Bernice L. Neugarten, ed.
Chicago: The University of Chicago Press, 1968.
In their review of the literature on the aging
female, and of their own findings based on 152
socio-sexual histories of women aged 51 and over
and their clinical experience, Masters and Johnson
note the importance of opportunity for regularity
of sexual expression as a factor in sexual performance
levels of aging women, and the great variety of
clinical symptoms of menopausal distress, and
discuss the factors that may account for the
increased sex drive of some women in their early
fifties. They conclude that there seems to be no
physiological reason why the frequency of sexual
expression found satisfactory for the younger woman
should not be carried over into the post-menopausal
years--in short, there is no time limit drawn by
the advancing years to female sexuality. In their
section on the aging male, they discuss six general
categories of bases for alteration of male
responsive ability--based on 212 socio-sexual histories
of men aged 50 and over--as: monotony of a repetitious
sexual relationship, preoccupation with career or
economic pursuits, mental or physical fatigue,
overindulgence in food or drink, physical and
mental infirmities, and fear of failure in performance.

*815. Parron, E. "Relationships in Black and White Golden
Wedding Couples." Diss., Rutgers University, 1979.

816. Pineo, Peter C. "Disenchantment in the Later Years
of Marriage." In *Middle Age and Aging: A Reader
in Social Psychology*, pp. 258-62, Bernice L.

Neugarten, ed. Chicago: The University of Chicago
Press, 1968. Data from the third interviewing, the
Middle Years of Marriage Study, of 400 couples
married up to 20 years from the sample of 1,000
couples studied by Burgess and his associates, appear
to indicate four predominant processes: there is
a general decline in marital satisfaction and
adjustment; there is a loss of intimacy; personal
adjustment and reports of personality characteristics
are relatively unaffected by disenchantment or loss
of intimacy; certain forms of marital interaction
are found to change as the frequency of sexual
intercourse diminishes and the amount of sharing of
activities declines, without any major link to
disenchantment. Pineo's interpretation is that the
grounds upon which a person decides to marry
deteriorate over time, and the fit between two
persons, which leads them to marry, is reduced with
time. The empirical finding is that marital
satisfaction declines with the passage of time.

817.   Powers, Edward A., and Gordon L. Bultena. "Sex
       Differences in Intimate Friendships of Old Age."
       In *The Older Woman: Lavender Rose or Gray Panther*,
       pp. 190-204, Marie Marschall Fuller and Cora Ann
       Martin, eds. Springfield, Illinois: Charles C.
       Thomas, 1980. A study of late life intimate
       friendships; data are based on a 1960 statewide
       study in Iowa, and a 1971 (interview) re-study
       of 235 persons in five representative counties, of
       whom 70% were women. Findings are that the social
       worlds of men and women in late life are distinct,
       in that men have more frequent social contact,
       but limit it to family and friends, in that men
       are less likely than women to have intimate friends
       and less likely to replace lost friends, and in that
       women have a diverse social world, and many have
       intimate ties outside the family. Powers and
       Bultena note the irony of the precariousness of
       the last years of men's lives in a society in which
       men's positions have been more privileged than
       women's.

818.   Rollins, Boyd C., and Kenneth L. Cannon. "Marital
       Satisfaction Over the Family Life Cycle: A Re-
       evaluation." *Journal of Marriage and the Family*
       (May 1974) 36(2):271-82. Two major studies of the
       trend of marital satisfaction over the family life

cycle arrived at contradictory conclusions--one
(Blood and Wolfe, 1960) found a general decline, and
the other (Rollins and Feldman, 1970) a U-shaped
curve. A sample of 800 married Mormons, with 50
males and 50 females at each of Duvall's eight
stages of the family life cycle, were measured by
instruments from the two studies. Results--i.e.,
a U-shaped curve for *both* husbands and wives--
suggested that *measurement* differences rather than
population differences account for the apparent
contradictions. Evidence is presented indicating
that the Blood-Wolfe Composite Index of Marital
Satisfaction is not a valid measurement technique.
It is reported that the practical importance of the
trend of marital satisfaction over the family life
cycle that was found in a secondary analysis of the
data was minimal, that the idea of sex differences
in marital satisfaction over the family life cycle
has been overplayed, and that it is questionable
that family life cycle should be pursued further as
an independent variable in research on marital
satisfaction. Role theory--specifically, a theory
of role strain--may explain the shallow U-shaped
trend of marital satisfaction over the family life
cycle. A focus on antecedents of role strain in
terms of the family career has both theoretical and
practical value, i.e., value for developing
predictors of marital satisfaction and alternative
preventive strategies if decline seems to be imminent.

819.   Safilios-Rothschild, Constantina. "Sexuality, Power,
       and Freedom Among 'Older' Women." In *Looking Ahead:
       A Woman's Guide to the Problems and Joys of Growing
       Older,* pp. 162-6, Lillian E. Troll, Joan Israel
       and Kenneth Israel, eds. Englewood Cliffs, New
       Jersey: Prentice-Hall, Inc., 1977. While older
       women in contemporary society may continue to look
       young and attractive, their overall subordinate
       status, discriminatory practices against them, and
       their internalized "feminine" stereotypes prevent
       them from achieving sexual fulfillment. We need
       to know how older women can reach the point where
       they will feel comfortable acknowledging their
       sexual needs and finding ways to fulfill them.
       As women are free to develop their intelligence and
       talents, they may become able to enjoy being sexual
       and to defy time and age.

820.   Saltz, Rosalyn.   "Fostergrandparenting: A Unique
       Child-Care Service." In *Looking Ahead: A Woman's
       Guide to the Problems and Joys of Growing Older*,
       pp. 126-32, Lillian E. Troll, Joan Israel and
       Kenneth Israel, eds. Englewood Cliffs, New Jersey:
       Prentice-Hall, Inc., 1977. Fostergrandparents are
       low-income persons over age 60 who are part-time
       caregivers in group settings for children. This
       paper provides evidence that the program seems to
       be achieving its goal of improving life adjustment
       and satisfaction for aging persons. Older women
       may have special motivation and qualifications for
       serving a quasi-family function for children
       despite their awareness that it is temporary.
       Unlike younger caregivers, older people may see
       the present as more important than the future with
       respect to achieving close, loving relationships,
       because they believe "The future is *now*."

821.   Shanas, Ethel.   "The Family as a Social Support System
       in Old Age." *The Gerontologist* (April 1979)
       19(2):169-74. Surprising as this may be, a major
       finding of social research in aging in all Western
       societies is the discovery and demonstration of the
       important role of the family in old age. This paper
       reports research findings on two aspects of the
       family as a social support system: family care for
       the elderly in time of illness, and family visiting
       patterns. Data are derived from a national
       probability survey of non-institutionalized persons
       aged 65 and over, conducted in 1975. They clearly
       indicate that the immediate family of the old
       person, spouses and children, is the major social
       support of the elderly in time of illness, and that
       the extended family of the old person--children,
       siblings and other kin--through face-to-face visits,
       serves as the major tie of the elderly to the
       community. These patterns indicate the mutual
       expectations of each generation. Old persons turn
       first to their families for help, then to neighbors,
       and, finally, to bureaucratic replacements for
       families, because they expect families to help in
       case of need. Family members respond to the needs
       of the elderly as best as they can.

822.   Shanas, Ethel.   "Social Myth as Hypothesis: The Case
       of the Family Relations of Old People." *The
       Gerontologist* (February 1979) 19(1):3-9. The

Robert W. Kleemeier Award Lecture, this paper presents evidence collected over the last 25 years that refutes the widely held belief that old people in the U.S. today are alienated from their families, especially from their grown children. This fiction, which has informed much social gerontology research for the past 30 years, is reminiscent of the Hydra: each time evidence has been presented showing that old people are not alienated from their families, new adherents of the myth rise up among the mass media, writers for the popular press, researchers, and even the elderly themselves. The term "family" is often confused with "household," but nothing in the definition of the family as a group to whom older people are related by blood or marriage implies that a family must live under the same roof. The family is still the first resource of both older and younger members for emotional and social support, crisis intervention, and bureaucratic linkages. As a refuge and private place for its adult members, the family may be more important today than ever before. Survey data collected in 1957, 1962 and 1975 validate Talcott Parsons's belief that the family is the primary basis of security for adults in later life, that older parents do see their adult children often, that the modified extended family-- siblings, nieces and nephews, etc.--is the dominant family form for old people in the U.S. and is very much alive, and that family help in providing long-term care for the elderly persists despite the alternative sources available in 1975, which were not available in 1962. Recommendations for research and policy "in the wake of the slain myth" are proposed.

*823. Shanas, Ethel, and Marvin B. Sussman, eds. *Family, Bureaucracy and the Elderly*. Durham, North Carolina: Duke University Press, 1977. Multidisciplinary perspectives on the family as a major source of social support, with thirteen original contributions.

*824. Sommers, Tish, and Laurie Shields. *The Disillusionment of Divorce for Older Women*. Gray Paper #6, Oakland, California: Older Women's League Educational Fund, 1980.

*825. Starr, Bernard D., and Marcella Bakur Weiner. *The Starr-Weiner Report on Sex and Sexuality in the*

Mature Years. New York: Stein and Day, 1981. A
questionnaire survey of 800 men and women aged 60
to 91 from the four regions of the U.S. found that
the frequency of sexual activity does not necessarily
decline with aging, as long as an opportunity
exists for its expression.

826. Stinnett, Nick, Linda M. Carter and James E.
      Montgomery. "Older Persons' Perceptions of Their
      Marriages." In *The Older Woman: Lavender Rose or
      Gray Panther*, pp. 113-23, Marie Marschall Fuller
      and Cora Ann Martin, eds. Springfield, Illinois:
      Charles C. Thomas, 1980. This article includes a
      review of studies concerning older persons'
      perceptions of their marriage relationships and
      present period of life and a report of a study of
      the perceptions of older spouses concerning their
      marriages and present life, based upon responses to
      questionnaires given by 408 older husbands and
      wives. Concludes that the greatest proportion of
      the respondents rated their marriages as very happy
      or happy, and that the majority reported that their
      marriages had become better over time. Research
      findings, among them that companionship and being
      able to express true feelings to one another were
      most often chosen as the most rewarding aspects of
      the present marriage relationship, are related to
      findings of other studies. It is stated that the
      results of this investigation suggest that progressive
      marital disenchantment over the life cycle may be
      a myth.

827. Tavris, Carol. "The Sexual Lives of Women Over Sixty."
      Ms. (July 1977) VI(1):62-5. Her analysis of the
      results of a national magazine survey of responses
      of 100,000 middle-American women to a study of
      female sexuality challenged the misconception Tavris
      held since her teens that women's sexual desire
      declines once they reach menopause. She examines
      the sources of the assumption that older people are
      sexless, and documents the claim that sexual response
      and pleasure continue into late life for many women,
      and the validity of the rule, "practice prolongs
      performance." She sees signs that age prejudice
      and the double standard of aging as applied to
      sexuality are changing, and states that one does
      not outgrow either love or lust.

828. Treas, Judith, and Anke Van Hilst. "Marriage and
      Remarriage Rates Among Older Americans." In
      Dimensions of Aging: Readings, pp. 208-13, Jon
      Hendricks and C. Davis Hendricks, eds. Cambridge,
      Massachusetts: Winthrop Publishers, Inc., 1979.
      U.S. Vital Statistics data for 1970 indicate that
      older persons constituted 1% of all brides and 2%
      of all grooms. Estimates for the 1960s suggest
      that the *propensity* of older people to marry has
      shown no change over time. Data show that older
      men have a substantial edge over women in the
      marriage market, and that marital forecasts differ
      for those with different marital histories, and
      also differ by region. Information about the marital
      choices of older people--that the widowed are the
      most usual marital choices, regardless of previous
      marital status--and about the wedding ceremony (older
      people attach the same symbolic import to their
      nuptials as younger brides and grooms, and prefer
      to solemnize their vows with a religious ceremony)
      provide insights into personal sentiments and social
      customs. The authors doubt that late-life unions
      will rise in the near future above the low levels
      they observe here.

829. Troll, Lillian E. "The Family of Later Life: A Decade
      Review." *Journal of Marriage and the Family*
      (May 1971) 33(2):263-90. The 1960s literature on
      the family of middle age and old age is discussed
      under the headings of marital interaction and cross-
      generation and intra-generation interaction;
      widowhood is treated separately. Conclusions
      are that there is a modified extended kin structure
      in the U.S. which includes older family members,
      that the post-parental couple or widow is not isolated
      from the family, that disengagement of the elderly
      is *into* rather than *away from* the family, and that
      the developmental approach is the most suited to
      studying the contracting family, which should be
      viewed along a dimension of time.

830. Troll, Lillian E. "Intergenerational Relations in
      Later Life: A Family System Approach." In
      Transitions of Aging, pp. 75-91, Nancy Datan and
      Nancy Lohmann, eds. New York: Academic Press, Inc.,
      1980. Troll discusses the value of a family system
      approach to intergenerational relations. She shows
      how the diversity of intergenerational relationships

can be traced to diversity in family boundaries
and family themes. Thus, if family members value
communication, they would tend toward self-disclosure
and the sharing of confidences with one another.
If its boundary is strong, it might also exclude
nonfamily members from the sharing of confidences,
although theme and boundary are not necessarily
correlated. So far as family boundaries are
concerned, it may be that aging people from tightly-
knit families are not disposed to take part in
indiscriminately gregarious senior centers or
nutrition sites, nor to make new friends easily
in nursing homes. Since most older people do have
families, the kind of family to which they belong
is very important. Troll also considers rural-
urban differences (and differences from one rural
area to another), the reasons for the persistence
of parent-child relationships throughout life, and
the importance of period effects for studying
relationships between the generations. Extensive
bibliography.

*831. Troll, Lillian E. "The Salience of Members of
       Three-Generation Families for One Another."
       Paper presented to the American Psychological
       Association, Honolulu, 1972.

*832. Troll, Lillian E., S. Miller and Robert Atchley.
       Families in Later Life. Belmont, California:
       Wadsworth Publishing Co., Inc., 1978.

 833. Uhlenberg, Peter. "Cohort Variations in Family Life
       Cycle Experiences of U.S. Females." *Journal of
       Marriage and the Family* (May 1974) 36(2):284-92.
       Five life cycle courses: "early death," "spinster,"
       "childless," "broken marriage--with children," and
       "preferred," were described, and the distribution
       of white and nonwhite females in birth cohorts
       from 1890-94 through 1930-34 were calculated.
       Among the findings were declining variability
       of white female life cycle experiences, due to
       mortality decline for women aged 15 to 50, younger
       age at marriage, increased marriage rates, and
       decline in childlessness, as well as a decline of
       mortality rates for nonwhite females from 1890
       to 1934 (but not at the same pace as for white
       females), an increase in nonmarriage rates for non-
       whites, and higher rates for broken marriages among

nonwhites. The number of more traditional types
of family life cycles has increased in part because
of declines in mortality rates and childlessness.

834. Youmans, E. Grant. "Family Disengagement Among Older
Urban and Rural Women." *Journal of Gerontology*
(April 1967) 22(2):209-11. Assessing disengagement
in family life by analyzing data on visiting patterns
with children and siblings, and on helping relationships with kin, from a cross-sectional survey of
two age groups (60 to 64 and 75 and over) of older
women in urban and rural areas in Kentucky, slight
but statistically significant disengagement was
found in the rural area only, in responses to two
items: the older women visited slightly less often
with their children than the younger women, and a
slightly smaller proportion of older than younger
women said they helped their siblings.

See also: 145, 146, 155, 191, 289, 300, 301, 325, 364, 368,
401, 402, 405, 431, 457, 477, 478, 480, 481, 482, 483, 507,
522, 523, 584, 631, 647, 650, 654, 665, 666, 670, 671, 672,
677, 679, 690, 691, 692, 694, 696, 698, 704, 706, 712, 713,
714, 716, 718, 732, 744, 835, 848, 850, 851, 853, 855, 856,
877.

B. Widowhood

835. Arling, Greg. "The Elderly Widow and Her Family,
Neighbors, and Friends." In *The Older Woman:
Lavender Rose or Gray Panther*, pp. 170-89, Marie
Marschall Fuller and Cora Ann Martin, eds.
Springfield, Illinois: Charles C. Thomas, 1980. A
review of studies and report of findings from 409
questionnaires administered as household interviews
to elderly widows in South Carolina. Items that
were used to measure family involvement, friendship
and neighboring, and morale are listed. It was
found that the family items are essentially unrelated
to any of the indices of morale. Respondents with
children living nearby have no higher morale than
those who either have no living children or have
none within an hour's drive. Similarly, the
frequency of contact with children has no significant
correlation with morale. If any one of the family

items has an impact, it is the variable measuring
contact with kin other than children. In contrast,
the neighbor-friendship variables are significantly
related to morale. In discussion of the findings,
it is observed that certain intergenerational
barriers are inevitable, but that conflicts between
aged parents and adult children may be exacerbated
by such conditions as poverty and ill health. This
study, which adds to the body of evidence that
contact between older persons and family members
is not directly associated with higher morale or
greater personal satisfaction, concludes with
suggestions of avenues for further research.

836.   Atchley, Robert C. "Dimensions of Widowhood in Later
       Life." *The Gerontologist* (April 1975) 15(2):176-8.
       Data are derived from responses to mail questionnaires
       by retired employees of a large midwestern phone
       company and retired public school teachers, sampled
       as part of an earlier study of retirement. Findings
       from data on 902 men and women aged 70 to 79 suggest
       that overarching generalizations about *psychological*
       reactions to or consequences of widowhood, should
       be made with great caution for both sexes. On
       social variables, however, there were significant
       differences by sex and marital status. In general,
       widowers fared better than widows. Among former
       phone company women, especially operators, widows
       were significantly worse off than widowed people
       in the other three sex and industry categories;
       they were likely to have inadequate incomes.
       Economic circumstances are a powerful factor
       influencing the social situation of widows. Thus,
       income adequacy is an essential component of any
       theory of adjustment to widowhood. Data also suggest
       that men have economic supports that for the most
       part tend to offset the effects of other social and
       psychological factors. Future research should be
       guided by findings that widowhood combines with
       sex and industry groups to produce income inadequacy;
       income inadequacy in turn affects car driving and
       social participation; income inadequacy and social
       isolation combine to produce anxiety.

837.   Barrett, Carol J. "Women in Widowhood." *Signs*
       (Summer 1977) II(4):856-68. Psychologist Barrett
       surveys the demography of widowhood, and the
       research studies on its stresses (grief, the

economic burden, social factors, physical and mental
health, individual variations). In discussing
social policy implications--education, government
and institutional support and social change--she
reports on her own research and clinical experience,
and on her program of group interventions for widows
in the Los Angeles area. She recommends broad-scale
public education dealing realistically with widowhood,
since most women may spend 18 or more years in this
final stage of the life cycle. Two themes recur
in the advice widows have for women whose husbands
are still living: financial and emotional preparation for widowhood.

*838. Barrett, Carol J., and Schneiweis, K.M. "An Empirical
Search for Stages of Widowhood." Paper presented
at the Gerontological Society, New York, 1976.

*839. Baum, Joanne. "An Exploration of Widowhood: Coping
Patterns Adopted By a Population of Widows."
Diss., University of Wisconsin at Madison, 1979.

*840. Cohn, A.R. "Influences of Selected Characteristics
on Widows' Attitudes Towards Self and Others."
M.A. thesis, Department of Psychology, Illinois
Institute of Technology, 1973.

841. Cosneck, Bernard J. "Family Patterns of Older
Widowed Jewish People." *The Family Coordinator*
(October 1970) 19(4):368-73. Of the widowed subjects,
29 men and 74 women over the age of 60, about one-
third lived in a home for the aged which accepted
people who were active and independent, another
one-third lived in the city but spent some leisure
time in the home for the aged, and the remainder
were completely independent of these two groups.
Most who lived alone--13 men and 25 women--did so
because they preferred it that way; of the 16 women
and 6 men who were living with their children, 10
women and 4 men were living in three-generation
households, and while the men seemed to be satisfied
with this, 6 women complained because of lack of
privacy and because they felt they were "captive"
baby sitters. Only about one-fourth of the sample
said they would consider remarriage. Responses
to the question about subjects' reactions toward
being alone are classified into five groups--those
who felt freed; relieved; accepting; the sensitive

(who showed more affect when discussing the
deceased mate--41% of the sample); and the
"dejected and traumatized."

*842. Foss, Hazel M., and F.G. Scott. *Developing a Widowed
       Services Program*. Eugene, Oregon: University of
       Oregon, 1977.

*843. Fowles, Donald G. *Elderly Widows*. U.S. Department
       of Health, Education and Welfare, Statistical Memo
       No. 33. Washington, D.C.: U.S. Department of
       Health, Education and Welfare, 1976.

 844. Gerber, Irwin, Roslyn Rusalem, Natalie Hannon, Delia
       Battin and Arthur Arkin. "Anticipatory Grief and
       Aged Widows and Widowers." *Journal of Gerontology*
       (March 1975) 30(2):225-9. Analysis of effects of
       anticipatory grief. Sample consisted of 81 survivors
       of acute illness death (20%) and chronic illness
       death (80%), and included 47 widows and 34 widowers;
       mean age was 67. Three medical variables were used
       as indicators of bereavement adjustment: number of
       physician office visits; number of times when ill
       without contacting a physician; number of psycho-
       tropic medications used. Open-ended questionnaire
       findings were that exposure to anticipatory grief
       has no appreciable impact on aged survivors' medical
       adjustment six months after their loss, that the
       period of anticipatory grief is dysfunctional for
       the aged *male* bereaved, and that length of experience
       with anticipatory grief had a significant *negative*
       effect on survivors' medical adjustment. Practical
       implications are discussed. Among these are that
       realistic *social* planning should be considered as
       important as emotional preparation for good medical
       adjustment of those undergoing an extended death
       watch, and that crisis intervention services should
       be very much concerned about the aged male bereaved.

 845. Harvey, Carol D., and Howard M. Bahr. "Widowhood,
       Morale and Affiliation." *Journal of Marriage and
       the Family* (February 1974) 36(1):97-106. Data from
       Almond and Verba's "The Five Nation Study" obtained
       from 4,892 respondents, including 476 widowed
       persons in the United Kingdom, Mexico, Germany,
       Italy and the U.S., and data from two earlier
       studies, including 378 widowed persons among 4,876
       respondents, indicate that the negative, long-term

consequences of widowhood seem to derive from socioeconomic deprivation rather than from widowhood
itself. Thus, researchers must control for
economic status, if social and psychological effects
of widowhood are to be separated from the effects
of poverty.

846.   Jacobson, Solomon G., Recorder. "The Woman Alone." In
       *No Longer Young: The Older Woman in America, Work
       Group Reports*, pp. 1-4. Ann Arbor, Michigan: The
       Institute of Gerontology, The University of Michigan-
       Wayne State University, 1974. The focus of this
       session was the widow. It was observed that the
       widow has not chosen her single state, and that
       adjustment to it is difficult. Widows have spent
       very little time as a woman alone before bereavement,
       and widowhood is a long period of aloneness. The
       tendency to over-react and to undertake many changes
       was noted, as well as the lack of preparation for
       widowhood, and societal discouragement of open
       expressions of grief. The middle-class widow who
       has no career may suffer a double loss of status,
       both from that ascribed by her husband's position
       and from a sudden move into the class of the
       unskilled worker. The concept of multiple anchors
       was introduced into the discussion to suggest how
       much of the trauma of the change in status from wife
       to widow may be avoided. The capacity to be future-
       oriented appears to be the basis for success as
       a woman alone.

847.   Kahana, Ralph J., M.D. "On Widowhood." *Journal of
       Geriatric Psychiatry* (1975) 8(1):5-8. In his
       Introduction to the two papers on the subject in
       this issue (pp. 9-59), Kahana summarizes their
       contents. One is by a social worker and her aide,
       and the other is by a sociologist. The papers are
       followed by a discussion of their content by
       psychiatrists. In the first paper, Phyllis R.
       Silverman and Adele Cooperband describe and evaluate
       a program offering "mutual help for the widowed,"
       a program that is part of *community psychiatry.*
       In the second paper, Helena Z. Lopata examines
       bereavement and grieving from a sociological
       perspective.

848.   Lopata, Helena Znaniecki. "The Meaning of Friendship
       in Widowhood." In *Looking Ahead: A Woman's Guide*

to the Problems and Joys of Growing Older, pp. 93-105,
Lillian E. Troll, Joan Israel and Kenneth Israel,
eds. Englewood Cliffs, New Jersey: Prentice-Hall,
Inc., 1977. This paper reports on a study of the
role of friendship in the support systems of urban
widows; the sample consisted of over 1,000 widows
living in the Chicago area. Americans idealize
friendship (although they are cautious about it),
and it is assumed that women will turn to friendship
when they are freed from their roles as wife and
mother. But most Chicago-area widows did not follow
this pattern. Few women were deeply involved in
relationships with friends. Some widows--in general,
the least educated and most disadvantaged--were
socially isolated; some were able to retain sex-
segregated friendships after widowhood; and some,
accustomed to couple-companionate interaction, had
difficulties maintaining these friendships after
widowhood. Relationships considered "close" appear
to be socially superficial. Friends, although very
helpful during and immediately after bereavement,
did not provide economic, service, or even emotional
supports for many widows. Apparently, undertaking
social activities with old or new friends does not
convert itself into deeper involvement in these
support systems. Blue-collar or working-class
ideology restricts friendships of women more than
does middle-class ideology. Feminism may promote
deeper and more gratifying friendships among women,
and thus widows may feel less stigma in the future.

849.   Lopata, Helena Znaniecki. "Role Changes in Widowhood:
       A World Perspective." In *Aging and Modernization*,
       pp. 275-303, Donald O. Cowgill and Lowell D. Holmes,
       eds. New York: Appleton-Century-Crofts, 1972. A
       cross-cultural perspective on widowhood in a
       sociological framework that focuses on role
       shifts in the lives of widows, acknowledging the
       limitations imposed by fragmentary data collected
       for other research purposes. Research indicates
       that the image of expanding circles of engagement
       is oversimplified. Widowhood is one example of many
       life breaks and role shifts which leave the affected
       persons to their own resources in rebuilding their
       lives. Societies and situations vary in the degree
       to which re-engagement is expected, but every society
       develops a limited number of standardized alternative
       life styles available to its wives and widows, thus

providing "solutions" to widowhood. Changes
effected by widowhood largely depend upon a woman's
involvement with the role of wife and the way this
role is inter-related with other roles. Widowhood
in Africa, in middle-class America (based upon data
from a study of Chicago-area widows), in traditional
India, and in China are described. Three forms of
life changes--*suttee*, automatic remarriage and
automatic levirate--are placed on a continuum. The
major difference between the widow in the U.S. and
her counterparts in other societies is the fact that
directions and forms of life changes are left up
to her, and that there is little institutionalized
guarantee of, or enforcement into, any one pattern.
Because of culture change and culture lag, the open-
ness of available choice is often problematic.
Factors influencing role changes in widowhood are:
societal characteristics affecting the life style
alternatives developed; the family institution; and
characteristics of the widow (age at marriage, age
at widowhood, ages of children, circumstances
surrounding the death of the spouse, and individual
personality). Widowhood causes disorganization in
the life of the survivor in every society, and in
most societies, it is institutionalized into similar
stages, although each has developed its own life
styles for widows after re-engagement.

850. Lopata, Helena Znaniecki. "The Widowed Family Member."
In *Transitions of Aging*, pp. 93-118, Nancy Datan
and Nancy Lohmann, eds. New York: Academic Press,
Inc., 1980. The conversion of social engagement of
adult members of American society from ascribed to
voluntaristic participation is especially evident
in the lives of the widowed. Lopata identifies three
types of widowed persons: those able to re-engage,
those for whom widowhood results in further disengagement, and those who are embedded in a support system.
Her topics are: widowhood as a neglected aspect of
family sociology; a comparison of widows with
widowers; the influence of education and social
class on widowhood; early problems of widowhood;
the reconstruction of social life space in widowhood;
remarriage and other relations with the opposite
sex; support systems; role changes. Extensive
bibliography.

851.   Lopata, Helena Znaniecki. *Widowhood in an American City*.
       Cambridge, Massachusetts: Schenkman Publishing Co.,
       Inc., 1973. Sociological analysis of widowhood in
       Chicago. Variables studied include age, education,
       ethnic, racial and religious affiliation of widows,
       their socio-economic status, and their residential
       location. Explores widows' relationships to children
       and in-laws, the social roles of friend and worker,
       and community participation. Predicts an increase
       in Chicago-area widows living in social isolation and
       on low incomes; shows the relationship between social
       isolation and such societal traits as independence
       of women, mobility, social voluntarism, and loose
       or non-existent extended kin ties; challenges
       disengagement theory; recommends ways to meet the
       needs of urban widows.

852.   Lopata, Helena Znaniecki. "Widowhood: Societal
       Factors in Life-Span Disruptions and Alternatives."
       In *Life-Span Developmental Psychology: Normative
       Life Crises*, pp. 217-34, Nancy Datan and Leon H.
       Ginsberg, eds. New York: Academic Press, Inc., 1975.
       The situation of widows is reviewed in comparative
       and historical perspective, and shown to be symbolic
       of the influence of societal changes upon their
       members. As social roles and resources expanded,
       the lives of women, except for the few in the upper
       classes, became more restricted than they had been
       in agricultural and nomadic social units. Women
       may be changing their levels of commitment to and
       involvement in roles outside the home, but many
       social and psychological constraints are placed
       upon widows. Studies of a heterogeneous sample of
       widows of all ages in metropolitan Chicago indicate
       that few are "liberated" and able to lead the multi-
       dimensional lives of social engagement expected of
       widows whose children are no longer young. Many
       are socially isolated because they lack support
       systems. However, the major spearhead of the next
       wave of change in human societies may come from the
       nonmarried women who have the opportunity to find
       new directions for their lives.

853.   Lopata, Helena Znaniecki. *Women as Widows: Support
       Systems*. New York: Elsevier North Holland, Inc.,
       1979. A report of eight years of reading, research
       and writing by Lopata about widowhood, in particular
       about widows in the Chicago metropolitan area. In

Part One, she presents a review of theoretical, cross-
cultural (based on the Human Relations Area Files),
historical and demographic perspectives on widowhood,
followed by chapters on Resources and Support Systems
of Widows, and Widowhood and Husbands in Memory (with
a section on husband sanctification). Part Two,
Main Contributors, has chapters on: Boyfriends and
New Husbands (only 6% remarried); Children as
Resources (daughters are much more significant in
the lives and support systems of these widows than
are sons); Friends; Others (findings were an absence
of siblings and the under-representation or absence
of extended kin, neighbors, co-workers, co-members
of voluntary and religious groups, and religious
personnel and members of other helping professions
from their support systems); Personal Resources and
Supports; Supports from the Economic Institutions
(only 25% of these widows were employed at the time
of the study; over 40% were living on incomes at
or below the poverty level); and a summary chapter
with profiles and implications. Tables, Appendix
of interviewing schedules (1,169 interviews were
conducted), and bibliography. Lopata states that
most older urban widows have been caught between
two styles of life, the one in which they were
socialized and the one in which they now live. She
believes that these cohorts of older women are unique
in many ways, and that newer generations of women
will not face many problems typical of today's
older widow. She reports that many of those women
studied here have adjusted slowly and often painfully
to appalling circumstances.

854. Silverman, Phyllis R. "Widowhood and Preventive
Intervention." *The Family Coordinator* (January
1972) 21(1):95-102. Aspects of what it means to
be widowed. The discussion is based primarily on
the experiences of widows under age 60 with the
Widow-to-Widow program. The focus is on those
women who wanted the additional assistance offered
to make the transition from wife to widow. For
these women, the most important fact was that the
intervener was another widow. The widow caregiver
is the most effective intervener. Education for
those recently widowed is not academic, but a matter
of providing concrete direction to become involved
in new activities.

*855. Steinhart, F. "The Social Correlates of Working
        Widows." Paper presented at the Midwest Sociological
        Society, Chicago, 1975.

 856. Wakin, Edward. "Living As a Widow: Only the Name's
        the Same." In *The Older Woman: Lavender Rose or Gray
        Panther*, pp. 151-7, Marie Marschall Fuller and Cora
        Ann Martin, eds. Springfield, Illinois: Charles C.
        Thomas, 1980. An overview of problems and needs
        of widows, and of programs and organizations pro-
        viding assistance to widows, among them the Widow-
        to-Widow program, and Naim, an organization for
        widowed Catholic men and women, which has chapters
        in a number of dioceses. Sociologist Helena Z.
        Lopata is quoted as recommending that those who
        want to help widows should help them become independent,
        and as citing the needs of widows as: grief work,
        companionship, solution of immediate problems, the
        building of competence and self-confidence, and
        help in re-engagement in their social world.

See also: 253, 286, 287, 418, 457, 567, 660, 663, 667, 702,
761, 779, 784.

XVII. SELECTED BIBLIOGRAPHIES

*857. *The Aged in Minority Groups*. Washington, D.C.: The
National Council on the Aging, Inc., 1973. Annotated;
19 pages.

*858. Astin, Helen S., Allison Parelman and Anne Fisher.
Sex Roles: A Research Bibliography. Washington,
D.C.: U.S. Government Printing Office, 1975.

859. Bachmann, Donna G., and Sherry Piland. *Women Artists:
An Historical, Contemporary and Feminist Bibliography*.
Metuchen, New Jersey: The Scarecrow Press, Inc.,
1978. Section I lists General Works--Books,
Periodicals and Catalogues; Section II provides
biographical sketches and bibliographies of
Individual Artists--Fifteenth Century and Earlier,
Sixteenth Century, Seventeenth Century, Eighteenth
Century, Nineteenth Century, and Twentieth Century;
Section III provides A Selected Bibliography on
Needlework.

*860. Baumhover, Lorin A., and Joan Dechow Jones, eds.
Handbook of American Aging Programs. Westport,
Connecticut: Greenwood Press, 1977.

861. Biblowitz, Iris, Liza Bingham, Frances M. Goodstein,
Julia Homer, Jill Janows, Ann Kautzmann, Peggy
Kornegger, Virginia Rankin MacLean, Jane Tuchscherer
and Judy Wynn, eds. *Women and Literature: An
Annotated Bibliography of Women Writers*. Cambridge,
Massachusetts: Women and Literature Collective,
1976.

862. Block, Marilyn R., Janice L. Davidson, Jean D. Grambs
and Kathryn E. Serock. *Uncharted Territory: Issues
and Concerns of Women Over Forty*. College Park,
Maryland: The University of Maryland Center on
Aging, 1978. Includes an Annotated Filmography,

pp. 187-206; a list of Film Distributors, pp. 207-9;
and a bibliographical listing, pp. 211-69, of
approximately 1,000 books and articles on older
women. Bibliographical headings: cultural/social
images and attitudes; demographic data; menopause
and sexuality; health and medical issues; psychological
issues; life patterns; family relationships; social
networks; widowhood and death; legal issues;
employment and retirement; social security and
pensions; continuing education; ethnic and racial
variations; other.

*863.   Cirksena, Kathy, and Fran Hereth, compilers, and Rita
         M. Costick, ed. *Continuing Education: Reentry and
         the Mature Woman—Annotated Selected References and
         Resources*. San Francisco, California: Far West
         Laboratory for Educational Research and Development,
         1977. (Women's Educational Equity Communications
         Network, sponsored by the U.S. Department of Health,
         Education, and Welfare.) This is the second
         publication in a bibliography series issued by the
         Women's Educational Equity Communications Network
         (WEECN). The first bibliography of the series,
         *Women's Educational Equity: Annotated Selected
         References and Resources*, was developed to provide
         an introductory overview of some of the major resources
         concerned with the elimination of sex role stereo-
         typing in the field of education. It includes an
         annotated listing of relevant journals, newsletters/
         resource publications, and library collections. A
         section covering books, reports and bibliographies
         contains entries related to elementary and secondary
         education, higher education, continuing education,
         and vocational or career education. This second
         publication includes information resources in the
         area of continuing education and the reentry woman,
         although it does not attempt to list them compre-
         hensively. The third bibliography in the series
         will be concerned with career counseling for women;
         individual components on various topics will include
         counseling minority women; women in specific
         occupations and professions; testing; specific
         career counseling programs for women; and counselor
         training, strategies, and techniques.

*864.   Cisler, Lucinda. *Women: A Bibliography*. New York:
         published by the Author, 1970.

865. Edelstein, Beth, and Liz Segedin. *Age is Becoming: An Annotated Bibliography on Women and Aging.* Berkeley, California: Interface Bibliographers, 1977. 50 pp., 250 entries approx. Second (expanded) edition of selected bibliography of current literature on the impact of aging on women in contemporary America. Material is primarily American, published from 1970 to 1975; the second edition includes an updated appendix of material published from 1975 to 1977. (The first edition was a project of the Task Force on Older Women, Oakland, California, National Organization for Women.)

*866. *A General Bibliography on Aging.* Washington, D.C.: The National Council on the Aging, Inc., 1972.

*867. Haber, Barbara. *Women in America: A Guide to Books, 1963-1975, with an Appendix on Books Published 1976-1979.* The original clothbound edition included annotations for 450 books, divided among eighteen subject categories. In this first paperback edition, Haber evaluates her initial effort and adds a bibliographical essay accounting for nearly 200 titles published since 1976.

868. Hollenshead, Carol, with Carol Katz and Berit Ingersoll. *Past Sixty: The Older Woman in Print and Film.* Ann Arbor, Michigan: The Institute of Gerontology, The University of Michigan-Wayne State University, 1977. 52 pp. A list of 289 selected books, journal and magazine articles, pamphlets, and films, with annotations of the publications and the films, focusing on the woman over age 60. Sections: Social and Psychological Issues; The Older Woman's Role in Marriage and the Extended Family; Widowhood; The Older Woman and Health; Sexuality; Legal and Economic Issues; Ethnic Background and the Older Woman; Approaches through the Humanities; The Older Woman in Film and Videotape; Distributors' Addresses. Section on the Older Woman and Health by Linda Bennett.

*869. Hughes, Marija Matich. *The Sexual Barrier: Legal, Medical, Economic and Social Aspects of Sex Discrimination.* Buffalo, New York: William S. Hein and Co., Inc., Hughes Press, 1977. Hughes, law librarian of the U.S. Commission on Civil Rights,

published her original bibliography in 1970, which,
supplemented in 1971 and 1972, contained 1,000 entries.
The 1977 edition contains more than 8,000 annotated
items, selected from 1960-75 publications, and arranged
in 17 chapters subdivided into 268 sections.
(Winner of the 1978 Joseph L. Andrews Award for
Outstanding Bibliography.)

*870.   Jones, J.E.   "Art and the Elderly: An Annotated
        Bibliography of Research and Programming."
        Art Education 31(7) 1978.

 871.   Kellam, Constance E.   *A Literary Bibliography on Aging.*
        New York: Council on Social Work Education,
        1968.   Originally compiled for social work education
        and training, this Bibliography was published for
        a wider audience, with the view that literature
        may serve as a primary source for all persons
        engaged in the human service professions.

*872.   Lerner, Gerda.   *Bibliography in the History of
        American Women*, a Sarah Lawrence College Women's
        Studies Publication.   Bronxville, New York: Sarah
        Lawrence College, 1978.   Lists bibliographical
        guides and sources in historiography of Women's
        History; Theories of Women; History of American
        Women; Family History; Motherhood; Sexuality; Women
        and Work; Women and Education; Women and Law;
        Women and Crime; Women and Art; Black Women; Other
        American Minority Women; and Biography and Auto-
        biography: Immigrant Women.

*873.   *Literary Writings in America: A Bibliography.*   Millwood,
        New York: KTO Press, 1977.   Eight volumes with over
        200,000 previously "lost" citations to works by and
        about American authors.   A photo-offset reproduction
        of 250,000 cards compiled as a post-Depression
        project of the Historical Records Survey program of
        the Federal Works Progress Administration.   An
        index to writings in over 2,000 volumes of magazines,
        as well as in over 600 volumes of literary history,
        criticism, and bibliography.   Full names and dates
        of over 600 authors are arranged in one alphabetical
        sequence; writings by and about an author are
        classified under the person's name and categorized
        as to type of writings; reviews are accessible by
        name of reviewer, name of author of reviewed book,
        and, in the case of literary biography and criticism,

name of the subject of the book. Provides access
to the writings of all major and minor American
writers from 1850 through 1942 that were published
in thousands of issues of American periodicals
never before included in existing indexes.

874. Mason, Elizabeth B., and Louis M. Starr, eds.
*Columbia University: The Oral History Collection
of Columbia University.* New York: Oral History
Research Office, 1973. This third edition of the
Oral History Collection is a guide to 360,000 pages
of typewritten transcripts of taped reminiscences,
generally edited for accuracy by the oral author.
The catalogue describes the largest hoard of
unpublished reminiscence in the world. The Oral
History collection, founded by historian Allan Nevins
in 1948, is the "largest and most diversified memory
bank of its kind in 20th century American life."

875. Meckler, Alan M., and Ruth McMullin, eds. *Oral
History Collections.* New York: R.R. Bowker Co.,
1975. This is the first edition of Oral History
Collections, prepared a quarter-century after the
inception of the oral history movement. The
introductory statement presents an overview of
developments in the field. The Bowker questionnaire
was sent to over 5,000 libraries and institutions;
cut-off date for accepting information was January
1974.

876. Moss, Walter G., ed. *Humanistic Perspectives on
Aging: An Annotated Bibliography and Essay.* Ann
Arbor, Michigan: The Institute of Gerontology, The
University of Michigan-Wayne State University, 1976.
Major categories are: Aging Around the World:
Non-Fiction, Past and Present; Reflections of the
Aging: Autobiographies by Older Authors; Literature
on Aging and Old Age (Drama, Essays, Novels, Poetry
and Short Stories); Reflections on Death. Also
includes Resources: Films and Videotapes, and Toward
a Humanistic Gerontology: Other Explorations.

877. Mueller, Jean E., and Margaret L. Kronauer. "A
Bibliography of Doctoral Dissertations on Aging
from American Institutions of Higher Learning,
1977-79." *Journal of Gerontology* (July 1980)
35(4):603-17. The original title by Jean E.
Mueller covered the years 1934-69; 1969 to 1979

have been covered in seven supplements to this date.
Major headings are: Biological Aspects; Behavioral
Aspects; Social Aspects; Health and Health Services;
Education.

*878.   Place, Linna Funk, Linda Parker and Forrest J.
        Berghorn. *Aging and the Aged: An Annotated
        Bibliography and Library Research Guide*. Boulder,
        Colorado: Westview Press, 1981.

*879.   Rooke, M. Leigh, and C. Ray Wingrove. *Gerontology:
        An Annotated Bibliography, 1966-1977*. Washington,
        D.C.: University Press of America, 1977.

*880.   Sharma, P.C. *Studies on Aging and Aged in America;
        a Selected Research Bibliography*. Monticello:
        Council Planning Library, 1976. (Exchange Bib-
        liography No. 714.)

 881.   Shock, Nathan W. "The List of Current Publications in
        Gerontology and Geriatrics." *Journal of Gerontology*
        (November 1980) 35(6):961-86. The subject categories
        are those in *A Classified Bibliography of Gerontology
        and Geriatrics* by Nathan W. Shock, published by
        Stanford University Press, in 1951. Major headings,
        excluding all Geriatrics headings, include:
        Gerontology; Psychological Processes; Social and
        Economic Aspects (Accidents, Crime, Demography,
        Economic Problems, including Employment and
        Retirement and Pensions); Education; Housing and
        Care; Legal Problems; Medical Care; Social Problems;
        Social Groups; Social Security; Social Services and
        Social Work; Popular Articles. The first appearance
        of this list was in April 1950, and this listing,
        in November 1980, is the last.

*882.   Shumway, Gary L. *Oral History in the U.S.--A Directory*,
        compiled by Gary L. Shumway. Oral History Association,
        1971. A compilation of all oral history materials
        in existence in the U.S. by state, so far as the
        Oral History Association was able to uncover them.
        (Carl Ryant, in No. 550 of this Bibliography,
        provides the address of the Executive Secretary
        in 1981 as: Ronald E. Marcello, Executive Secretary,
        North Texas State University, P.O. Box 13734,
        N. T. S. U. Station, Denton, Texas 76203.)

*883. Wilkinson, C.W. *Comprehensive Annotated Bibliography on the Rural Aged (1975-1978).* West Virginia University Gerontology Center, Occasional Papers on the Rural Aged, 1, 1978.

*884. Williamson, Jane. *New Feminist Scholarship: A Guide to Bibliographies.* Old Westbury, New York: The Feminist Press, 1979. Annotated bibliography of bibliographies (approximately 400), organized by 30 subject headings, including Anthropology and Sociology, Child Care, Lesbians, Third World Countries, and Work.

885. "Women In the South: A Bibliography. *Southern Exposure* (Winter 1977) IV(4):98-103. This Bibliography is included in the issue on Generations: Women in the South, and is described as an eclectic survey of topics and time periods intended to serve as an indication of available written sources and a stimulus to further research. Headings are: Theory; General; Autobiographies, Biographies, Memoirs; Literature.

NAME INDEX

*Name appears as author or editor or
recorder or translator or in title
of work
**Name appears in the body of the work